"Joseph Barber Lightfoot has been, for me, in many ways the epitome of what the commentator on New Testament and early church texts can and should aspire to. His detailed knowledge of the literature of the time was unsurpassed, and his ability to shed the light of that knowledge on the New Testament writings was without peer. His commentaries on New Testament texts and the early Fathers retain a relevance and a value to this day almost unique for nineteenth-century scholarship. That a fuller publication of his writings is now available in these volumes is a wonderful bonus for those who want to hear these New Testament and early church texts as they were first heard."
James D. G. Dunn, Emeritus Lightfoot Professor of Divinity, University of Durham

"The discovery and publication of previously unpublished commentaries on the New Testament by Joseph Barber Lightfoot is a highly significant event in the history of New Testament scholarship. For a start, these shed valuable light on the reception of the New Testament in the nineteenth century, representing the work of the foremost English scholar of that era whose linguistic and historical skills exhibit a quality of scholarship that few today can match. Not all of his historical, literary or theological judgments look fully convincing today, but his acute reading of the Greek text and his phenomenal range of knowledge can still contribute greatly to contemporary exegesis. Ben Witherington, Todd Still and Jeanette Hagen are to be warmly congratulated for their remarkable success in making such a significant voice from the past resound again today."
John M. G. Barclay, Lightfoot Professor of Divinity, University of Durham

"The discovery of hitherto unknown exegetical works by J. B. Lightfoot is a rare gift, full of potential for fresh insight both about the man himself (acknowledged worldwide as the leading scholar of his day) and, as he would have wished, about texts which he knew so well and which themselves express the heart of the gospel. Hearty congratulations to finder, editor and publisher on an unexpected and exciting addition to the core library of seminal biblical studies."
N. T. Wright, University of St. Andrews and formerly Bishop of Durham

"From Bede, the greatest European scholar of the seventh century, to today's world-class university sharing a world heritage site with a majestic cathedral, creative and careful study has long stood alongside prayer and worship here in Durham. It is therefore fitting that this amazing discovery of Lightfoot's handwritten manuscripts was made by one of the world's leading biblical scholars in the cathedral library. For within these pages, Lightfoot embodies that Durham tradition—outstanding independent scholarship offered humbly in the service of God."
David Wilkinson, Durham University

"We are greatly in debt to Ben Witherington, Todd Still and their collaborators for bringing this material to light for our day."
Steve Walton, Tyndale House, Cambridge

"Thanks to Witherington and his associates and to IVP for bringing this cache of material from the great J. B. Lightfoot into the public domain. His previously published works have remained important (his multivolume study of the apostolic fathers is essential for these writings), and this hitherto unpublished material will now also likely come to be seen as a valuable resource."
Larry Hurtado, University of Edinburgh

"Harnack said it best: Lightfoot was a true liberal for he was 'an independent, free scholar . . . in the absolute sense of the word. He has never defended tradition for the tradition's sake.' We need more liberals like that today!"
Daniel B. Wallace, Dallas Theological Seminary

J. B. LIGHTFOOT

The Gospel of St. John
A Newly Discovered Commentary

THE LIGHTFOOT LEGACY SET

◆

Volume 2

Edited by
BEN WITHERINGTON III
and **TODD D. STILL**

Assisted by
JEANETTE M. HAGEN

IVP Academic
An imprint of InterVarsity Press
Downers Grove, Illinois

InterVarsity Press
P.O. Box 1400, Downers Grove, IL 60515-1426
ivpress.com
email@ivpress.com

InterVarsity Press® is the book-publishing division of InterVarsity Christian Fellowship/USA®, a movement of students and faculty active on campus at hundreds of universities, colleges and schools of nursing in the United States of America, and a member movement of the International Fellowship of Evangelical Students. For information about local and regional activities, visit intervarsity.org.

Cover design: Cindy Kiple
Interior design: Beth McGill
Images: Joseph B. Lightfoot: Joseph Lightfoot, English theologian and Bishop of Durham, Lock and Whitfield
(19th century) / Private Collection / © Look and Learn / Elgar Collection / Bridgeman Images
recycled paper: © tomograf/iStockphoto
glossy insert page images courtesy of Durham Cathedral Library / © Chapter of Durham Library

ISBN 978-0-8308-2945-3 (print)
ISBN 978-0-8308-9898-5 (digital)

Library of Congress Cataloging-in-Publication Data
Lightfoot, J. B. (Joseph Barber), 1828-1889.
The gospel of St. John : a newly discovered commentary / J. B. Lightfoot ; edited by Ben Witherington III and Todd D. Still ; assisted by Jeanette M. Hagen.
pages cm. -- (The Lightfoot legacy set ; Volume 2)
Includes bibliographical references and index.
ISBN 978-0-8308-2945-3 (hardcover)
1. Bible. John--Commentaries. I. Witherington, Ben, III, 1951- editor. II. Still, Todd D., editor. III. Title.
BS2615.53.L54 2015
226.5'07--dc23
2015033920

P	23	22	21	20	19	18	17	16	15	14	13	12	11	10	9	8	7	6	5	4	3	2	1
Y	35	34	33	32	31	30	29	28	27	26	25	24	23	22	21	20	19	18	17	16	15		

BISHOP LIGHTFOOT'S BOOKPLATE

This shews the Bishop's own coat of arms impaled with those of the See, and the Mitre set in a Coronet, indicating the Palatinate dignity of Durham.

Though the Bookplate is not the Episcopal seal its shape recalls the following extract from Fuller's *Church History* (iv. 103):—'Dunelmia sola, judicat ense et stola.' "The Bishop whereof was a Palatine, or Secular Prince, and his seal in form resembleth Royalty in the roundness thereof and is not oval, the badge of plain Episcopacy."

Figure 1. Bishop Lightfoot's Bookplate

Quotations Regarding
J. B. Lightfoot and His Work

"His editions and commentaries . . . as well as his critical dissertations have an imperishable value, and even where it is impossible to agree with his results, his grounds are never to be neglected. The respect for his opponent which distinguishes him . . . has brought him the highest respect of all parties. . . . There never has been an apologist who was less an advocate than Lightfoot. . . . He [was] an independent, free scholar . . . in the absolute sense of the words. He has never defended a tradition for the tradition's sake. But how many times, when the tradition was previously defended inadequately and so threatened to lose its reputation, has he saved the tradition with sweeping reasons!"[1]

Adolf von Harnack

"In the great bulk of his literary work Bishop Lightfoot depended entirely on his own labours. He never employed an amanuensis; he rarely allowed anyone else even to verify his references. The only relief which he would accept was the almost mechanical correction of the proof/sheets of the new editions, as they were called for, of his Epistles of St Paul."[2]

H. E. Savage

"His lectures on the Greek New Testament were distinguished not only by their ability but also by their spiritual power. A pupil who attended one of the earliest courses remarks: 'I remember well how much the class was impressed, when, after giving us the usual introductory matter, Lightfoot closed the book and said, "After all is said and done, the only way to know the Greek Testament properly is by prayer" and dwelt further on this thought.'"[3]

The Cambridge Review

"We are glad to be able to hope, from hints which have from time to time reached the public ear, that a large portion of the whole field was covered by Dr. Lightfoot's

---

[1]F. J. A. Hort, "Lightfoot, Joseph Barber," *Dictionary of National Biography, 1885–1900* (London: Smith, Elder & Co), 33:239.

[2]G. R. Eden and F. C. Macdonald, eds., *Lightfoot of Durham* (Cambridge: Cambridge University Press, 1932), p. 110.

[3]Cited by Eden and Macdonald, *Lightfoot of Durham*, p. 13.

labours, and that some of the MSS. which are in the care of his literary executors will in due course be published; for even if they are only posthumous fragments, the student . . . will thankfully welcome them."

Anonymous obituary to Lightfoot in the *Contemporary Review*, 1890

To all the doctoral students past and present

who have studied under the remarkable scholars who have

taught in Durham's theology department

over the last century.

Contents

ABBREVIATIONS

BIBLICAL VERSIONS

ℵ*	Original text of the Codex Sinaiticus
A/al.	Codex Alexandrinus
Arm.	Armenian
A.V.	Authorized Version
B	Codex Vaticanus
B.M.T.	Byzantine Majority Text
C	Codex Ephraemi Syri Rescriptus
C*	Redaction of Codex Ephraemi Syri Rescriptus
Δ	Codex Sangallensis 48
D	Codex Bezae Cantabrigiensis
E	Codex Basilensis
Ethiop.	Ethiopian
E.V.	English version
G	Codex Seidelianus I/Codex Harleianus
Goth.	Gothic
H	Codex Wolfii B
Harcl.	Harclean Syriac
K	Codex Cyprius
L	Codex Regius
Lact.	Lactantius
Lat.	Latin
M*	Codex Campianus
Memph.	Memphis
Peshit.	Peshitta
Symach.	Symmachus
Syr.	Syriac
Teb.	Tebtunis
T.R.	Textus Receptus
Vulg.	Vulgate
X	Codex Monacensis

ANCIENT AUTHORS AND WORKS

Aelian

An.	*De natura animalium*

Aeschylus
    Sept.   *Septem contra Thebas*
Ambrose
    Ep(ist).   *Epistulae*
    Comm. in Luc.   *Expositio evangelii secundum Lucam*
Apost(l). Const(it).   *Apostolic Constitutions*
Aristot.   Aristotle
    Rhet.   Rhetoric
Aristophanes
    Vesp.   *Vespae*
Augustine
    c. Faust.   *Contra Faustum Manichaeum*
    de conj. adult.   De adulterinus conjugiis
    Op.   *De opera monachorum*
    Sermo.   *Sermones*
Basil
    ad Eunom.   *Adversus Eunomium*
B.T.   Babylonian Talmud
Can. Mur.   Canon Muratoni
Chron. Pasch.   *Chronicon Paschale*
Cicero
    Prov. Cons.   *De provinciis consularibus*
Clem. Hom.   *Clementine Homilies*
Clem. Recog(n).   Clementine Recognitions
Clement of Alexandria
    Quis div. salv.   *Quis dives salvetur*
    Strom.   *Stromata*
Cyprian
    Adv. Jud.   *Adversus Judaeos* (Pseudo-Cyprian)
    Epist.   *Epistulae*
Demosthenes
    Phorm.   *Pro Phormio*
Dionysius Areopagiticus
    de eccles. hierarch.   *De ecclesiastica hierarchia*
Ephraem
    Haer.   *Against Heresies*
Epiph.   Epiphanius
    De mens. et pond.   *De mensuris et ponderibus*
    Haer.   *Adversus haereses*

Hom.	*Homilies*
Erub.	ʿErubim
1 Esdr	1 Esdras
Eusebius of Caesarea	
Chron.	*Chronicon*
Demonstr. Evang.	*Demonstratio evangelica*
Hist. Eccles.	*Historia ecclesiastica*
Onam(astic)./Onom.	*Onomasticon*
Praep. Ev(ang).	*Praeparatio evangelica*
Fabricius	
Cod. Apoc. N. T.	Johann Albert Fabricius, *Codex Apocryphus Novi Testameni*
Gregory of Nyssa	
Cant.	*In Canticum Canticorum*
Eunam.	*Contra Eunomium*
Heliod.	Heliodorus
Hippol.	Hippolytus
c. Noet.	*Contra haeresin Noeti*
Haer./Refut.	*Refutatio omnium haeresium*
Ign.	Ignatius
Eph(es).	*Epistle to the Ephesians*
Magn.	*Epistle to the Magnesians*
Phil(ad).	*Epistle to the Philadelphians*
Polyc.	*Epistle to Polycarp*
Rom.	*Epistle to the Romans*
Smyrn.	*Epistle to the Smyrnaeans*
Trall.	*Epistle to the Trallians*
Iren.	Irenaeus
Jerome	
Matth./Comm. in Matt.	*Commentariorum in Matthaeum*
Vir. Ill(ustr).	*De viris illustribus*
Josephus	
Ant.	*Antiquitates judaicae*
Bell. Jud.	*Bellum judaicum*
c. Apion.	*Contra Apionem*
Vit.	*Vita*
Justin	
Apol.	*Apology*
Dialog./Dial. Trypho	*Dialogue with Trypho*
Lactant.	Lactantius
Inst.	*Divinarum institutionum*

1 Macc	1 Maccabees
Mart. Polyc.	*Martyrdom of Polycarp*
Orac. Sybll.	*Oracula Sibyllina*
Orest.	Euripides, *Orestias*
Origen	
Comm. in John.	*Commentarii in evangelium Joannis*
c. Celsum	*Contra Celsum*
Philastrius	
Haer.	*Diversarum Hereseon Liber*
Philo	
Fragm.	*Fragments*
de cherub.	*De cherubim*
de. Confus. Ling.	*De confusione linguarum*
de Festo Cop.	*De festo cophini*
de Migra. Abr.	*De migratione Abrahami*
de Poster. Ca.	*De posteritate Caini*
de Spec. Leg.	*De specialibus legibus*
Flacc.	*In Flaccum*
Leg. All.	*Legum allegoriae*
quod omn. prob.	*Quod omnis probus liber*
Plato	
Gorg.	*Gorgias*
Sympos.	*Symposium*
Tim.	*Timaeus*
Plautus	
Asinar.	*Asinaria*
Pliny the Elder	
Nat. Hist./H. N.	*Naturalis historia*
Plutarch	
de Alex.	*Alexander*
Moral.	*Moralia*
Pomp.	*Pompeius*
Pseudo-Ignatius	
Philadel.	*Epistle to the Philadelphians*
Ruinart	
Sanhed(r).	*Sanhedrin*
Seneca	
Epistl.	*Epistulae morales*

Shepherd of Hermas

Mand.	Mandates
Sim.	Similitudes
Vis.	Visions

Sir — Sirach

Suetonius

Jul.	Divus Julius
Vesp.	Vespasianus

Syncellus

Chron.	Chronicle of Theophanes

Tacitus

Hist.	Historiae

Tertull. — Tertullian

adv. Hermos	Adversus Hermogenem
adv. Judaeos	Adversus Judaeos
adv. Marc.	Adversus Marcionem
Adv. Prax.	Adversus Praxean
de carn Chr.	De carne Christi
de praescr./Praescr. Haer.	De praescriptione haereticorum
de pud.	De pudicitia
Test. Twelve. Pat. Levi	Testament of the Twelve Patriarchs, Levi

Theod. Mops. — Theodore of Mopsuestia

praef. in Epist. ad Ephesos	Preface to the Commentary on Ephesians

Theodoret

H(aer). F(ab).	Haereticarum fabularum compendium

Theophilus

ad Autol.	Ad Autolycum

Vict. Ant. — Victor of Antioch

ap. Cramer Cat. in Marc.	John Cramer, Catena in Marcum

Wis. Sol. — Wisdom of Solomon

Xenophon

Anab.	Anabasis
Mem.	Memorabilia

Modern Sources and Persons

Alford	Henry Alford, The New Testament for English Readers, 4 vols. (London: Rivingtons, 1866)

Anc. Syr. Documents	Ancient Syrian Documents
Assem., *Bib. Or.*	Assemani, *Bibl. Orient.*
Bengel	Johannes Bengel
Boeckh, *C. I. G.*	Philipp August Boeckh, *Corpus Inscriptionum Graecarum*
Bretschneider, *Lex.*	Karl Gottlieb Bretschneider, *Lexicon manuale Graeco-Latinum in libros Novi Testamenti*
BSHST	*Basler Studien zur historischen und systematischen Theologie*
Bunsen *Hippolytus*	C. J. Bunsen, *Hippolytus and His Age* (1852)
A. Buttmann	Alexander Buttmann
Cave	William Cave, *Primitive Christianity*
Clinton, *Fast. Rom.*	Henry Fynes Clinton, *Fasti Romani*
Cotelier, *Patr. Apost.*	Jean-Baptiste Cotelier, *Patres Apostolici*
Credner, *Canon*	Carl August Credner, *The History of the Canon of the New Testament*
Cureton, *Spicileg. Syr.*	William Cureton, *Spicilegium Syriacum*
Cureton, *Anc. Syr. Documents*	William Cureton, *Ancient Syrian Documents*
Ewald	W. H. A. Ewald, *Kritische Grammatik der hebräischen Sprache* (1827)
GCS	Die griechischen christlichen Schriftsteller der ersten [drei] Jahrhunderte
Gesenius	W. Gesenius, *Hebräisches u. Chaldäisches Handwörterbuch* (1812)
Lightfoot *Hor. Heb.*	John Lightfoot, *Horae Hebraicae*
Lipsius, *de Grace*	Justus Lipsius, *De Grace*
Meyer	H. A. W. Meyer
Migne, *Pat. Graec.*	*see* PG
PG	*Patrologiae Cursus Completus: Series Graeca*. Edited by Jacques-Paul Migne. 162 vols. (Paris, 1857–1886)
PTS	Patristische Texte und Studien
Renan, *Vie de Jesus*	Ernest Renan, *The Life of Jesus* (London: Trübner & Co., 1864)
Robinson	Armitage Robinson
Scrivener, *Collatio Cod. Sinait.*	Frederick Henry Ambrose Scrivener, *Collations of the Codex Sinaiticus*
Smith's Dictionary	William Smith, *Dictionary of the Bible*
Stud. und Krit.	*Studien und Kritiken*
Tisch./Tischendorf	Constantin von Tischendorf
Tregelles	S. P. Tregelles, *Account of the Printed Text of the Greek New Testament* (1854)
Trench (*Syn./New Testament Synon.*)	R. C. Trench, *Synonyms of the New Testament*, 9th ed. (London: Macmillan, 1880)
Trench, *Miracles*	R. C. Trench, *Notes on the Miracles of our Lord* (1883)

Turpie	*The Old Testament in the New* (1868)
Westcott, *Canon*	B. F. Westcott, *A General Survey of the History of the Canon of the New Testament* (1855; revised 1875)
Westcott, *Introd. to the Gospels*	B. F. Westcott, *Introduction to the Study of the Gospels* (1860; revised 1866)
Wettstein	J. J. Wettstein, Novum Testamentum Graecum editionis receptae cum lectionibus variantibus codicum manuscript (1751)
Winer	G. B. Winer, *Grammatik des N.T. Spachidioms und Biblisches Realworterbuch*
Zahn, *Ignatius*	Theodore Zahn, *Ignatius of Antioch*

Miscellaneous

A.U.C.	Ab urbe condita
Comp. fol.	Compare folio
l.c.	loco citato
lxx	Septuagint
MS/MS.	manuscript
sq./sqq.	the following one(s)
t.r.	textus receptus
v.l.	varias lectiones

FOREWORD

In 1978, I was in the Durham Cathedral cloister visiting the Monk's Dormitory that then, as now, served as a display room for important artifacts and manuscripts. It was also something of an archival library. I was a young doctoral student of Charles Kingsley Barrett and had already come across the name of J. B. Lightfoot on various occasions. Indeed, I had bought a reprint of his classic Philippians commentary while I was still in seminary in Massachusetts several years earlier. While perusing the various display cases, I came across an open notebook that displayed Lightfoot's comments on a notoriously difficult passage in Acts 15, and I wondered whether more of this sort of meticulous exegetical material existed, written in Lightfoot's own hand, somewhere else in that library.

Naturally, I was interested, since there were no publications by Lightfoot that directly dealt with Acts, and certainly no commentaries by Lightfoot on Acts. I mentioned this discovery to Professor Barrett, who himself was an admirer of J. B. Lightfoot. In fact, in the early 1970s he had written a *Durham University Journal* article in which he praised Lightfoot as arguably the foremost scholar of the New Testament of his era.[1] Somehow, however, nothing more happened in regard to this matter, and in truth, I forgot about it.

I mentioned in passing seeing this material some years later to Professor J. D. G. Dunn, who was then (the Lightfoot Professor of Divinity) at Durham University. Still, nothing more came of it. Yes, there was a celebration of the centennial of Lightfoot's death in 1989, planned and organized by the tireless

---

[1]C. K. Barrett, "Joseph Barber Lightfoot," *Durham University Journal* 64 (1972): 193-204.

efforts of Professor Dunn, that produced a fine special issue of the *Durham University Journal*, published in 1990, with various articles about the legacy of Lightfoot.[2] There was even a fine monograph done by G. R. Treloar on Lightfoot as a historian.[3] Although it was clear that Treloar had read and studied some of Lightfoot's unpublished work on Acts, the primary sources had not been completely read or studied, much less published.

On my sabbatical in the spring of 2013, when I was scholar-in-residence in St. John's College at Durham University, I decided to try and see just what Lightfoot materials might still be gathering dust in the Cathedral library. I must confess, I was not prepared for what I found. There, in the Monk's Dormitory in a tall bookcase—whose lower compartment was crammed with Lightfoot files, folders, letters, pictures, inkwells and more—sat not only three brown notebooks of Lightfoot's detailed exegetical lectures on Acts numbering over 140 pages, but also a further gigantic blue box full of hundreds of pages of additional Acts materials, including a lengthy excursus on the authenticity of the Stephen speech. But even that was not all.

There was also a whole blue box full of hundreds of pages of Lightfoot's exegetical studies on the Gospel of John, lectures on 2 Corinthians two notebooks on 1 Peter, and finally a further notebook of Lightfoot's reflections on early Judaism. All were in Lightfoot's own hand, all done in great detail and none of it, except the first four or five pages of the introduction to Galatians contained in the first Acts notebook (which Kaye and Treloar excerpted and published in a *Durham University Journal* article in the 1990[4]), has ever been published—until now.[5]

---

[2]Professor Dunn edited this special edition of the journal, which includes articles by David M. Thompson on Lightfoot as a churchman, Martin Hengel on Lightfoot's interaction with the Tübingen school on the Gospel of John and the second century, C. K. Barrett on Lightfoot as a biblical commentator, and James D. G. Dunn on the contributions of Lightfoot to church and academy.

[3]G. R. Treloar, *Lightfoot the Historian: The Nature and Role of History in the Life and Thought of J. B. Lightfoot*, Wissenschaftliche Untersuchungen zum Neuen Testament 2.103 (Tübingen: Mohr Siebeck, 1998).

[4]B. N. Kaye and G. R. Treloar, "J. B. Lightfoot and New Testament Interpretation: An Unpublished Manuscript of 1855," *Durham University Journal* 82 (1990): 160-75 (on 171-75).

[5]There are a few other exceptions to this remark: (1) Three articles on Acts, which appear in the appendices to volume one of this series (*Acts of the Apostles: A Newly Discovered Commentary*), were previously published in periodicals and dictionaries but have long since been out of print and are in the public domain, and (2) Lightfoot's essays on the authenticity of the Gospel of John, examining both the external and internal evidence, were published, but not his exegesis of John.

It is important to say at this juncture that this material would still be unpublished were it not for (1) the capable help of the Durham Cathedral Library staff, especially Catherine Turner (now retired) and Gabrielle Sewell; (2) the hard work of a current doctoral student at the University of Durham, Jeanette Hagen, who did some of the painstaking work reading and transcribing this material, as well as Andy Stubblefield, who made the indexes; (3) the generosity of Asbury Seminary, Baylor University (through an Arts and Humanities Faculty Development Program Grant administered by the office of the vice provost of research) and Willard J. Still, who helped to pay for the digitalization and transcription of these materials; and (4) our friends at InterVarsity Press, in particular Andy Le Peau, Jim Hoover, Dan Reid and David Congdon, who saw the value of letting this material see the light of day so it might provide valuable help for our understanding of the New Testament, help from an unexpected quarter.[6]

From where exactly did this material come? The answer is from Lightfoot's lecture notebooks. When Lightfoot served as fellow (1851), Hulsean Professor of Divinity (1861) and Lady Margaret's Professor (1875) at Cambridge University, he gave several series of lectures on Acts, the Gospel of John, 1 Peter and 2 Corinthians (among other subjects). The first Acts notebook, which also includes notes on Galatians, begins with these words—"Lenten Term, 1855." Over time, as he continued to lecture on these great New Testament texts, Lightfoot would revise his lectures, further annotate them, change his mind on a few things and add things.

When Lightfoot became bishop of Durham in 1879, he brought all of his Cambridge work on the New Testament, and much else, with him. This is how these materials eventually came into the possession of the Durham Cathedral Library. Lightfoot had been lecturing on Acts and John and other parts of the New Testament for more than twenty years when he left Cambridge for Durham, and the impression one gets from these unpublished manuscripts is that, having already published commentaries on Galatians (1865), Philippians (1868), and Colossians and Philemon (1875), Lightfoot's views on Acts, John, 2 Corinthians and 1 Peter were mostly formed by the

---

These essays were first published posthumously by Macmillan in 1893. Baker republished them in 1979 with a fresh introduction by Philip Edgecumbe Hughes under the title *Biblical Essays*.
[6]Todd Still joined this ambitious project at the invitation of BW3 in early June 2013.

time he came to Durham. Indeed, one finds in these same Acts notebooks some of the materials that went into Lightfoot's Galatians commentary and his fragmentary commentaries on certain Pauline letters (namely, Romans, the Corinthian and Thessalonian correspondences, and Ephesians).[7]

Our hope is that these materials will be as rewarding for you in your reading and studying as they have been for us. To be sure, it is an honor to work on these long-lost manuscripts from a great exegete and historian who set in motion a long line of great New Testament scholars in Durham. Scholars who, like Lightfoot, left their mark in Durham include Lightfoot's contemporary and friend B. F. Westcott as well as Alfred Plummer, William Sanday, H. E. W. Turner, C. K. Barrett, C. E. B. Cranfield, J. D. G. Dunn, J. M. G. Barclay, Stephen Barton and Francis Watson. These are but a few of those who have followed in the footsteps and in the tradition of Lightfoot, *focusing on detailed historical, exegetical and theological study of the text.* This volume, and the one to follow, continue that Durham legacy and contribution to New Testament scholarship.

Ben Witherington III
St. John's College, Durham, England
Pentecost 2013

Todd D. Still
Baylor University/Truett Seminary, Waco, Texas
Advent 2013/Epiphany 2014

---

[7]Lightfoot's comments on these Pauline letters were published posthumously as *Notes on the Epistles of St. Paul* (London: Macmillan, 1895).

Editors' Introduction

J. B. Lightfoot
as Biblical Commentator

No one could match Lightfoot for "exactness of scholarship,
width of erudition, scientific method, sobriety of
judgment and lucidity of style."[1]

William Sanday

"No one ever loitered so late in the Great Court that he did not see
Lightfoot's lamp burning in his study window, though not many
either was so regularly present in morning Chapel at seven o'clock
that he did not find Lightfoot always there with him."[2]

Bishop Handley C. G. Moule

Joseph Barber Lightfoot (1828–1889) was in many ways ideally suited to be a commentator on the New Testament. He had mastery of at least seven ancient and modern languages (German, French, Spanish,

---

[1]William Sanday, "Bishop Lightfoot," *The Expositor* 4 (1886): 13-29 (on 13). Sanday was also a Durhamite, most well known for producing the International Critical Commentary on Romans with Arthur Headlam.
[2]Lightfoot's successor (with one in between) as bishop of Durham.

Italian, Latin, Classical Greek, Koine Greek, and the Greek of the church fathers) and a good working knowledge of many others, including Hebrew, Aramaic, Syriac, Armenian, Ethiopic and Coptic. Some of these languages he taught himself. It was clear enough from early on that Lightfoot had a gift for languages. He once asked a friend whether he did not find it to be the case that *one forgets what language one is reading* when one becomes absorbed in a text![3] There have been precious few biblical scholars over time that could have candidly made such a remark about so many different languages.

Lightfoot also had a keen interest in history and understood its importance for the study of a historical religion such as Christianity. He was a critical and perspicuous thinker and writer with few peers in any age of Christian history. Furthermore, Lightfoot was able to devote himself to the study of the New Testament in ways and to a degree that few scholars before or since his time have been able to do, not least because he never married and had no family for whom to care.[4] Yet when we look at the list of his publications, we may be somewhat surprised that there are not more works of biblical exegesis. Here is a list of his works that were first published in the nineteenth century.

• *Saint Paul's Epistle to the Galatians* (London: Macmillan, 1865)

• *Saint Paul's Epistle to the Philippians* (London: Macmillan, 1868)

• *S. Clement of Rome* (London: Macmillan, 1869)

---

[3]He made this remark to J. R. Harmer. See G. R. Eden and F. C. Macdonald, eds., *Lightfoot of Durham: Memorials and Appreciations* (Cambridge: Cambridge University Press, 1932), pp. 118-19. Apparently, Lightfoot also knew Arabic. It is a great pity that no proper biography has ever been written on Lightfoot. What we have in *Lightfoot of Durham* is some fond remembrances of the man by a few of the people who knew him. Only a portion of the volume discusses his academic work, and even then only very cursorily. Do see, however, pp. 105-22 and the brief discussions by H. E. Savage and Bishop J. R. Harmer (Lightfoot's chaplain, secretary and proofreader for some years, before becoming a bishop himself). Note also the essays by the dean of Wells and the bishop of Gloucester (pp. 123-41). Notice that there are *no scholars* writing essays in this volume. This speaks volumes about Lightfoot's work for and impact on the church. There is a nice anecdote about how as a boy at school, when someone asked how he was coming along with his German, the reply given from the school was: "Oh he's mastered German, he's moved on to Anglo-Saxon!"
[4]If one wonders why someone like Lightfoot agreed to take a post like the episcopal seat in Durham after a thriving academic life in Cambridge and after having turned down becoming bishop of Litchfield, the answer in part is family connections. He had a great love for the "north" of England, as his mother was from Newcastle and his family on his father's side was from Yorkshire. He saw it, in one sense, as returning to his ancestral home.

- *Fresh Revision of the English New Testament* (London: Macmillan, 1871)
- *Saint Paul's Epistles to the Colossians and Philemon* (London: Macmillan, 1875)
- *Primary Charge* (London: Macmillan, 1882)
- *The Apostolic Fathers, Part 2, S. Ignatius, S. Polycarp*, 3 vols. (London: Macmillan, 1885–1889)
- *Essays on Supernatural Religion* (London: Macmillan, 1889)
- *The Apostolic Fathers, Part 1, S. Clement of Rome*, 2 vols. (London: Macmillan, 1890)
- *Cambridge Sermons* (London: Macmillan, 1890)
- *Leaders in the Northern Church* (London: Macmillan, 1890)
- *Ordination Addresses* (London: Macmillan, 1890)
- *Apostolic Fathers Abridged* (London: Macmillan, 1891)
- *Sermons Preached in St. Paul's* (London: Macmillan, 1891)
- *Special Sermons* (London: Macmillan, 1891)
- *The Contemporary Pulpit Library: Sermons by Bishop Lightfoot* (London: Swan Sonnenschein, 1892)
- *Dissertations on the Apostolic Age* (London: Macmillan, 1892)
- *Biblical Essays* (London: Macmillan, 1893)
- *Historical Essays* (London: Macmillan, 1895)
- *Notes on the Epistles of St. Paul from Unpublished Commentaries* (London: Macmillan, 1895)

Compare this to the inventory created by B. N. Kaye after inspecting everything the Durham Cathedral Library had in handwritten script by Lightfoot:

- Lecture notes on Acts
- Lecture notes on Ephesians
- Script on the destination of Ephesians (published in *Biblical Essays*)
- Lecture notes on 1 Corinthians 1:1–15:54
- Lecture notes on 1 Peter

- Internal evidence for the authencity and genuineness of St. John's Gospel (printed in *Biblical Essays*)

- External evidence for the authenticity and genuineness of St. John's Gospel (printed in *Biblical Essays*)

- External testimony for St. John's Gospel (rough notes worked up in *Biblical Essays*)

- Second set of notes on internal evidence (printed in *The Expositor* [1890])

- Notes on introduction to John and John 1:1–12:2

- Notes on introduction to Romans and Romans 1:1–9:6 and a separate set of incomplete notes briefly covering Romans 4–13

- Notes on Thessalonians

- Preliminary text for William Smith's *Dictionary of the Bible* article

- Chronology of St. Paul's life and epistles

- The text of St. Paul's epistles

- St. Paul's preparation for the ministry

- Chronology of St. Paul's life and epistles (printed in *Biblical Essays*)

- The churches of Macedonia (printed in *Biblical Essays*)

- The church of Thessalonica (printed in *Biblical Essays*)

- Notes on the genuineness of 1 and 2 Thessalonians

- Unlabeled notes on the text of 1 and 2 Thessalonians

From even a cursory comparison of these two lists, several things become apparent: (1) There is a good deal of material on Acts, John, Paul and 1 Peter that never saw the light of day; and (2) Lightfoot wrote as much, and as often, for the sake of the church and its ministry and about the church and its ministry as he did on subjects of historical or exegetical interest. But where had Lightfoot gained all his knowledge and erudition? What sort of education and what teachers produced such a scholar and churchman?

THE GROOMING OF A SCHOLAR

C. K. Barrett reminds us that Lightfoot in the first instance gained his skills as a commentator on the Bible from studying at King Edward's School in

Birmingham under James Lee Prince. Such study gave him a thoroughgoing training in both Greek and Latin, with wide reading in classical literature and history. When Lightfoot went to study at Trinity College, Cambridge, he worked with B. F. Westcott, who was three years his senior. In 1851 he took the Classical Tripos and came out as a Senior Classic.[5] Barrett relates the well-known story that Lightfoot wrote his tripos exam without a single mistake, which Barrett thinks refers to his work on the language parts of the exam. Afterward, Lightfoot was elected to a fellowship at Trinity and went on to teach languages to other students at Trinity. In his "spare" time he was learning theology and reading the Apostolic Fathers.[6]

At the tender age of thirty-three, Lightfoot was named Hulsean Professor of Divinity and was the mainstay of the faculty there, even with the addition of Westcott and Hort. Of his lectures in Cambridge, F. J. A. Hort reports,

> They consisted chiefly, if not wholly, of expositions of parts of books of the New Testament, and especially of St. Paul's Epistles, with discussions and leading topics usually included in "Introductions" to these books. Their value and interest were soon widely recognized in the university, and before long no lecture-room then available sufficed to contain the hearers, both candidates for holy orders and older residents; so that leave had to be obtained for the use of the hall of Trinity.[7]

His commentaries on what we now call the later Pauline letters (Philippians, Colossians and Philemon) as well as on Galatians began to come out in the 1860s, but it is clear that already in the 1850s, based on his Cambridge lecture notes, which we can now inspect, that Lightfoot had already sorted out his view of Acts and its relationship to the Pauline corpus as well as Pauline chronology. He had also done extensive work on the Gospel of John and 1 Peter. Indeed, we find some of his Galatians commentary in the same notebook as his lecture notes on Acts. In other words, Lightfoot's previously unpublished work on Acts, John, 1 Peter and some of Paul's letters was produced when he was at the height of his

---

[5]A tripos is an exam taken for the BA degree with honors at Cambridge University.
[6]C. K. Barrett, "J. B. Lightfoot as Biblical Commentator," *Durham University Journal* (1992): 53-70 (on 54).
[7]F. J. A. Hort, "Lightfoot, Joseph Barber," *Dictionary of National Biography, 1885–1900* (London: Smith, Elder & Co), 33:232-40, on p. 233.

powers and commentary-writing ability. *These heretofore unpublished are often as detailed as the published commentaries and are from the same period of Lightfoot's life.*

If we ask why some of this material was not published during Lightfoot's lifetime, the answer is ready to hand—it is incomplete. None of these unpublished manuscripts were full commentaries on the books in question. But there are further reasons why Lightfoot did not publish his voluminous materials on Acts and John. As Barrett notes, Lightfoot, Westcott and Hort had agreed to divide up the New Testament among them and to write commentaries on each book.[8] Lightfoot was tasked with treating the Pauline corpus, not the Gospels, Acts or 1 Peter.[9] Furthermore, the last of his published commentaries (on Colossians and Philemon) came out less than four years before Lightfoot became bishop of Durham in 1879, a work in which he became almost totally absorbed for the rest of his life, which proved to be ten years.[10] Regarding Lightfoot's commentary work, Hort remarks:

> Technical language is as far as possible avoided and exposition, essentially scientific, is clothed in simple and transparent language. The natural meaning of each verse is set forth without polemical matter. The prevailing characteristic is . . . good sense unaccompanied by either the insight or delusion of subtlety. Introductions, which precede the commentaries,

---

[8]At an earlier point in time, Lightfoot, Westcott and Hort were meant to write commentaries for the Smith's Commentary series. Although this plan did not pan out, it is of present import to note that Lightfoot was supposed to have commented on Acts for this series.

[9]It was Alexander Macmillan who suggested to Westcott the possibility of a Cambridge commentary on the entire New Testament. Westcott in turn enlisted Lightfoot and Hort for the project, to be based on the Westcott and Hort Greek text.

Until beginning this work on Lightfoot, I had not realized that the original attempt to have a Cambridge Bible Commentary on the whole New Testament had begun with this agreement, although it never came to full fruition. In the 1960s and '70s, C. F. D. Moule, the relative of the successor of Lightfoot in the Durham episcopacy (H. G. C. Moule), revived the attempt to have a Cambridge Bible Commentary on the Greek New Testament, but it too was destined not to be completed. Indeed, it produced only a couple of notable volumes, C. E. B. Cranfield's volume on Mark and Moule's on Colossians and Philemon. This brings us to the turn of the twenty-first century when I, another Durham man, was named editor of the New Cambridge Bible Commentary series, along with my Asbury colleague Bill Arnold, who is the Old Testament editor. This third attempt has now produced volumes on both Old and New Testament books, but there is still much to be done, and more volumes are forthcoming. (BW3)

[10]For example, he became absorbed in training ordinands for the Anglican ministry, in setting up the diocese of Newcastle and in paying for churches to be built.

handle the subject-matter with freshness and reality, almost every section being in effect a bright little historical essay. To each commentary is appended a dissertation, which includes some of Lightfoot's most careful and thorough work.[11]

There was one gargantuan academic project Lightfoot continued to work on even after he became bishop—his monumental and groundbreaking studies on the apostolic fathers, though he mostly only found time to work on this project during holidays and while traveling.

> There are vivid descriptions of Lightfoot being found in a boat or railway carriage with an Armenian or Coptic grammar in hand or calmly correcting proofs while being driven down precipitous paths in Norway. . . . But above all the secret lay in his ability to switch off, giving himself totally to what was before him. As his chaplain [J. R. Harmer] put it . . . "His power of detachment and concentration was extraordinary. I have seen him break off from an incomplete sentence for a momentous interview with one of his clergy, give him his undivided and sympathetic attention followed by the wisest counsel and final decision, and almost before the door was closed upon his visitor become once more absorbed in his literary work."[12]

Lest we worry that in later life Lightfoot went off the boil as he labored away on the apostolic fathers, Stephen Neill assuages such concern. "If I had my way," Neill maintains, "at least five hundred pages of Lightfoot's *Apostolic Fathers* would be required reading for every theological student in his first year. I cannot imagine any better introduction to critical method, or a better preparation for facing some of the difficult problems of New Testament interpretation that yet remain unsolved."[13]

There was probably, however, another reason why Lightfoot never published his work on John and Acts. His friend, colleague and original Cambridge mentor B. F. Westcott *was* producing a commentary on John. Lightfoot would likely have regarded it as bad form to publish something that competed with his colleague's work, especially when they had already agreed regarding the division of labor when it came to the New

---

[11]Hort, "Lightfoot," pp. 237-38.
[12]John A. T. Robinson, "Joseph Barber Lightfoot" (Durham Cathedral Lecture, 1981), p. 13.
[13]Stephen C. Neill, *The Interpretation of the New Testament 1861-1961* (Oxford: Oxford University Press, 1966), p. 57.

Testament. Furthermore, his other colleague F. J. A. Hort was scheduled to do Acts.

Turning to another academic matter, we learn early on what kind of man Lightfoot was when it came to collegiality. Having become Hulsean Professor of Divinity at Cambridge at the remarkably young age of thirty-three, when the Regius Professorship of Divinity became open in 1870, it was assumed that he would take it. But when Lightfoot learned that Westcott would be returning to Cambridge after fulfilling an ecclesiastical assignment, he turned down the post so that it might be given to Westcott.

> Lightfoot used all his influence to induce his friend Westcott to become a candidate and resolutely declined to stand himself. After Lightfoot's death, Dr. Westcott wrote, "He called me to Cambridge to occupy a place which was his own by right; and having done this he spared no pains to secure for his colleague favorable opportunities for action, while he himself withdrew from the position which he had so long virtually occupied."[14]

This speaks volumes about the character of the man.

Instead of becoming Regius Professor, five years later Lightfoot accepted the Lady Margaret's chair. As such, Lightfoot focused on his exegetical work, work that went into his lectures. These labors remained largely unknown after he died, since they were mostly unpublished. In fact, Lightfoot never fully revised any non-Pauline materials into commentary form since there was neither time nor opportunity to do so once he became bishop of Durham. Then, he died prematurely.

So it was that these invaluable Cambridge New Testament notes of Lightfoot remained unpublished. They were presumably first moved to Bishop Auckland Palace (the residence of the bishop of Durham) when Lightfoot moved to Durham. Following his death, they were transported to the Durham Cathedral Library.[15] There, they have barely seen the light of day since 1889, with only a handful of scholars and clerics even reading a

---

[14]Hort, "Lightfoot," p. 234.

[15]Hort ("Lightfoot," p. 237) says that Lightfoot's library was divided between the divinity school at Cambridge and the University of Durham. What he does not tell us is what happened to his papers, letters and unpublished manuscripts. We now know that they stayed in Durham in a cupboard in the Monk's Dormitory in the Cathedral close.

Doctrine of the Logos

The expression unintelligible in itself. Evidently had a previous
The Apostles use old terms to enunciate the better unity.
λόγος (λέγω) speech, language. this was a necessity of their position —
diff. from Φίλων — to apply, select, arrange.
their adaptation. see letter to Ign. Rom.
Consequently it always has reference to the subject
matter.
speech — account — reason of a thing.

And from this last sense. it got to signify
the faculty of reason — regarded Logos as
an energy & rest as a potentiality.

We too have here meanings of λόγος like are
'speech' & 'reason'.

Combin. of speech & reason: both special
characteristics of man.

How far is the one coextensive the other?
that a separate child or are combined

Applying λόγος to the Divine Being —
It will involve two prominent ideas, corresponding
to these (1) Wisdom, creative & sustaining —
Providence.
(2) Revelation.

These are the prominent ideas which the expression λόγος τοῦ Θεοῦ could involve.

But as the expression etymologically considered
under two ideas, so also in its historical
progress we trace the union of two distinct
lines of development of thought.

ἐπίστευσεν. The δοῦλος seem to show that the ... of the ... and was interternal. In A.V. 'believed', 'commit'. The same could be preserved in both clauses here.

25. περὶ τοῦ ἀνθρώπου & ἐν τῷ ἀνθρώπῳ whereas A.V. should testify of man, for he knew what was in man.

It specializes the particular man, with whom at any ... supposed here the had dealings

δοῦλος. ... translated in the A.V. which has also omitted to translate the preceding δοῦλος. The ... is 'of Himself': here 'on His part.

ὃ χρείαν εἶχεν ἵνα

III
---

1. Νικόδημος. A name ... common among the Jews See Joseph. Ant. XVIII. 3. 2. Bell. Jud. ii. 17. 10.
See Buxtorf pp. 15, 28,
Comp. Νικόλαος.

Perhaps Theudas = Matthias. Act V. 36. See Wieseler p 90.

Nicodemus was called ... has ... of same Jewish name (...Theodorus, Theodotus, Petrus, Matthias, &c.) or a modification of same Jewish name as Alphaeus, Jason, Simon, a second name adopted as John Hyrcanus, Herod Agrippa &c.

The Talmud ... Nicodemus whose name was Bunai ... one of the ... richest men when Jerusalem was taken by Titus. He was born ...
See Lightfoot here

Lightfoot's learned notes on Sychar (John 4:5)

55. ...

53. ...

Expansive comments by Lightfoot on the eucharistic overtones of John 6:53ff.

(1) Commentary
(2) authenticity

(31
(a

VII. 53 — VIII. 11.

This pericope cannot be genuine.

(1) External Evidence

(a) 1st century in
Several old MSS omit it
[a] אABCTLXΔ 33. Of these [...] in AC, Lt
for these it [...]:
(b). Versions. Pesh. etc. Memph. + Theb. both. Arm.
[...] a (Euc. sae. IV) [(Bux. sae. VI)]

(c) Nicon. IV. p. 299 for his comment [...]
[...] for VII. 52 [...] viii. 12.
Tertull. de pudic. 6, [...]
[...] if he had had [...]
Cyprian? [...] this pericope in his text.

He [...] Greek [...] of the 4th & 5th centuries
Euc. Chrysost. Apollin.*, Theod. Mops., Cyr. Alex.
† See the note in Cod. 1.

Importance of teaching of
[...]

[...] No Evidence that it [...]
& If. Then before the 4th century [...]
(ii) When it does occur, it is found in at least three

(2) Internal Evidence.
narrative
(a) The authorship of connexion [...]
At the beginning καὶ ἐπορεύθησαν ἕκαστος [...]
At the end πάλιν οὖν αὐτοῖς ἐλάλησεν
ὁ Ἰησοῦς. To what? There can be no [...]
there.

(b) The style. [...]
The connexion of sentences. St. John very
frequently omits all connecting particles. When

Lightfoot's remarks on Jesus as the "Good Shepherd" (John 10:11)

Martha the house.

2 ἦν δὲ Μαρία
St John afterwards relates the incident
xii. 2.
But here he assumes that his readers know it
already.   This accords with the language of
the other Evangelists Matt. XXVI. 13, Mark. XIV. 9

The forms Μαρία & Μαριάμ seem to be used indiffe-
-rently by St John. Here the reading is doubtful.

4 ὅτι ἐστὶν πρὸς θάνατον
Let us take it its prima facie meaning.
For a || see above on vii. 8

Τῆς δόξης κ. τ. λ.
For the glory of the Son is the glory of the
Father also. XIII. 31 sq, XIV. 13, XVII. 1 sq

5. ἠγάπα   The notice seems the earliest here
            'λαϊδεγατην
quite as well & correctly considers Judas (as
though It is remaining case of indifference), as
explain u. 11.
                Judas
R— ἀγαπάω, φιλέω, See Trench N.T. Syn. p. 4[?]
    D salighten   ἐφίλει. doubtless for which is important

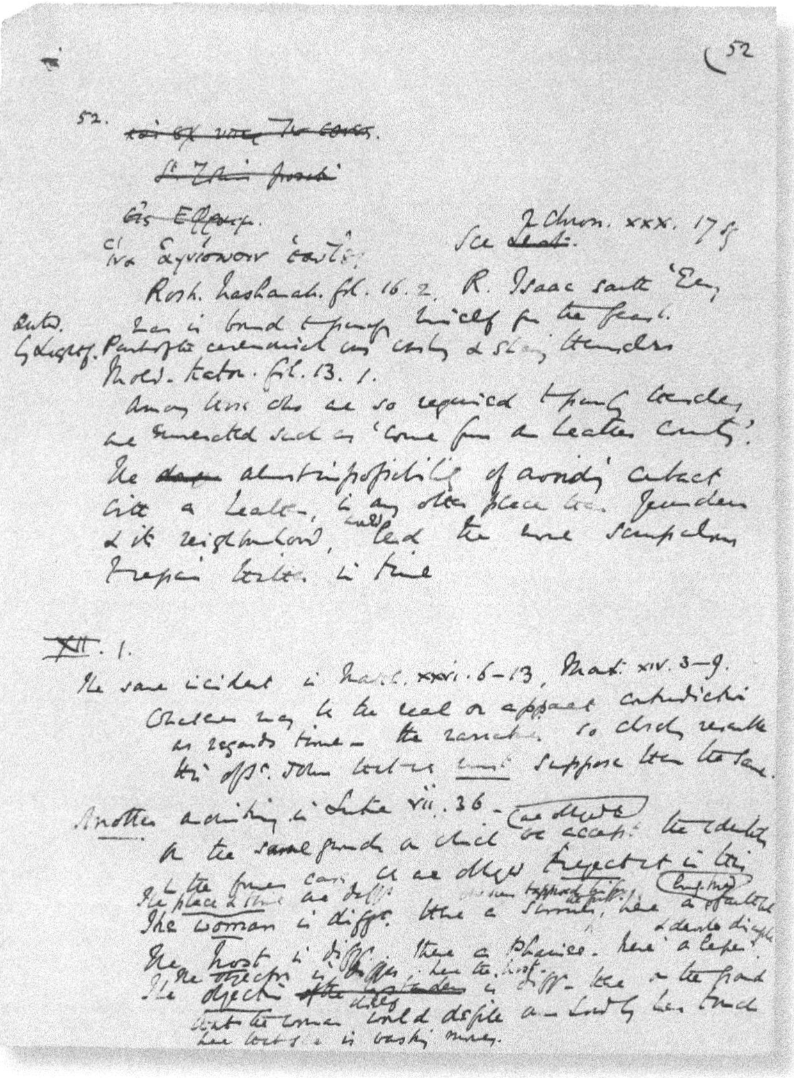

52.

~~[struck-through text]~~

~~[struck-through text]~~

εἰς Ἔφεσον.

Cl. [?]   2 Chron. xxx. 17 §
ἵνα ἁγνίσωσιν ἑαυτοὺς   See [?].

Rosh. hashanah. fil. 16. 2   R. Isaac saith 'Ἐν
[?] [?]

[marg: cuts.]
[marg: Galilary] Perhaps the ceremonial was costly & slow, therefore

Moed. katon. fil. 13. 1.

[illegible handwritten lines]

XII. 1.

The same incident in Matt. xxvi. 6-13, Mark xiv. 3-9.
[illegible handwritten lines]
... John [?] [?] suppose them the same.

Another anointing in Luke vii. 36 —
[illegible handwritten lines]
The place & time are diff[?].
The woman is diff[?].
The host is diff[?], there a Pharisee, here a leper.
The [?] is diff[?].
[illegible handwritten lines]

The incomplete commentary of Lightfoot on John's Gospel concludes with six pages of introductory comments on Mary's anointing of Jesus. The above image is the first.

small part of these materials over the last 150 years.[16] We trust that these Lightfoot volumes will remedy this regrettable neglect.

LIGHTFOOT'S METHOD

Lightfoot learned early on about the value of writing out one's thoughts about the Scriptures. He once advised: "Begin to write as soon as you possibly can. That was what Prince Lee [his headmaster at King Edward's, Birmingham] always said to us. This is the way to learn. Almost all I have learnt has come from writing books. If you write a book on a subject, you have to read everything that has been written about it."[17]

As Robinson stresses, "One turns back with relief to his patient, inductive method after so many of the pre-judgments and unexamined assumptions of form- and redaction-criticism. . . . Lightfoot would have been horrified to think that serious scholarship could by-pass the historical questions or suppose they could be settled *a priori* by the theological."[18] *This is because Lightfoot believed wholeheartedly that nothing could be theologically true that was historically false when it comes to matters involving a historical religion such as Christianity.*

If we ask about Lightfoot's particular modus operandi with respect to commentary writing, his approach is basically the same inductive method: (1) Establish the text by dealing with the text-critical issues, including the textual variants. (2) Offer necessary grammatical and syntactical notes and discussions. (3) Proceed with exegesis proper. For Lightfoot, this sometimes entailed long excursi on special topics and more exegetically problematic matters as well as translations of key phrases into English. (4) Deal with theological issues and larger topics that might involve several New Testament documents.

Lightfoot assumed that his audience would know enough Greek and

---

[16]Barrett ("Lightfoot as Biblical Commentator," p. 55) observes, "Three commentaries [i.e., Galatians, Philippians and Colossians] were published in Lightfoot's lifetime. He left lecture notes, and other notes, on other epistles which doubtless he would have used in published work had he lived, and had his interest not become absorbed in what must be regarded as his greatest work, that on the text of 1 Clement and the Epistles of Ignatius (with 2 Clement and Polycarp thrown in for full measure)—not to mention his conscientious, time-consuming work as bishop of Durham."

[17]Robinson, "Lightfoot," p. 13.

[18]Ibid., p. 16.

scholia to be able to figure out his elliptical references to parallels in other
Greek texts and the like as well as his brief (and sometimes infrequent)
footnotes referencing the work of other scholars. "The permanent value of
Lightfoot's historical work depends on his sagacity in dealing with the materials out of which history has to be constructed. He was invariably faithful
to a rigorous philological discipline, and was preserved by native candor
from distorting influences."[19]

It may be asked at this juncture, What is the value of this material today,
since many good commentaries on Acts, John, 2 Corinthians and 1 Peter
have been written since the time of Lightfoot? The answer to this question
is twofold. First, there is Lightfoot's encyclopedic knowledge of early Greek
literature, a knowledge that is probably unequaled to this day by any subsequent commentator on the New Testament.[20] As Barrett points out,
Lightfoot did not have, nor did he need, a lexicon to find parallels to New
Testament Greek usage. As a close look at his Galatians commentary
shows: "He knows Origen, Ephraem Syrus, Eusebius of Emesa, Chrysostom, Severianus, Theodore of Mopsuestia, Theodoret, Euthalius, Gen-
nadius, Photius, Victorinus, Hilary, Jerome, Augustine, Pelagius, Cassio-
dorus, John of Damascus," not to mention all the pagan Greek literature
and later catenae of Greek and Latin sources.[21] Lightfoot was a walking
lexicon of Greek literature of all sorts, and not infrequently he was able to
cite definitive parallels to New Testament usage that decided the issue of
the meaning of a word or a phrase.

Second, as Dunn notes, time and again Lightfoot *"clearly demonstrates
the importance of reading a historical text within its historical context, that
the meaning of a text does not arise out of the text alone, but out of the text
read in context and that the original context and intention of the author is a*

---

[19]Hort, "Lightfoot," p. 239.
[20]The only New Testament scholar I have ever met, studied with or talked to that was even close
to Lightfoot in these skills was Bruce Metzger, with whom I studied the apostolic fathers in a
summer course at Princeton. He too had a vast panoply of languages at his command as well as
an encyclopedic knowledge of Greek and early Christian literature. It appears he had a photo-
graphic memory, and one wonders whether Lightfoot did as well. Savage (*Lightfoot of Durham*,
p. 110) seems to confirm this conjecture when he speaks of Lightfoot's "remarkable accuracy of
memory which enabled him to apply it readily. Page after page was written *currente calamo* with
few or no books of reference at hand, and with only a 'ver.' here and there in the margin, where
future verification was required." (BW3)
[21]Barrett, "Lightfoot as Biblical Commentator," p. 57.

determinative and controlling factor in what may be read or heard from such a text. . . . Lightfoot would certainly have approved a referential theory of meaning: that that to which the language of the text refers determines and controls the meaning of the text."[22]

This approach is sorely needed today as commentators increasingly dismiss or ignore the importance of original-language study and of the original historical context of a document, or who try to do "theological interpretation" of the text without first having done their historical homework to determine the original contextual meaning of the text, whether theological in character or not. It may be hoped that this series of volumes will revive an interest in the full gamut of subjects relevant to the study of the New Testament, not least ancient history, including social history; the classics; a precise knowledge of Greek, including its grammar and syntax and rhetoric; and, of course, the theology and ethics of the material itself. Doubtless Lightfoot himself would be pleased if this were one outcome of the publication of his long-lost exegetical studies on the New Testament.[23]

Finally, this commentary shows exactly the way Lightfoot approached his study of the New Testament—carefully, prayerfully and, in his own words, with "the highest reason and the fullest faith." Not one or the other, but both. Time and again Lightfoot's intellect and his piety shine through in these lost manuscripts. He shows us repeatedly that faith and reason need not be at odds with each other, especially if it is *fides quaerens intellectum* ("faith seeking understanding"). Honesty about early Christianity and its Lord need not be feared by a person of Christian faith, whether then or now. Taken for what it is, this commentary will not merely "tease the mind into active thought" (a phrase made famous by C. H. Dodd, a Cambridge man like Lightfoot)[24] but also nourish the soul.

---

[22]James D. G. Dunn, "Lightfoot in Retrospect," *Durham University Journal* (1992): 71-94 (here 75-76), italics added for emphasis.

[23]It is possible that he might be a bit miffed to see all this material published since it is incomplete. Lightfoot was nothing if not a perfectionist when it came to fully completing tasks to the best of his ability. The numerous little parenthetical notes to himself to verify a reference or the check marks in the manuscript indicating a reference verified testify to this scholarly habit. Nevertheless, this material, even though incomplete, is extremely valuable, as even a casual reading of what follows should demonstrate.

[24]C. H. Dodd, *The Parables of the Kingdom*, rev. ed. (New York: Scribner's, 1961), p. 5.

Lightfoot and the Gospel of John

If there was one commentary J. B. Lightfoot most wanted to write and publish, it was a commentary on the Gospel of John. There were many reasons for this hope and inclination. First of all, Lightfoot regularly lectured on this Gospel at Cambridge and knew the literature on it well. He loved teaching this material and thought it exceedingly important for understanding the real character of early Christian thought. He once remarked that while the Synoptics presented the facts about the Jesus of history, John's Gospel presented the profound commentary.

Second, for much of his career Lightfoot was deeply concerned about the negative impact of the radical criticism of early Christianity, especially criticism of the historical trustworthiness of documents like the Gospel of John, emanating from the successors of F. C. Baur at Tübingen in his own day. Lightfoot was too much of a historian and too much of an apologete for Christian orthodoxy to be silent for long about the sort of cannonading that resounded all the way to the United Kingdom from the Tübingen school.

And besides, he read critically and took seriously German scholarly works to a degree seldom seen in nineteenth-century British biblical scholarship. He was the ideal person to attempt a deconstruction of the "new" edifice erected by Baur and others. It is clear that what radical critics were saying about Lightfoot's favorite Gospel struck a nerve. You do not write two hundred or so pages defending the authenticity and genuineness of the Gospel of John if you are not exercised about the subject and motivated to present a different view—especially to the views then making inroads all across Europe.[25]

In view of all this, why exactly did all those detailed Cambridge lectures notes on the background and text of the Gospel of John never see the light of day before now? One reason, already noted above, was that Lightfoot's

---

[25]On which see the introductory material below. Some of that material first appeared in 1890 in a periodical called *The Expositor* just after Lightfoot's death. It was then collected together with Lightfoot's additional lecture notes on the subject and published by Macmillan of London in 1904 under the title *Biblical Essays*. Finally, it was reprinted in a volume of the same name by Baker Books in 1979. As the information at the website Project Canterbury makes clear, the material is out of print and in the public domain. We are pleased to reprint the materials here in their original form.

sometime mentor, colleague at Cambridge and friend B. F. Westcott was writing such a commentary.

Nevertheless, I can say now with some assurance that he continued to work on John throughout the period he was at Cambridge, beginning with the Michaelmas term in 1848, when he first began teaching the Gospel of John, and continuing until 1879, when he was "called up North." I say this for three primary reasons: (1) Lightfoot's notes on John are more fulsome than his notes on some of the material in the other two volumes of this series. (2) His notes on John are in several different inks and in some cases in pencil, signaling ongoing work. This is clear because although the original date at the beginning of the manuscript is 1848, we have, for example, a comment on John 7:35 with an article title and author penciled in from 1853. What is interesting is that only rarely is anything crossed out, indicating Lightfoot had later changed his mind on something. And (3) Lightfoot was convinced that the Gospel of John was the most important Gospel theologically, chronologically and historically for a whole host of reasons, not least its clarity on the doctrine of the incarnation. In times when the authenticity and veracity of the Gospel of John were being challenged both at home (by the author of *Supernatural Religion* and others) and abroad (by the successors of F. C. Baur), Lightfoot strongly felt that his Cambridge students, especially the divinity students, needed a hearty sampling of the Gospel meat served up by the Beloved Disciple, and he was going to be sure they did not miss that meal. The massive amount of work he did on authenticity and genuineness of John (see appendix A and appendix B below) reveals Lightfoot's protracted commitment to vindicating the Gospel.

Thus Lightfoot continued to work on this Gospel time and again, revising his notes and updating his references. Perhaps he hoped for a day when all of his material on the Gospel might see the light of day, once Westcott's commentary had "had a good innings," as cricketers would say. These notes come from before and during the period Westcott was working on John, and unfortunately they were never published, until now. If Lightfoot did have a hope that one day this rich material would emerge into the light of day, we are delighted to be able to fulfill that hope, even if this commentary is born out of due season. As it turned out, the Cambridge commentary series did not get very far. No other volumes on the Gospels emerged other than the one by Westcott, and Lightfoot himself did not finish the work on the Pauline epistles. There were two other matters pressing in on him.

The first of these is that Lightfoot was convinced the *big* issue when critiquing the Tübingen approach to early Christianity was *history*. Baur developed, and his successors built on, a particular interpretation of the first four centuries of early Christianity according to which neither the New Testament nor the apostolic fathers could be taken at face value historically. These texts had to be read critically and with a certain degree of skepticism when it came to *Geschichte* as well as *Historie*.

While Lightfoot agreed that critical analysis was required, he did not think that the highest reason necessarily led to a radical deconstruction of the nature and character of Jesus, the New Testament and early Christianity.[26] As a historian, Lightfoot became convinced that he needed to present a very different picture of early Christianity, which in turn led him to focus on providing a definitive critical edition and commentary on the apostolic fathers. To counter the influence of the Tübingen school, one needed to provide better readings not only of the New Testament but also of the earliest successors to the original apostles—the apostolic fathers. To this latter task Lightfoot devoted most of his time and academic attention in the 1870s and 1880s. Indeed, he was still working on revisions of a later edition of his Clement volume just before he died prematurely in 1889.[27]

Lightfoot's election as bishop of Durham in 1879 left him no time to write more biblical commentaries. He had previously turned down an offer to take up episcopal office elsewhere in Britain, but when the chance to "go up North" came, from where various of his ancestors and in particular his mother (who was from Newcastle) had come, he simply could not refuse it. With the exception of his work on the apostolic fathers, from 1879 on his time was consumed with ministerial duties. He even turned down opportunities to lecture (something he loved to do) at Durham. But there are ways for the dead to continue to address us. One way is by pub-

---

[26]One of his favorite expressions or mottos was "the highest reason and the fullest faith."
[27]For a reprint edition of his work on the apostolic fathers, see J. B. Lightfoot, *The Apostolic Fathers*, 5 vols. (Peabody, MA: Hendrickson, 1989).

lishing their lost, misplaced, forgotten or long-out-of-print works that are still of enormous value. Lightfoot's commentary on John is one such lost treasure.[28]

---

[28]The following is a note from Dr. Catherine Turner, the former librarian of Durham Cathedral Library. Her last act before retirement was to digitize all of the unpublished notes of Lightfoot found in these three volumes, last of all the Lightfoot notes on John. We owe her a great debt of gratitude. Here is her parting note, written on August 13, 2013:

> The digital copies of these notes by J. B. Lightfoot were taken in the sequence in which they were stored in the bundles of his notes in the cathedral library.
>
> These bundles were held together with brass fastenings, and had apparently not been separated for many years—by implication since Lightfoot himself had compiled them.
>
> The pages are all numbered, in Lightfoot's hand, but there are frequent jumps and omissions in the pagination. I have assumed that Lightfoot assembled these bundles from earlier sequences of notes to draw together his thoughts and analysis of the Gospel of St. John and did not repaginate the pages when he did so.
>
> I have labelled the images so that they fall into the sequence they had in their fastened bundles in the Lightfoot archive, and I have added in brackets the page number if it does not match this pagination.

Introduction

External and Internal Evidences of the Authenticity and Genuineness of the Fourth Gospel

The Author Explains Himself[1]

This lecture originally formed one of a series connected with Christian evidences, and delivered in St George's Hall in 1871. The other lectures were published shortly afterwards; but, not having been informed beforehand that publication was expected, I withheld my own from the volume. It seemed to me that in the course of a single lecture I could only touch the fringes of a great subject, and that injustice would be done by such imperfect treatment as alone time and opportunity allowed. Moreover I was then, and for some terms afterwards, engaged in lecturing on this Gospel at Cambridge,[2] and I entertained the hope that I might be able to deal with the subject less inadequately if I gave myself more time. Happily it passed into other and better

---

[1]Reprinted from the *Expositor* of January–March, 1890.

[2]In fact, Lightfoot's long-lost lecture notes on John, which form the commentary proper below, give us some precise information on this point—the lectures are labeled Michaelmas Term 1848, and then this is crossed out and labeled 1868 in pencil, suggesting all the pencil additions and corrections come from the later delivery of the lectures on John. What this in turn means is that this introductory material was written and published after Lightfoot had been lecturing on the Fourth Gospel in Cambridge for some time. It appears to have been written first in 1871, with the additional preface from 1889, the year Lightfoot died.

hands [i.e., Westcott's], and I was relieved from this care.

A rumor got abroad at the time, and has (I am informed) been since re-peated, that I did not allow the lecture to be published, because I was dis-satisfied with it. I was only dissatisfied in the sense that I have already ex-plained. It could not be otherwise than unsatisfactory to bring forward mere fragmentary evidence of an important conclusion, when there was abundant proof in the background. The present publication of the lecture is my answer to this rumor. I give it after eighteen years exactly in the same form in which it was originally written, with the exception of a few verbal alterations. Looking over it again after this long lapse of time, I have nothing to withdraw.

Additional study has only strengthened my conviction that this narrative of St. John could not have been written by any one but *an eye-witness*.[3] As I have not dealt with the external evidence except for the sake of supplying a statement of the position of antagonists, the treatment suffers less than it would otherwise have done from not being brought down to date. I have mentioned by way of illustration two respects in which later discoveries had falsified Baur's contentions. The last eighteen years would supply several others. I will single out three: (1) The antagonists of the Ignatian Epistles are again put on their defense. The arguments which were adduced against the genuineness of these epistles will hold no longer. Ignatius has the testimony of his friend and contemporary Polycarp, and Polycarp has the testimony of his own personal disciple Irenaeus. The testimony of Irenaeus is denied by no one; the testimony of Polycarp is only denied because it certifies the Ig-natian letters. Before we are prepared to snap this chain of evidence rudely, and to break with an uninterrupted tradition, we require far stronger reasons than have been hitherto adduced; (2) Justin Martyr wrote before or about the middle of the second century. His use of the Fourth Gospel was at one time systematically denied by the impugners of its apostolic authorship. Now it is acknowledged almost universally, even by those who do not allow that this evangelical narrative was written by St. John himself; (3) The Diates-saron of Tatian was written about A.D. 170, and consisted of a 'Harmony of

---

[3]Recent treatments of the Fourth Gospel have begun to consider again this possibility in one form or another after such an idea had been regularly dismissed for some decades. See, e.g., the com-mentaries by Keener, Lincoln, Witherington and the detailed work of Richard Bauckham in his monograph titled *Jesus and the Eyewitnesses* (Grand Rapids: Eerdmans, 2006).

Four Gospels.' Baur and others contended that at all events St. John was not one of the four. Indeed how could it be? For it had not been written, or only recently written, at this time. The Diatessaron itself has been discovered, and a commentary of Ephrem Syrus upon it in Armenian has likewise been unearthed within the last few years, both showing that it began with the opening words of St. John. [1889]

EXTERNAL EVIDENCE FOR JOHN'S AUTHENTICITY BRIEFLY REVIEWED

The fourth of our canonical Gospels has been ascribed by the tradition of the Church to St. John the son of Zebedee, the personal disciple of our Lord, and one of the twelve apostles. Till within a century (I might almost say, till within a generation) of the present time, this has been the universal belief, with one single and unimportant exception, of all ages, of all churches, of all sects, of all individuals alike. This unanimity is the more remarkable in the earlier ages of the Church, because the language of this gospel has a very intimate bearing on numberless theological controversies that started up in the second, third, and fourth centuries of the Christian era; and it was therefore the direct interest of one party or other to deny the apostolic authority, if they had any ground for doing so. This happened not once or twice only, but many times.

It would be difficult to point to a single heresy promulgated before the close of the fourth century, that might not find some imaginary points of coincidence or some real points of conflict, some relations whether of antagonism or of sympathy, with this gospel. This was equally true of Montanism in the second century, and of Arianism in the fourth. The Fourth Gospel would necessarily be among the most important authorities, we might fairly say the most important authority, in the settlement of the controversy, both from the claims which it made as a product of the beloved apostle himself, and from the striking representations which it gives of our Lord's teaching. The defender or the impugner of this or that theological opinion would have had a direct interest in disproving its genuineness and denying its authority. Can we question that this would have been done again and again, if there had been any haze of doubt hanging over its origin, if the antagonist could have found even a *prima facie* ground for an attack?

And this brings me to speak of that one exception to the universal tradition to which I have already alluded. Once, and once only, did the disputants in a theological controversy yield to the temptation, strong though it must have been.

A small, unimportant, nameless sect, if indeed they were compact enough to form a sect, in the latter half of the second century, denied that the Gospel and the Apocalypse were written by St. John. These are the two canonical writings which especially attribute the title of the Word of God, the Logos, to our Lord: the one, in the opening verses, 'In the beginning was the Word, and the Word was with God, and the Word was God'; the other, in the vision of Him who rides on the white horse, whose garments are stained with blood, and whose name is given as the 'Word of God.'[4] To dispose of the doctrine they discredited the writings.

Epiphanius calls them *Alogi*, 'the opponents of the Word,' or (as it might be translated, for it is capable of a double meaning) 'the irrational ones.' The name is avowedly his own invention. Indeed they would scarcely have acknowledged a title which had this double sense, and could have been so easily turned against themselves. They appear only to disappear. Beyond one or two casual allusions, they are not mentioned; they have no place in history. This is just one of those exceptions which strengthen the rule.

What these *Alogi* did, numberless other sectaries and heretics would doubtless have done, if there had been any sufficient ground for the course. But even these *Alogi* lend no countenance to the views of modern objectors. Modern critics play off the Apocalypse against the Gospel, allowing the genuineness of the former, and using it to impugn the genuineness of the latter. Moreover there is the greatest difference between the two. The modern antagonist places the composition of the Fourth Gospel in the middle or the latter half of the second century; these ancient heretics ascribed it to the early heresiarch Cerinthus, who lived at the close of the first century, and was a contemporary of St. John. Living themselves in the latter half of the second century, they knew (as their opponents would have reminded them, if they had found it convenient to forget the fact) that the Gospel was not a work of yesterday, that it had already a long history, and that it went back at

---

[4]See Jn 1:1; Rev 19:13 respectively.

all events to the latest years of the apostolic age; and in their theory they were obliged to recognize this fact. I need hardly say that the doctrine of the Person of Christ put forward in the Gospel and the Apocalypse is diametrically opposed to the teaching of Cerinthus, as every modern critic would allow. I only allude to this fact, to show that these very persons, who form the single exception to the unanimous tradition of all the churches and all the sects alike, are our witnesses for the antiquity of the Gospel (though not for its authenticity), and therefore are witnesses against the modern impugners of its genuineness.

With this exception, the early testimony to the authenticity and genuineness of the Gospel is singularly varied. It is a remarkable and an important fact, that the most decisive and earliest testimony comes, not from Fathers of the orthodox Church, but from heretical writers. I cannot enter upon this question at length, for I did not undertake this afternoon to speak of the external evidence; and I ask you to bear in mind, that any inadequate and cursory treatment necessarily does a great injustice to a subject like this; for the ultimate effect of testimony must depend on its fullness and variety. I only call attention to the fact that within the last few years most valuable additions have been made to this external testimony, and these from the opposite extremes of the heretical scale.

At the one extreme we have Ebionism, which was the offspring of Judaizing tendencies; at the other, Gnosticism, which took its rise in Gentile license of speculation and practice. Ebionism is represented by a remarkable extant work belonging to the second century, possibly to the first half of the second century, the *Clementine Homilies*. The greater part of this work has long been known, but until within the last few years the printed text was taken from a MS mutilated at the end; so that of the twenty Homilies the last half of the nineteenth and the whole of the twentieth are wanting. These earlier Homilies contained more than one reference to gospel history which could not well be referred to any of the three first evangelists, and seemed certainly to have been taken from the fourth. Still the reference was not absolutely certain, and the impugners of St. John's Gospel availed themselves of this doubt to deny the reference to this gospel.

At length, in the year 1853, Dressel published for the first time, from a Vatican MS., the missing conclusion of these Homilies; and this was found to contain a reference to the incidents attending the healing of the man born blind, related only by St. John, and related in a way distinctly characteristic of St. John—a reference so distinct, that no one from that time has attempted to deny or to dispute it. So much for the testimony of Ebionism, of the Judaic sects of early Christianity. But equally definite, and even more full, is the testimony which recent discovery has brought to light on the side of Gnosticism. Many of my hearers will remember the interest which was excited a few years ago by the publication of a lost treatise on heresies, which Bunsen and others ascribed (and, as is now generally allowed, correctly ascribed) to Hippolytus, in the earlier part of the third century. This treatise contains large and frequent extracts from previous Gnostic writers of diverse schools—Ophites, Basilideans, Valentinians; among them, from a work which Hippolytus quotes as the production of Basilides himself, who flourished about A.D. 130–140. And in these extracts are abundant quotations from the Gospel of St. John. I have put these two recent accessions to the external testimony in favor of the Fourth Gospel side by side, because, emanating from the most diverse quarters, they have a peculiar value, as showing the extensive circulation and wide reception of this gospel at a very early date; and because also, having been brought to light soon after its genuineness was for the first time seriously impugned, they seem providentially destined to furnish an answer to the objections of recent criticism.

If we ask ourselves why we attribute this or that ancient writing to the author whose name it bears—why, for instance, we accept this tragedy as a play of Sophocles, or that speech as an oration of Demosthenes, our answer will be, that it bears the name of the author, and (so far as we know) has always been ascribed to him. In very many cases we know nothing, or next to nothing, about the history of the writing in question. In a few instances we are fortunate enough to find a reference to it, or a quotation from it, in some author who lived a century or two later. The cases are exceptionally rare when there is an indisputable allusion in a contemporary, or nearly contemporary, writer. For the most part, we accept the fact of the authorship, because it comes to us on the authority of a MS. or MSS. written several centuries after the presumed author lived, supported in some cases by quotations in a late lexicographer, or grammarian, or collection of extracts. The external testimony in favor of St. John's Gospel reaches back much nearer to the writer's own time, and is far more extensive than can be produced in the case of most classical writings of the same antiquity.

From the character of the work also, this testimony gains additional value; for where the contents of a book intimately affect the cherished beliefs and the practical conduct of all who receive it, the universality of its reception, amidst jarring creeds and conflicting tendencies, is far more significant than if its contents are indifferent, making no appeal to the religious convictions, and claiming no influence over the life. We may be disposed to complain that the external testimony is not so absolutely and finally conclusive in itself that no door is open for hesitation, that all must, despite themselves, accept it, and that any investigation into the internal evidence is superfluous and vain.

But this we have no right to demand. If it is as great, and more than as great, as would satisfy us in any other case, this should suffice us. In all the most important matters which affect our interests in this world and our hopes hereafter, God has left some place for diversity of opinion, because He would not remove all opportunity of self-discipline. If then the genuineness of this gospel is supported by greater evidence than in ordinary cases we consider conclusive, we approach the investigation of its internal character with a very strong presumption in its favor. The *onus probandi* rests with those who would impugn its genuineness, and nothing short of the fullest and most decisive marks of spuriousness can fairly be considered sufficient to counterbalance this evidence.

As I proceed, I hope to make it clear that, allowing their full weight to all the difficulties (and it would be foolish to deny the existence of difficulties) in this gospel, still the internal marks of authenticity and genuineness are so minute, so varied, so circumstantial, and so unsuspicious, as to create an overwhelming body of evidence in its favor. But before entering upon this investigation, it may be worthwhile to inquire whether the hypotheses suggested by those who deny the genuineness of this gospel are themselves free from all difficulties. For if it be a fact (as I believe it is) that any alternative which has been proposed introduces greater perplexities than those which it is intended to remove, we are bound (irrespective of any positive arguments in its favor) to fall back upon the account which is exposed to fewest objections, and which at the same time is supported by a continuous and universal tradition.

We may take our start from Baur's theory, for he was the first to develop and systematize the attack on the genuineness of the Fourth Gospel. According to Baur it was written about the year 170. The external testimony however is alone fatal to this very late epoch; for, after all wresting of evidence and post-dating of documents, it is impossible to deny that at this time the gospel was, not only in existence, but also received far and wide as a genuine document; that it was not only quoted occasionally, but had even been commented upon as the actual work of St. John. Consequently the tendency of later impugners has been to push the date farther back, and to recede from the extreme position of this, its most determined and ablest antagonist.[5]

Hilgenfeld, who may be regarded as the successor of Baur, and the present representative of the Tübingen school (though it has no longer its headquarters at Tübingen), would place its composition about the year 150; and Tayler, who a few years ago (1867) reproduced the argument of Baur and others in England, is disposed to assign it to about the same date. With a strange inconsistency he suggests, towards the close of his book, that its true author may have been John the presbyter, though John the presbyter is stated by Papias (who had conversed with this John, and from whom all the information we possess respecting him is derived) to have been a personal disciple of our Lord, and therefore could hardly have been older than John the apostle, and certainly could not have been living towards the middle of the second century. This tendency to recede nearer and nearer to the evangelist's own age shows that the pressure of facts has begun to tell on the theories of antagonistic criticism, and we may look forward to the time when it will be held discreditable to the reputation of any critic for sobriety and judgment to assign to this gospel any later date than the end of the first century, or the very beginning of the second.

---

[5]Lightfoot, of course, lived before the discovery of various Greek fragments of the Gospel of John, probably dating to the second century, particularly P[52]. This would have further supported his case about the dating of the Fourth Gospel. On the other hand, another piece of evidence brought to light by M. Oberweis ("Das Martyrium der Zebedaiden in Mk. 10.35-40 (Mt. 20.20-3) und Offb 11.3-13," *New Testament Studies* 44 [1998]: 74-92) provides us with a reference to the possible early demise of John son of Zebedee, suffering a fate like his brother, who died in A.D. 44.

THE INTERNAL SILENCES AND NOTICES[6]

But meanwhile, let us take the earliest of these dates (A.D. 150) as less encumbered with difficulties, and therefore more favorable to the opponents of its genuineness, and ask whether a gospel written at such a time would probably have presented the phenomena which we actually find in the fourth canonical gospel. We may interrogate alike its omissions and its contents. On this hypothesis, how are we to account for what it has left unsaid, and for what it has said? Certainly it must be regarded as a remarkable phenomenon, that on many ecclesiastical questions that then agitated the minds of Christians it is wholly silent, while to others it gives no distinct and authoritative answer. Our Lord's teaching has indeed its bearing on the controversies of the second century, as on those of the fourth, or of the twelfth, or of the sixteenth, or of the nineteenth, but, as in these latter instances, its lessons are inferential rather than direct, they are elicited by painful investigation, they are contained implicitly in our Lord's life and person, they do not lie on the surface, nor do they offer definite solutions of definite difficulties.

Take, for instance, the dispute concerning the episcopate. Contrast the absolute silence of this gospel respecting this institution with the declarations in the Epistles of Ignatius. A modern defender of the episcopate will appeal to the commission given to the apostles (John 20:22, 23). I need not stop here to inquire to what extent it favors his views. But obviously it is quite insufficient by itself. It would serve almost equally well for an apostolically ordained ministry of any kind, for a presbyteral as for an episcopal succession. Is it possible that a writer, composing a gospel at the very time when the authority of this office had been called in question, if a supporter of the power of the episcopate, would have resisted the temptation of inserting something which would convey a sanction, if an opponent, something which would convey a disparagement, of this office, in our Lord's own name?

Or, again: take the Gnostic theories of emanations. Any one who has studied the history of the second century will know how large a place they occupy in the theological disputes of the day; what grotesque and varied forms they assume in the speculations of different heretical teachers; what diverse arguments, some valid, some fanciful, are urged against them by

---

[6]See the excursus below (pp. 109-11) at the end of John 1 on these matters.

orthodox writers. Would a forger have hesitated for a moment to slay this many-headed hydra by one well-aimed blow? What can we suppose to have been the object of such a forger, except to advance certain theological views? And why should he have let slip the very opportunity, which (we must suppose) he was making for himself, of condemning the worst forms of heresy from our Lord's own lips? It is true that you and I think we see (and doubtless think rightly), that the doctrine of God the Word taught in St. John's Gospel is the real answer to the theological questionings which gave rise to all these theories about aeons or emanations, and involves implicitly and indirectly the refutation of all such theories. But it is only by more or less abstruse reasoning that we arrive at this conclusion. The early Gnostics did not see it so; they used St. John's Gospel, and retained their theories notwithstanding.

A forger would have taken care to provide a direct refutation that it was impossible to misunderstand. Or, again, about the middle of the second century the great controversy respecting the time of celebrating Easter was beginning to lift up its head. For the latter half of this century the feud raged, bursting out ever afresh and disturbing the peace of the Church again and again, until it was finally set at rest in the fourth century at the Council of Nicaea.

Was the festival of the Lord's resurrection to be celebrated always on the same day of the week, the Sunday? Or was it to be guided by the time of the Jewish Passover, and thus to take place on the same day of the month, irrespective of the day of the week? Each community, each individual, took a side in this controversy. Unimportant in itself, it seriously endangered the existence of the Church. The daring adventurer who did not hesitate to forge a whole gospel would certainly not be deterred by any scruple from setting the matter at rest by a few strokes of the pen. His narrative furnished more than one favorable opportunity for interposing half a dozen decisive words in our Lord's name, and yet he abstained. Thus we might take in succession the distinctive ecclesiastical controversies of the second century, and show how the writer of the Fourth Gospel holds aloof from them all, certainly a strange and almost incredible fact, if this writer lived about the middle, or even in the latter half, of the century, and, as a romancer, was not restrained by those obligations of fact which fetter the truthful historian who is himself a contemporary of the events recorded!

But if the omissions of the writer are strange and unaccountable on the assumption of the later date of the Gospel, the actual contents present still greater difficulties on the same hypothesis. In the interval between the age when the events are recorded to have taken place and the age in which the writer is supposed to have lived, a vast change had come over the civilized world. In no period had the dislocation of Jewish history been so complete. Two successive hurricanes had swept over the land and nation. The devastation of Titus had been succeeded by the devastation of Hadrian. What the locust of the first siege had left the cankerworm of the second had devoured. National polity, religious worship, social institutions, all were gone. The city had been razed, the land laid desolate, the law and the ordinances proscribed, the people swept into captivity or scattered over the face of the earth. 'Old things had passed away; all things had become new.'

Now let us place ourselves in the position of one who wrote about the middle of the second century, after the later Roman invasion had swept off the scanty gleanings of the past that had been spared from the earlier. Let us ask how a romancer so situated is to make himself acquainted with the incidents, the localities, the buildings, the institutions, the modes of thought and feeling, which belonged to this past age and (as we may almost say) this bygone people. Let it be granted that here and there he might stumble upon a historical fact, that in one or two particulars he might reproduce a national characteristic. More than this would be beyond his reach.

For, it will be borne in mind, he would be placed at a great disadvantage, compared with a modern writer; he would have to reconstruct history without those various appliances, maps and plates, chronological tables, books of travel, by which the author of a historical novel is so largely assisted in the present day. And even if he had been furnished with all these aids, would he have known how to use them? The uncritical character of the apostolic age is a favorite commonplace with those who impugn the genuineness of the canonical Scriptures, or the trustworthiness of the evangelical narratives. I do not deny that the age (compared with our own) was uncritical, though very exaggerated language is often used on the subject. But obviously this argument has a double edge. And the keener of these two edges lies across the very throat of recent negative criticism. *For it requires a much higher flight of critical genius to invent an extremely delicate fiction than to detect it when invented. The age which could not expose a coarse forgery was incapable of constructing a subtle historical romance.*

This one thing I hope to make clear in the short time that is allowed me this afternoon. The Fourth Gospel, if a forgery, shows the most consummate skill on the part of the forger; it is (as we should say in modern phrase) thoroughly in keeping. It is replete with historical and geographical details; it is interpenetrated with the Judaic spirit of the times; its delineations of character are remarkably subtle; it is perfectly natural in the progress of the events; the allusions to incidents or localities or modes of thought are introduced in an artless and unconscious way, being closely interwoven with the texture of the narrative; while throughout, the author has exercised a silence and a self-restraint about his assumed personality which is without a parallel in ancient forgeries, and which deprives his work of the only motive that, on the supposition of its spuriousness, would account for his undertaking it at all. In all these respects it forms a direct contrast to the known forgeries of the apostolic or succeeding ages. I will only ask my hearers who are acquainted with early apocryphal literature to compare St. John's Gospel with two very different and yet equally characteristic products of the first and second centuries of the Christian era—with the *Protevangelium, or Gospel of the Infancy of Jesus*, on the one hand, and with the *Clementine Homilies*, on the other. The former, a vulgar daub dashed in by a coarse hand in bright and startling colors; the other, a subtle philosophical romance, elaborately drawn by an able and skillful artist. But both the one and the other are obviously artificial in all their traits, and utterly alien to the tone of genuine history. Such productions as these show what we might expect to find in a gospel written at the middle or after the middle of the second century. If then my description of the Fourth Gospel is not overcharged (and I will endeavor to substantiate it immediately), the supposition that this gospel was written at this late epoch by a resident at Alexandria or at Ephesus will appear in the highest degree incredible; and, whatever difficulties the traditional belief may involve, they are small indeed compared with the improbabilities created by the only alternative hypothesis.

THE POSITIVE INTERNAL EVIDENCE

I have already proved that the absence of certain topics in this gospel seems fatal to its late authorship. I shall now proceed to investigate those phenomena of its actual contents which force us to the conclusion that it was written by a Jew contemporary with and cognizant of the facts which he relates, and more especially those indications which fix the authorship on the Apostle St. John. It is necessary however to premise by way of caution, that exhaustive treatment is impossible in a single lecture, and that I can only hope to indicate a line of investigation which any one may follow out for himself.

First of all then, the writer was a Jew. This might be inferred with a very high degree of probability from his Greek style alone. It is not ungrammatical Greek, but it is distinctly Greek of one long accustomed to think and speak through the medium of another language. The Greek language is singularly rich in its capabilities of syntactic construction, and it is also well furnished with various connecting particles. The two languages with which a Jew of Palestine would be most familiar—the Hebrew, which was the language of the sacred Scriptures, and the Aramaic, which was the medium of communication in daily life—being closely allied to each other, stand in direct contrast to the Greek in this respect. There is comparative poverty of inflexions, and there is an extreme paucity of connecting and relative particles. Hence in Hebrew and Aramaic there is little or no syntax, properly so called. Tested by his style then, the writer was a Jew.

Of all the New Testament writings the Fourth Gospel is the most distinctly Hebraic in this respect. The Hebrew simplicity of diction will at once strike the reader. There is an entire absence of periods, for which the Greek language affords such facility. The sentences are co-ordinated, not subordinated. The clauses are strung together, like beads on a string. The very monotony of arrangement, though singularly impressive, is wholly unlike the Greek style of the age. More especially does the influence of the Hebrew appear in the connecting particles. In this language the single connecting particle is used equally, whether co-ordination or opposition is implied; in other words, it represents 'but' as well as 'and.' The Authorized Version does not adequately represent this fact, for our translators have exercised considerable license in varying the renderings : 'then,' 'moreover,' 'and,' 'but,' etc.

Now it is a noticeable fact, that in St. John's Gospel the capabilities of the Greek language in this respect are most commonly neglected; the writer falls

back on the simple 'and' of Hebrew diction, using it even where we should
expect to find an adversative particle. Thus 5:39, 40, 'You search the Scriptures, for in them you think that you have eternal life, and they are they
which testify of Me: and you will not come to Me'; 7:19, 'Did not Moses give
you the law, and none of you keeps the law?' where our English version has
inserted an adversative particle to assist the sense, 'and yet'; 7:30, 'Then they
sought to take Him, and no man laid hands on Him,' where the English
version substitutes 'but no man'; 7:33, 'Then said Jesus unto them. "Yet a little
while am I with you, and I go to Him that sent Me,"' where again our translators attempt to improve the sense by reading 'and then.' And instances
might be multiplied.

The Hebrew character of the diction moreover shows itself in other ways—
by the parallelism of the sentences, by the repetition of the same words in
different clauses, by the order of the words, by the syntactical constructions,
and by individual expressions. Indeed so completely is this character maintained throughout, that there is hardly a sentence which might not be translated literally into Hebrew or Aramaic, without any violence to the language
or to the sense. I might point also to the interpretation of Aramaic words, as
Cephas, Gabbatha, Golgotha, Messias, Rabboni, Siloam, Thomas, as indicating knowledge of this language.

On such isolated phenomena however no great stress can fairly be laid,
because such interpretations do not necessarily require an extensive acquaintance with the language, and when the whole cast and coloring of the diction
can be put in evidence, an individual word here and there is valueless in
comparison. There are however two examples of proper names in this Gospel
on which it may be worthwhile to remark, because the original is obscured
in our English Bibles by a false reading in the Greek text used by our translators, and because they afford incidentally somewhat strong testimony to the
writer's knowledge both of the language and of contemporary facts.

The first of these is Iscariot. In the other three Gospels this name is attributed to the traitor apostle Judas alone. In St. John's Gospel also, as represented in the received text and in our English version, this is the case. But
if the more correct readings be substituted, on the authority of the ancient
copies, we find it sometimes applied to Judas himself (12:4, 13:2, 14:22), and
sometimes to Judas' father Simon (e.g. 6:71 'He spoke of Judas the son of

Simon Iscariot'; 13:26, 'He gives it to Judas the son of Simon Iscariot'). Now this shows that the evangelist knew this not to be a proper name strictly so called, but to describe the native place of the person, 'the man of Kerioth,' and hence to be applicable to the father and the son alike. The other instance which I shall give, at first sight presents a difficulty; but when further investigated it only adds fresh testimony to the exact knowledge of the Fourth Evangelist.

In St. Matthew, Simon Peter is called Bar-Jona (Matt. 16:17); i.e. son of Jona (or Jonan or Jonas). Accordingly, in the received text of St. John also he appears in not less than four passages (1:42, 11:15-17) as Simon son of Jona (or Jonan or Jonas). But there can be no reasonable doubt that the correct reading in all these four passages is 'Simon son of Joannes'—the Hebrew and Aramaic Johanan, the English John, and that later transcribers have altered it to make it accord with the form adopted by St. Matthew. Here there is an apparent discrepancy, which however disappears on examination; for we find that Jona or Jonan or Jonas is more than once used in the LXX version of the Old Testament as a contracted form of the name Johanan, Johannes, or John. Thus the statements of the two evangelists are reconciled; and we owe it to the special knowledge derived from the Fourth Gospel that the full and correct form is preserved. For, when we have once got this key to the fact, we can no longer question that John was the real name of Peter's father, since it throws great light on our Lord's words in St. Matthew.

The ordinary name Jonah, which was borne by the prophet, and which is generally supposed to be the name of Simon's father, signifies 'a dove,' but the name Johanan or John is 'the grace of God.' Hence the Baptist is called not Zechariah, as his relatives thought natural, but John, in accordance with the heavenly message (Luke 1:13), because he was specially given to his parents by God's grace. So too the call of St. Peter (John 1:42) becomes full of meaning: 'Thou art Simon the son of the grace of God; thou shalt be called Cephas,' and the final commission given to the same apostle is doubly significant, when we interpret the thrice repeated appeal as 'Simon son of God's grace, lovest thou Me?' for without this interpretation the studied repetition of his patronymic seems somewhat meaningless.

Bearing this fact in mind, we turn to the passage of St. Matthew (16:17, 18) 'Jesus answered and said unto him, "Blessed art thou, Simon Bar-Jona (son of the grace of God), for flesh and blood hath not revealed it unto thee, but My Father which is in heaven. And I say unto thee—That thou art Peter, and upon this rock I will build My Church.'" His name and his surname alike are symbols and foreshadowings of God's special favor to him in his call and commission. This is only one of many instances in which the authenticity of the statements of the Fourth Gospel is confirmed by the fact that they incidentally explain what is otherwise unexplained in the narrative of the synoptic evangelists.

Another evidence that the writer was acquainted with the Hebrew language is furnished by the quotations from the Old Testament. This evangelist, like St. Paul, sometimes cites from the current Greek version of the Seventy, and sometimes translates directly from the Hebrew. When a writer, as is the case in the Epistle to the Hebrews, quotes largely and quotes uniformly from the LXX version, this is at least an indication that he was not acquainted with the original; and hence we infer that the epistle just mentioned was not written by St. Paul, a Hebrew of the Hebrews, but by some disciple, a Hellenistic Jew, thoroughly interpenetrated with the apostle's mind and teaching, but ignorant of the language of his forefathers. If on any occasion the quotations of a writer accord with the original Hebrew against the LXX version, we have a right to infer that he was acquainted with the sacred language, was, in fact, a Hebrew or Aramaic-speaking Jew.

Several decisive examples might be produced, but one must suffice. In 19:37 is a quotation from Zechariah 12:10, which in the original is, 'They shall look upon Me whom they pierced.' Accordingly it is given in St. John, 'They shall look on Him whom they pierced' (Ὄψονται εἰς ὃν ἐξεκέντησαν). But the LXX rendering is, 'They shall gaze upon Me, because they insulted' where the Greek rendering has not a single word in common with St. John's text. In 12:40 again, the evangelist quotes Isaiah 6:10, 'Because that Esaias said again, He hath blinded their eyes, and hardened their heart, that they should not see with their eyes,' etc. Now this quotation is far from being verbally exact, for in the Hebrew the sentence is imperative, 'Make fat the heart of this people, and make heavy their ears, and close their eyes, that they should not see with their eyes,' etc. Yet, on the other hand, it does not contain any of the characteristic renderings of the LXX, and this is one distinct proof that, however loosely quoted, it was derived, not from the

LXX, but from the original. For the LXX translators, taking offense, as it would seem, at ascribing the hardening of the heart to God's own agency, have thrown the sentence into a passive form: 'The heart of this people was made fat, and with their ears they heard heavily, and their eyes they closed' etc., so as to remove the difficulty. If therefore the evangelist had derived the passage from the LXX, it is inconceivable that he would have reintroduced the active form, thus wantonly reviving a difficulty, unless he had the original before him.

I will only add one other example. In 13:18 occurs a quotation from Psalm 41:9 (40:10). Here the expression that in the original signifies literally 'made great' or 'made high his heel' is correctly translated 'lifted up his heel' (ἐπῆρεν ἐπ' ἐμὲ τὴν πτέρναν αὐτοῦ), as in the A.V. of the Psalms. The LXX version however gives 'he multiplied (or increased) tripping up with the heel,' or 'treachery,' that has given rise to the paraphrastic rendering in our Prayer-Book version, 'laid great wait for me.' Here again it is obvious that the evangelist's quotation could not have been derived from the LXX, but must have been rendered either directly from the Hebrew, or (what for my purpose is equally decisive) indirectly through some Chaldee Targum.

If therefore we had no other evidence than the language, we might with confidence affirm that this Gospel was not written either by a Gentile or by a Hellenistic Christian, but by a Hebrew accustomed to speak the language of his fathers. This fact alone negates more than one hypothesis which has been broached of late years respecting its authorship, for it is wholly inconsistent with the strictly Gentile origin which most recent theories assign to it. But, though irreconcilable with Gentile authorship, it is not wholly inconsistent with the later date, for we cannot pronounce it quite impossible that there should be living in Asia Minor or in Egypt, in the middle or after the middle of the second century, a Judaic Christian familiar with the Hebrew or Aramaic language, however rare such instances may have been.

Having thus established the fact that the writer was neither a Gentile nor a Hellenist, but a Hebrew of the Hebrews, we will proceed to inquire further whether he evinces an acquaintance with the manners and feelings, and also with the geography and history (more especially the contemporary history) of Palestine, which so far as our knowledge goes (and in dealing with such questions we must not advance one step beyond our knowledge) would be

morally impossible with even a Hebrew Christian at the supposed date, long
after the political existence of the nation had been obliterated, and when the
disorganization of Jewish society was complete.

As I am obliged to compress my remarks within the space of a single
lecture, I cannot place the evidence fully before you;[7] but my hope is, that I
may indicate the lines of investigation which will enable you to answer it
more completely for yourselves. I will only say, that we obtain from the
Fourth Gospel details at once fuller and more minute on all these points
than from the other three. Whether we turn to the Messianic hopes of the
chosen people, with all the attendant circumstances with which imagination
had invested this expected event, or to the mutual relations of Samaritans,
Jews, Galileans, Romans, and the respective feelings, prejudices, beliefs,
customs of each, or to the topography as well of the city and the temple as
of the rural districts—the Lake of Gennesaret, and the cornfields and
mountain ridges of Shechem, or to the contemporary history of the Jewish
hierarchy and the Herodian sovereignty, we are alike struck at every turn
with subtle and unsuspicious traces, betokening the familiarity with which
the writer moves amidst the ever-shifting scenes of his wonderful narrative.

This minuteness of detail in the Fourth Evangelist is very commonly overlooked, because our gaze is arrested by still more important and unique
features in this Gospel. The striking character of our Lord's discourses as
recorded in St. John—their length and sequence, their simplicity of language,
their fullness and depth of meaning—dazzles the eye of the critic and blinds
him to the historical aspects of the narrative. Only by concentrating our view
on these latter shall we realize the truth that the evangelist is not floating in
the clouds of airy theological speculations, that though with his eye he peers
into the mysteries of the unseen, his foot is planted on the solid ground of
external fact; that, in short, the incidents are not invented as a framework
for the doctrine, but that the doctrine arises naturally out of, and derives its
meaning from, the incidents.

One example will serve at once to illustrate the double characteristic of
this Gospel, the accurate historical narrative of facts which forms the basis
of the Gospel, and the theological teaching which is built as a superstructure

---

[7]He was, however, able to write a lengthy essay on the external evidence in more detail, which can
be found in appendix A below.

upon this foundation, and which the evangelist keeps distinctly and persistently in view in his selection and arrangement of the facts, and also to introduce the investigation which I purpose instituting.

The narrative and the discourses alike are thoroughly saturated with the Messianic ideas of the time. The Christ, as expected by the Jews, is the one central figure round which all the facts are grouped, the one main topic on which all the conversations hinge. This is the more remarkable, because the leading conception in the writer's own mind is not the Messiah, but the Word, the *Logos*—not the deliverance of Israel, but the manifestation of God in the flesh. This main purpose is flung out at the opening of the Gospel, and it is kept steadily in view in the selection of materials throughout the work. But it does not once enter into the mind of the Jews, who are wholly absorbed in the Messianic idea. Nay, the word *Logos* does not once occur even on our Lord's own lips, though the obvious motive of His teaching is to enforce this higher aspect of His person, to which they were strangers. And I cannot but think that this distinct separation is a remarkable testimony to the credibility of the writer, who, however strongly impressed with his mission as the teacher of a great theological conception, nevertheless keeps it free from his narrative of facts, though obviously there would be a very strong temptation to introduce it, a temptation which to a mere forger would be irresistible.

The Messianic idea, for instance, is turned about on all sides, and presented in every aspect. On this point we learn very much more of contemporary Jewish opinion from the Fourth Gospel than from the other three. At the commencement and at the close of the narrative—in the preaching of the Baptist and in the incidents of the Passion—it is equally prominent. In Galilee (1:41, 46, 49; 6:15, 28, 30 sq.), in Samaria (6:25, 29, 42), in Judaea (5:39, 45 sq.; 7:26 sq., 40-43; 8:30 sq.; 10:24), it is the one standing theme of conversation. Among friends, among foes, among neutrals alike it is mooted and discussed. The person and character of Jesus are tried by this standard. He is accepted or He is rejected, as He fulfills or contradicts the received ideal of the Messiah.

The accessories also of the Messiah's coming, as conceived by the Jews, are brought out with a completeness beyond the other Gospels. I will only ask you, as an illustration of this, to consider the discourse on the manna

in the sixth chapter. The key to the meaning of the conversation is the fact
that the Jews expected a miracle similar to the gift of manna in the wilderness, as an accompaniment of the appearance of the great deliverer. This
expectation throws a flood of light on the whole discourse. But the fact is
not communicated in the passage itself. There is only a bald, isolated
statement, which apparently is suggested by nothing, and itself fails to
suggest anything: 'Our fathers did eat manna in the wilderness.' Then
comes an aposiopesis. The inference is unexpressed. The expectation, which
explains all, is left to be inferred, because it would be mentally supplied by
men brought up among the ideas of the time. We ourselves have to get it by
the aid of criticism and research from rabbinical authorities. But, when we
have grasped it, we can unlock the meaning of the whole chapter. Connected with Messiah's coming are other conceptions on which it may be
worthwhile to dwell for a moment. One of these is the appearance of a
mysterious person called 'the prophet.' This expectation arose out of the
announcement in Deuteronomy 18:15, 'The Lord thy God will raise up unto
thee a prophet from the midst of thee, like unto me.' To this anticipation we
have allusions in not less than four places in St. John (1:21, 25; 6:14; 7:40), in
all of which 'the prophet' is mentioned, though in the three first the dis-
tinctness of the expectation is blurred in the English version by the rendering 'that prophet.' In all these passages the mention of 'the prophet'
without any explanation is most natural on the lips of contemporary Jews,
whose minds were filled with the Messianic conceptions of the times, while
such language is extremely unlikely to have been invented for them more
than a century after the date of the supposed occurrences. But the point
especially to be observed is, that the form which the conception takes is
strictly Jewish, and not Christian. Christian teachers identified the prophet
foretold by Moses with our Lord Himself, and therefore with the Christ.
This application of the prophecy is made directly in St. Peter's speech (Acts
3:22), and inferentially in St. Stephen's (Acts 7:37); and later Christian
teachers followed in their steps. But these Jews in St. John's Gospel conceive
'the Christ' and 'the prophet' as two different persons. If He is not 'the
Christ,' they adopt the alternative that He may be 'the prophet' (1:21, 25); if
not 'the prophet,' then 'the Christ' (7:40). It is hardly conceivable to my
mind that a Christian writer, living in or after the middle of the second

century, calling on his imagination for facts, should have divested himself so absolutely of the Christian idea and fallen back on the Jewish.

But before I have done with 'the prophet,' there is yet one more point worthy of notice. After the miracle of feeding the five thousand, we are told that 'those men who had seen the miracle that Jesus did said, "This is of a truth the prophet that should come into the world"' (6:14). The connection is not obvious, and the writer has not explained himself. Here again the missing link is supplied by the Messianic conception of the age. The prophet foretold was to be like Moses himself. Hence, it was inferred that there must be a parallel in the works of the two. Hence a repetition of the gift of the manna—the bread from heaven—might be expected. Was not this miracle then the very fulfillment of their expectation? Hence we read that on the day following (after several incidents have intervened, but with the miracle still fresh on their minds), they seek Him out, and still try to elicit a definite answer from Him: 'What sign do you then? Our fathers did eat manna in the desert.' Thus a casual and indistinct reference in one part of the chapter is explained by an equally casual and indistinct reference in another, and light emerges from darkness.

From the Messianic ideas I turn to the Jewish sects and the Levitical hierarchy. The Sadducees, with whom we are familiar in other Gospels, are not once mentioned by the Fourth Evangelist. How are we to account for this fact? Have we here a discrepancy, or (if not a discrepancy) at least an incongruity? Is there in St. John's picture an entire omission of that group which occupies a prominent place on the canvas of the other evangelists, especially of St. Matthew?

The common connection, when describing the adversaries of our Lord, is 'the Pharisees and Sadducees' in the Synoptic evangelists, 'the chief priests and the Pharisees' in St. John. In the comparison of these phrases lies the solution. The high priests at this time belonged to the sect of the Sadducees. How this happened we do not know. It may be that their Roman rulers favored this party, as being more lukewarm than the Pharisees in religious matters, and therefore less likely to give trouble to the civil powers. At all events, the fact appears distinctly from more than one notice in the narrative of the Acts (4:1; 5:17); and the same is stated in a passage of Josephus (*Ant.* xx.9.1). Thus, a real coincidence arises from an apparent incongruity.

But Josephus elsewhere (*Ant.* xviii.1.4) makes another statement respecting the Pharisees, which throws great light on the narrative of the Fourth Evangelist. He tells us that the Sadducees were few in number, though of the highest rank; and that when they were in office, they were forced, even against their will, to listen to the Pharisees, because otherwise they would not be tolerated by the people. Now this is precisely the order of events in St. John. The Pharisees (with one single exception) always take the initiative; they are the active opponents of our Lord, and the chief priests step in to execute their will.

The single exception is remarkable. Once only we find chief priests acting alone and acting promptly (12:10). They form a plot for putting Lazarus to death. This was essentially a Sadducees' question. It was necessary that a living witness to the great truth, which the high-priestly party denied, should be got rid of at all hazards. Hence they bestir themselves and throw off their usual apathy; just as, turning from the Gospels to the Acts of the Apostles, they have taken the place of the Pharisees as the foremost persecutors of the new faith, because the resurrection from the dead was the cardinal topic of the preaching of the Apostles.

But there is one other notice of the Jewish historian with which the narrative of the Fourth Evangelist presents a striking but unsuspicious coincidence. We are somewhat startled with the outburst of rudeness that marks the chief of the party on one occasion (11:49, 50). 'One of them, Caiaphas, being high priest that year, said unto them. "You know nothing at all, and you do not reflect that it is expedient for you that one man should die for the people, and that the whole nation should not perish." As a comment on this, take the words of Josephus: 'The behavior of the Sadducees to one another is not a little rude, and their intercourse with their peers is brusque, as if addressing strangers' (*Bell. Jud.* ii.8.14).

These coincidences need little comment. I will only add that the Fourth Evangelist does not himself give us the key to the incidents, that the references have been gathered from three different parts of Josephus, that the statements in the evangelist are not embroideries on his narrative, but are woven into its very texture and that nevertheless all these several notices dovetail together and create one harmonious whole, which bears the very impress of strict historical truth.

After reviewing these coincidences, it will appear strange that from the passage last quoted, Baur derived what he obviously considered to be one of his strongest arguments against the authenticity of the Gospel. Because the evangelist three times speaks of Caiaphas as 'high priest that year' (11:49, 51; 18:13), he argues that the writer supposed the high priesthood to be an annual office, and therefore could not have been the Apostle John. Now unless I have entirely misled you and myself, this is incredible. You cannot imagine that one who shows an acquaintance, not only with the language, but also with the customs, feelings, history, topography of the race, even in their minute details, should yet be ignorant of this most elementary fact of Jewish institutions. Whether the Gospel is authentic or whether it is not, such a supposition is equally incredible. If the writing is a forgery, the forger was certainly highly informed and extremely subtle; he must have ransacked divers histories for his facts; and yet here he is credited with a degree of ignorance which a casual glance at a few pages of his Old Testament or his Josephus would at once have served to dissipate. Suppose a parallel case. Imagine one, who writing (we will say) a historical work, shows a subtle appreciation of political feeling in England, and a minute acquaintance with English social institutions, and yet falls into the error of supposing that the premier is elected annually by vote of the people, or that the lord-mayoralty is a hereditary office tenable for life.

If therefore this supposition is simply impossible, we must explain the expression, 'high priest that year,' in some other way. And the explanation seems to be this—the most important duty of the high priest was an annual function, the sacrifice and intercession for the people on the great day of atonement. 'Once every year,' says the writer of the Epistle to the Hebrews (9:7), 'the high priest alone enters into the second tabernacle (the inner sanctuary), not without blood, which he offers for himself and for the errors of the people.' The year of which the evangelist speaks was the year of all years, 'the acceptable year of the Lord,' as it is elsewhere called; the year in which the great sacrifice, the one atonement, was made, the atonement which annulled once and for ever the annual repetitions. It so happened that it was the duty of Caiaphas, as high priest, to enter the holy of holies, and offer the atonement for that year. The evangelist sees, if we may use the phrase without irreverence, a dramatic propriety in the fact that he of all men should make this declaration. By a Divine irony he is made unconsciously to declare the truth, proclaiming Jesus to be the great atoning sacrifice, and himself to be instrumental in offering the victim. This irony of circumstances is illustrated in the case of Pilate, as in the case of Caiaphas. The latter, the representative of the Jewish hierarchy, pronounces Jesus the great atoning sacrifice; the former, the representative of the civil power, pronounces Him as the sovereign of the race, 'Behold your King!' The malignity of Caiaphas and the sneer of Pilate alike bear witness to a higher truth than they themselves consciously apprehend.

From the sects and the hierarchy we may turn to the city and the temple. Here too we should do well to bear in mind how largely we owe the distinctive features of the topography and architecture with which we are familiar to the Fourth Gospel. Within the sacred precincts themselves the Porch of Solomon, within the Holy City the pools of Bethsaida,[8] and Siloam, are brought before our eyes by this evangelist alone. And when we pass outside the walls, he is still our guide. From him we trace the steps of the Lord and His disciples on that fatal night crossing the brook Kidron into the garden; it is he who, relating the last triumphal entry into Jerusalem, specifies 'the branches of the palm trees' (the other evangelists use general expressions, 'boughs of the trees,' or the like), 'the palm trees' on which he had so often gazed, of which the sight was still so fresh in his memory, which clothed the eastern slopes of Olivet, and gave its name to the village of Bethany, 'the house of dates.' How simple and natural the definite articles are on the lips of an eye-witness I need not say. How awkward they sound to later ears, and how little likely to have been used by a later writer, unfamiliar with the scene itself, we may infer from the fact that in our own version they are suppressed, and the evangelist is made to say, 'they took branches of palm trees.'

Moreover the familiarity of the Fourth Evangelist, not only with the site and the buildings of the temple, but also with the history, appears in a striking way from a casual allusion. After the description of the cleansing of the temple by our Lord—a description which though brief is given with singular vividness of detail—the Jews ask for some sign, as the credential

---

[8]"Bethsaida" or "Bethzatha" should probably be read in St. John 5:2 rather than "Bethesda."

which might justify this assumption of authority and right of chastisement. His answer is, 'Pull down this temple, and in three days I will build it up.' Their astonishment is expressed in their reply, 'This temple has been forty-six years in building, and will you raise it again in three days?' (2:19, 20). Now I think it will be allowed that this mention of time is quite undesigned. It has no appearance of artifice, it occurs naturally in the course of conversation, and it is altogether free from suspicion, as having been introduced to give a historical coloring to a work of fiction. If so, let us examine its historical bearing.

For this purpose it is necessary to follow two distinct lines of chronological research. We have to investigate the history of the building of the Herodian temple, and we have to ascertain the dates of our Lord's life. Now by comparison of several passages in Josephus, and by the exercise of historical criticism upon them, we arrive at the conclusion that Herod commenced his temple about A.U.C. 735, i.e. 18 B.C. It took many years in building, and was not finally completed until A.U.C. 817, i.e. A.D. 64. Thus the works were going on during the whole of the period comprised in the New Testament history. If we add forty-six years to the date of its commencement (A.U.C. 735) we are brought down to A.U.C. 781 or 782, i.e. A.D. 28 or 29.

The chronology of Herod's temple involves one considerable effort of historical criticism. The chronology of our Lord's life requires another. Into this question however I need not enter into detail.[9] It is sufficient to remind you that the common date of the Christian era is now generally allowed to be a little wide of the mark, and that our Lord's birth actually took place three or four years before this era. The point to be observed here is, that St. Luke places the baptism of our Lord in or about the fifteenth year of Tiberius, which comprised the interval between the autumn of 781 and the autumn of 782. Now the occurrence related by St. John took place, as we may infer from his narrative, in the first Passover after the baptism; that is, according to St. Luke's chronology probably at the Passover of 782. Thus we are brought to the same date by following two lines of chronology; and we arrive at the fact that forty-six years there or thereabouts had actually elapsed since the com-

---

[9]On which see pp. 76-78 in the commentary below.

mencement of Herod's building to this point in our Lord's ministry. I am anxious not to speak with too great precision, because the facts do not allow it. The exact number might have been forty-five or forty-seven years, for fragments of years may be reckoned in or not in our calculation, and the data are not sufficiently exact to determine the date to a nicety. But, after all allowance made for this margin of uncertainty, the coincidence is sufficiently striking.

And now let us suppose the Gospel to have been written in the middle of the second century, and ask ourselves what strong improbabilities this hypothesis involves. The writer must first have made himself acquainted with a number of facts connected with the temple of Herod. He must not only have known that the temple was commenced in a particular year, but also that it was still incomplete at the time of our Lord's ministry. So far as we know, he could only have got these facts from Josephus.

Even Josephus however does not state the actual date of the commencement of the temple. It requires some patient research to arrive at this date by a comparison of several passages. We have therefore to suppose, first, that the forger of the Fourth Gospel went through an elaborate critical investigation for the sake of ascertaining the date. But, secondly, he must have made himself acquainted with the chronology of the Gospel history. At all events, he must have ascertained the date of the commencement of our Lord's ministry. The most favorable supposition is, that he had before him the Gospel of St. Luke, though he nowhere else betrays the slightest acquaintance with this gospel. Here he would find the date that he wanted, reckoned by the years of the Roman emperors. Thirdly, after arriving at these two results by separate processes, he must combine them; thus connecting the chronology of the Jewish kings with the chronology of the Roman emperors, the chronology of the temple erection with the chronology of our Lord's life.

When he has taken all these pains, and worked up the subject so elaborately, he drops in the notice that has given him so much trouble in an incidental and unobtrusive way. It has no direct bearing on his history; it does not sub-serve the purpose of his theology. It leads to nothing, proves nothing. Certainly the art of concealing art was never exercised in a more masterly way than here. And yet this was an age which perpetrated the most crude and bungling forgeries, and is denounced by modern criticism for its utter incapacity of criticism.

Nor, when we travel beyond the city and its suburbs, does the writer's knowledge desert him. One instance must suffice, but it is, if I mistake not, so convincing, that it may well serve in place of many. The country of the Samaritans lay between Judaea and Galilee, so that a person journeying from the one region to the other, unless he were prepared to make a detour, must necessarily pass through it. This was the case with our Lord and His Apostles, as related in the fourth chapter. The high-road from Jerusalem passes through some very remarkable scenery. The mountain ridges of Ebal and Gerizim run parallel to each other from east to west, not many hundred feet apart, thus inclosing a narrow valley between them. Eastward this valley opens out into a plain, a rare phenomenon in this country—'one mass of corn unbroken by a boundary or hedge,' as it is described by one who has seen it.

Up the valley westward, shut in between these mountain barriers, lies the modern town of Nablus, the ancient Shechem. The road does not enter the valley, but traverses the plain, running at right angles to the gorge, and thus touching the eastern bases of the mountain ridges as they fall down into the level ground. Here at the mouth of the valley is a deep well, even now descending 'to a depth of seventy feet or more,' and formerly, before it had been partially filled with accumulated rubbish, we may well believe deeper still. In the words of Dean Stanley:

> Of all the special localities of our Lord's life in Palestine, this is almost the only one absolutely undisputed. By the edge of this well, in the touching language of the ancient hymn, '*quaerens me sedisti lassus*.' Here on the great road through which 'He must needs go' when 'He left Judaea, and departed into Galilee,' He halted, as travellers still halt, in the noon or evening of the spring day by the side of the well. Up that passage through the valley His disciples 'went away into the city,' which He did not enter. Down the same gorge came the woman to draw water, according to the unchanged custom of the East. . . . Above them, as they talked, rose 'this mountain' of Gerizim, crowned by the temple, of which vestiges still remain, where the fathers of the Samaritan sect 'said men ought to worship.' . . . And round about them, as He and she thus sat or stood by the well, spread far and wide the noble plain of waving corn. It was still winter, or early spring, 'four months yet to the harvest,' and the bright golden ears of those fields had not yet 'whitened' their unbroken expanse of

verdure. But as he gazed upon them, they served to suggest the glorious vision of the distant harvest of the Gentile world, which with each successive turn of the conversation unfolded itself more and more distinctly before Him, as He sat (so we gather from the narrative) absorbed in the opening prospect, silent amidst His silent and astonished disciples.

The scrupulous accuracy of the geographical and archaeological details in St. John's account of the conversation with the Samaritan woman will have appeared already from this quotation. I will only ask you to consider for a moment how naturally they occur in the course of the narrative, so naturally and so incidentally that without the researches of modern travellers the allusions would be entirely lost to us. I think that this consideration will leave but one alternative. Either you have here written, as we are constantly reminded, in an uncritical age and among an uncritical people, the most masterly piece of romance-writing which the genius and learning of man ever penned in any age; or you have (what universal tradition represents it to be) a genuine work of an eye-witness and companion of our Lord. *Which of these two suppositions does less violence to historical probability I will leave to yourselves to determine.*

Follow then the narrative in detail. An unknown Traveller is sitting at the well. His garb, or His features, or His destination, show Him to be a Jew. A woman of the country comes to draw water from the well, and He asks her to give Him to drink. She is surprised that He, a Jew, is willing to talk so freely to her, a Samaritan. And here I would remark that the explanation which follows, 'For the Jews have no dealings with' (or rather, 'do not associate with') 'the Samaritans,' is the evangelist's own, a fact obscured by the ordinary mode of printing in our English Bibles. Hitherto, though the scene is very natural and very real, there is nothing which a fairly clever artist might not have invented. But from this point onwards follow in rapid succession various historical and geographical allusions, various hints of individual character in the woman, various aspects of Divine teaching on our Lord's part, all closely interwoven together, each suggesting and suggested by another, in such a manner as to preclude any hypothesis of romance or forgery. 'Thou wouldest have asked, and I would have given thee living water.' 'Sir, Thou hast nothing to draw with, and the well is deep. . . . Art Thou greater than our father Jacob?' And so the conversation proceeds, one point suggesting the next in the most natural way. Take, for instance, the reference to Gerizim. 'Sir, I perceive that Thou art a prophet. Our fathers worshipped in this mountain.' Observe that there is no mention in the context of any mountain in the neighborhood; that even here, where it is mentioned, its name is not given, but suddenly the woman, partly to divert the inconvenient tenor of the conversation, partly to satisfy herself on one important point of difference between the Samaritans and the Jews, avails herself of the newly found prophet's presence, and, pointing to the over-hanging heights of Gerizim, puts the question to Him. The mention of the sacred mountain, like the mention of the depths of the well, draws forth a new spiritual lesson. 'Not in this mountain, nor yet at Jerusalem. . . . God is a spirit.' The woman says, 'When Messiah comes. He will tell us all things.' Jesus says, 'I that speak unto thee am He.'

At this point the disciples approach from the valley, with the provisions which they had purchased in the city, and rejoin their Master. They are surprised to find Him so engaged. Here again an error in the English version obscures the sense. Their marvel was, not that He talked with the woman, but that He talked with *a* woman. It was a rabbinical maxim, 'Let no man talk with a woman in the street (in public), no, not with his own wife.' The narrowness of His disciples was shocked that He, their own rabbi, should be so wanting to Himself as to disregard this recognized precept of morality. The narrator assumes the knowledge with which he himself was so familiar. So the conversation with the woman closes. With natural eagerness she leaves her pitcher, and hurries back to the city with her news. With natural exaggeration she reports there that the stranger has told her all things that ever she did.

A conversation with the disciples follows, which is hardly less remarkable, but from which I must be content to select one illustration only. I think that it must be allowed, that the reference to the harvest is wholly free from suspicion, as regards the manner of its introduction. It is unpremeditated, for it cannot be severed from the previous part of the conversation, out of which it arises. It is unobtrusive, for the passage itself makes no attempt to explain the local allusion (which without the experience of modern travellers would escape notice): 'There are yet four months, and then cometh the harvest. Behold, I say unto you. Lift up your eyes, and look on the fields; for they are white already to harvest.' And yet, when we once realize the scene, when in imagination our eye ranges over that vast expanse of growing corn—so unusual in Palestine, however familiar in corn-growing England—we are at once struck with the truthfulness and the significance of this allusive parable.

I have thus endeavored to show, by taking a few instances, the accuracy of the writer's knowledge in all that relates to the history, the geography, the institutions, the thoughts and feelings of the Jews. If however we had found accuracy, and nothing more, we might indeed have reasonably inferred that the narrative was written by a Jew of the mother-country, who lived in a very early age, before time and circumstance had obliterated the traces of Palestine, as it existed in the first century; but we could not safely have gone beyond this. But unless I have entirely deceived myself, the manner in which this accurate knowledge betrays itself justifies the further conclusion that we have before us the genuine narrative of an eye-witness, who records the events just as they occurred in natural sequence.

I have discussed the accuracy of the external allusions. Let me now apply another test. The representation of character is perhaps the most satisfactory criterion of a true narrative, as applied to an age before romance-writing had been studied as an art. We are all familiar with the principal characters in the Gospel history: Peter, John, Philip, Thomas, Pilate, the sisters Mary and Martha, and several others which I might mention; each standing before us with an individuality, that seems to place him or her within the range of our own personal knowledge.

Have we ever asked ourselves to which evangelist above the rest we owe this personal acquaintance with the actors in this great drama? When the question is once asked, the answer cannot be doubtful. It is true indeed that we should have known St. Peter without the narrative of the Fourth Evangelist, though he adds several minute points, which give additional life to the portrait. It is true that Pilate is introduced to us in the other Gospels, though without St. John we should not have been able to read his heart and character, his proud Roman indifference and his cynical scorn. But, on the other hand, take the case of Thomas. Of this Apostle nothing is recorded in the other Evangelists, and yet he stands out before us, not as a mere lay figure, on whose stiff, mechanical form the artist may hang a moral precept or a doctrinal lesson by way of drapery, but as a real, living, speaking man, at once doubtful and eager, at once hesitating and devoted—sceptical, not because his nature is cold and unsympathetic, but because his intellect moves more cautiously than his heart, because the momentous issues which belief involves bid him pause before he closes with it; at one moment endeavoring to divert his Master's purpose of going up to Jerusalem, where certain destruction awaits Him; at the next, ready to share the perils with Him, 'Let us also go with Him'; at one moment resisting the testimony of direct eye-witnesses and faithful friends to his Master's resurrection; at the next, overwhelmed by the evidence of his senses, and expressing the depth of his conviction in the earnest confession 'My Lord and my God.'

I must satisfy myself with one other example. The character of the sisters Martha and Mary presents a striking contrast. They are mentioned once only in the other Gospels, in the familiar passage of St. Luke, where they appear respectively as the practical, bustling housewife, who is busied about many things, and the devout, contemplative, absorbed disciple, who chooses the one thing needful. In St. John also this contrast reappears, but the characteristics of the two sisters are brought out in a very subtle way. In St. Luke the contrast is summed up, as it were, in one definite incident; in St. John it is developed gradually in the course of a continuous narrative. And there is also another difference. In St. Luke the contrast is direct and trenchant, a contrast (one might almost say) of light and darkness. But in St. John the characters are shaded off, as it were, into each other. Both alike are beloved by our Lord, both alike send to Him for help, both alike express their faith in His power, both alike show deep sorrow for their lost brother. And yet, notwithstanding this, the difference of character is perceptible throughout the narrative. It is Martha who, with her restless activity, goes out to meet Jesus, while Mary remains in the house weeping. It is Martha who holds a conversation with Jesus, argues with Him, remonstrates with Him, and in the very crisis of their grief shows her practical common sense in deprecating the removal of the stone.

It is Mary who goes forth silently to meet Him, silently and tearfully, so that the bystanders suppose her to be going to weep at her brother's tomb; who, when she sees Jesus, falls down at His feet; who, uttering the same words of faith in His power as Martha, does not qualify them with the same reservation; who infects all the bystanders with the intensity of her sorrow, and crushes the human spirit of our Lord Himself with sympathetic grief. And when we turn to the second occasion in which the two sisters are introduced by St. John, the contrast is still the same. Martha is busied in the homely duties of hospitality towards Jesus and her other guests; but Mary brings her choicest and most precious gift to bestow upon Him, at the same time showing the depth of her humility and the abandonment of her devotion by wiping His feet with her hair.

In all this narrative the Evangelist does not once direct attention to the contrast between the two sisters. He simply relates the events of which he was an eye-witness without a comment. But the two were real, living persons, and therefore the difference of character between them develops itself in action.

I have shown hitherto that, whatever touchstone we apply, the Fourth Gospel vindicates itself as a trustworthy narrative, which could only have proceeded from a contemporary and an eye-witness. But nothing has hitherto been adduced which leads to the identification of the author as the Apostle St. John. Though sufficient has been said to vindicate the authenticity, the genuineness is yet untouched. It is said by those who deny its apostolic origin, that the unknown author, living in the middle of the second century, and wishing to gain a hearing for a modified gospel suited to the wants of his age, dropped his own personality and shielded himself under the name of St. John the son of Zebedee.

Is this a true representation of the fact? Is it not an entire though unconscious misrepresentation? John is not once mentioned by name throughout the twenty-one chapters of this Gospel. James and John, the sons of Zebedee, occupy a prominent place in all the other Evangelists. In this Fourth Gospel alone neither brother's name occurs. The writer does once, it is true, speak of the 'sons of Zebedee,' but in this passage, which occurs in the last chapter (21:2), there is not even the faintest hint of any connection between the writer himself and this pair of brothers. He mentions them in the third person, as he might mention any character whom he had occasion to introduce.

Now is not this wholly unlike the proceeding of a forger who was simulating a false personality? Would it not be utterly irrational under these circumstances to make no provision for the identification of the author, but to leave everything to the chapter of accidents? No discredit, indeed, is thrown on the genuineness of a document by the fact that the author's name appears on the forefront. This is the case with the histories of Herodotus and Thucydides; it is the case also with the Epistles of Paul and Peter and James, and with the Apocalypse of John. But, on the supposition of forgery, it was a matter of vital moment that the work should be accepted as the genuine production of its pretended author. The two instances of early Christian forgeries which I brought forward in an earlier part of this lecture will suffice as illustrations.

The *Gospel of the Infancy* closes with a distinct declaration that it was written by James. The *Clementine Homilies* affirm the pretended authorship in the opening words, 'I Clement, being a Roman citizen.' Even if our supposed forger could have exercised this unusual self-restraint in suppressing the simulated author's name, would he not have made it clear by some allusion to his brother James, or to his father Zebedee, or to his mother Salome? The policy which he has adopted is as suicidal as it is unexpected.

How then do we ascertain that it was written by John the son of Zebedee? I answer, first of all, that it is traditionally ascribed to him, as the *Phaedo* is ascribed to Plato, or the *Antigone* to Sophocles; and, secondly, that from a careful examination of indirect allusions and casual notices, from a comparison of things said and things unsaid, we arrive at the same result by a process independent of external tradition. But a forger could not have been satisfied with trusting to either of these methods. External tradition was quite beyond the reach of his control. In this particular case, as we shall see, the critical investigation requisite is so subtle, and its subject-matter lies so far below the surface, that a forger, even supposing him capable of constructing the narrative, would have defeated his own purpose by making such demands on his readers.

For let us follow out this investigation. In the opening chapter of the Gospel there is mention of a certain disciple whose name is not given (1:35, 37, 40). This anonymous person (for it is a natural, though not a certain inference, that the same is meant throughout) reappears again in the closing scene before and after the passion, where he is distinguished as 'the disciple whom Jesus loved.' At length, but not till the concluding verses of the Gospel, we are told that this anonymous disciple is himself the writer: 'This is the disciple who testifies of these things, and wrote these things.'

In accordance with this statement we find that those particular scenes in which this anonymous disciple is recorded as taking a part are related with peculiar minuteness and vividness of detail. Such is the case, for instance, with the notices of the Baptist and of the call of the earliest disciples. Such again is the case with the conversation at the Last Supper, with the scene over the fire in the hall of Caiaphas's house, with certain other incidents connected with the crucifixion, and with the scene on the Lake of Galilee after the resurrection.

Who then is this anonymous disciple? On this point the Gospel furnishes no information. We arrive at the identification, partly by a process of exhaustion, partly by attention to some casual incidents and expressions. Comparing the accounts in the other Gospels, it seems safe to assume that he was one of the inner circle of disciples. This inner circle comprised the two pairs of brothers, Peter and Andrew, James and John—if indeed Andrew deserves a place here. Now he cannot have been Andrew, because Andrew appears in company with him in the opening chapter, nor can he have been Peter, because we find him repeatedly associated with Peter in the closing scenes. Again, James seems to be excluded; for James fell an early martyr, and external and internal evidence alike point to a later date for this Gospel. Thus by a process of exhaustion we are brought to identify him with John the son of Zebedee.

With this identification all the particulars agree. First—He is called among the earliest disciples; and from his connection with Andrew (1:40, 44) it may be inferred that he was a native of Bethsaida in the neighborhood. Secondly—At the close of his Master's life, and after his Master's resurrection, we find him especially associated with Simon Peter. This position exactly suits John, who in the earliest days of the Church takes his place by the side of Peter in the championship of faith. Thirdly—Unless the beloved disciple be John the son of Zebedee, this person who occupies so prominent a place in the account of the other Evangelists, and who stood in the foremost rank in the estimation of the early Church as a pillar Apostle, does not once appear in the Fourth Gospel, except in the one passage where 'the sons of Zebedee' are mentioned and summarily dismissed in a mere enumeration of names. Such a result is hardly credible. Lastly—Whereas in the other Evangelists John the Baptist is very frequently distinguished by the addition of this surname, and always so distinguished where there is any possibility of confusing him with the son of Zebedee, in this Gospel alone the forerunner is never once called John the Baptist. To others some distinguishing epithet seemed needed. To the son of Zebedee there was only one famous John; and therefore when he had occasion to mention him, he naturally spoke of him as John simply, without any addition. Is it conceivable, I would ask, that any forger would have lost sight of himself so completely, and used natural language of John the son of Zebedee with such success, as to observe this very minute and unobtrusive indication of personality?

I have addressed myself more directly to the theory of the Tübingen school, either as propounded by Baur, or as modified by later critics, which denies at once the historical character of this Gospel and its apostolic authorship, and places it in the middle or latter half of the second century. But there is an intermediate position between rejecting its worth as a historic record and accepting St. John as its author, and this position has been taken up by some. They suppose it to have been composed by some disciple or disciples of St. John from reminiscences of their master's teaching, and thus they are prepared to allow that it contains some historical matter which is valuable. You will have seen however that most of the arguments adduced, though not all, are equally fatal to this hypothesis as the other. The process by which, after establishing its authenticity, we succeeded in identifying its author is, if I mistake not, alone sufficient to overthrow this solution. Indeed this theory is exposed to a double set of objections, and it has nothing to recommend it. I have already taken up more time than I had intended, and yet I feel that very much has been left unsaid. But I venture to hope that certain lines of investigation have been indicated, which, if carefully and soberly followed out, can only lead to one result. Whatever consequences may follow from it, we are compelled on critical grounds to accept this Fourth Gospel as the genuine work of John the son of Zebedee.

Some among my hearers perhaps may be disappointed that I have not touched on some well-known difficulties, though these have been grossly exaggerated. Some have to be satisfactorily explained; of others probable, or at least possible, solutions have been given; while others still remain on which we are obliged to suspend judgment until some new light of history is vouchsafed. *It is not from too much light, but from too little light, that the historical credibility of this Gospel has suffered.* Each new discovery made, each old fact elucidated, sets at rest some disputed question. If the main fact of the genuineness be established, the special difficulties can well afford to wait.

One word more, and I conclude. I have treated this as a purely critical question, carefully eschewing any appeal to Christian instincts. As a critical question I wish to take a verdict upon it. But as I could not have you think that I am blind to the theological issues directly or indirectly connected with it, I will close with this brief confession of faith: I believe from my heart that the truth which this Gospel more especially enshrines—the truth that Jesus Christ is the very Word Incarnate, the manifestation of the Father to mankind—is the one lesson which, duly apprehended, will do more than all our feeble efforts to purify and elevate human life here by imparting to it hope and light and strength, the one study which alone can fitly prepare us for a joyful immortality hereafter. [1871]

THE CHRONOLOGY OF OUR LORD'S LIFE

[In addition to the remarks above, it is necessary to say something about the rather different chronology of Jesus' life one finds in St. John,[10] when compared to the Synoptics, not least because of its bearing on the historical trustworthiness of the Fourth Gospel.][11] In three respects, the Fourth Gospel can be contrasted with the Synoptic portrait of Jesus when it comes to matters of chronology and history: 1) the scene of the ministry; 2) the characterization of the preaching; and 3) the duration of the ministry. The chronology of the ministry is derived wholly from St. John himself (i.e. not from the Synoptics). One must take into account the writer, the scenes, and the persons for whom the narrative is written.

There are at least three passages which help us at this juncture: 1) 2:13; 2) 4:4; 3) 12:1, and possibly 5:1. The upshot of close scrutiny of such passages is that they suggest that Jesus' ministry involved the great part of three years, or at least more than two. What we know from St. Luke (3:1) is that the

---

[10]See now the excursus by Lightfoot on this on pp. 120-21 below.

[11]This transitional sentence is my own, based on numerous comments by Lightfoot elsewhere (see below, e.g., in appendix A), in order for what follows to comport with and fit with what has come before. (BW3)

ministry began in the fifteenth year of Tiberius—A.U.C. 781 or 782 thus, in A.D. 28 or 29. How much longer it went beyond two years is impossible to say, the uttermost limit of course being the end of Pilate's rule in Judaea in A.D. 37, coincident with the accession of Gaius. Tiberius died in March of A.U.C. 790 (A.D. 37). As for our Lord's age when he began the ministry we have the notice in Luke 3:23—about thirty.

As for the structure of this Gospel, after the Prologue on the *Logos*, there are two great parts: 1) the description of the ministry climaxing with 'the conspiracy of the Jews' in 11:45-57, and 2) followed in John 12ff. the history of the Paschal week, the death, the resurrection, the appearances. We must focus on the crucial juncture in the narrative in John 7, and ask a crucial question.

In more detail we have to ask and answer where do most of the Galilean events reported in the Synoptics fit in? I am disposed to think they fit immediately after John 7:1. I must emphasize the importance of this epoch. When the Evangelist says in a very general way 'and he went about in Galilee' it seems reasonable that it would be here that we must place most of the Synoptic events. There were a considerable number of events between Jesus' second and third visits to Jerusalem. As for the ministry at Jerusalem and the neighborhood, we have a gap between 7:2 and 7:3. It is unlikely that a third visit to Jerusalem followed hard upon the second one especially since 7:1 says the Jewish authorities were looking for an opportunity to kill him, and so 'instead' of returning to Jerusalem at that time, he went about in Galilee.

So what of the ministry in Jerusalem between the second and third visits? We have: 1) the visit to Jerusalem during the Feast of the Tabernacles (Tishri—October) as reported John 7:1-13—the confrontation with the brothers, but he does in due course go up to Jerusalem; 2) 7:14-36—teaching and conversation in the Temple during the latter days of the Festival; 3) 8:1-11 must be omitted; 4) 7:37–8:30—preaching on 'the Great Day' of the Festival (day eight) near the Temple treasury on two topics: 1) the water 7:37; 2) the light 8:12; 5) 8:31-59—other conversations. This then leads to . . .

9:1–10:21—the healing of the blind man on the Sabbath day with the ensuing discourse on the door and the sheepfold.

10:22-39—Jesus at Jerusalem at the Feast of Dedication (December), teaching at the Porch of Solomon.

10:40-42—He returns beyond the Jordan.

1)   The 11th chapter as a whole—Jesus at Bethany, the raising of Lazarus

11:45-57—the conspiracy of the 'Jews'

THE COMMENTARY ON JOHN

The Logos Doctrine

My purpose in this initial examination is to show how the religious phraseology, and to some extent, the religious thought, of the time had prepared the way for the promulgation of the Gospel.

The expression ὁ Λόγος is unintelligible in itself. It evidently had a pre-history. The Apostles used old terms to enunciate new truths. This was a necessity of their position. Λόγος (λέγω) refers to speech, language, and is different from φωνή, as applying selection, arrangement, adaptation. See my notes on Ignatius, *Rom.* Consequently, it always has reference *to the subject matter.* As enunciate of speech it conveys an account, the reasons of a thing, and from this last sense it even gets to signify the faculty of reason, regarded however as an energy, and not as a potentiality. The two extreme meanings of Λόγος then are speech and reason. See Plato's *Theaetetus.*

What is the connection between reason and speech? Both are special characteristics of man. The connection is not only etymological but a fact, but this must be substantiated. How far would the one exist without the other is not a subject with which we are concerned. But what of applying Λόγος to the Divine Being? There are two prominent ideas corresponding to this connection: 1) Wisdom—active and substantive Providence; 2) Revelation. These are the primary ideas that the phrase ὁ Λόγος τὸν Θεόυ would convey. But as the expression etymologically coincided with two ideas, so also in its historical progress we trace the union of two distinct lines of de-

velopment of thought: 1) Old Testament Revelation, and 2) Platonic speculative Philosophy.

1) Old Testament Revelation. We have expressions such as 'God spoke'
(see Luther's comment in his Table Talk), and 'the Word of the Lord came
unto' etc. See e.g. 1 Sam 3:1 and Amos 8:11. The expression in the Hebrew is
generally דְּבַר יְהוָה; In the LXX it is translated Λόγος κυρίῳ or ὁ Λόγος
κυρίῳ. It is a Hebrew expression comprising of any revelation of God's will
and a man's heart or understanding whether by direct speech or otherwise.
Much more rarely (cf. 1 Sam 9:27; 1 Kngs 12:22; 1 Chron 17:3; comp. Prov 30:5;
Is 40:8) we have 'the Word of God' (cf. Ps 33:6).

2) Platonic Philosophy. It refers to the creative demiurgic reason. The
original plan or conception of the Creator, which was evolved in the creation
and government of the world. Also it refers to the eternal archetype in the
divine mind, of which the material world, both in its design and in its continuance, is a copy. These thoughts are to be traced back to Plato's *Timaeus*.
It is the λογισμός of the demiurge. The word Λόγος itself however is not
prominent in the *Timaeus*, in fact one could ask does it occur at all, in this
sense? Grote, *Plato III*, p. 285 reviews the usage in detail up through the
patristic usage and later, even commenting on the extravagance of the Cambridge Platonists. Λόγος is that which impresses itself on matter. It includes
the definitions, ideas of things—λόγοι.

It will be seen that in 1) the sense speech enunciation is prominent, in
2) the sense reason is prominent. These then correspond roughly to the two
derived meanings of Λόγος as indicated above. *The doctrine of the Logos as
it had been developed at the time of the Christian era arose out of the union
of these two influences. And its object was to bridge over the gulf between the
Infinite and the finite, between the Creator and the created, between the Governor and the governed.*

Alexandria was the local center where this union was cemented. Alexandria was the meeting point between East and West, the point of contact
between Greek philosophy and Jewish religion. In a sense Alexander's mind,
his plan, was impressed upon Alexandria. At other points as well however
the fusion would take place, more or less completely. And from Alexandria
the idea would spread. Even if the use was not generated separately elsewhere, one must not expect to find it confined to Alexandria. On the one

hand, Old Testament revelation declared that God was not only a creator but a very present ruler in the universe, and the religious instincts accorded with this belief. It represented his agency in the only way it could be represented to human faculties, under the form of human similitudes, as e.g. it spoke of the hand of God, of the eyes of God, and so forth, of God appearing to men and speaking to them.

On the other hand, Greek philosophy maintained (and intellectual thought was on its side) that God the Infinite Being was incomprehensible, and that in his Absolute Nature we could know nothing of Him, could hold no communion with Him. How were these two apparently contradictory ideas about the divine nature to be combined?

Moreover, it would be natural to expect that the relative proportions of the two elements would vary at different times and in different places and this is also confirmed by fact. In some places the Hebrew element predominated, in some the Greek. In Palestine, the question is heard more from the Old Testament side, and in Alexandria more from the side of Greek philosophy. In Palestine, the Word of God is the presence of Yahweh who reveals his will to his saints, the prophets; in Alexandria it is the informing design of the Creator which impresses itself upon and expresses itself in the universe, which sets the world in motion and keeps it so. I will now proceed to give illustrations of what has been said.

1) Palestine. The Palestinian teaching was probably derived from the Egyptian. The Targums. In their present form, they are not older than the 3rd or 4th century A.D. but they are founded on older oral targums. In Targum Onkelos on the Pentateuch, the 'Word of the Lord' is substituted again and again for God or the Lord where manifestations of God are mentioned. The term used is *Memra*. In fact the characteristic teaching of the Targum is this substitution of language, using some periphrasis for God. Sometimes the substitution involves an angel (see. e.g. Gen 32:30—'the angel of the Lord'), or 'the Glory' i.e. the Shekinah, but most especially it is 'the Word of the Lord.'[1] For example, see Gen 21:20, 22: 'The Word of the Lord was an aid to the boy . . .' or Exod 19:17: 'And Moses

---

[1] See Sporer, Jahrbuch der Hesch, pp. 292, 308.

brought forth the people out of the camp to meet the Word of the
Lord'; or Exod 25:22: 'And I will place My Word for you there, and
I will speak with you'; or Lev 26:9, 11, 12: 'And I will look upon
you through my Word' (vs. 9); or 'And my Word shall not abhor
you' (vs. 11); and 'I will make my Shekinah to dwell among you'
(vs. 12).[2] Or Numb 23:4—'And the Word from before the Lord met
Balaam'; Deut 4:24—'The Lord thy God whose Word is a con-
suming fire' (comp. 9:3). Deut 5:3—'I stood before the Word of the
Lord, and between you.' Or consider Jonathan ben Uzziel on the
prophets—e.g. Isaiah 1:14, 16, 20, and Is. 9:8, especially 42:1.[3] This
last passage is especially important as showing the distinction between Messiah and the Word.

2)   Alexandria—The LXX especially Exod 14:9-11.[4] The exposition of
      Aristobulus (about 150 B.C. under Ptolomais Philo) is important
      here, and there are quotes from his work in Clement of Alexandria,
      and Eusebius, though some are of doubtful authenticity. But at all
      events, the type of interpretation dates to before the Christian era.
      There is an important passage in Eusebius *Praep Evang.* viii.10, p.
      292 (Garif. ??) and another on Ezekiel in *Praep Evang.* ix.29, p. 412
      which seems to have escaped the writers on this subject.[5] Then
      there is Wisdom of Solomon which probably dates to 120–80 B.C.,
      and note its Platonic character.[6] In this work, the personification
      is however of Wisdom, not of the Word. This is necessary for the
      writer's design. He speaks in the name of Solomon. The *personifi-
      cation* however which was begun in Proverbs (see especially 8:22),
      and carried on in Sirach especially 1:1sq. and Sir. 14, is here still
      more advanced. See especially Wis. Sol. 7, 8, 9 on the genesis and
      work of Sophia. It is co-ordinated with the Word (9:1, 2; comp.
      18:14, 15). This then leads to the discussion of Philo and his in-
      fluence on the language of Christian theology and the methods of

---

[2]See Etheridge, p. 230.
[3]Sporer, pp. 312, 313.
[4]See Sporer, *Philo*, p. 10.
[5]The date is uncertain, see Ewald, iv. p. 297.
[6]See the article by Westcott in Smith's Dictionary, p. 781.

Christian interpretation. When it comes to his use of Λόγος we must talk about the strongly philosophical side of the doctrine and this philosophical Greek side obscures the Hebrew religious side of the concept.[7] Thus we must talk about the union of the Palestinian and Alexandrian sides of the discussion. Note that there is nothing in Philo about Messiah in such discussions. The doctrine of the Messiah and the doctrine of the Word [in Judaism] were basically separate.[8] The two converge in Christianity (see St. Paul and the Epistle to the Hebrews). But it is St. John who insists that the Λόγος is a divine Person, and that the Λόγος was made flesh, and that the Λόγος was Messiah.

The Christian doctrine of the Λόγος was the synthesis of the two influences. A distinction must be made between Deity Absolute and Deity Manifest. The former is ὁ Θεός, the latter is ὁ Λόγος τοὺ Θεόυ. The adoption of these terms, rather than any other, to denote Deity Manifest, is due to the fact already explained that both on the side of the Old Testament revelation and on the side of Platonic philosophy the same word Λόγος had an established usage which was an approach to the meaning required. In Old Testament revelation, God spoke to the prophets, in the Platonic cosmogony, the word of God was the medium or instrument of creation. The doctrine of the Logos cannot be regarded as the solution of a difficulty, it is rather the recognition of the fact that both sides of the antithesis are true. The intellectual objection is valid, while the religious instinct still remains.

The doctrine of the Λόγος grew up between the close of the Old Testament era and the opening of the New. It was an important period of preparation, the value of which cannot be overrated. The seething of all the diverse elements, the fusion of opposites in the order of thoughts, it was when the 'fullness of time' (τὸ πλήρωμα τοῦ χρόνου—Gal. iv.4) had come, that 'God sent into the world his Son, born of woman.' The more one studies history, the more one feels the force and significance of St. Paul's expression. Whether considered morally, or socially, or politically, or philosophically, or religiously, it was essentially the fullness of time. Even an unbeliever must

---

[7]See the quotations from him in Ritter and Priester.
[8]See in Westcott, p. 141.

allow, the Christian era has been the turning point of world history. This is not a matter of theory, but of fact. Whether we consider the actions of Rome, or the intellect of Greece, or the religious aspirations of Judaea, the expression 'fullness of time' is apt.

The Prologue and the Preparation;
the Word and the Witness
(John 1)

John 1:1-19 may be called the Preface about the Word, the link between God and Man, and covers the following matters: 1) the Word's eternal relations, his divinity; 2) his work in Creation and the sustaining of the physical world; 3) his work in the heart and conscience of men; 4) his special revelation of himself to the chosen people; and 5) his Incarnation and humanity, the new dispensation. These truths are set forth through a contrast between the Word and the Witness.

Vs. 1 Ἐν ἀρχῇ There is doubtless here a reference to Gen 1:1. In a sense the Gospel is to Genesis as the book of Revelation is to Malachi. It is the work of the Old Testament to provide the revelation of the absolute, sole supremacy of God, and of the New to provide the revelation of the connecting link between God and Man. The leading doctrine of the Old Testament is *monotheism*, of the New *theanthropism*. As the Old advanced in time, new words were prepared for the New, but monotheism necessarily preceded. This fundamental truth of the unity and independence of God must first be established before the supplemental truth of the communion of God and man could be promulgated. The Incarnation was the historical manifestation, the culminating act of the communion. The contrast between the Old and the New is again brought out as a contrast of Law (the absolute fact of

---

As a general rule Lightfoot does not give headings and titles in his notebooks, so I have created some in these volumes to make finding the divisions in the manuscripts easier. (BW3)

a supreme ruler) and grace (the condescending love of fatherly goodness).

Ἐν ἀρχῇ So Col 1:15; Heb 1:10. Compare the language used of Wisdom in Prov 8:22 (however ἔκτισέν would not be applicable here). See Sirach 24:9 which is taken from Proverbs. See especially Rev 3:18. Ἐν ἀρχῇ in itself does not necessarily imply past eternity, but it does so in its present relation.

ὁ Λόγος the 'Word' however no adequate translation of Λόγος is possible. It implies both 'reason' and 'language' i.e. it represents both the counsels proceeding from God and the manifestation to man. The oldest Latin translation represented it by *sermo* (*adv. Hermos* 20), but Tertullian pleaded for *ratio* (*adv. Prax.* 5). Ultimately *verbum* was chosen and it appears in all the existing manuscripts.[1] Yet *sermo* is a more adequate representation than *verbum* which is primarily a way to render ῥῆμα.

ὁ Λόγος is applied to our Lord elsewhere in Rev 19:13 and in the Epistle of St. John 1:1—περὶ τοῦ Λόγου τῆς ζωῆς. The Christology of the Gospel and Revelation is the same. In Col 1:25 the expression τὸν λόγον τοῦ Θεοῦ occurs of the revelation, not of the person revealed. See Heb 4:12, 13. *It is never used in the Bible as an equivalent for the Scriptures, the written word.* The common restriction of the word is calculated to mislead. The 'Word of God' includes the γραφή and much more.

πρὸς τὸν Θεόν—not ἐν τῷ Θεῷ because of the distinction of person, not σύν τῷ Θεῷ lest it should seem to divide the Godhead. Comp. 1:18; 17:5 (and see the references to πρός in Lücke, p. 297). In Prov 8:30 it is παρ' αὐτῷ in Sir 1:1 it is μετ' αὐτοῦ but perhaps a different preposition purposely chosen here.

καὶ Θεὸς ἦν ὁ Λόγος. Θεὸς is undoubtedly the predicate here, because of the analogy of the order of the usage of the article, and the confusion of sense that would otherwise be introduced. See John 4:24; 1 John 4:8, 16. The gradations of possible meaning are: 1) the eternal pre-existence; 2) the divinity; 3) the deity of the Word. These nuances of the Greek cannot be reproduced in English. Here it is Θεός not ὁ Θεός. The latter would be the absolute God, the Father (see Origen on this). In terms of word order, καὶ Θεὸς ἦν ὁ Λόγος makes the word Θεός emphatic. The restatement of the relationship of the Word to God is given in vs. 2, introducing the idea of the instrumentality of the Word in the work of creation.

[1] See Westcott, *Canon*, p. 218.

Vs. 2 Going from πρὸς τὸν Θεόν in vs. 2 to δι' αὐτοῦ in vs. 3 transitions us from his relationship to God to his relative relationship to the work of creation.

Vs. 3 πάντα δι' αὐτοῦ The English 'by' is ambiguous as a translation here. The same preposition as here (διά) is used 1) in the Old Testament and Apocrypha of Wisdom (Prov 8:22sq.; Wis Sol 9:1, 2); 2) in Philo of the Word (*de cherub*. 34, p. 162; *Leg. All*. iii.31, p. 106); 3) of the Lord in other parts of the New Testament (Heb 1:2; Col 1:16). Contrast this with ὑπό or ἀπό used of the Father.

χωρὶς αὐτοῦ A strengthening of the preceding proposition by the negating of its opposite.

ὃ γέγονεν Should this be attached to the foregoing sentence or the following sentence? In favor of the latter is all of antiquity. Perhaps this unanimity is due to the influence of the first commentator, Heracleon.

1) The Fathers—*Directly*: Western—Valentinius cited in Irenaeus; Eastern—Valentinius in *Exe. Uxod.*; in Clement and Origen; Ambrosiaster in *Hipp*. v.8 (p. 1075) and *Hipp*. v.16, where the added explanation is decisive. *Indirectly*: By ending the quotation with the words οὐδὲ ἕν—Tatian, Theophilus, Hippolytus, Ptolemais, Clement, Tertullian, etc. So large an array of witnesses for an interpretation or reading is rare.

2) The Versions—Old Latin, Egyptian, Curetonian Syriac. The Peshitto however is doubtful.

3) The Oldest Manuscripts—Either decisive as ℵ, A, C, D or doubtful as B, Δ.

There seems to be no ante-Nicene or immediately post-Nicene witness for the comma punctuation. We only have the printed texts of one or two passages in Eusebius (see Tregelles) and Cyprian (adv. Jud. II.3, p. 251). There is nothing in the context which requires it. In Eusebius *Praep. Ev.* xi.17, p. 540d it is quite clear from the interpretation that the words should be connected with what follows. The other reference in Tregelles is wrong, it should be p. 321d, and there is nothing in the context there to decide the punctuation.

Vs. 4 On the other hand, in favor of the common punctuation, all things have not only been created in Him but also sustained in Him. He is not only the origin but the sustainer of life, not only the Creator but the Preserver.

The sense is that that which has been made was life in Him. We do not want
a past tense here, but some however read ἐστί. Of this, more hereafter. We
have to take ζωή in the first place of the things endowed with life. This is no
difficulty in itself. But in the following clause, ἡ ζωή is the principle of life.
And the translation is in the highest degree awkward.

The real issue is the usage of St. John (see passage quoted in Alford). The
manifest sense of the text must take precedent over early tradition, and
therefore we should acquiesce with the now common punctuation which
attaches ὃ γέγονεν with what goes before (cf. 11:25; 14:12; 1 John 5:11). To what
is the change in punctuation to be attributed? The more modern (and I think
more correct) punctuation seems to have been introduced to cut the ground
from under the Manichaeans. They maintained that the Holy Spirit was
created because St. John perhaps said πάντα etc. It is to be noted that St.
Basil, in reply to this view is still unacquainted with the modern punctuation
(see *ad Eunom.* p. 278a, 303d, 308a; the text does not seem to be quoted in
the *de Spiritus sancti*). Gregory of Nyssa still quotes the text with the older
punctuation (*Cant.* I, p. 495a). In another passage it may seem to suggest he
adopted the new punctuation (*Eunam.*? II.T.II, p. 461) but this is not necessarily required by the language there, and is otherwise improbable. Chrysostom on the other hand has adopted the correct modern punctuation.

ἦν v.l. ἐστί So the authorities in Tregelles (I.IV, p. 7) and add ℵ.

A reading of the second century. If we take the punctuation ὃ γέγονεν ἐν
αὐτῷ then ἐστί seems to be required. And perhaps it was adopted as a
necessary consequence of the faulty punctuation (if indeed it was faulty).

ἐν αὐτῷ ζωὴ ἦν Life was in Him, was sustained in and through Him. The
manner of the 'Logos' and his action is described by διά, his sustaining of
things by ἐν. Comp. Col 1:17, 18.

ζωή life, the life physical but as leading to and merged with the life moral
and spiritual. The expression starts from the idea of the natural life, and loses
itself in the idea of the spiritual life. See Ignatius, *Rom.* 7. βίος would be out
of place here. The 'Logos' is the sustainer of life natural as well as life spiritual.
The ζωή prepares the way for the φῶς. In the next clause it is no longer ζωή
but rather ἡ ζωή.

Vs. 5 φαίνει 'shines' but we should have expected 'shone,' but the Apostle
would speak of its eternal, absolute, unchangeable character, hence the

present tense. This is substituted for by an aorist in the next clause (κατέλαβεν) where an historical fact is stated.

οὐ κατέλαβεν See Sir 15:1—ὁ ἐγκρατὴς τοῦ νόμου καταλήψεται αὐτήν (i.e. Wisdom). The sense of over-powered has been suggested and would have a parallel in [John] 12:35 μὴ σκοτία ὑμᾶς καταλάβῃ. In itself the meaning 'over-powered' makes excellent sense here, but it does not seem to be wanted here, see especially vss. 10, 11.

Vs. 6 The introduction of the Witness is a fit prelude to the Incarnation of the Word. Ἐγένετο ἄνθρωπος, ἀπεσταλμένος παρὰ Θεοῦ, ὄνομα αὐτῷ Ἰωάννης· The preposition παρά denotes the source of his commission. Note it is not ἀπό here.

Vss. 7-8 It was necessary to the theological purpose of St. John that he distinguish between the office of Jesus and of John. At the same time, he may have been determined by *historical* reasons to lay stress on the distinction. See vs. 8 and the emphatic language there, and vss. 15 and 20—καὶ ὡμολόγησεν καὶ οὐκ ἠρνήσατο. See 1 John 5:6-8 and compare the whole narrative in John 1:19-23; 3:22-36; 4:1; 5:33-36; 10:40-42. On the disciples of John in Asia Minor see Acts 19:2-4. Here we may have an indication of where the Gospel was written.[2] See also *Orac. Sybll.* iv.160; *Clem. Hom.* ii.23; Hegesippus in Eusebius *Hist. Eccles.* iv.22; Ephraem, *Haer.* 17. The importance of John as a teacher was recognized by Josephus, *Ant.* xviii.5.2.

Vs. 7 δι' αὐτοῦ i.e. through John.

Vs. 8 comp. 5:35: ἐκεῖνος ἦν ὁ λύχνος ὁ καιόμενος καὶ φαίνων, ὑμεῖς δὲ ἠθελήσατε ἀγαλλιαθῆναι πρὸς ὥραν ἐν τῷ φωτὶ αὐτοῦ.

ἀλλ' ἵνα see 9:3; 13:18; 15:25; 1 John 2:19 (a reference from Meyer). We must not therefore understand ἦλθεν (vs. 7) definitely.

Vs. 9 Two ways of taking the passage: 1) ἐρχόμενον εἰς τὸν κόσμον, 'was coming into the world' i.e. was on the point of manifesting itself to the world; 2) πάντα ἄνθρωπον ἐρχόμενον. The latter is to be preferred for reasons given hereafter, but observe: 1) ἦν must be 'there was' not 'it' or 'he was'; 2) ἐρχόμενον is not 'who comes' but 'when he comes.'

There existed *already* the true light.

ἐρχόμενον εἰς τὸν κόσμον i.e. the capacity of truth and holiness, the light

---

[2]See Ewald, *Johann. Schrift.* I, p. 13; *Gesch.* v, p. 9; vii, p. 152.

of conscience, which is innate in man. This interpretation is to be preferred
to the other for three reasons: 1) There is a contradiction in terms between
Ἦν . . . ἐρχόμενον εἰς τὸν κόσμον, and ἐν τῷ κόσμῳ ἦν (vs. 10) [if they refer
to the same thing]. Is there anything in the form of the sentence to show that
the latter is intended as a corrective of the former? 2) Ἦν . . . ἐρχόμενον εἰς
τὸν κόσμον are too far separated. Mark 2:18 is no parallel. In itself, indeed,
John would hardly have said 'the light was coming at the world,' inasmuch
as the whole theme of this prologue was to show that the light was there
from the beginning.

τὸ ἀληθινόν 'the true' i.e. the essential, the original light, the source and
fountain of light. It does not imply that all other lights are false, in the sense
of being no light at all, but that they are only faint, imperfect, fragmentary,
reflections or emanations of the true light. See 1 John 2:8; comp. John 6:32;
15:1. This word is one of the points of resemblance between this Gospel, the
Epistle, and the Apocalypse. See Rev. 3:7, 14. On this word, see Trench sec. viii.

Vs. 10 ἐν τῷ κόσμῳ ἦν The Logos was in the world at large. The natural
capacities of the human spirit, the work of the conscience, the yearning towards a higher life.

δι' αὐτοῦ ἐγένετο repeated from vs. 2, emphasizing the topic of gratitude.

οὐκ ἔγνω means they did not recognize, appreciate, appropriate the offer
of his.

κόσμος A favorite word of St. John. It occurs more frequently in his
writings than in all the rest of the New Testament together. It is curious to
note that the word κόσμος never has the sense of 'the universe' or 'the world'
in the LXX of the Old Testament. Sometimes we find κόσμος with a qualifier,
e.g. Deut 4:19; comp. Gen 2:1, but there it represents the hosts, the angels
(צָבָא). In the Apocrypha, especially in the Platonic Wisdom of Solomon this
sense first comes. In the Latin word *mundus* the idea of beauty precedes, the
idea of order is secondary though present. κόσμος involves not only the idea
of order (τάξις), but also of beauty. It is a very beautiful word in its origin.
The Pythagoreans tell a story about this, but Pythagoreus is too much of a
mythical, mystical person. It is Plato who makes a great step philosophically—*Tim.* p. 886B and 28B; cf. Isocrates, *Panes*, p. 78. There seems to be
three stages: 1) it seems to have been invented (and is frequently so used) in
reference to the regular motion of the stars so that sometimes ὁ κόσμος

signifies the heavens as opposed to 'the earth'; 2) sometimes more comprehensive, and of course the comprehensive sense would encroach on and supercede the other sense, as the prevalence of law and order in the terrestrial, the material universe; 3) inasmuch as the immediate neighborhood of the speculative plenaera (?) was recognized . . . hence ultimately ὁ κόσμος gets to be almost a synonym for 'the lower world' not indeed to the exclusion of the more comprehensive sense as the material universe, but to the description of it, more specifically referring to the world with its inhabitants, its interests, its tendencies etc.; Hence, 4) the moral sense, in which it is used by the Apostles (and by them, for the first time I believe). The Apostles felt themselves in an exceptional position. They were placed *outside* the common interests and tendencies of society of the age, of the world. It was wholly opposed to them. Hence κόσμος is used in contrast to the light, to the truth, to the kingdom of heaven. *Thus, from signifying 'order and beauty' has come round to the direct opposite meaning, signifying what is directly opposed to order, to beauty.*

There is a parallel case with the word φιλοσοφία that is likewise a Pythagorean word. See Diogenes Laertius, *Prom. Sec.* 12. But from being an expression of modest diffidence, of humble truth-seeking, the word got debased in time. It got to signify the very opposite of this—what was conceited, self-opinionated, not truth-seeking but untrue, fallacious. Comp. Col 2:8.

Vs. 11 εἰς τὰ ἴδια The manifestation of the Logos in the Old Testament dispensation. One must observe that the Incarnation is not brought forward until vs. 14 and there as something distinctly new—Καὶ ὁ Λόγος σὰρξ ἐγένετο. The sequence is: 1) his revelation to the conscience of mankind generally; 2) his revelation of himself to the Hebrew race especially; and 3) his distinct and definite revelation of Himself as man Incarnate.

τὰ ἴδια . . . καὶ οἱ ἴδιοι The A.V. here is inadequate. The Vulgate on the other hand has preserved the difference in gender of these terms but not the identity of the Word. *In propria venit, et sui eum non receperunt.* His own inheritance, his own people (or servants). Comp. Matt 21:33-34. The ἀμπελῶνα is τὰ ἴδια, the γεωργοῖς are οἱ ἴδιοι. On τὰ ἴδια see John 16:32, 19:27. On οἱ ἴδιοι see 13:1. On the latter phrase see also Deut 14:2, 26:10; Ps 35:4.

But the work of the Logos is not confined to the sending of the Son in the parable in Matt 21, but comprises the sending of the servants. For the Logos manifested Himself through the prophets, as well as in the Incarnation, in the Man, Christ Jesus.

Παρέλαβον 'received as their own, received as *directly offered to them.*' This is the force of the preposition. The ἔλαβον of the following verse is comprehensive. Where natural opposition is implied 1) κατέλαβεν (vs. 5) is used; 2) where natural alliance is implied παρέλαβον (vs. 11) is used; 3) where there is neutrality, the simple word ἔλαβον (vs. 12 from λαμβάνειν) is used.

Vs. 12 ὅσοι δέ, i.e. whether Jew or Gentile, whether through the medium of the natural conscience or the Old Testament revelation. We find that the meaning of the sentence is well illustrated by 1 Cor 2:23, 24, except that St. John is speaking of the Word pre-Incarnate, St. Paul of the Word Incarnate, the man Jesus Christ. This will give a meaning to the following verse—οὐκ ἐξ αἱμάτων οὐδὲ ἐκ θελήματος σαρκὸς etc.

ὅσοι δέ The grammar, placed absolutely not the relative with αὐτοῖς, this would require τούτοις as e.g. Matt 7:24, see references in Meyer.

ἔδωκεν Not merely 'he made it possible for them' but 'he empowered them'; cf. 5:27; 17:2.

τέκνα Θεοῦ The nature of this new birth is stated afterwards. The idea of 'children of God' in St. John is the moral and spiritual endowment derived from the Father (see 1 John 3:9), in St. Paul rather the privileges to which the child is entitled as heir (Rom 8:16sq.—without, again, excluding the other idea). See Deut 14:1. Each idea implies the other, but the starting point of the two Apostles is different. Frequently in St. Paul we have υἱοὶ Θεοῦ, never in St. John. See Gal 3:26; 4:7 (the son of the family as opposed to the slave). The natural relationship has furnished the metaphor to St. John, the legal relationship to St. Paul. And against the exclusiveness of the Jewish boast of Abrahamic descent we have here, τοῖς πιστεύουσιν εἰς τὸ ὄνομα αὐτοῦ. See the parallel in Rom 9:7, 8; Matt 3:9; comp. Luke 3:8.

εἰς τὸ ὄνομα αὐτοῦ This is the only expression which presents any obstacle to referring the passage to the work of the Logos prior to the Incarnation, and the obstacle here is only apparent. No doubt, elsewhere 'in the name of Jesus Christ, of the Son of God' is a common phrase (2:23; 3:18; 1 John 3:23; 5:13). But, 'the name of God' is also a common phrase, and Logos here takes the place of God, for 'name' signifies title, majesty, honor, office, the original idea of mere 'appellation' having passed out of sight (see Phil 2:9).

Vs. 13 οἳ etc. not referring to τέκνα Θεοῦ as the antecedent (with Meyer) but to τοῖς πιστεύουσιν. In the expressions that follow there is a gradation: 1) the blood; 2) the passions or affections; 3) the choice of rational men. Hence οὐδὲ . . . οὐδὲ. But observe that we have here not ἄνθρωπος but ἀνδρός, not *homo* but *vir* Comp. Is 2:9, 5:15; 31:9. Note the very early reading ὅς ἐγεννήθη, an example of what we said, namely that the text has had a history before it emerges.

The Apostle here has in view Abraham, the hero, the patriarch of the race. His object is not to deprecate but to exalt, but the spiritual birth may be much more exalted by the contrast. Comp. 8:33.

αἵματα See Euripides, *Ion* 693, which is the only instance given in the lexicons of this sense. In classical usage the term means 'bloodshed,' which also has an analogy in the Hebrew—דָּמִם and therefore it is more usual in Hebraic Greek. The explanation of the use of the plural is the same in the one case (Greek) as in the other (Hebrew).

ἐκ Θεοῦ absolutely, as more emphatic, not ἐκ θελήματος Θεοῦ.

Vs. 14 Καί 'and then,' 'and at length'—a new stage, a new aspect of the operation of the Word.

σὰρξ ἐγένετο See Clem., *Rom.* II.9. The Word appeared under the limitations of mere human nature, for the σὰρξ implies the perfect [or unfallen] humanity. It is not σὰρξ ἐνεδύσατο, but stronger, σὰρξ ἐγένετο.

καὶ ἐσκήνωσεν apparently an unimportant word, but in fact, it is a summary of a people's past history, and contains in itself the substance of a people's hope. The tabernacle, מִשְׁכָּן from שָׁכַן to settle down, inhabit, dwell. The abode, the visible symbol of the Almighty God, the heart of the religious worship of the Israelites, the center, the focus of the nation.

The Greek rendering σκήνη adopted for it in the LXX (σκήνη is אֹהֶל more probably). This word chosen partly no doubt to the similarity in sound. I cannot find that there is any etymological connection, though there may be. Hence σκήνη used especially of the divine Majesty dwelling in the midst of the chosen race, as being a very present help to His people, as manifesting Himself especially to them. See especially Sirach 24:8-10. Hence the latter Chaldee word, *Shekinah*, to denote the visible representation of Deity, the manifestation of Yahweh to His people. This derived form established a still stronger connection between the Hebrew and the Greek. In sound they were almost identical. A fact, not to be overlooked. Thus the Shekinah of the Lord becomes a synonym for the Word of the Lord. See especially Is 6:5, 6 (and Smith's *Dictionary* article on Shekinah s.v.). It is in fact (as defined in Smith's *Dictionary*) a periphrasis for God, whenever he is said to dwell on Zion amongst Israel, between the cherubim and so on. The Shekinah, said the Jewish teachers, was wanted in the second Temple, but it would be returned in the days of Messiah (cf. Hagg 1:8; Zech 2:10; 8:3; Ezek 43:7).

The Incarnation of the Logos, the birth of Jesus Christ in the flesh was, says St. John, the reappearing of the Shekinah, the restoration of the visible symbol of the divine Majesty, after which the Jewish teachers from every generation had yearned.

Similar doubtless was the application that St. Stephen would have made of the σκήνη (Acts 7:44) when he was rudely interrupted. Similar is the application made of the σκήνη in Heb 8, 9 see especially 8:5, 7, 8; 9:11. The restoration of the σκήνη, the Shekinah, had taken hold of the national mind. The Christian Apostles and early teachers respected this sentiment. They thought however that the σκήνη was only a type, a shadow, a foreshadowing of the good things to come, and that the Incarnation of the Son of God was the true fulfillment of these yearnings. But nowhere has the definite idea and definite image so close a parallel as in the Apocalypse. The restoration of the σκήνη is a prominent idea there. See 7:15; 8:6; 15:5; especially 21:3. The word σκηνόω is used nowhere else in the New Testament than in John's Gospel and the Apocalypse. Note Shekinah/σκήνη compare מְאוּם/ μῶμος. Hebrew and Greek sound alike words with similar meanings.

ἐθεασάμεθα see 1 John 1:1; 4:14.

τὴν δόξαν αὐτοῦ The explanation of σκήνη prepares the way for the explanation of δόξα. Δόξα in the New Testament has the idea of visible splendor, brilliant light. See Luke 2:9; Acts 7:55; especially Acts 22:11; 1 Cor 15:41; Rev 18:1. It is used especially of visible brightness, which symbolized the presence of the divine Majesty within the σκήνη. See Rom 9:4; Heb 9:5. Hence it is used especially in connection with the Shekinah in the Targums. See again the passages already mentioned Is 6:6; Hagg 1:8; Ezek 43:7. This is the meaning here as well. And the concidence with the Apocalypse can be noted—Rev 15:8, in connection with the σκήνη as here. See Rev 21:11, 23; 22:5; and John 2:11 (more references in Meyer).

ὡς μονογενοῦς 1:18; 3:16, 18; 1 John 4:9; comp. Heb 9:17; Ps 21:21; Ps 34:20, see especially Wis. Sol. 7:22. On πρωτότοκος see Col 1:15; Heb 1:6. It means here the sole representative, the sole heir of the Father. The phrase 'eternal generation' is an expression and an idea borrowed from finite human relations.

παρὰ Πατρός with μονογενοῦς see also 6:46; 7:29; 16:27. The point is the generation of the Word/Son is something different from that of the τέκνα Θεοῦ, not the transmission of ethical characteristics, but the communication of the absolute nature.

πλήρης Two possible accounts of the construction here: 1) a parenthesis consisting of καὶ ἐσκήνωσεν ἐν ἡμῖν, καὶ ἐθεασάμεθα τὴν δόξαν αὐτοῦ, δόξαν ὡς μονογενοῦς παρὰ Πατρός; 2) an absolute nominative. The first seems somewhat too intricate for the simple constructions of St. John. The second accords with the language of the Apocalypse (see 1:4, 5). See Winer, sec. lix, p. 557. The reason for the nominative is the same here as there. It gives emphasis, puts forward the reason (?) absolutely. πλήρης elsewhere, as though indeclinable (an alternative to this offered by Hort); see Mark 4:28 (B, D and compare the t.v. in C*); Acts 6:5, again with two main textual variants.

χάριτος καὶ ἀληθείας A tacit contrast with the Law. See vs. 17.

Vs. 15 The witness [i.e., John] 'cries,' καὶ κέκραγεν, not as the E.V. has it 'cried.' An indirect reference perhaps to Isaiah 40:3—φωνὴ βοῶντος. See vs. 23. But whether or not there is this allusion, the point is that the testimony of John to the Messiahship of Jesus was clear and distinct.

Οὗτος ἦν ὃν εἶπον etc. The Baptist has announced Him before he saw Him. See vss. 30, 33. Comp. Matt 3:11; Mark 1:7; Luke 3:16.

Ὁ ὀπίσω μου ἐρχόμενος ἔμπροσθέν μου γέγονεν 'Has been set before me.'

ὅτι πρῶτός μου ἦν 'He was first in respect of me.' πρῶτος is used rather than πρότερος because not only relative but absolute priority is intended. πρῶτος is substituted for ἔμπροσθεν, ἦν for γέγονεν. πρῶτος is not simply πρότερος. In Aelian (?), *An.* ix. 12 (in Herder p. 8). John 15:18 πρῶτον ὑμῶν is hardly a parallel, because the plural makes a difference. Again Luke 2:2 cannot be so taken. Cf. Herm. on *Elus.* (*Ned.* v.67, p.343); Herm. *Opus.* III, p. 168. See e.g. Orch. (?) *Etem.* 30. See Winer, *Gramm.* sec. xxxv, p. 258. The sense of πρῶτος here is the same as the thrust of 8:58.

The doctrine here has a parallel in Phil 2:6sq. ἐν μορφῇ Θεοῦ ὑπάρχων compares to πρῶτός μου ἦν. The ἔμπροσθέν μου γέγονεν here compares to διὸ καὶ ὁ Θεὸς αὐτὸν ὑπερύψωσεν in Phil 2:9. The original glory pertained to the Logos in his absolute personality. The subsequent glory to the Logos Incarnate, the God man Jesus Christ.

Vs. 16 The testimony of John closes with vs. 15. This is clear from the distinct reference to the work of Christ as a *historical* past (ἡμεῖς πάντες) and more especially from the aorist ἐλάβομεν.

Πλήρωμα His plenitude. See my notes of Ephes. i.22.

ἡμεῖς πάντες 'we all,' whether Jews as in 1 John, or Gentiles as in 'you my disciples.'

χάριν ἀντὶ χάριτος See Philo, *de Poster. Ca.* sec. 43, p. 254 M.

Vs. 17 ἡ χάρις καὶ ἡ ἀλήθεια The grace is opposed to the rigor, the narrowness, the strictness of the Law, as in Aristotle's famous contrast between the ἀκριβοδίκαιον and the ἐπιεικές.

The ἀλήθεια is opposed to the typical, partial, temporary character of the Law. On the σκιά ('shadow') as opposed to the σῶμα ('body') see especially Col 2:17. ἀλήθεια is more frequently opposed to idol-worship, as the substantial and the true as opposed to the purely imaginary and false, as e.g. in Rom 1:25. The contrast there is more direct, but still in an inferior degree it holds here. Observe the definite articles ἡ χάρις καὶ ἡ ἀλήθεια, perhaps a reference to vs. 14.

Ἰησοῦ Χριστοῦ, no longer 'Logos' but the historical manifestation, the Incarnate Word.

ἐγένετο not ἐδόθη for the function of Jesus Christ in the one case was different from the function of Moses, in the other Moses was only the medium of the transmission of the old covenant, Jesus Christ was the historic center, the creative agency of the new. He Himself was the grace, was the truth. For a similar distinction see Gal 3:19—ἐν χειρὶ μεσίτου.

Vs. 18 From the οἰκονομία of the new dispensation, the Apostle passes on to the θεολόγια. Having spoken of the Gospel, as superceding the Law, he speaks of the Logos as the Revealer of God. Thus in these two senses, the Christian dispensation is viewed in two aspects: 1) as an answer to the prophetic Jew, the realization of the Messianic hopes; 2) as an answer to the philosophic heathen, the solution of his difficulty of the unknowable Absolute Being.

Observe the order here, Θεὸν οὐδεὶς ἑώρακεν πώποτε. Comp. Gal 2:6, πρόσωπον ὁ Θεὸς ἀνθρώπου οὐ λαμβάνει.

ἑώρακεν Comp 6:45, 46 and 14:7 and Sir 43:41. The word is plainly not used in a physical sense merely, but in an intellectual sense. Even in the most striking of the Old Testament theophanies, this truth is not forgotten—see Exod 33:20.

μονογενὴς Θεὸς or ὁ μονογενὴς υἱός? 1) Both readings are found as early as the latter half of the second century. In Irenaeus they occur on successive pages (pp. 255, 56); 2) As a matter of authority, unquestionably Θεός is better supported than υἱός; 3) On the other hand, the sense seems to require υἱός of the two. Unless the verbal paradox was intentional (which is quite possible), we are at a loss to reconcile Θεὸς οὐδείς with Θεὸς ἐξηγήσατο. Nor again is μονογενὴς Θεός an expression we should expect. There is however the expression in Philo about the δεύτερος Θεός. 4) ΘC and VC are abbreviations and the one might be substituted for the other. 5) μονογενὴς υἱός occurs several times—John 3:16, 18; 1 John 4:9, but μονογενὴς Θεός never elsewhere. It is very unlikely then that a scribe would substitute Θεός for υἱός, though quite naturally he might do the converse. On the whole, if the choice were just between Θεός and υἱός, the former would seem to have greater claims, *but* 6) there is some authority for reading μονογενής or ὁ μονογενής only.

Pseudo-Ignatius, *Phil.* 2 however is not decisive. In Tris (?) iv, p. 102 the quote is not direct, whereas in the context where it is directly quoted it is in the form μονογενὴς υἱός and all the other passages in Ignatius seem to be equally *indecisive.* Moreover, we have υἱός Θεὸς, *Clement* p. 956 and elsewhere *filius dei.*

εἰς τὸν κόλπον τοῦ Πατρὸς expresses intimate union with the Father. The present participle denotes his eternal relationship with the Father.

ἐκεῖνος See Meyer.

ἐξηγήσατο See Plato's *Republic* iv, p. 448C and *Eum.* 565, 579.

Vs. 19 The beginning of the narrative proper. The preaching of John hitherto has been directed to contrasting the Word and the Witness, and thus has been subservient to the theological purpose of the Evangelist, in developing the doctrine of the Person of Christ. The commencement of the historical narrative seems as that of the Synoptic Gospels.

τοῦ Ἰωάννου The other Gospels style him John the Baptist, in the Fourth Gospel he is never so called. This may be a slight indication of authorship. There was no *third* John from whom it was necessary to distinguish him.

οἱ Ἰουδαῖοι 'the Jews,' characteristic of the Fourth Gospel. See 2:6, 13, 18; 4:9; 5:1 etc. What is the inference—that the writer was not a Jew? This is contradicted by the language and the tenor of the Gospel throughout. But it shows that the writer, when he wrote, was widely separated in time and place from the national life of the Jews. The aged Apostle, writing at the close of the first century (thirty years after the fall of the Temple and the polity of the Jews) and writing moreover in a Gentile city, and mostly for Gentile converts who would naturally use this mode of speech.

Σὺ τίς εἶ; Note the emphatic Σύ. 'Art thou one of these imposters, these false Messiahs who from time to time have been disturbing the peace and imperiling the existence of the nation?'

Baptizing, cleansing was connected in the popular conception with the preparation for the Messiah's kingdom. See Ezek 36:26; Zech 8:1, hence their anxiety to know what his baptism portended.

Vs. 20 καὶ ὡμολόγησεν The words are omitted in ℵ. Reiterated obviously with a view to making the declaration emphatic, and thus directed against the Henobaptists. These Henobaptists must have formed, not a large, but an appreciable sect at the time when and in the neighborhood where John wrote. The Evangelist is not content with reaffirming his view by merely denying the negative.

Ἐγὼ οὐκ εἰμί The correct word order as in the best manuscripts and versions, and the most appropriate as well. The T.R. has οὐκ εἰμὶ Ἐγώ. Perhaps this order would form a better reply to the question, but the Baptist's answers are not direct replies. They are so framed as to lead his inquirers into some further truth. See vs. 25. Therefore he does not reply 'I am *not* the Christ' but rather '*I* am not the Christ' i.e. 'the Christ is here, but I am not he.'

Vs. 21 Ἠλίας See Mal 4:5, 6. See Smith's Dictionary s.v. p. 531. Comp. Luke 9:8.

σὺ Ἠλίας εἶ; The true word order is expressive. Some contempt and disappointment expressed in the emphatic σύ.

Οὐκ εἰμί Not in the sense in which the question was asked. He is not the same person, but nevertheless, he was the fulfillment (or rather a fulfillment) of the prophecy of Malachi (see Matt 11:12; 17:12; Mark 9:3), for he came in the spirit and power of Elijah (Luke 1:17).

Ὁ προφήτης The one predicted in Deut 18:15, 18. See below on 6:14; 7:40. This figure was sometimes connected with and (mis)identified with the Messiah in national expectations. According to some, here Jeremiah was foretold (see Smith's Dictionary s.v. p. 970). The Apostles set forward our Lord as the fulfillment of this prediction, see Acts 3:22; 7:3 and this is perhaps the allusion below in 1:46.

Vs. 22 Τίς εἶ; All these conjectures are exhausted, and the questioner is put in despair.

Vs. 23 Ἐγὼ the emphatic position of the word points to the suppressed contrast. 'A voice of one crying.' The distinction here is clear, and the difference of reference between φωνή and Λόγος. See my notes on Ignatius, *Rom.* 2 and *Smyrn.* 4.7 (Trench, *Syn.* xxxix, p. 172, who seems silently to endorse this view). But though the words are each appropriate in their proper place, there is nothing to show that the Evangelist had this distinction between the two words in his mind. There is no emphatic contrast of φωνή and Λόγος here.

On the other hand, by the form of expression ἔφη Ἐγὼ φωνὴ βοῶντος it is probable that the Baptist intends to represent himself simply as the mouthpiece of the divine will and that the Evangelist in quoting his words lays stress on this fact. Notice it does not say 'my voice' or 'in the voice of' but '*I am a voice.*' It is a voice clearly articulate indeed, and intensely significant, but nothing more. His *message, his witness* is all in all. The Witness must decrease and the Word must increase.

βοῶντος means shouting, loud and clear in its utterance. See κέκραγεν in vs. 15. We have here an abridged quotation of Is. 40:3. In regard to its form in the original, the parallel clauses seem to suggest that 'in the wilderness' ought to be taken with what follows. Otherwise, the order is in favor of the common punctuation. The LXX reading retains the order, but omits 'in the desert' perhaps because the translator could not readily find another synonym for ἔρημος. This facilitates taking ἐν τῇ ἐρήμῳ with what goes before, inasmuch as it removes the reason for taking it otherwise.

The Evangelists preserve the order, and to some extent the words of the LXX (as here cf. Matt 3:3; Mark 1:3; Luke 3:4sq.). It is therefore still open to

us to take ἐν τῇ ἐρήμῳ with what follows, as e.g. Tregelles does. Both the
order and application will admit this, but the other seems more natural in
itself, at least more natural in the Synoptics but perhaps less natural in John
(see Ewald, p. 135). We must ask about the meaning of the passage as it
occurs in its original context.

Here are some points of contact between the prophecy and its application:
1) There is the superficial resemblance. The solitary voice in the desert. In
both cases ἔρημος, but two different regions are intended in the two cases.
On the locale of the Baptist's preaching see *Sinai and Palestine*, p. 304;
2) There is the true and fundamental resemblance—the harbinger of a great
deliverance. The key here is that the prophecy was pitched sufficiently
broadly that it could have designated something more than a temporary
deliverance. The immediate fulfillment was, and was felt to be, *inadequate*.
The prophecy was not exhausted by safe passage over the wasteland and
deliverance from the land of captivity. Now the true link of connection between the prophecy and its fulfillment had to do with the Messianic hope of
the nation. The superficial resemblance in 1) [see above] struck the minds
of the contemporaries of the Apostles. It appealed to the mode of thought
of the age, and consequently the Apostles and the Evangelists lay a stress on
this sort of coincidence that is hardly intelligible to us, which does not take
any hold upon our minds.

On the other hand, all study of Jewish history and all criticism of Scriptural books seems only to bring out more clearly the strong Messianic
yearnings of the Jews. If the angst brought on by individual texts becomes
weaker, the angst from the national history becomes stronger. The whole life
of the nation was one loud, clear, unbroken prophecy. It was a remarkable
utterance and is a remarkable occurrence. It was answered by the most
striking incident, by the appearing of the foremost character (to say nothing
more at present), that has ever appeared on the stage of this world's history
by the greatest moral emancipation that the human race has ever encoun-
tered—prophecy and fulfillment conceived as lock and key.

Vs. 24 ἀπεσταλμένοι v.l. with the definite article added before the word,
but the former is better supported. Observe the naturalness with which this
notice comes in. 'And they were sent from the Pharisees' not 'and they were
persons sent.' The point seems to be the jealousy of the Pharisees at any inter-

ference with their authority. Comp. 7:47, 48.[3] They were the self-constituted guardians of religious community power. Notice no reference here to the careful observance of ritual practices.

Vs. 25 Neither the Christ nor one of his expected forerunners or companions.

Vs. 26 Ἐγὼ βαπτίζω Notice there is no direct answer to the question asked. The answer is indirect indeed, so far as being a reply to the question, but the Baptist has the further design to lead their thought to some ulterior truth, as Heracleon truly saw and Origen vainly disputed.

ἐν ὕδατι The contrasting clause is suppressed. 'Another baptizes with a higher baptism.' See vs. 33; Matt 3:11; Mark 1:8; 3:16; especially Acts 1:5; 4:16; comp. 19:4.

στήκει probably the right reading here, this or ἕστηκεν.

οὐκ οἴδατε 'know not' i.e. in His true person. See vs. 31. In a lower sense they may or may not have known him.

Vs. 28 Βηθανίᾳ Note the form of this reading. The general (almost unanimous) consent of the old manuscripts, etc. supported by the assertion of Origen, and see e.g. Heracleon. However, the reading Βηθαβαρᾶ (T.R.) has the following in its favor: 1) the fact that no such Bethany is mentioned in either the Old Testament or the New Testament and that Origen who lived in Palestine did not know of any such place in that locale; 2) There is the tradition mentioned by Origen at Bethabara was the place of the baptism. In the days of Eusebius (*Onamastic.* s.v.) it was still seen as the traditional location and resorted to by persons wanting baptism; 3) the higher probability that Bethany would be substituted for Bethabara, a less familiar name, rather than the converse; 4) the few manuscripts contemplated by Origen— the Cureton Syriac (this must have been independent). Later manuscripts may have been influenced by Origen's criticism. The Ethiop. has both readings. In any case the name Bethabara signified ferry house. See Beth-barah (Judg 7:24), Beth-arabah (Josh 15:61). Neither identification has much to recommend it. Note in Mark 7:27 there is a confusion between Bethany and somewhere else.

Vs. 29 Τῇ ἐπαύριον The notice of time here is very precise. Comp. vss. 35, 44; 2:1. Afterwards they are looser, see 2:12: Μετὰ τοῦτο κατέβη εἰς

---

[3]See however Ewald, *Geni* (?) v, p. 192; vii, p. 400.

Καφαρναοὺμ αὐτὸς καὶ ἡ μήτηρ αὐτοῦ καὶ οἱ ἀδελφοὶ καὶ οἱ μαθηταὶ αὐτοῦ, καὶ ἐκεῖ ἔμειναν οὐ πολλὰς ἡμέρας, and 3:22: Μετὰ ταῦτα ἦλθεν ὁ Ἰησοῦς καὶ οἱ μαθηταὶ αὐτοῦ εἰς τὴν Ἰουδαίαν γῆν, καὶ ἐκεῖ διέτριβεν μετ᾽ αὐτῶν καὶ ἐβάπτιζεν, and 4:3: ἀφῆκεν τὴν Ἰουδαίαν καὶ ἀπῆλθεν πάλιν εἰς τὴν Γαλιλαίαν, and note vss. 44, 45, 54 refer to Galilee.

The baptism and the temptation, where are they to be placed? The baptism is placed before all the events just mentioned, comp. 1:26, 31, 32. The temptation seems to follow immediately (Matt 4:1—Τότε; Mark 1:12—εὐθύς; Luke 4:1—ὑπέστρεψεν ἀπὸ τοῦ Ἰορδάνου, καὶ ἤγετο) after the baptism. This is not however absolutely certain from these expressions. The narrative of St. John from vs. 28 onwards seems to give *continuously* our Lord's *public life* and there seems to be no room for his retirement [to the desert]. We must suppose it also took place before the point in time where St. John's narrative commences.

ὁ Ἀμνὸς τοῦ Θεοῦ The reference is to Is. 53. See especially vs. 7 for Ἀμνὸς and for ὁ αἴρων τὴν ἁμαρτίαν τοῦ κόσμου see vss. 4, 12. This passage was commonly interpreted of the Messiah, apparently before the Christian era (see Brown's [?] *Sermons* p. 98). Thus the Baptist's expression would be a natural sequel to the revelation which he had received that Jesus was the Messiah. The two points in the expression are: 1) the humility, tenderness of his character; 2) the sacrificial character of his career. The first of these was realized in the actual character of Jesus as he was standing before John. The second followed from the circumstances of the cases. All the great prophets and reformers had in some sense been sacrifices to the cause of God, had in some sense borne the sins of the people, more especially those who had died in the righteous cause (see the passages quoted by Alford about the seven brethren). Whether John also foreknew how Jesus would, in a special and unique sense, bear the sins of the world we cannot say. He may have uttered the words without a full and entire consciousness of their deep meaning.

The Fifty-Third Chapter of Isaiah is again and again applied in the New Testament to Jesus (see especially Acts 8:32, Philip; 1 Pet 1:19 compared with 2:22-24). But this was after the passion and crucifixion had given a new meaning to the application of the prophecy. St. John here delights to reveal how the Baptist at the commencement of our Lord's career had applied the text that afterwards was so signally fulfilled, hence the repetition in vs. 36. Not once only did he announce this truth.

αἴρων The idea here is twofold: 1) to take up, lift up, bear; 2) to take away, remove i.e. it involves the idea of 1) with the suffering of the victim, and 2) the release of the sinners. i.e. the scapegoat concept. See my notes on Gal 3:13; comp. 1 John 3:5; 1 Sam 15:24; 25:28. In 1 Pet 2:24, ἀνήνεγκεν after the LXX of Isaiah, adding ἐπὶ τὸ ξύλον. Perhaps St. John had the same idea in αἴρων.

τὴν ἁμαρτίαν viewed as one. 'As in Adam all die, so in Christ all shall be made alive.'[4] Is there any reference here to the Paschal lamb? Perhaps not, as John the Baptist used the words, but probably yes as John the Evangelist repeats them. For the coincidence of time, not at once here suggested by the connection Jesus is the slain lamb of Isaiah's prophecy, and Jesus dies on the first day of Unleavened Bread, hence in St. Paul and elsewhere. And in St. John comp. 19:36 from Exod 12:46.

Again there is the coincidence with the Apocalypse, τὸ ἀρνίον, about thirty times. It is as if it is the designation under which Jesus was first introduced to his disciples. See vs. 15. The words were said before Jesus had come to be baptized and therefore before he was revealed to John as Messiah. John's commission was to preach that the Kingdom of Heaven was at hand, i.e. to preach the near approach of Messiah. Not without the sign revealed from heaven did he know *who* was the Messiah.

Vs. 31 κἀγὼ οὐκ ᾔδειν αὐτόν i.e. did not know his true personality. So St. John uses οἶδα elsewhere—4:10; 7:28; especially 8:19; 20:9. This is perfectly consistent with: 1) the relationship between Jesus and John as recounted by the other Evangelists. Even supposing (though of this there is no evidence and all of the circumstances actually related i.e. the descent to Egypt, the abode of John in the wilderness) that the two cousins were brought up together, as the Italian painters represent it.[5] For ᾔδειν does not refer to actual knowledge but to spiritual appreciation. And as Jesus' own brothers, even at a later period, did not in this sense know him (John 7:5) so John may have been equally ignorant of Him, until the special revelation came to him;

---

[4]See 1 Cor 15:22.
[5]Not a few Italian painters pair John the Baptist with John the Evangelist. They include Agnolo Gaddi (1350–1396), Sandro Botticelli (1445–1510), Domenico Ghirlandio (1449–1494), Defendente Ferrari (d. ca. 1540), Dosso Dossi (1490–1542) and Guido Reni (1575–1642). The pair also appears in works by Hans Memling (1430–1494), Juan de Joanes (1475–1545) and El Greco (1541–1614).

2) Matt 3:14, for this only implies moral superiority and not necessarily any recognition of his Messiahship.

ἀλλ' 'not withstanding my ignorance of who was the Messiah, I was sent (this much I knew) baptizing that messiah (whoever he was) might be made manifest.' See the Jewish tradition in Justin, *Dial. Trypho* p. 226B.

ἐγώ 'I am not the Christ,' the 'I' emphatic here, keeping up the contrast.

ἐν ὕδατι The water as opposed to the Spirit, the reading here however is more than doubtful.

Vs. 32 ἐμαρτύρησεν, a favorite word and thought of St. John's. Again a point of contact with the Apocalypse.

Τεθέαμαι Whether this vision was confined to John or not we cannot safely infer from the expression itself. There is nothing in the narrative of significance which implies it was seen by others or indeed that anyone else was present on the occasion. N.B. St. John's narrative here *assumes* the account in the Synoptics, and the history of the Baptism. This is only one of several instances, e.g. the Lord's Supper, that is the most remarkable of all the stories St. John wrote to supplement the other Gospels and is also an exaggeration of a fact. He did not write to supply deficiencies but rather from a different point of view, he assumed facts already known.

Is περιστερὰν ἐξ οὐρανοῦ mere resemblance to the language of St. Matthew and St. Mark?

ἔμεινεν ἐπ' αὐτόν On its special force see John 3:34.

Vs. 33 κἀγὼ οὐκ ᾔδειν αὐτόν emphatic repetition.

οὗτός ἐστιν ὁ βαπτίζων again the Synoptic narrative is assumed (Matt 3:11; Mark 1:8; Luke 3:16).

ἐπ' αὐτόν is determined by the καταβαῖνον. The baptism with the Holy Ghost, was fulfilled on the day of Pentecost and in subsequent similar manifestations.

Vs. 34 κἀγὼ ἑώρακα, καὶ μεμαρτύρηκα A connection not only within the Gospel, but with 1 John 1:1, 2; comp. 4:16.

ὁ Υἱὸς τοῦ Θεοῦ not a Son of God. For to him is given the Spirit without measure (3:34). The v.l. ὁ ἐκλεκτός in Syr., ℵ, some Latin mss., Syr. Harcl. Comp. Luke 9:35. Tregelles, Tisch., and Alford do not mention the v.l.

Vs. 35 Observe the part the disciples of John play in this Gospel.

Vs. 37 ἠκολούθησαν τῷ Ἰησοῦ Was it this fact and a less remembered incident in John's connection with our Lord that suggested the phraseology in Rev 11:4? This however was only a temporary following, as appears in vs. 40. Note the connection of following and the lamb in the Apostle's memory.

The *call* comes later (Matt 4:18sq.; Mark 1:16sq.; comp. Luke 5:1sq.). It appears from the Synoptic narrative (or at least it seems probable) that they had some acquaintance with Jesus before. Otherwise his abruptness and their ready response seems hardly intelligible.

Vs. 39 ὄψεσθε the correct reading. ἴδετε doubtless an emendation to make the grammar uniform.

ὡς δεκάτη A v.l. ἕκτη. The question is, is this a Jewish reckoning of time?

Vs. 40 ὁ ἀδελφός older or younger? Probably younger if we may judge from the order of the lists of the Apostles. This however is not conclusive since the list may be geared to preserve the precedence of St. Peter. Epiphanius, *Haer.* 51, sec. 17, p. 440 makes Andrew the elder. See Cave, p. 4. The name Andrew is Greek. Does it represent some similar Hebrew name just as 'Simon' is similar to Simeon? At all events it is probable that the brothers spoke Greek as well as Aramaic.

The Apostles were called ἀγράμματοί καὶ ἰδιῶται (Acts 4:13), but this does not exclude all culture. We know that it was customary even for those of the class of fishermen to be educated. See the article in the *Quarterly* on Talmudim.

εἷς ἐκ τῶν δύο The other doubtless John himself: 1) compare the way he speaks of himself elsewhere; 2) the incidents are very precise and doubtless related by an eyewitness. The succession of days, even the hour of this critical event in the writer's life.

Vs. 41 πρῶτος (so ℵ and others). Some excellent authorities (A, B) read πρῶτον but this is obviously a correction of an apparently awkward reading. He was the *first* to find him. The word is obviously emphatic. This is a reply, we may suppose, to some inquiry from the writer's disciples, or a corrective of some false impression derived from an earlier Gospel narrative. There is a possibility that Alford's explanation is correct.

τὸν ἴδιον explaining πρῶτον, so Alford.

Εὑρήκαμεν As though John was following him from a distance, and at least assuming that Simon would know they had been together.

τὸν Μεσσίαν comp. 4:25. St. John alone uses the Jewish equivalent of 'the Christ.' In both passages it is in the mouth of another. Elsewhere in the A.V. it occurs only in Dan. 9:25, 26.

Vs. 42 ὁ υἱὸς Ἰωάνου The name of Peter's father as given by John is
Ἰωάννης or the more correct form Ἰωάνης. So here and at 21:15, 16, 17. In all
places however, most ancient authorities have Ἰωάνα, as it is read in the
Received Text. This however is plainly an adaptation to Matt 16:17—Σίμων
Βαριωνᾶ. John is doubtless the reading in the Fourth Gospel. There is a
temptation to change from Ἰωάννης to Ἰωάνα, not convincingly however.
How then are we to explain the difference? The Greek Ἰωάνας or Ἰωάνα is
used to represent two different Hebrew names—יוֹנָה the prophet's name,
Jonah (meaning dove), and also יוֹחָנָן Johanan meaning the grace or gift of
God, and so abbreviated as 'John.' This latter word appears in Greek under
diverse forms:

1) Ἰωανάν—1 Chron 3:15 (a son of Joash); 1 Chron 12:4 (one of
   David's captains); 1 Chron 6:9, 10 (son of one Azariah and father
   of another); 1 Chron 3:24 (a different person); 1 Chron 12:12 (a
   different person); Neh 12:23; Ezek 8:12; 2 Chron 17:15; 23:1; Luke
   3:27, but sometimes it is Ἰωάνναν (especially A in Jeremiah),
   1 Macc 2:2; v.l. Luke 3:27; Ezek. 10:28; Neh. 12:13, 23, 42.

2) Ἰωνάν—dropping the first α as it is liable to be slurred over, the
   accent falling on the last syllable. See 1 Chron 12:12 (א has Ἰωάν
   a corruption) Neh. 4:18 (but א has Ἰωάννav). Cf. 1 Esdr 9:1; Ezek
   5:6; 1 Chron 26:3; Luke 3:27 v.l.; Luke 3:30 v.l.

3) Ἰωανάς A in 1 Chron 6:10.

4) Ἰωάνης or Ἰωάννης—1 Esdr 8:38; 1 Macc 2:1 (and vs. 2a); 1 Macc
   8:17; 9:36sq.; 13:53; 16:1; 2 Macc 4:11; 11:17.

5) Ἰωνά—2 Kngs 25:23; Luke 3:30.

6) Ἰωννά—v.l. Luke 3:27.

7) Ἰωνάς—1 Esdr 9:23 but perhaps a corruption see Smith's
   Dictionary I, p. 1120.

At all events it is doubtful what Hebrew name is represented thereby. The
English equivalent (A.V.) are Jehohanon, Johanan, Joannan (Esdr 9:1),
Joanna (Luke 3:27), Jonan (Luke 3:30), Joannan (1 Macc 2:2), Jona (John 1:42
comp. Matt 16:17), and Jonas (John 21:15sq.). The name 'James' is also explained sometimes as = Johannes, John but this is more than doubtful. From

all this it will appear that Βαριωνᾶ is only the equivalent of 'son of John' ('Ιωάννης). In an old list of Apostles we hear about the father'Ιωνά and the mother'Ιωννά (see Cotcher, *Nam. Ap.* (?) I p. 275). This is obviously a mistaken attempt to reconcile the account in St. John and St. Matthew, an attempt based on ignorance. The Codex Am. has 'Johanna' here.[6]

Why is this stress laid on his parentage, son of John, son of Jonas here and in John 21:15sq. and Matt 16:17? It appears from this repetition that the Lord delighted to dwell on the expression. Is it: 1) simply to distinguish him from others e.g. Simon the Zealot? This is a supposition. Is it 2) to describe his natural position and contrast his loftiness in the Kingdom of grace? 'Simon son of the poor fisherman John thou shalt become the foundation stone of the Kingdom of Heaven.' Is it 3) to try out the significance of the name John— 'the grace gift of God'? So Zecharias consents that his heaven given son shall be called 'John.' Comp. τοῦ Πατρός μου τοῦ ἐν τοῖς οὐρανοῖς (Matt 7:21).

Κηφᾶς the name is new, for the first time given here. Matt 16:17 refers to a later occasion. It is there said not 'thou shalt be called Peter' but rather 'thou art Peter.' Κηφᾶς only here and in St. Paul (1 Cor. Gal.).[7] The names and verbage of this Gospel are much more Jewish than the Synoptics.

EXCURSUS: EVIDENCE OF THE AUTHENTICITY AND AUTHORSHIP OF THIS GOSPEL

The narrative unit concluded in relation to the question of the authenticity and genuineness of this Gospel: 1) We have the precision of detail, the precision of an eyewitness might be inferred, yet we are not told that the author is an eyewitness. 2) Nevertheless, there is room for such an eyewitness. One of the two persons is mentioned by name, Andrew, and the other is not. Still there is not the slightest indication that the anonymous person is the author. 3) Looking at other parts of the book however we find that an anonymous person appears and reappears in the narrative. He is the disciple whom Jesus loved, and sometimes simply 'the other disciple.' Still however not a word about the authorship. The fact that he is never named is the more remarkable considering that he is a very important and prominent character. 4) At

---

[6]See Scrivener's *Introd.* p. 125; Origen, *Op.* III p. 671sq. See also the Gospel of the Hebrews, and Nickles (?) *Evang. Apoc.* p. 43, 417.

[7]I.e., 1 Cor 3:22; 9:5; Gal 2:9.

length in a postscript to the Gospel (Joh. 21:24, 25) written apparently at a later date, (by a different hand), it is stated that this disciple is the one 'who bore this testimony and wrote it down.' Still even there, the name is withheld. This is confirmed by the knowledge of certain anonymous witnesses. 5) John the son of Zebedee is the only prominent disciple of Jesus who does not appear by name, and therefore, independently of the tradition, it would seem probable that we must identify the anonymous disciple with him. 6) The eldest tradition has held this to have been John son of Zebedee. 7) No one critical incident in his life would dwell on his mind. He would recall the minute circumstances, even the hour of the day. All this forms a very convincing body of evidence, being convincing because it is of the most auspicious kind. The mode of procedure is wholly unlike that of a forger. The Apocryphal Gospels declare at their opening in the most explicit terms who was the author. This is not only unlike a forger, it is wholly unintelligible on such a supposition. For in order to produce its result, it supposes a control over the traditions of the writers of a succeeding generation, and yet makes no effort to give them the desired direction.

But it is quite intelligible and quite natural on the supposition that the writer was known to those among whom the Gospel was first circulated and that their own knowledge would supply all that was wanted in regard to the person, the circumstances, and the opportunities of the writer. In other words, it is quite natural on the supposition that St. John wrote as tradition says he wrote to instruct a body of disciples who had gathered about him, and with whom he lived on familiar terms. And (it may be added), it is natural *on this supposition alone.* But 8) A certain prominence is given to Andrew in this narrative as though he was a person in whom the reader would be especially interested. Moreover, he is spoken of in such a manner, as to suggest that a certain chapter in his past ministry had been the subject of arguing or perplexity. He was the first to find his own brother (εὑρίσκει οὗτος πρῶτον τὸν ἀδελφὸν τὸν ἴδιον Σίμωνα—1:41) and to reveal the Messiah to him. What is the account of this? It does not explain itself but supposes some previous occurrence. Was it that the call of the Apostles Peter and Andrew as related in the Synoptics had seemed to clash with information derived from Andrew himself or from those around him? And that St. John was anxious to correct these misapprehensions and to give the honor due to Andrew as the first to call his more famous brother Peter, the leading Apostle, to the side of Messiah? He thus relates an incident prior to the formal call, in which Andrew plays the chief part.

And here we are reminded of the notice contained in the earliest tradition related to the writing of St. John's Gospel. It is there stated that Andrew was instructed by revelation that John should write his Gospel. The tradition may not be true, probably is not true, in the dress that it now wears. But it bears testimony at least to the fact that Andrew in the earliest witness was believed to have been a companion of St. John in Asia Minor and to have had some influence on the writing of this Gospel. Andrew also appears first in the list of Papias' oral authorities.

Vs. 44—Introduction of Philip. Note his prominence in the Gospel of John—here, 12:21, 22; 14:8, 9. In fact we know nothing of him from any other source than St. John's Gospel. As is the case with Andrew, may we not trace some historical connection with St. John's Gospel? He too has a prominent place in the list of Papias, coming right after Andrew and Peter. Moreover, he is related by Polycrates of Ephesus to have lived at Hierapolis, and he is quite clear it is the Philip who is one of the Twelve and mention is made of his three daughters. In the mention of the daughters there is apparently a confusion with Philip the Evangelist (see Eusebius, *Hist. Eccles.* v.24. Philip the Evangelist and his daughters certainly lived in these parts for Papias is concerned with the daughters—Eusebius, *Hist. Eccles.* iii.39). But the confusion is perhaps best explained by the supposition that both the Philips were in Asia Minor. The confusion is not confined to Polycrates. The *Acts of Philip* take him to Hierapolis and make him preach in Phrygian Asia.

Vs. 45 The three mentioned together as in Papias—Andrew, Peter, Philip. Note the naturalness of the narrative in vss. 44-46. He is starting for Galilee. He finds Philip who is a native of Bethsaida. Philip, when or where we are not told, finds Nathanael and the next incident occurs at Cana in Galilee.

There is nothing very remarkable in this, but at the close of the Gospel (21:2) Nathanael is described (quite incidentally) as ὁ ἀπὸ Κανᾶ τῆς Γαλιλαίας. Here at length we have the explanation of the occurrence.[8] The writer unconsciously assumes on the part of his readers a fact well known

---

[8]On Nathanael cf. Gretch. (?) *Ursprach. Theolog.* 1868, p. 248.

to himself which makes the whole sequence of events intelligible, namely that Nathanael lives at Cana and so he omits to explain how the notice ἠθέλησεν ἐξελθεῖν εἰς τὴν Γαλιλαίαν (vs. 43) bears on the incident following. The key to the explanation is found in a wholly different place.

Βηθσαϊδά house of fish, therefore a common name on a lakeside. There was another Bethsaida on the east side of the lake where the 5,000 were fed (Luke 9:10sq.).

Vs. 46 Ναθαναήλ Identified with Bartholomew? This is probable but not certain. Bartholomew like Barnabas, Barabbas, Barjona, Bartimaeus, Barjesus is simply a patronymic, not a proper name. He therefore must have had some other name. Now it would appear from 21:2 that he was one of the personal followers of Christ, most probably one of the Twelve. But if so, which one? In all three lists of the Twelve, Philip and Bartholomew are named and connected together (see Matt 10:3; Mark 3:18; Luke 4:14). In Clem. *Recog.* i.59 (from the Ascent of James), Bartholomew takes up the argument against an opponent of Philip. In the *Acts of Philip* (see Tisch.) Philip the Apostle and Bartholomew (who however is called one of the '70'), travel and preach together.

Ὃν ἔγραψεν Μωϋσῆς ἐν τῷ νόμῳ καὶ οἱ προφῆται εὑρήκαμεν i.e. we have found the Messiah. Doubtless a reference to the passage in Deut 18:15.

υἱὸν τοῦ Ἰωσήφ Alford says, 'This expression seems to show previous acquaintance on the part of Philip with Jesus.' Hardly so. The narrative is not complete. Many things must have occurred. Many conversations had been held with Jesus and with others between the Ἀκολούθει μοι (vs. 43) and εὑρίσκει Φίλιππος τὸν Ναθαναήλ (vs. 45), so that no inference can be drawn of this kind. υἱὸν τοῦ Ἰωσήφ τὸν ἀπὸ Ναζαρέτ speaks to how he appeared to men. See Matt. 13:55—ἐστιν ὁ τοῦ τέκτονος υἱός. This occurs in the same Gospel that records his genealogy (Matt 1) and see Luke 2:49—'your father and I seek you.' The inference therefore that the Fourth Gospel writer did not believe (perhaps did not know of) the miraculous conception is false. John certainly knew of it. Philip may not have known of it. The people of the place certainly did not know of it.

Vs. 46 Ἐκ Ναζαρέτ? Not from the smallness or insignificance of the town (this might be inferred from the passage here standing alone), as Alford. Rather Nazareth had a bad reputation. It is not the size but the quality ἀγαθόν that Nathanael remarks on. The Nazarenes appear as a violent, unscrupulous, irreligious people (Luke 4:16, 29; Matt 13:12, 58). This is perhaps the simplest explanation of Matt 2:23. There is an irony in the inscription over the cross—'Jesus of Nazareth, King of the Jews.' See 'the sect of the Nazarenes' (Acts 24:5). Nazarene was a contemptuous appellation of the Christians in early as in later times. Generally applied by the Jews to the Christians, hence the Palestinian Christians called this by the Emperor Julian the Apostate. 'This last conquered Nazarene' is his uttered last exclamation.

Vs. 47 Ἰσραηλείτης This is the retort for Nathanael's contempt of the Nazarenes. ἀληθῶς Ἰσραηλείτης, Ἰσραηλ being the correct name of Jacob, Israelites being the people of the covenant. 'Men of Israel' is the Jewish equivalent to the Roman 'Quirites.' *Non possum ferre, Quirites.* See Acts 21:28: Ἄνδρες Ἰσραηλεῖται, βοηθεῖτε· cf. Acts 5:35 from Gamaliel: Ἄνδρες Ἰσραηλεῖται. So too the Apostles when they seek to elicit a favorable hearing—see Acts 2:22; 3:12. See also 2 Cor 11:22. The term Ἰσραηλείτης in St. Paul's case is on the religious side what 'Romanos' is on the political side.

Vs. 48 με γινώσκεις; ὄντα etc. goes with what follows. ὑπό in this context 'beneath.'

τὴν συκῆν συκῆ is the tree, συκῆ with a final accent, the fruit, Palestinian fig. Cf. 1 Kngs 4:25; Micah (?) 4:4; Zech 3:10—תְּאֵנָה from the Hebrew verb meaning to stretch out. Whether Nathanael was or was not in sight is a matter of little question. We need not stop to imagine whether Jesus saw him with his outward eyes. The fact that he read his heart is alone important. All this would appear to have happened before Nathanael's own house.

Vs. 49 σὺ εἶ ὁ Υἱὸς τοῦ Θεοῦ, σὺ Βασιλεὺς εἶ τοῦ Ἰσραήλ i.e. the Messiah described on both sides, in his relation to God, and in his relation to man. On ὁ Υἱὸς τοῦ Θεοῦ as Messiah see Ps 2:7; John 11:27. The Evangelist takes the expression in a deeper sense than that in which Nathanael uttered it. It was the consciousness that his thoughts were real, which dictated his reply to Nathanael. It is called forth in what was implied by our Lord's words, rather than what was actually said.

There is the same apparent inconsequence, the same deep-rooted connection, and significant fullness, in the connection between our Lord and his mother at the marriage feast. The unexpressed thoughts must be supplied before the sequence is complete. Nathanael has been convinced by this single isolated manifestation of the divine Spirit in Jesus. He shall see here-after how heaven and earth are connected in Him, how he is the Jacob's ladder by which God's grace descends on man and man's spirit rises to God. Nathanael's expression of faith has its counterpart in the promise, the descending angels correspond to the 'Son of God,' the ascending to the 'King of Israel.'

Vs. 50 εἶπεν αὐτῷ It is an answer to Nathanael but it is also addressed to the others present also—Philip, and probably Peter, Andrew, and John.

Vs. 51 On 'the heavens opened' i.e. God revealed, cf. Acts 7:56—Ἰδοὺ θεωρῶ τοὺς οὐρανοὺς διηνοιγμένους καὶ τὸν Υἱὸν τοῦ ἀνθρώπου ἐκ δεξιῶν ἑστῶτα τοῦ Θεοῦ. On the angels descending and ascending see Gen 28:12. The narrative of Jacob's dream is here used figuratively. No external, visible appearance is meant. The figure receives its explanation in such passages as John 3:23; 11:38; 13:13; 14:10, 20; 16:28; 17:21sq. The idea pervades John's Gospel in diverse forms.

ἐπὶ τὸν Υἱὸν τοῦ ἀνθρώπου Nathanael had called him the Son of God. Both are titles of the Messiah. The one is the necessary counterpart to the other. The Son of Man, derived originally from Dan 7:13, 14. He is the typical ideal man, the representative head, the crown, the absolute sovereign of the human race (see Herzog [?] on Daniel, p. 114). 'Son of Man' was the common Aramaic expression where we would simply say 'man.' The Son of Man is 'the Man.' In St. John it seems to be used formally (always?) in connection with the exaltation either of Jesus Himself or of the human race through Jesus. Jesus is the second Adam, the man in whom all men are quickened.

The Beginning of the Signs
of the Messianic Times
(John 2)

In John 2 we turn to the first miracle narrative, and it is a festive occasion. This declares the character of his teaching—the Son of Man came eating and drinking (Matt 21:18-19). Here we have a practical comment on the saying recorded in the Synoptics. This word 'came' especially in its contrast to the way John came; seems to point to such a commencement of our Lord's ministry as this. It is especially significant, too, that the first miracle was wrought to bless the one human relation that his later followers, for centuries afterwards, were only too ready to depreciate. The unconscious Manicheanism of medieval Christianity finds no countenance in the teachings of the Savior. It is instructive as well to compare the opening of his ministry with the close.

Vs. 1 τῇ ἡμέρᾳ τῇ τρίτῃ i.e. reckoning from the last mentioned day.

Κανᾶ Cureton Syr. (see John 4:46) and this is also the form in the Peshitto. As the Syriac generally retains the original Aramaic name which has been transformed in the Greek, e.g. Simeon, Johanan, so probably here as well. If so, in identifying the place the form *Catna* ought to be kept in view, though possibly the 't' has dropped out in the modern (Arabic) dialect, as it had in the Greek. It was to be identified with Kefer Kenna, but Robinson identified it with Kana Elilet (?), about nine miles from Nazareth. This is more probable. It has *koph* and not a *caph* but the 't' is not regarded.

γάμος a marriage feast, the feast being the most important part of the ceremonial. See Tobit 8:19: καὶ ἐποίησεν αὐτοῖς γάμον ἡμερῶν δεκατεσσάρων; Esther 4:22: ἐν γὰρ ταύταις ταῖς ἡμέραις ἀνεπαύσαντο οἱ Ἰουδαῖοι ἀπὸ τῶν ἐχθρῶν αὐτῶν καὶ τὸν μῆνα, ἐν ᾧ ἐστράφη αὐτοῖς (ὃς ἦν Ἀδὰρ) ἀπὸ πένθους εἰς χαρὰν καὶ ἀπὸ ὀδύνης εἰς ἀγαθὴν ἡμέραν, ἄγειν ὅλον ἀγαθὰς ἡμέρας γάμων καὶ εὐφροσύνης, ἐξαποστέλλοντας μερίδας τοῖς φίλοις καὶ τοῖς πτωχοῖς; and Gen 29:22: συνήγαγεν δὲ Λαβαν πάντας τοὺς ἄνδρας τοῦ τόπου καὶ ἐποίησεν γάμον, where ἐποίησεν γάμον is a non-literal translation of וַיַּעַשׂ מִשְׁתֶּה whereas the literal would be συμπόσιον. And see the other references in Smith's *Dictionary*, p. 251. See also Matt 22:2: ὅστις ἐποίησεν γάμους τῷ υἱῷ αὐτοῦ. This usage is classical but with γάμος rather than γάμον ποιεῖν. In Hellenistic Greek either is good.

ἡ μήτηρ τοῦ Ἰησοῦ ἐκεῖ She is never named in St. John's Gospel, and he never names himself, nor does he name his brother James (though James is named repeatedly in the other three Gospels). Mary's husband Joseph appears to be already dead. This may be inferred from the silence of the Evangelists and from the expression in Matt 13:55. The explanation for the suppression of the name of Jesus' mother is found in 19:26. The same delicate reason which would not permit him to mention his own or his brother's name led him to suppress the name of her who had become his adopted mother. But were such fine shades of artfulness at the command of a fisher? If he had thought of the device in one case, would he have remembered it in the other? Would it have occurred to him moreover to introduce so inauspiciously an incident that only explains his reticence? This was probably John's first introduction to her whose adopted son he was to become. The mother takes precedence over the son here, but it would be the son who would be glorified (vs. 23).

καί also, referring to what goes before. Comp. for the καί (separated from the καί which follows), Phil 4:3—μετὰ καὶ Κλήμεντος καὶ τῶν λοιπῶν συνεργῶν μου.

Vs. 2 καὶ οἱ μαθηταὶ αὐτοῦ i.e. Andrew, Peter, Philip and Nathanael, and John.

Vs. 3 λέγει ἡ μήτηρ τοῦ Ἰησοῦ πρὸς αὐτόν Said half in perplexity half in expectation that he might render aid. Obviously there is expectation, and some faith in a supernatural power that dictates the question. Such might be expected of her who held the secret of his divine parentage, who kept all these things in her heart (Luke 2:19, 51), even if she had not heard (which she must have done) about John the Baptist's announcement. She is decisive that he should manifest forth his glory. There is some alloy mixed up with the faith perhaps, parental ambition, perhaps eager impatience, which he checks.

Compare the answer in Luke 2:49 to 'your father and I . . .' namely 'I must be about my Father's business.' We have the same separation of himself from her here. Note the substantial unity of the different Gospels here.

Vs. 4 γύναι No want of respect here. Nothing harsh in this term meaning 'lady' or 'madam.' No other term would be used. μήτηρ would have been inconsistent with Τί ἐμοὶ καὶ σοί. But still there is *a certain tone of reserve*. Comp. Matt 19:26.

On Τί ἐμοὶ καὶ σοί cf. Matt 8:29; Luke 8:28; Mark 5:7; Jud. 15:12. 'What have you and I in common? What is there between us two? My ways are not your ways.[1] I know when it is fit to work a miracle, and when it is fit to withhold, but you do not.' Here is the rebuke.

οὔπω ἥκει ἡ ὥρα μου The reference is not so much to lapse of time absolutely, as to the opportuneness of the occasion relatively, and the fitness of things. More especially it has to do with the frame of mind, the spirit of the witnesses, and above all of her who asks the question.

Vs. 5 From eager impatience, from parental ambition, she is at once corrected to humble submission and to unquestioning faith. The ὥρα which a moment before was far off, has at once arrived. The change of mind has made the distant, present. He will not work a miracle and gratify those who from ambition or curiosity seek a sign (see Mark 8:12; Matt 16:1sq.; Luke 4:16sq.), but to humble faith the response is at once given.

Vs. 6 λίθιναι ὑδρίαι ἓξ κατὰ τὸν καθαρισμόν See Mark 7:3. See the relevant section in the Mishnah on purifications.

τῶν Ἰουδαίων It occurs rarely in the other Gospels (Matt 28:15; Mark 7:3; Luke 7:3 [ἀπέστειλεν πρὸς αὐτὸν πρεσβυτέρους τῶν Ἰουδαίων, but of the centurion]; and 13:51 [πόλεως τῶν Ἰουδαίων]). But it is characteristic of St. John. Note the altered circumstances and the lapse of time, and the probable residence among Gentiles, and the fall of the city of Jerusalem and the Jewish polity.

ἀνὰ μετρητὰς δύο ἢ τρεῖς. μετρητάς is the equivalent to the Hebrew

---

[1] An allusion to Is 55:8.

'bath.' The Attic μετρητάς contained 72 xestae (?) and the Hebrew 'bath' contained 72 'lgs' (?). This seems to point to some common source of measurement, perhaps Egyptian (see Smith's *Dictionary*, p. 1736). On the amount of water necessary for each unit, see that prescribed in the Mishnah (VI, p. 480 Sarentin?). The Attic measurement μετρητάς was 8.66 gallons. Josephus identifies the 'bath' with the μετρητάς. See *Ant.* viii.2.9 where he says it is equal to 72 xestae. The estimate of the later rabbis makes it 4.4286 gallons (Smith's *Dictionary*, p. 1742). Probably the Greek term μετρητάς here means the Hebrew bath, not the Attic measurement. It stands for it in the LXX in 2 Chron 4:5. Was there a Greek μετρητάς different from the Attic μετρητάς? The jars might or might not have been empty to start with so we do not know if they filled them full. Cf. Sir 35:1, 22:1 to Heliod. *Athn.* vii.27. See Gruter, p. 578 no.1, and 474.4 and 579.7 (the same as Muratori p. 924.1). The 'triclinardes' (often a slave) was the chief of the *tricliniarii* (see Gruter, p.576.6). We find them also in Petronius, M. Beker, Chancl. II, p. 252.

Vs. 9 ὡς δὲ ἐγεύσατο This does not mean (as Alford seems to think) that he was a guest. He does the work of a 'progustator.'

οἶνον γεγενημένον 'When it had been made wine.'

Vs. 10 ὅταν μεθυσθῶσιν 'When men have drunk deep.' See Pliny, *Nat. Hist.* xiv.13.

Vs. 11 ἀρχὴν τῶν σημείων as a beginning of his signs. Probably omit τήν before ἀρχήν (in the B.M.T. and the T.R.) but this is uncertain. τὰ σημεῖα is a favorite word in St. John. This is significant. He never uses δύναμις, as is common in the Synoptics. Every incident, every discussion in this Gospel is a σημεῖον. Also τέρατα is a favorite word in Acts, but in the Gospels only occasionally (cf. Matt 24:24; Mark 13:22; John 4:48).

Ταύτην ἐποίησεν This again seems to be some kind of answer to a question from St. John's disciples. Comp. above on 1:41 and below on 4:46, 54. The precision with which these miracles in Cana are related is noteworthy.

τὴν δόξαν αὐτοῦ See on 1:14. He appears as the divine Logos. He gives proof that by Him all things were made.

It is worth remarking on the striking character of the miracle. So St. John always. He does not record many miracles but they are always the most striking of their class, each distinct types. The difficulty in miracles is not enhanced by the scale. *The many gallons of water made wine may startle the imagination, but the creative power that could turn one drop of water into wine could with the same ease turn the whole.* It may seem strange that the impression on those present was not greater. But we are apt to exaggerate the probable effect of such an exhibition of power. There are many ways of thrusting aside the practical implications, many ways of explaining away the divine interposition, which, no doubt, even in our own days men would have recourse to—'and they said that he cast out demons by Beelzebub the prince of the devils'[2] which was a recourse available then but would not be now, which would cover any case. We must mention the moral condition of the witness, his capacity of *discerning* the spirits, his receptivity of divine teaching, was the only safe-guard of belief, even when a miracle was wrought.

Vs. 12 Μετὰ τοῦτο After this, how long is not said.

Κατέβη for Capernaum was on the lakeside, Cana in the hill country, 4:46. So Luke 4:31, from Nazareth.

Καφαρναούμ The best supported form (ℵ, B, Orig.). See the Syriac in Cureton on 4:46, and Peshitto. It means Caphar village opposite to a large town, Capharsalama (1 Macc 7:31). See Lenz, p. 383. It seems to mean the village of refreshment. This was probably the original force of the proper name.[3] The word means resuscitation or revivification hence either consolation or resurrection or both. This might be alluded to in Luke 4:23. The important point is that in St. Luke mention is made of his having been 'of Capernaum' too. Observe the change from 2:1—he has taken his right place, he has increased but she has decreased.

οἱ μαθηταὶ αὐτοῦ Probably those mentioned before.

οὐ πολλὰς ἡμέρας The reason explained in the following verse.

Vs. 13 τὸ πάσχα τῶν Ἰουδαίων For πάσχα see Lenz, p. 276, explained ὑπέρβασια in Josephus, *Ant.* ii.6. The natural confusion with πάσχειν, hence the Latin Fathers translate it *pasias*. The form is the Aramaic emphatic. Comp. Satan-Satana (whence *Satanas*). Note σάββατα that becomes a plural.

---

[2]See Lk 11:15.
[3]While Lightfoot is certainly right about the word "Caphar" = village, it seems clear at this juncture that "naum" = Nahum, the village of Nahum the prophet.

Excursus: The Chronology of St. John and the Synoptists

'He went up to Jerusalem.' Note the number of visits to Jerusalem. The visits to Jerusalem are the signal posts of St. John's chronology: 1) here (cf. 4:13) a Passover—the first Passover. Cleansing of the Temple, discourse with Nicodemus; 2) There is a Festival (5:1). Irenaeus p. 147 says it was a Passover, as does Origen (IV, p. 250), though it is not stated. Several uncial manuscripts read ἡ ἑορτή. The article is apparently added to define it as 'the' Passover (as e.g. here). But in 7:1 the Feast of the Tabernacles is called ἡ ἑορτή. The use elsewhere of the definite article seems to show that it was not the Passover. 3) The healing at the Pool of Bethesda—the two verses prepare. He is in Galilee (6:4). So in 7:2, 14, 37 we have the Feast of the Tabernacles (October), preaching of Jesus, [woman taken in adultery], healing of the blind man; 4) 10:22. Apparently a separate visit for the term τὰ ἐνκαίνια, the Feast of Dedication (winter), and the raising of Lazarus; 5) 11:55; 12:1, 2. The Passover. So from John 12:10 onwards, almost everything takes place at Jerusalem or in that neighborhood. Hence, St. John has been called the Jerusalem Gospel, the other three the Galilean Gospels.

From St. John, we derive the backbone of the chronology of our Lord's life. These Jewish festivals are so many vertebrae. But even here we cannot be sure that the chronology is continuous. Jesus may have paid more visits to Jerusalem than are recorded. His active ministry may have extended over more than *three* Passovers. There is nothing in St. John's narrative that excludes this. From 8:57 Irenaeus (ii.22.6) infers that our Lord was not far from fifty years old, at all events that he was over forty. There would be some ground for this if the Jews knew our Lord's age. As it was, they would simply state the extreme possible limit. The 'man of sorrows' might well look older than an ordinary man—'You have not lived half a century, and have you seen Abraham?' Irenaeus gives as his reason Jesus lived forty years or more that this is the *mature* time of life, neither unripe as a youth, nor decayed as old age. He is arguing against the Valentinian chronology, which supposed that Jesus died *complens trigesiorum annum* [about 30 years of age]. See their argument in Irenaeus. He appeals to the elders who were disciples of St. John, but what it was exactly that they testified is not clear. Whether it was said that Jesus' ministry extended several years after his baptism (after his thirtieth year), or that he was over forty years old at his Passion, is not clear.

There is nothing in St. John's Gospel that directly contradicts the view that he was between forty and fifty years old when he died, but there is also nothing which *requires* it. On the other hand, the narrative suggests a shorter ministry, three or four years. If Irenaeus meant that the elders said this (but Jesus was forty or fifty years old), it is probable that he misrepresented them (confusing his own interpretations with their tradition), or that they misrepresented the statement of St. John. But it is by no means clear that he did mean this.

Altogether, St. John's chronology is thoroughly natural. There is no symmetrical arrangement in it, no appearance of artifice. It is altogether irregular, and there are also great gaps in the history (e.g. 7:1; 10:40), long stretches of days about which nothing is rendered (see Sabatier, p. 56). This again is evidence of authenticity. So much for St. John's chronology absolutely, and now to compare it to the other three Gospels.

The Synoptics exhibit no chronological certainty. Occasionally incidents are linked together as occurring at about the same time, but there is *no chronological backbone* here. In the general chronology then there is no conflict because there is no contact. The Synoptics *might suggest* only one year of ministry, and the Valentinians and others have drawn this inference from them, but it is an inference drawn only from their *silence*, and is valueless against any facts on the other side. Because only one Passover is mentioned in the Synoptics, we cannot conclude that only one occurred during our Lord's ministry. On the other hand, the various *effects* of our Lord's ministry as represented in the Synoptics seem to require more than a year. One must remember the fragmentary character of these three Gospels. They are not biographies but incidences from our Lord's life and teaching, gathered and grouped together for catechetical purposes. The great *prima facie* difference is in the number of visits to Jerusalem. Only one is recorded in the Synoptics, and yet even here they give indication of their fragmentary character. There are incidents, there are expressions of our Lord which presuppose previous visits: 1) he does not come to Jerusalem as a stranger (see Sabatier, pp. 85-86 and on the Sermon on the Mount also); 2) we have a distinct statement in Matt 13:37/Luke 13:34 ('how often'); 3) the allusions in Luke 13:6, 9, 33 especially in their connection. As for the sort of argument used against such data (Mark 10:32), see Sabatier, p. 84.

Ἱεροσόλυμα See Josephus, *Bell. Jud.* vi.10 of Melchizedek ('Its original founder was a Canaanite chief called in the native tongue 'righteous King' for such indeed he was. In virtue thereof, he was the first to officiate as priest of God and being the first to build the temple, gave the city, previously called Solyma, the name of Jerusalem.') but *Ant.* i.10.2 is more vague. Eupolemius from Alexander Polyhistor quoted in Eusebius, *Praep. Ev.* ix.34sq. speaks of the building of the Temple in Jerusalem (by Solomon).

Vs. 14 ἐν τῷ ἱερῷ, not the ναός comp. 10:23. See Josephus, *Ant.* viii.3.9 and see Trench's *Synonyms*. On 'between the temple/ναός and the altar,' see Matt 23:35. On the τοὺς πωλοῦντας βόας (merchants), see Mishnah, *Shekalim* 7.2. καθήμενος, a positive characteristic of bankers, hence the ἐπικαθήμενος, the money changers, see Demosthenes, *Phorm.* p. 946.

Vs. 15 ἐκ σχοινίων This feature does not occur in the Synoptic accounts. Σχοινίον is a rope made of rushes or reeds in the LXX as well as in classical Greek. See Josh 2:15 LXX; 2 Sam 8:2.

τά τε πρόβατα probably 'and' as πάντας rather than πάντα seems to show. On τῶν κολλυβιστῶν, see John Lightfoot on Matt 21:12. See Surentus (?) Vol. II, p. 176sq. κολλύβος is the payment to the moneychanger, a fee paid to him to change the money. The half (Tyrian) shekel payment to the temple was on the first of Adar, collected in the provinces on the fifteenth. On the twenty-fifth the bankers sat in the sanctuary. The money was supposed to be all collected before the end of the Jewish year (?). On the fourteenth Zina (?) was he present? This would explain ἐγγὺς ἦν in vs. 13, but probably the money-changers sat in the sanctuary at other times as well to accommodate the purchase of victims etc. There were precise directions about the chests for receiving the money and for the banking.

ἐξέχεεν aorist (perhaps) see Lobeck, *Phyrm.* p. 222.

Vs. 16 Πατρός μου See Luke 2:49; comp. John 5:18; 8:19. The claiming of God as his Father is one of the stresses.

οἶκον ἐμπορίου The language at the close of the ministry is more severe—σπήλαιον λῃστῶν ('house of thieves'—see Matt 21:13).

Vs. 17 ἐμνήσθησαν οἱ μαθηταί perhaps at a later date as in vs. 22.

Ὁ ζῆλος see Ps 69:9.

καταφάγεταί E.V. wrong here 'hath eaten.' The future here is substituted for the aorist to bring out the prophetic reference. καταφαγέται does not refer to outward persecution. On the form see Lobeck, *Phyrm.* 327. As for the reference of this Psalm to the Messiah see elsewhere in John 15:25 compared to vs. 4 and 19:28 compared to vs. 21. So also in the other Evangelists and see Acts 1:20—vs. 25. See Perowne (?), p. 367.

An incident of the same kind is recorded in the Synoptics as happening at the close of our Lord's ministry (Matt 21:12; Mark 11:15; Luke 19:45). If it were necessary to identify the one with the other, St. John would have the higher claim to be the historic truth, the Synoptics must yield absolute deference to it. The Synoptics are to be interpreted by St. John and not conversely, for St. John is precise and definite. But the incident may well have occurred twice, the same scene of profanation calling forth the same feeling of righteous anger, would produce the same results.

Vs. 18 We are ill-fitted by our conventional mode of life for judging of the character of an incident so thoroughly unconventional. It would not startle the Jews as it would startle us. It would seem a not unnatural (though somewhat extraordinary) act of a religious zealot. The many incidents recorded in Josephus' narrative of zealotry in these days will offer confirmation. The Jews are impatient of such a proceeding. They require to see Jesus' credentials. They resent it, but not more than this.

ἀπεκρίθησαν 'Answered' is too narrow for the word. 'Remonstrated' would express the meaning here, but this again would not include other passages. This verb is used for replying to an *act*, as well as replying to a speech.

The ναός is the body of Christ but it is also the Herodian temple. With the death of Christ was involved the abolition of the Jewish polity, the destruction of the Jewish temple which was the symbol and center of that polity. With the resurrection arose a new, a spiritual, Temple not made with hands, the Christian Church. The Christian Church is symbolized by, and in some sense is the body of Christ.

Compare the form in which the accusation is brought against our Lord in Mark—Ἡμεῖς ἠκούσαμεν αὐτοῦ λέγοντος ὅτι Ἐγὼ καταλύσω τὸν ναὸν τοῦτον τὸν χειροποίητον καὶ διὰ τριῶν ἡμερῶν ἄλλον ἀχειροποίητον οἰκοδομήσω (14:58).

As Christ's body died a natural body and rose a spiritual body, so on the ruins of the material temple was built the spiritual edifice of the Church. Out of the ashes of the Israel according to the flesh arose the Israel according to the Spirit.

To this saying of the Lord in vs. 18 (interpreted in some such way), we may refer the words of St. Stephen that was alleged as a charge against him (see Acts 6:14). The idea of a body as a temple, because in it the Spirit of God resides, or should reside, is familiar from St. Paul. To our Lord it was applicable as to no one else see Col 2:9—ὅτι ἐν αὐτῷ κατοικεῖ πᾶν τὸ πλήρωμα τῆς Θεότητος σωματικῶς.

St. Mark tells us that the false witnesses did not agree with one another (Mark 14:58). The saying was sufficiently obscure in itself for unscrupulous men to wrest both the form and the meaning to their own purposes. Of the double meaning, the primary meaning is to some external act or thing, the secondary reference is to some spiritual truth symbolized literally. St. John's Gospel will afford many instances (e.g. 3:13) where there is an allusion to the actual Incarnation and actual resurrection but there is also a reference to the spiritual descent and ascent.

Vs. 22 ἐπίστευσαν τῇ γραφῇ The passage in view is not as listed by Alford. See Gal 3:22. St. John very frequently refers to a particular γραφῇ without specifying which one it is. This may be regarded as almost his special peculiarity. The meaning of this is that he wrote for those who did not require this information, who probably had heard the application from his own lips, who at all events lived in an age when the application had become recognized, had become in a manner stereotyped. So here cf. 17:12; 19:28; 20:9. But in all cases the reference can be determined with high probability. Thus 17:12 refers to Ps. 41:10; see John 13:18. John 19:28 refers to Ps 69:22 as appears from the incident itself and from the other Evangelists.

The reference here and in 20:9 will be the same. What is it then? The words 'when then he arose from the dead, the disciples remembered and believed the Scripture.' What Scripture did the disciples so apply soon after the resurrection? St. Luke's narrative supplies the answer—Acts 2:27, 31 citing Ps 16:10. Recollect that this was said by St. Peter on a very notable occasion (the most notable occasion of preaching recorded in the history of the Church), not very long after the resurrection and in the presence of St. John.

Vs. 23 The three uses of ἐν here: 1) local; 2) temporal; 3) pragmatical. The last however in the phrase ἐν τῇ ἑορτῇ is very doubtful. On א, B comp. 6:4.

Let us ask ourselves the meaning of the change from Scriptures to Scripture (singular). This is not insignificant. There was gradual insensibility to the variety of Scriptures. The diversity was lost sight of in the unity. This has been going on in John, in other words. *Instrumentum* and bibliotheca have both disappeared as names for the Scriptures. They used to be called 'the books,' τὰ βιβλία. This was transferred to Latin—*Bibliaorum*, but in late medieval Latin *Biblia, Bibliae*. And in modern languages *la Biblia, la Bible, die Bibel*. Whether the feminine first appeared in the Latin or the Romances languages, deserves inquiring into. I should think the latter. The transference into another language would facilitate the change of gender and the Romance dialects would react on the Latin. There is a gain in the clear concept of unity, but a definite loss in the absence of any sense of variety. Modern criticism has taken its revenge. A one-sided conception has produced a one-sided reaction. And the critics have found nothing but divergences, discrepancies, oppositions.

ἐπίστευσαν εἰς To 'believe in' not the same as to believe.

τὸ ὄνομα αὐτοῦ This refers to his dignity, his claim to deference. Yet the belief was not very deep-seated as appears from the next verse.

Vs. 24 Ἰησοῦς οὐκ ἐπίστευεν αὐτὸν αὐτοῖς as Luke 16:11. See Bretschneider, *Lex.* s.v πιστεύειν, p. 277.

αὐτόν not αὐτόν here, but perhaps to be aspirated here; comp. 19:17; Acts 14:17; Rev 8:6; 18:7. See the note in A. Buttmann, p. 98. Yet perhaps αὐτόν here can be treated like the English 'he bethought himself.' The αὐτόν seems to show that the repetition of the same word was intention. In the A.V. ἐπίστευεν 'believe.' The same word should be rendered in both clauses 'trust.'

Vs. 25 περὶ τοῦ ἀνθρώπου and ἐν τῷ ἀνθρώπῳ not as A.V. 'should testify of man for he knew what was in a man.' It specifies the particular man with whom at any time he had dealings.

αὐτός Not translated in the A.V. that also chose not to translate it in the previous verse. Here it is 'of Himself' there 'on his part.'

ὅτι οὐ χρείαν εἶχεν ἵνα

NICODEMUS AND THE NEW BIRTH
(JOHN 3)

Vs. 1 Νικόδημος A name not uncommon amongst the Jews, see Josephus, *Ant.* xviii.3.2, *Bell Jud.* ii.17.10. See Simons (?) pp. 15, 28. Comp. Νικόλαος. Nicodemus was either a translation of some Jewish name (like Theodorus, Theodotus, perhaps Theudas = Matthias, Acts 5:36, see Wiesler, p. 90), or a modification of some Jewish name like Alphaeus, Jason, Simon, or a second adopted name like John Hyrcanus or Herod Agrippa. The Talmud mentions one Nicodemus whose real name was Baar, and elsewhere Baar is called a disciple of Jesus, one of the three eldest men when Titus took Jerusalem. He was ben Gorion. On this see John Lightfoot. The Nicodemus of Josephus (*Bell. Jud.* s.v.) was father of Gorion. See Delitzsch, *Zeitschrift fur Luth. Theol.* 1854, p. 643.

In regard to the character of Nicodemus, comp. 7:50 and 19:39. And see the Gospel of Nicodemus chapters 5, 7, 15.

ἄρχων τῶν Ἰουδαίων A member of the Sanhedrin, comp. 7:50.

Vs. 2 διδάσκαλος A very qualified confession of the Person of Jesus.

Vs. 3 ἀπεκρίθη This is the reply to ἐλήλυθας διδάσκαλος. Nicodemus seems to ask 'what have you to teach us?' The reply is, 'I don't cast a lesson here or a lesson there, but an entire change of life, a being born again.'

ἄνωθεν 'again, anew' as in Gal 4:9. This is the right translation for: 1) this is how Nicodemus takes it, on the supposition that it was spoken in Aramaic (which however is more than doubtful. The mistake in reference would be impossible); 2) the analogy of the New Testament; 1 Pet 1:3, ἀναγεννήσας, having fathered again (cf. vs. 23); Titus 3:5, παλινγενεσίας, regeneration. There is no doubt in our Lord's reply that Nicodemus had understood the word ἄνωθεν, at all events. So too καινή κτίσις, καινός ἄνθρωπος, a Jewish mode of speaking, about proselytes. For an early interpretation of this we turn to Justin Martyr, *Apol. I* chapter 61: 'For Christ also said, "Except ye be born again, ye shall not enter into the kingdom of heaven." Now, that it is impossible for those who have once been born to enter into their mothers' wombs, is manifest to all. . . . Since at our birth we were born without our own knowledge or choice, by our parents coming together, and were brought up in bad habits and wicked training; in order that we may not remain the children of necessity and of ignorance, but may become the children of choice and knowledge, and may obtain in the water the remission of sins formerly committed, there is pronounced over him who chooses to be born again, and has repented of his sins, the name of God the Father and Lord of the universe.' Cf. Cureton Syriac at this juncture, and Peshitto.

It is no argument that in 3:31, 21:11 (19:23 can hardly be quoted) ἄνωθεν means 'from above.' No doubt more frequently ἄνωθεν does mean 'from above.' But because it means so twice is not reason why it should mean so thrice, in a third place.

Vs. 4 What is the nature of the answer? The expression 'being born anew' was familiar to the educated Jews. But the expression would never be used of one born a Jew. A proselyte who was admitted into the covenant was said to be born anew, regenerated. He ceased to be a Gentile; he was born an Israelite. But with this meaning, so Nicodemus thought and spoke, the phrase could have no reference to himself, nor none to the Jews about him. They would not be born again. The spirit therefore which dictated the reply is akin to that which said, 'We have Abraham as our father.'[1]

Vs. 5 ἐξ ὕδατος καὶ Πνεύματος the water, the visible; the Spirit, the invisible grace. The καὶ Πνεύματος distinguishes the baptism of which our Lord speaks from the baptism of John. St. John has been called the sacramental Gospel.

Vs. 6 τὸ γεγεννημένον etc. There is an Israel after the flesh and there is an Israel after the Spirit. 'The one you are, the other you must become.'

---

[1]See Jn 8:39; cf. Mt 3:9; Lk 3:8.

σάρξ ἐστιν partakes of the character of, preserves the nature of that from which it sprung. For this natural external conception of your religious pedigree it is the necessary consequence, the inevitable result that your whole religious life should be final, external.

Vs. 7 Δεῖ ὑμᾶς Is there not some force in this word ὑμᾶς? Is it not in fact the key to the whole force of the context? 'Because I said that *you*, the children of Abraham, the children of the covenant, so proud of your national descent, so satisfied with your stainless pedigree?' Of the poor proselyte who needed to be born anew, as one of the covenant people, such words were intelligible, but as applied to themselves the words seemed to have no meaning. See 8:31sq. and the remainder of the chapter.

τὸ πνεῦμα The motions of the flesh can be seen and felt, can be described in words, can be explained and known. Not so the motions of the Spirit. Of the operations of the Spirit we are conscious. But there the awareness and knowledge ends. The before and after, the mode and the sequence of the operation, are unknown to us. It is this characteristic of the wind τὸ πνεῦμα, the רוּחַ that made it a portender (?) of the Spirit as e.g. John 20:22. This is a symbolism not confined to any one nation of family of nations. See Xenephon, *Mem.* iv.3.14. It is Indo-European (cf. *inspiro*). It expresses: 1) invisibility; 2) freedom; 3) incomprehensibility. The only other passage in the New Testament where πνεῦμα means wind is Heb 1:7 (and even there it is doubtful).

It is a pity that the word 'ghost' has gone out of use except in the phrase 'yielded up the ghost.' Matt 27:50, ἀφῆκεν τὸ πνεῦμα. There we can make no distinction between ἄνεμος and πνεῦμα. Comp. Eccles 11:5: ἐν οἷς οὐκ ἔστι γινώσκων τίς ἡ ὁδὸς τοῦ πνεύματος. ὡς ὀστᾶ ἐν γαστρὶ κυοφορούσης, οὕτως οὐ γνώσῃ τὰ ποιήματα τοῦ Θεοῦ, ὅσα ποιήσει σὺν τὰ πάντα.

οὕτως ἐστὶν The regular combination see Matt 13:45.

Vs. 10 ὁ διδάσκαλος There are two mistaken interpretations in Alford. ὁ διδάσκαλος does not mean *the* teacher. It does not require that he should have been 'pre-eminent,' 'the one whom men call *the* teacher.' ὁ διδάσκαλος τοῦ Ἰσραήλ is a rabbinical expression. See John Lightfoot and the sources he cites—'art thou a wise man in Israel.' Another instance of the Hebrew coloring in the Gospel.

γινώσκεις discernment, the process.

Vs. 11 οἴδαμεν 'We know,' the absolute fact as often in St. John. See *Journal of Philology* III, p. 116. οἴδαμεν 'I and mine.' ὃ οἴδαμεν, Hebrew parallelism. As very frequently in the second clause, each word is an advance upon the corresponding word in the first clause. ἑωράκαμεν is more vivid than οἴδαμεν, μαρτυροῦμεν is stronger than λαλοῦμεν.

Vs. 12 τὰ ἐπίγεια 'These facts of the new birth which are enacted on earth, of which, if you cannot explain the operation, you can at least see the results.'

τὰ ἐπουράνια e.g. the Sonship of Christ, the nature of his Kingdom, of which you can have no earthly experience. See Wis. Sol. 9:16; and comp. Heb 6:1.

Vs. 13 The verse is a comment on ἐπουράνια. No one else can teach you τὰ ἐπουράνια. 'I, only I, who came down from heaven, who therefore who can ascend into heaven, can rise to the mysteries of the higher world and carry you thither with me.' It is the answer to the question in Prov 30:4—'Who ascends into heaven and comes down.' Comp. Eph 4:9, 10.

ἀναβέβηκεν εἰς τὸν οὐρανὸν The actual Ascension is only a symbol of the spiritual ascension of the Son of Man that is continuous. Thus ἀναβέβηκεν includes the idea expressed in the Collect for Ascension Day—'In heart and mind hither ascend.' This is also the explanation of the perfect ἀναβέβηκεν and compare 1:52.

ὁ υἱὸς τοῦ ἀνθρώπου The Man, the typical Man, the representative of the race, in whom is seen the image of God, in all its completeness and definiteness of nature. In this or that man, it is blurred and confused, only partially and inadequately represented. In *the* Man alone is the impress perfect. Thus, the Son of Man can be none other than the Son of God, the Word of God incarnate.

ὁ ὢν ἐν τῷ οὐρανῷ A reference to Dan 7:13. In reference to mankind he may be said to ascend and descend, to carry up their souls to heaven, and to bring down the divine grace upon them. But in his own Person he dwells continually in heaven. He *is* in heaven. Thus ὁ ὢν ἐν τῷ οὐρανῷ is a corrective to the idea of ascent and descent that seems to limit his divinity, his Heavenly being.

Vs. 14 καὶ καθώς The Ascension suggests the Crucifixion, the lifting up as common to both.

ὕψωσεν τὸν ὄφιν A symbolical meaning given. See Philo, *Leg. Alleg.* ii.19, I p. 80M. He made it Edom in one case, σωφροσύνη. For Patristic passages see my notes on *Barnabas* 12. See Justin Martyr, *Dialog.* 94 on this type of sign (see John Lightfoot on this), comp. Wis. Sol. 16:5 where it is seen as an arbitrary sign, a sign of God's power. The point of comparison is: 1) the lifting up, and 2) the healing. Other lessons (e.g. in Alford) may be derived therefrom. These may be legitimate applications but they do not appear in the narrative.

By man came death, by man came also the resurrection of the dead, 1 Cor 15:20, in the likeness of the flesh of sin, Rom 8:3. The lifting up of the crucifixion suggests a lifting up in a higher sense (see 12:32sq.).

Vs. 16 There is possibly a reference to Gen 22:2 (comp. Heb 11:17) in vs. 16, but I question it.

Does our Lord's discourse continue, or is this St. John's commentary on it? Probably the latter. We must imagine this Gospel as written for, almost as spoken to, the disciples gathered about the veteran teacher. This will explain how there is no distinct line of demarcation between the original speaker's own words and the comments of the narrator. The speaker's tones, gestures, his own and his hearers' vivid imaginations, supplies what is wanted in the form of the narrative. Comp. 1:16-18. And I am not sure but that this principle should be applied much more widely e.g. vss. 13-14.

So too St. Paul in Gal 2:14sq. and Acts 1:16sq. Certainly, 1) they all seem spoken as of the past, and 2) they all strongly resemble St. John's own language and St. John's own Epistle e.g. 1 John 4:8. But when Alford says that this would be to accuse St. John of an imposture, a forgery, this is an entire misconception. Imposture and forgery imply an *intent to deceive.* Such an intent has no place here.

Vs. 17 ἵνα κρίνῃ τὸν κόσμον This was the Jewish conception. Messiah was the avenger of his people, the punisher of the heathen.

Vs. 18 ἤδη κέκριται The fact itself is his condemnation. His state of soul is his punishment, judged and by implication, condemned. See Rom 14:23; Gal 2:11.

ὅτι μὴ πεπίστευκεν Because the sole perfect image of divine grace and holiness has been presented to him and he has rejected it.

The idea of μονογενής, 'the sole Son,' is that of *perfect* representation. The graces, the power of the Father are not divided among many, so that each is a partial reflex of the Divine Original, but are concentrated and coexist in

One. Comp. 1:14, 18 for the idea of concentration of Divinity, not as Alford has it.

Vs. 19 Not this is the reason, the ground, of the condemnation but this *is* the condemnation. The closing of the eyes to the light (it was a Biblical blindness as we would say) was indeed the cause of the punishment, but it was the punishment itself as well.

ἦν γὰρ αὐτῶν The hypocrisy, the pride, the impurity, the selfishness of men, they shrunk from Jesus in his earthly life, as the same vices have always shrunk from the presence of the Ideal, of the same moral holiness. See esp. Eph 5:14.

Vs. 20 ἐλεγχθῇ exposed.

Vs. 21 ποιῶν τὴν ἀλήθειαν To do evil is the opposite of 'to do the truth.' Comp. Rev 21:27; 22:15.

Vs. 22 Μετὰ ταῦτα The interval may have been long or short. We cannot assume the continuity of the history. This is a common chronological notice in St. John denoting an uncertain period, comp. 5:1, 14; 7:1; 21:1; and with μετὰ τοῦτο 11:7, 11; 19:28.

εἰς τὴν Ἰουδαίαν γῆν See my note on Gal 1:22.

ἐβάπτιζεν Explained at 4:2, but notice the natural way it is stated here and left without explanation.

ἐν Αἰνὼν ἐγγὺς τοῦ Σαλείμ See the Cureton Syriac and the Peshitto. Σαλείμ ℵ, B, L, Origen; Σαλήμ—B.M.T.

It is not at all implied in the narrative that St. John and our Lord were baptizing at or near the same place, only that they were baptizing at the same time. In Josh 15:32 we have καὶ Λαβὼς καὶ Σαλή in the mention of the tribes of Judah, but the name is not the same. These places are moreover in the arid country south of Judaea. See Smith's *Dictionary* article, II, p. 1093, on Salim. The most probable location of Salim seems to be that assumed by Jerome and Eusebius (see John Lightfoot, ii, p. 499), near the Jordan sight or nine miles south of Scythopolis. In Jerome's time it was called Saliminias. A Salim has been discovered by Van der Welde exactly in the position (six English miles south of Bethshan) and two miles west of Jordan. See Smith's *Dictionary*, p. 1093. There is 'much water' there, comp. the name Aenon.

John apparently moves gradually northward in his baptizing. See Smith's *Dictionary* s.v. Jordan, Vol. I, p. 1127sq. He is probably 1) at the lower fords of the Jordan at Jericho (John 10:40; comp. 11:1; comp. Matt 3:1); 2) at Beltabara/ Beltany John 1:29sq. the upper fords; 3) Aenon near Salim. John's native home was in the hill country of Judaea (Luke 1:39). He was apprehended by Herod Tetrarch of Galilee and therefore must have been under his jurisdiction at that time. This also points to a northward movement.

ὕδατα πολλά Therefore not on the river Jordan. It seems to be about midsummer (comp. 2:23; 4:3; 5:1).

παρεγίνοντο

Vs. 24 οὔπω γὰρ ἦν etc. Correcting some misapprehension? On the Synoptic narrative see Meyer.

Vs. 26 See 1:28.

μεμαρτύρηκας The perfect is expressive. The surprise is that after bearing witness to Jesus, and thus deferring to Him, he should still be baptizing, though Jesus had commenced his ministry.

Vs. 27 'The authority, the power, is given Him of God.' The words might also be taken to refer to the Baptist himself (so Alford), and would make excellent sense. 'I cannot assume a superiority which God has not given me.' But the former interpretation is more in accordance with St. John's language elsewhere see 5:19, 30; 9:33; 14:10. No argument can be based on the use of ἄνθρωπος that is quite unemphatic here, a Hebraism for τις. Heb 5:4 is a parallel but proves nothing.

Vs. 28 Οὐκ εἰμὶ ἐγὼ ὁ Χριστός, ἀλλ' ὅτι Ἀπεσταλμένος εἰμὶ ἔμπροσθεν ἐκείνου. The last word here does not refer to Χριστός but to a more remote subject, Jesus. Comp. 1:18, 33; 5:11, 39.

Vs. 29 Comp. Matt 9:15 (Mark 2:19; Luke 5:34); Matt 25:1 in answer to the disciples of John. They would recognize their master's metaphor. νυμφίος not ὁ νυμφίος. 'He that has the bride is the bridegroom; I am not a bridegroom.'

ὁ δὲ φίλος τοῦ νυμφίου To be distinguished from the οἱ υἱοὶ τοῦ νυμφῶνος (Matt 9:15; Mark 2:19; Luke 5:34). This is a translation of the Hebrew phrase 'the friend or companion of the bridegroom' who conducted all the preliminaries of the marriage, the betrothals etc. on behalf of the bridegroom (see John Lightfoot, I, p. 586). See Buxtorf, s.v. p. 2536.

Hence the propriety of the metaphor. John the Baptist is the φίλος. He arranges the preliminaries of the marriage. The disciples of Jesus are οἱ υἱοὶ, the guests and friends at the feast. See especially the illustration in Buxtorf l.c. The matrimonial contract between God and his people, taken from the law of Moses. The first one is torn up and new one made.

ἑστηκώς An attitude of expectation or of attention. 1 Cor 16:13—stand on the alert.

καὶ ἀκούων αὐτοῦ The exact point in time, whether on the approach or at the feast, is not clear, and it is not a matter of consequence.

χαρᾷ χαίρει See Lobeck, *Panal.* p. 524.

τὴν νύμφην νυμφίος A coincidence of exegesis with Rev 18:23. It is worth noticing too that the Church is spoken of as the bride only here and in Rev 21:2, 9, 17, though it is implied in the metaphor of the bridegroom elsewhere (e.g. Matt l.c.) and even expressed in other terms (e.g. 2 Cor 11:2; Eph 5:25sq. In the first of these passages Paul is the friend of the bridegroom). For the spiritual significance of the voice of the bridegroom, see Rev 22:21.

On ἡ χαρά See 15:11; 17:13; comp. Phil 2:2.

Vss. 31-32 The same difficulty confronts us here as in vss. 16ff. and the same answer perhaps must be given.

ὁ ὢν ἐκ τῆς γῆς ἐκ τῆς γῆς ἐστιν καὶ ἐκ τῆς γῆς λαλεῖ is of the earth. This is all that can be said of him. There is an end of it. Comp. John 19:22—Ὃ γέγραφα, γέγραφα. The A.V. has tried to relieve the expression from what seemed to be tautological, but which was really deliberately emphatic.

Observe the parallelism which brings out the emphasis:

ὁ ὢν ἐκ τῆς γῆς	ὁ ἐκ τοῦ οὐρανοῦ ἐρχόμενος
ἐκ τῆς γῆς ἐστιν	πάντων ἐστίν
ἐκ τῆς γῆς	ὃ ἑώρακεν καὶ ἤκουσεν
λαλεῖ	τοῦτο μαρτυρεῖ

Vs. 34 ἐκ μέτρου δίδωσιν τὸ Πνεῦμα See Col 1:19—πᾶν τὸ πλήρωμα. *Spiritus sanctus non habitant super prophetas nisi nemsma(?) quadrans.*

The Samaritan Woman
and the Courtier's Child
(John 4)

Vs. 1 ὁ Κύριος This designation of Jesus is not found in either St. Matthew or St. Mark, except Matt 21:3 and Mark 11:3 (Ὁ Κύριος αὐτοῦ χρείαν ἔχει), which is a doubtful exception. It occurs also in the later additions to St. Mark in 16:19, 20. In St. Luke it is found several times, e.g. 7:13 (where however there is a v.l. Ἰησοῦς); 11:39; 12:42; 13:15; 17:5 etc. and several times in St. John.

Ἰησοῦς πλείονας etc. repeating the direct words of the speaker so the present ποιεῖ καὶ βαπτίζει. The A.V. has 'made and baptized'; comp. Gal 1:23.

Vs. 2 καίτοιγε The statement has been made twice over—3:22; 4:1. At the repetition of it, it occurs to the writer to explain the strict fact. Another example of the naturalness, the *circumstantial* character of this Gospel. Jesus himself did not baptize. Baptism was left to the attendants. See Acts 10:48; 1 Cor 1:17. The subordinate position of John is implied thereby.

Vs. 3 πάλιν The better supported reading on the whole.

Vs. 4 Ἔδει It lay in his way, unless he made a long detour and went through Peraea. Comp. Josephus, *Ant.* xx.6.1. The whole narrative is an illustration of St. John's statement that Jews have no dealings with Samaritans. We find the Galileans leagued with the Judeans against the Samaritans. Samaria and the Samaritans are not mentioned in the first two Gospels (except Matt 10:5 where the 70 are prohibited from going into Samaria). St. Luke first recounts our Lord's dealings with these people—9:52; 10:33, the parable; and 17:11. It does not appear however that he did more than preach casually as he passed through Samaria from Galilee to Judaea, or conversely. This appears from the passages in St. Luke 9:52; 17:11 διήρχετο and from the narrative of St. John Ἔδει . . . διέρχεσθαι here and vs. 40, δύο ἡμέρας.

Συχάρ See Peshitto (Shochar). In the Cureton Syr. the word is missing but the manuscript is torn. This word has been made a difficulty for the authenticity of this Gospel. Yet the word certainly occurs in the Talmud, indeed it occurs in the connection the well or fountain at Sychar. See the passages in Delitzsch, Garenkis (?) *Zeitschrift Luth. Theol.* 1856, p. 243 (cf. *Zeit. Luth.* xxiv.6.53). It ceases therefore to have any bearing on the authenticity of this Gospel. It is simply a question of interpretation. The points to be observed from the Talmudic notices are: 1) it must have been a corn growing city; 2) it was far from Jerusalem; 3) the place was regarded as profane (by Jews); 4) the identifying of the place was difficult. This latter might have been wrong either: a) the fact of it being a mystical name or a nickname; b) or is it due to its comparative obscurity. If a) be the solution it would refer to Shechem itself, or if b) to such an obscure place as Askar. See John Lightfoot I, p. 597.

Sychar = Sychem = Shechem = Neapolis = Nablus? Neapolis however was not on the exact site of Shechem. So Beelezebub, Beelzebul. 'Drunkenness' Is 28:1—'the crown of pride, the garlands of Ephraim.' There is however speculation that the name 'Sychar' comes from the word for 'mendacium' see Hab 2:18. See Smith's *Dictionary of Biog.* II, p. 411b.

Against this Sychar = Shechem equation: 1) the expression εἰς πόλιν in vs. 5. But St. John was writing for Gentile Christians unacquainted with Palestine; 2) notice that this nickname was given to Shechem. The passage where Sychar is mentioned in the Talmud betrays no hint that Shechem is meant (see however Wiesler, p. 231); 3) the distance. Jacob's well is more than a mile from Shechem. In Nablus itself there were many springs. Yet the woman might have preferred the holy well. See John Lightfoot on Acts 7:16.

Let us suppose instead that Sychar is a place *near* Shechem (see *Palestinian Exploration*, July 1877, p. 149). 1) Early habitation separates Sychar from Shechem (see Eusebius), or at least from Neapolis. See Jerome, *Op* III, p. 279. He adds *ubi nunc ecclesia fabricate est.* On p. 265 he says that the city of Jacob is now a desert. Note that the Bourdeaux pilgrim is more explicit—see Smith's *Dictionary* s.v. He places Sychar at 1,000 paces from Shechem. 2) A place named Askar exists near the well. The differences in spelling not impossible (at least so Delitzsch). In manuscripts of the fourth and fifth centuries we have the spelling Esychar. Perhaps the Jews preferred so calling it, endorsing the Samaritan Nablus that it was the locale of Jacob's well. 3) This is in accordance with the notices in the Talmudic literature—the well of Sychar, the description of the place. In any case see Josephus, *Ant.* xi.8.6.

Vs. 5 χωρίον 'a parcel of ground' is a good translation. Comp. Acts 1:18; 4:34; 28:7. It ought to have been similarly translated in Matt 26:36; Mark 14:32, a place called Gethsemane.

ὃ ἔδωκεν a tradition, the fact is not recorded in the Old Testament. The reference is doubtless to the ground mentioned in Gen 33:19, comp. Josh 24:32; Gen 48:22. On Joseph as the first Samaritan patriarch see Josephus, *Ant.* ix.14.3, which shows the antipathy of the Jews. Two tombs of Joseph shown there. In Palestine it is better to determine the sites than try and mark the boundaries. The journeyings and sojourns of the patriarchs marked by wells.

Vs. 6 ἦν δὲ ἐκεῖ See *Sinai and Palestine*, p. 237; and especially Robinson, II, p. 282sq.; III, p. 132.

οὕτως 'without much ado.' See Ast. (?) *Lex. Plat.* II, p. 495 s.v.; see R+P, *Soph. Phil.* 1067.

ὥρα ἦν ὡς ἕκτη There were two modes of reckoning. It might be midday, or six o'clock in the evening. It is unimportant which is adopted here. Note rather the definiteness of the impression on the narrative.

Vs. 7 ἐκ τῆς Σαμαρίας i.e. a Samaritan, the country not the city (Sebaste) that was two hours distance. It is not said that she came from Sychar, perhaps it even implies the opposite. Nor can this be inferred from vs. 28. This disposes of some difficulties (for example if she was from Nablus there was water near at hand) whether Sychar be Shechem or not. See Buttmann, p. 58.

Vs. 9 οὐ γὰρ συνχρῶνται Ἰουδαῖοι Σαμαρείταις If this is part of the woman's own reply, it is a rude irony, perhaps it is one of the interjectional explanations of the Evangelist. But in either case, what exactly does it mean? How is it reconcilable with vs. 8 ἵνα τροφὰς ἀγοράσωσιν? See the article on the Samaritan Pentateuch in Smith's *Dictionary* II, p. 1117 and my *Galatians* p. 289.

Vs. 10 Εἰ ᾔδεις τὴν δωρεὰν τοῦ Θεοῦ, καὶ τίς ἐστιν ὁ λέγων σοι Δός μοι πεῖν Two things: 1) that God's gracious gift extends to all; and 2) that I am the administrator of it.

Vs. 11 ἄντλημα See another instance of this in Plutarch, *Moral.* p.974E.
On βαθύ see Robinson, p. 284.
τὸ ὕδωρ τὸ ζῶν See e.g. Gen 26:19; Lev 14:50sq. and 15:13.

Vs. 12 The Samaritan tradition.

Vs. 13 The question is only indirectly discussed. Contrast ὁ πίνων with ὃς
δ᾽ ἂν πίῃ (vs. 14).

Vs. 14 γενήσεται ἐν αὐτῷ πηγὴ ὕδατος ἁλλομένου εἰς ζωὴν αἰώνιον The
draught itself shall become a well, a fresh source, a fresh center of distri-
bution.

Vs. 20 οἱ πατέρες ἡμῶν Deut 37:4 v.l. Trisham's (?) testimony, p. 149. See the
passage in Bereshith Rabba 32 in John Lightfoot, II, p. 540. Comp. Gen 35:4.

Vs. 22 ὃ οὐκ οἴδατε This for two reasons: 1) the mixture of idolatry with
the worship of Yahweh among the Samaritans; 2) they were probably of
heathen origin. A sprinkling of Jews who remained in the land intermixed
with heathen. See 2 Kings 24:17sq. Note the name Cutheans, and this playing
fast and loose with the worship of Yahweh seems to have continued. See
Robinson, II, p. 290 note 3 and Josephus, *Ant.* xii.5.5. The mixture of hea-
thenism and Hebrew monotheism seems to have prevailed to a very late date,
e.g. the pagan elements in the teaching of Simon Magus (Helen of Troy etc.).
In actual correspondence with Antiochus of Syria the Samaritans: 1) actually
call themselves Sidonians, and renounce kinship with the Jews; 2) they say
their temple is not dedicated to anyone, and they request that the idol of
Zeus Ἑλλήνιός be given. Antiochus dedicates the temple to Zeus Ἑλλήνιός.
3) Even the Hebrew side of their religion was imperfect. They received only
the Pentateuch. Thus the thread of the progressive development of the revelation was broken. They knew nothing of the Πολυμερῶς καὶ πολυτρόπως
(Heb 1:1), more especially nothing of the ever-changing views of the Messianic person and office. The commentators seem to lay all the stress on 2)
and nothing on 1) which is more important.

ὅτι ἡ σωτηρία ἐκ τῶν Ἰουδαίων ἐστίν They preserved the continuity of
the divine revelation and from them in the fullness of time came Messiah.

ἡ σωτηρία The promised salvation which was implied in his own
name—Jesus as in his realized office, comp. e.g. Josh 3:17; Is 2:3; Micah
4:2; Obadiah 21 etc.

Vss. 23-24 ἀληθινοὶ comp. vs. 37.

Πνεύματι the spiritual comprehensive manifestations, ἀληθείᾳ, the archtype the realization of which makes the external worship only a shadow, an image, reflection as it were. Compare the ἡ χάρις καὶ ἡ ἀλήθεια.

Vs. 25 ὅτι Μεσσίας ἔρχεται On the nature of the Messianic expectations of the Samaritans see Westcott, *Introd. to the Gospels*, p. 149, and the references in Ewald, p. 189. The name of 'Messiah,' the 'guide' illustrates ἀναγγελεῖ ἡμῖν ἅπαντα. Compare the name of the Simonian book 'The Great Announcement.' How did they get their idea of Messiah? From: 1) the prediction in Deuteronomy; 2) contact with the Jews. But they would not recognize a Messiah who was a descendant of Judah, a son of David. Perhaps through them came the idea of Messiah being a son of Joseph, which the rabbis made a suffering Messiah.

ὁ λεγόμενος Χριστός comp. 1:41, a conventional explanation of the Evangelist himself.

Vs. 27 μετὰ γυναικός 'with a woman' (Alford all wrong here). The rabbinical maxims explain this. See Erub. Fol. 53.2. R. Jose the Galilean being on a journey found Berurea in the way, to whom he said, 'What way must we go to Lydda?' She answered: 'Oh thou foolish Galilean, have not the wise men taught, "do not multiply discourse with a woman"? You ought to have just said "Which way to Lydda?"' See Yoma fol. 66.2. fol. 240.2—'Let no one talk with a woman in the street, no not even with his own wife.'

Vs. 28 ἀπῆλθεν εἰς τὴν πόλιν Not necessarily 'went back.' See e.g. 6:1; 9:7, 11; 12:19 etc. When returning is directly expressed it is ἀπελθεῖν πάλιν e.g. 4:3; 10:40. She went to the city that she might talk with her neighbors.

Vs. 29 The natural exaggeration of language in one excited. Μήτι—not as the A.V. has it, but more perplexed, and doubtful, 'Surely this cannot be. . . .' Comp. vs. 32.

Vs. 30 ἤρχοντο Imperfect 'started on their way.' The imperfect explains the Ἐν τῷ μεταξύ in the next verse.

Vs. 31 ἠρώτων asked, not interrogated. See Trench, *New Testament Synonyms*, sec. 1 no. xl. Here however it may be said that an inquiring is *implied*. But not elsewhere—e.g. 4:40; 12:16; 16:23, 26; 17:9 etc.

Vs. 32 βρῶσιν Sacramental teaching. Not equal here to βρῶμα. It might well be so, but as βρῶμα itself.

Vs. 33 Μή τις 'Surely no one was here' etc.

Vs. 34 Comp. the quote in Deut 8:3 in Matt 4:4.

ποιῶ. . . . τελειώσω The change of tense is determined by the different meanings of the words. τελειώσω is 'accomplish once for all.' However there is a tendency to use a past tense of this verb. It cannot be an accident that though the word occurs twenty-three times in the New Testament, it is always in the past tense (aorist or perfect), except in Luke 8:32 (καὶ τῇ τρίτῃ τελειοῦμαι), where there is a special reason for the present tense.

Vs. 35 οὐχ ὑμεῖς λέγετε Comp. Matt 16:1, 2 which is the best comment on our passage. There is the same pointing to external nature, and the same spiritual application, the same contesting of his hearer's quick apprehension about times and seasons in their physical being and their dullness in forecasting the approach of times and seasons of spiritual import. If the time is less sure here it is because the hearers are less sensitive to it. And this explains the ὑμεῖς. 'Ye who are burdened with the things of this world, ye who are engaged with material cares, ye in your lower sphere.' Comp. 8:15 ὑμεῖς κατὰ τὴν σάρκα κρίνετε, ἐγὼ οὐ κρίνω οὐδένα. Alford gets on the wrong track here. 'Ye who just now misunderstood my allusion to the *food* and took it in a gross material sense.'

Ἔτι τετράμηνός ἐστιν The vividness of the image and our Lord's practice elsewhere of teaching from visible nature require that this should be taken as chronologically correct, i.e. that these words were spoken about four months before harvest time, just as above he started from actual 'living' water (vs. 13), and the actual food (vs. 31). On the time of the year, see Stanley, p. 239. The slight variations are unimportant, it was in what we would call winter, the end or the beginning of the year. Either is reconcilable with vs. 1.

Before going further, we may note: 1) the soundness and naturalness of the narrative. Note the gradations in the woman's feelings towards our Lord—contemptuous, ironic, respect mingled with curiosity, wonderment which has almost ripened into faith; 2) the relation of the Lord's teaching here to his teaching in the other Evangelists—see esp. vss. 34, 35; 3) the exact and lively picture which it conveys of the relations between Jews and Samaritans; 4) lastly, and not leastly, the topographical truth. See Stanley, p. 239.

ἐπάρατε τοὺς ὀφθαλμοὺς ὑμῶν καὶ θεάσασθε τὰς χώρας The χώρας here are the spiritual χώρας. The transition is as rapid as in vs. 13 and vs. 31.

λευκαί εἰσιν One of the earliest and most abundant crops was harvested by the Apostles from this very field of Samaria. Comp. Acts 1:8; 8:5 (εἰς τὴν πόλιν τῆς Σαμαρίας, the same place?), 14; 15:3.

Vs. 36 ὁ θερίζων i.e. the Apostles.

εἰς ζωὴν αἰώνιον This marks the transition from the natural to the spiritual harvest.

ὁ σπείρων

Vs. 37 A.V. wrong. 'Herein is that saying true . . .' The manuscript authority favors omitting ὁ, but the apparent difference may have caused the mistake—'Herein lies truth, the real proverb of which the vulgar sign is only a counterfeit.'

Vs. 38 ὁ λόγος ἐστὶν ὁ ἀληθινός comp. τὸ φῶς τὸ ἀληθινόν (1:9); τὸν ἄρτον ἐκ τοῦ οὐρανοῦ τὸν ἀληθινόν (6:32); ἡ ἄμπελος ἡ ἀληθινή (15:1). So that ὁ λόγος ἐστὶν ὁ ἀληθινός means 'the genuine or real proverb/maxim' comp. 4:33, which is the maxim taken in its higher, spiritual sense of which the lower physical sense is only a shadow, a counterfeit. Comp. Plato, *Tim.* p.26E on ἀληθινός.

ἀπέστειλα Their mission had commenced at their call, their commission. Possibly, the mission recorded in the other Evangelists was prior to this, see Luke 9:2; Matt 10:5.

ἄλλοι κεκοπιάκασιν Referring to himself primarily. The plural is for symmetry with ὑμεῖς, just as above ὁ θερίζων of a work for symmetry with ὁ σπείρων.

Vs. 42 διὰ τὴν σὴν λαλιάν 'your talk' and διὰ τὸν λόγον αὐτοῦ (vs. 41), not necessarily depreciating. See Meyer on 8:43, it designates more or less unrestrained familiar talk. Note the receptivity of the Samaritans as in Acts 8. The uncertainty of their belief καὶ οἴδαμεν ὅτι οὗτός ἐστιν ἀληθῶς would make them the more eager for some firm ground on which to stand. See Justin Martyr, *Apol.* I. 53. Their ready belief has a parallel in the centurion, and the Syrophoenician woman, both beyond the pale of the covenant people.

τοῦ κόσμου The universality of Messiah's kingdom would be more comfortable to Samaritan rather than to the Jewish people's presumptions, owing to their mixed origins and less rigorous exclusiveness. See Meyer.

ὁ Χριστός a later gloss in the B.M.T. and T.R. It is omitted in ℵ, B, C.

Vs. 43 Μετὰ δὲ τὰς δύο ἡμέρας '*the* two days,' not as A.V.

Vs. 44 Another back reference to the Synoptic narrative which is thus assumed. Matt 13:57; Mark 6:4; comp. Luke 4:24. But what is the connection here? There are various unsatisfactory solutions proposed. The explanation that the γάρ is dependent on the following clause is quite inadmissible. Alford's parallels are no parallels. Look at the Synoptic narratives. The πατρίς in this saying is Nazareth as distinguished from Capernaum. πατρίς there is decidedly not Galilee as a whole, but Nazareth specially. Still a difference remains, for Nazareth and Capernaum (the sea of Tiberias) both belong to Galilee. It cannot be imagined that the writer of the Fourth Gospel did not know that Nazareth belonged to Galilee, for he like the Synoptists speaks of the Lord as a Galilean (7:41, 52).

The explanation is to be sought in the circumstances under which the Gospel was written—its circumstantial character and probably its oral dictation. The writer has permanently in his mind that Jesus in returning to Galilee, avoids his own native town Nazareth. Thinking to mention this, he simply says Jesus went to Galilee without naming the part of Galilee, but he adds the explanation as though his hearers are acquainted with the circumstances that were so obviously present to his own memory, that Jesus carefully avoided Nazareth.

Vs. 45 ὅσα ἐποίησεν Comp. 2:23.

Vs. 46 βασιλικὸς A very frequent word in Josephus. See Kreitz (?), p. 144 and Wettstein here. The soldiers' attendants, courtiers of Herod, as distinguished from the Roman authorities and their attendants. Elsewhere sometimes βασιλικός means a prince. See Steph. *Thes.* s.v. Was he Herod's steward Chuza (Luke 8:3), or Herod's foster brother Manaen (Acts 13:1)? All this is conjecture.

Vs. 48 εἶπεν οὖν ὁ Ἰησοῦς πρὸς αὐτόν It was a reply to his entreaty, 'I will work a miracle,' but it was addressed to the bystanders—'Except you see miracles, you will not believe.'

Vs. 49 κατάβηθι as 2:12.

τὸ παιδίον μου 'My darling.' The tenderness of paternal affection. Before it was τὸν υἱόν in vs. 47 and in the Lord's reply (vs. 50). It does not appear that his son was very young.

Vs. 50 ἐπορεύετο 'Started on his way.' The imperfect preparing the way for ἤδη δὲ αὐτοῦ καταβαίνοντος as above vss. 30, 31.

Vs. 52 κομψότερον ἔσχεν As we would say, 'to get on nicely.' It was a doctor's expression. See Epictetus iii.10. Grammatical pedants objected to the expression. See Bekker, *Anecd.* p. 102.23. Archilochus (?) used κομψότερον of a sick man.

ὥραν ἑβδόμην Either at one o'clock or at seven o'clock. The probabilities of the case seem rather to favor the latter as the father would probably not delay on the road and spend the night out.

Vs. 53 ἐπίστευσεν More than is implied in vs. 30.

Vs. 54 δεύτερον σημεῖον a second miracle in Cana or in Galilee, for meanwhile he had wrought others in Jerusalem. The A.V. is loose and not very intelligible. Here again the writer seems to be answering some inquiries or solving some perplexities of his disciples.

This is not the same miracle as in Matt 8:5; Luke 7:1 for: 1) The place is there Capernaum, here Cana; 2) The petitioner is there a centurion, a Roman soldier, here a servant of Herod, a βασιλικός; 3) The sick person is there a servant (ὁ παῖς μου in Matt and τινος δοῦλος in Luke), here a son; 4) The sickness there is παραλυτικός, here the issue is a fever (ὁ πυρετός); 5) The centurion there asks Jesus not to enter his house but only to say the word, the courtier here entreats him to come down to his house, ere his child die; 6) The words of the centurion and the answer of the Lord are both so remarkable there, that they would not fail to be expected here if the incident were the same. The only thing in common is the healing at a distance but that is not peculiar to these miracles.

A Sabbath Healing
and the Aftermath
(John 5)

ἑορτή The definite article to be omitted here (against the B.M.T.) though it occurs in some excellent ancient sources (ℵ, C, II, L etc.). It seems however to have been inserted in order to define the feast as the Passover (as 2:23; 4:45; 6:4; one ms. adds a reference to 'unleavened bread' another to 'tabernacles' from 7:2). The feast in question is more probably Purim than any other. It seems to have been some festival between winter and the Passover (see 6:9), for though possible it is not probable that a Passover is indicated in St. John's narrative. For more exact calculations see Wiesler, *Chron.* p.192sq. We find our Lord at an equally obscure feast in John 10:22 (τὰ ἐνκαίνια). The absence of the article seems to show it was not an important festival.

Vs. 2 The destruction of Jerusalem in A.D. 70 was not so complete that a bath of medicinal waters should be destroyed. Indeed, it is not probable that St. John had seen Jerusalem since its fall.

ἐπὶ τῇ προβατικῇ κολυμβήθρα The sheep gate. An uncertain 'door' or 'porch' of the sheep is mentioned in Neh 3:1, 32; 12:38. A.V. has 'sheep market.' The words are omitted in the Cureton Syriac and ℵ and Peshitto.

ἐν τοῖς Ἱεροσολύμοις ἐπὶ τῇ προβατικῇ κολυμβήθρα and so other. It is clear that some understood κολυμβήθρα with προβατικῇ, but see Tisch.

Βηθεσδά According to Eusebius *Onam.*, it refers to a place where there are stoas, columns. See Robinson, I, p. 380, and this interpretation seems to have produced no other reading, as it has also altered Βεθεσδά. See Jerome, *Opus* III, p. 182. Jerome knowing the situation says '*quid vocabatur* προβατικῇ.' Perhaps some of these variant readings come from getting hold of the rabbinical word that refers to a 'bath.' See Buxtorf, p. 1796 here and Wettstein here. And may not this variant have come from the name of the gate προβατικῇ? See Sachs, *Sprache und Altesttumsforschung aus Judentum Quelle*, p. 199. But it does not follow that Eusebius and the Bourdeaux Pilgrim were right in the location. Βηθεσδά probably means 'the house of mercy' as Cureton Syriac and Peshitto make it, referring to the healing properties of the water. See Delitzsch however, *Zeitschrift fur Luth. Theolog.* 1856, pp. 622sq.

On St. John's way of rendering Hebrew names elsewhere see 19:13, 17; 20:16; comp. 1:39, 42, 43; 4:25; 9:7; comp Buxtorf (?), p. 1829. The only other reading which can come into competition with that one is ἡ ἐπιλεγομένη Ἑβραϊστὶ *Βηθζαθά* (so ℵ the text of that manuscript is obviously often correct, as here?) of which a variety of other readings are corruptions—e.g. Bethsaida, the reading of the Bourdeaux pilgrim which he corrects to Beltzalta, imperfectly pronounced. No doubt since Bethsaida was a common name this encouraged that particular reading. Yet I am disposed to think that Bethzatha is the correct reading here. It is read by ℵ and Eusebius. In favor of Bethesda however is: 1) the fact of its meaning; and 2) A, C, Cureton Syriac, etc.

But where is the locality? If we could fix the locale of the sheep gate then this would be approximately decided. This however is only roughly probable—somewhere near the Temple. Tradition identifies it with St. Stephen's gate, north of the Temple area. There are no sufficient grounds for this. See Robinson, I, p. 342 for his conjecture. The true (uninterpolated) account of St. John in all events accords with this, for there is nothing miraculous, only an intermittent (probably medicinal) healing spring. The case is analogous to that in Luke 8:43.

Vs. 3 Omit πολύ, in accord with the other interpolations that try to promote its extraordinary character, giving an exaggerated magnitude to the character of the story.

Omit from ἐκδεχομένων τὴν τοῦ ὕδατος κίνησιν all the way through ἄγγελος γὰρ κατὰ καιρὸν κατέβαινεν ἐν τῇ κολυμβήθρᾳ καὶ ἐτάρασσε τὸ ὕδωρ· ὁ οὖν πρῶτος ἐμβὰς μετὰ τὴν ταραχὴν τοῦ ὕδατος ὑγιὴς ἐγίνετο, ᾧ δήποτε κατείχετο νοσήματι in vs. 4. They are omitted in: 1) in the foremost ancient manuscripts ℵ, B, C, D; and 2) Cureton Syriac, the Egyptian versions, some manuscripts of the Old Latin, so that at that time these phrases do not seem to have been there. And yet the interpolation must have been early, see Tertullian.

What was the motive of the interpolator? To explain vs. 7 which seemed to need explaining and to heighten the effect. Perhaps it emanated from St. John's own school in Asia Minor. It does not however imply any different conception of the physical effect, except in the particular phrase 'which was first' which St. John does not say. The interpolation reflects a belief that all physical changes, whether regular or irregular were produced by angelic agency, e.g. the motion of the planets. This belief we find in Jewish writers, and again in the early Apologists. Comp. Justin Martyr, *Apolog.* II.5; Antenagoras 2a, p. 124 etc. It is as dogmatic to deny as to assert this.

Vs. 7 ἄνθρωπον οὐκ ἔχω, a Hebraism. There is nothing said about the necessity of being first. The people crowded in front of him so that he could not get into the water when it was in motion.

Vs. 8 κράβαττόν naturally it went into Latin as *grabatus*. Hence the reading is probably correct.

Vs. 10 Comp. Matt 12:8.

Vs. 14 ἐν τῷ ἱερῷ 'men at hand'

μηκέτι ἁμάρτανε not implying that his ailment was a direct punishment for his offense. Comp 9:2.

Vs. 18 ἔλυεν 'Would do away with?'

Vs. 21 οὓς θέλει ζωοποιεῖ, as he did in the case of Lazarus. The bodily raising is only a type of the spiritual raising implied in ζωοποιεῖ. Comp. 3:13. That this spiritual raising is prominent, appears from the context.

Vs. 24 ἔχει ipso facto. Then and there. There is no κρίσις, no discrimination, and *a fortiori* no condemnation, for none is needed. The state itself is the acquittal. The κρίσις is precluded, see also the expressions in vs. 29. Comp. μεταβέβηκεν and 1 John 3:14. Comp. Eph 2:4—the kingdom of Satan.

Vs. 25 καὶ νῦν ἐστιν ὅτε οἱ νεκροὶ ἀκούσουσιν τῆς φωνῆς τοῦ Υἱοῦ τοῦ Θεοῦ καὶ οἱ ἀκούσαντες ζήσουσιν. Here again a double sense as the καὶ νῦν ἐστιν shows.

On οἱ νεκροί see Matt 7:22; Rev 3:1 etc.

Vs. 26 ζωὴν ἔχειν ἐν ἑαυτῷ compared to ἔδωκεν αὐτῷ expresses the whole doctrine of the Person of Christ, derived from and yet subservient to the Logos doctrine, the eternal generation of the Son.

Vs. 27 Υἱὸς ἀνθρώπου ἐστίν, as the head, the representative of the race, he is also the judge of the race. Comp. Acts 7:31, where however it is ἐν ἀνδρί (not since he is Son of Man = Messiah), with a reference to Dan 7:13. Υἱὸς ἀνθρώπου became a title, hence the article omitted as e.g. Rev 1:13; 14:16.

Vs. 29 ποιήσαντες . . . πράξαντες See 3:21, 22. Comp. Gal 5:19, 22 τὰ ἔργα, καρπός, and Eph 5:2. Observe again the contrast of ζωή and κρίσις. The righteous are not judged even to be acquitted. Their state itself is their acquittal.

Vs. 30 ποιεῖν ἀπ᾿ ἐμαυτοῦ as coming from myself. The perfect work with the Father.

Vs. 31 Ἐὰν ἐγὼ μαρτυρῶ Supposing it possible that my own testimony could be separated from the Father's testimony, then do not accept my testimony, it is not the truth.

Vs. 32 ἄλλος ἐστὶν ὁ μαρτυρῶν God, not St. John here. This is clear here.

Vs. 33 ὑμεῖς You have disregarded the higher testimony, seeking out John's.

Vs. 34 ἀλλὰ ταῦτα λέγω But this I say; I refers to John's testimony.

Vs. 35 ὁ λύχνος ὁ καιόμενος καὶ φαίνων The lamp which is lighted and then gives light. ὁ λύχνος describes the type as e.g. 2 Cor 12:12 τὰ μὲν σημεῖα τοῦ ἀποστόλου. Cf. Gal 3:20; 4:1; John 10:11 (ὁ ποιμὴν ὁ καλός). 'Johannes lumen illuminatum, Christus lumen illuminary' (Augustine, *Serm.* 382). Comp. Strabo x.14, p. 642. Notice no reference here to any Old Testament prophecy or to Sir 48:1: καὶ ἀνέστη Ἠλίας προφήτης ὡς πῦρ, καὶ ὁ λόγος αὐτοῦ ὡς λαμπὰς ἐκαίετο. Contrast John 1:9; 8:12. ὁ καιόμενος must be understood under two ideas: 1) derived light; 2) corruption burning out. For καίεσθαι, see Luke 7:35; Rev 4:5; comp. Ip. (?) 509. Arist (?) *Vesp.* 1372. This misunderstanding has arisen due to a misinterpretation of the definite article. φαίνεται mistranslated as = φαίνειν in the A.V. in Matt 24:27; Phil. 2:15; Rev 18:23.

Vs. 37 οὔτε φωνὴν αὐτοῦ πώποτε ἀκηκόατε οὔτε εἶδος αὐτοῦ ἑωράκατε It is not by your outward senses that you can apprehend him. See 6:46.

Vs. 38 καὶ τὸν λόγον αὐτοῦ οὐκ ἔχετε ἐν ὑμῖν which revelation is necessary in order that by a natural affinity you may apprehend this testimony. The καί here almost = 'yet' as in vs. 40.

Vs. 39 ἐραυνᾶτε The form is certainly the indicative as the argument shows. 'You search the Scriptures, and they bear witness of me, and yet you will not come to me. . . .' ἐραυνᾶτε well describes the rabbinical mode of dealing with the Scriptures. דָּרַשׁ hence midrash. The word itself however does not imply a reproach. See 1 Pet 1:10. It was not the exactness, the diligence of their search which was blameworthy, but the direction in which that diligence was expended, the frivolity (?) of the objects, the arrangement, counting of the letters, the fantastical allegorical interpretation.

ὑμεῖς you of yourselves, you on your part.

δοκεῖτε See Schotter in Alford. Technically they were right, practically they were wrong. See Meyer.

Vs. 40 ζωὴν ἔχητε that life after which you are searching in your own blind way.

Vs. 41 Δόξαν παρὰ ἀνθρώπων If I did, I should have a favorable reception from you. I seek not glory (the recognition of my office), my title.

Vs. 42 On the one hand, this is the only testimony, the only recognition, the only cause that appeals to you. You cannot appreciate the higher recognition, God's recognition, because you have not the love of God in you. The yearning for God is necessary for the appreciation, the understanding of his testimony. See 1 John 3:17; 5:3.

τοῦ Θεοῦ is therefore an objective genitive—love for God.

Vs. 43 ἐὰν ἄλλος ἔλθῃ The Antichrist is meant. Those who came before our Lord are mentioned in 10:8. A diligent search has counted up 64 such deceivers (see Meyer, p. 208) since the time of Christ. Comp. Matt 24:24.

Vs. 44 οὗ μόνου Θεοῦ The only God. God the Supreme, the Omniscient (cf. 6: 15, 16). Not as A.V. Rom 16:27; 1 Tim 1:17.

Vs. 45 ἠλπίκατε Has restored your hopes. Comp. 1 Cor 15:19sq.; 2 Cor 1:10; 8:5. 1 Tim 4:10; 5:5 for the past tense.

Vs. 46 ἐπιστεύετε The continuous state.

Vs. 47 γράμμασιν 'letters,' a reproach is implied in the expression. Something, as we would say, written in black and white, something which appeals to the outward senses and therefore much more directly to gross carnal mind.

Bread on Earth,
Bread from Heaven
(John 6)

Vs. 1 The miracle related by all four Evangelists. See Auger (?), p. 103. The chronological bearing must be deferred.

πέραν τῆς θαλάσσης τῆς Γαλιλαίας τῆς Τιβεριάδος St. Luke (9:10) says in the neighborhood of εἰς πόλιν καλουμένην Βηθσαϊδά. The A.V. has Bethsaida, which is clearly wrong. It was not the Bethsaida of the Gospels, though in itself more important. Bethsaida means 'fishing station,' a common name near lakes and rivers (investigate this point further).[1] The common Bethsaida is on the west side of the lake. The place here mentioned is Beth Julias, on the northeast side of the lake, called Julias by Philip the Tetrarch. Perhaps this Bethsaida is meant in Mark 8:22.

Τιβεριάδος is in apposition with θαλάσσης. See Pausanias v.7.3, Eusebius *Onom.* The name Tiberias does not occur in the other Gospels. See 6:23 of the city, and 21:1.

Vs. 2 τὰ σημεῖα This shows that many unrecorded incidents took place.

Vs. 3 εἰς τὸ ὄρος The mountain country. See below vs. 15. Comp. Matt 5:1 ἀνέβη εἰς τὸ ὄρος with Luke 6:17.

In the corresponding narrative here it is εἰς ἔρημον τόπον κατ᾽ ἰδίαν. Matt 14:13; Mark 6:32; Luke 9:10. This is quite in accordance. The lonely places are among the mountains. Thus when our Lord wants to be alone, wants to pray,

---

[1]From time to time in the manuscript, Lightfoot makes a parenthetical note to himself to double-check an assertion he makes.

he returns to the mountains. Matt 14:23; 17:1; Mark 6:46 etc.

Vs. 4 ἦν δὲ ἐγγὺς τὸ πάσχα This accounts for the gathering crowds. They were pilgrims on their way to the festival in Jerusalem. This is the second of three Passovers mentioned by St. John. Our Lord does not spend this Passover, as he does the first and third at Jerusalem, but apparently in Galilee and the neighborhood. See 7:2. He goes up to Jerusalem at the less frequented Festival of Tabernacles and then in such a manner as to not attract observation. The Passover is mentioned because the discourse which follows has a reference to the Paschal ceremonial.

Vs. 5 Philip again mentioned here as 1:44sq.; 12:21sq.; 14:8. Remember his prominence in St. John's narrative and his connection with Asia Minor. It has been supposed that Philip was the steward and Judas the bursar of the little company.

ἀγοράσωμεν 'must we buy.' So ℵ, A, B, D. Not ἀγοράσομεν.

Vs. 6 πειράζων αὐτόν trying or testing him. The word 'tempt' properly means nothing more.

Vs. 7 ἄρτοι, loaves (A.V. 'bread') as vs. 9. Comp. 1 Cor 10:16, 17, where the right translation is of some importance.

Διακοσίων Two hundred shillings worth of loaves.

Vs. 8 Mentioned here in connection with Philip. So too 1:45; 12:22. They came from the same place and seem to have been friends.

Vs. 9 Terms expressive of poverty and meanness.

Παιδάριον, ὀψάρια the diminutive. The numbers ἕν, πέντε, δύο, the quality κριθίνους, barley. See Seneca, *Epistl.* 18; Pliny, *Nat. Hist.* xviii.14. Compare [Samuel] Johnson on the definition of oats, a grain which is frequently given to horses, but which in Scotland supports the people. See the long list of passages in Wettstein.

ὀψάρια See Plato *Symposium*, iv.4, p. 667. On this fish see Altem. (?) ix.35sq. p.385E. Dean Alford is unguarded if not wrong in characterizing it as of later Greek usage.

Vs. 10 τοὺς ἀνθρώπους the people.

δὲ χόρτος πολὺς The grass would be more abundant now than at any other time of year.

οἱ ἄνδρες comp. Mark 6:44. Not as before τοὺς ἀνθρώπους. The men only were counted. St. Matt 14:21 adds χωρὶς γυναικῶν καὶ παιδίων.

ὡς πεντακισχίλιοι How they were counted appears from the narrative of
Mark 6:39; Luke 9:14.

Vs. 11 διέδωκεν through the disciples, as is made clear in the Synoptic
narrative.

Vs. 13 κοφίνους All four Evangelists use the word here. On the other hand,
in the feeding of the four thousand, σπυρίδας is used. See Matt 15:37; Mark 8:8.
The same distinction is observed where the two miracles are mentioned together (Matt 16:9, 10; Mark 8:19, 20). Comp. Juvenal III.14, vi.54; Philo, *de Festo
Cop.* V. p.48. See the passages in Wettstein on Matt. 14:20. The *cophinus* was
characteristic of the Jews. It was generally a small handbasket. This was also
used as a measure, hence we are able to ascertain its general size. See Lampe,
II, p. 165. On the other hand, the σπυρίδας might be very large as Acts 9:25.

In the case of the miracle here, the crowd fed were Jews on the way to the
Festival. In the other feeding miracle they are inhabitants of the Decapolis
(Mark 7:31) and therefore half heathen.

ἐπερίσσευσαν The other reading, ἐπερίσσευσεν (B.M.T., T.R.), seems to
be a grammatical correction.

Vs. 14 ὁ προφήτης ὁ ἐρχόμενος comp. 1:21. The prophet of Deut 18:15; like
Moses, see vss. 31, 32. Comp. Midrash Qoheleth, folio 86: 'As the first redeemer made manna to descend, as it is said (Exo 16:4) "Behold I will make
bread from heaven to rain upon you," so the latter (second) redeemer (will
make) manna (to descend) as it is said (Ps 72:16) "and there shall be a handful
of corn on the earth"' (see Lampe II, p. 167, and John Lightfoot, II, p. 552 and
the quotes of other passages on p. 557).

Here we see the truthfulness of St. John's narrative. ὁ ἐρχόμενος is used
of the Messiah, Matt 11:3 (23:39); Luke 7:19, 20 (19:38 ὁ ἐρχόμενος, ὁ
Βασιλεύς); John 11:27; 12:13; see Bruder s.v.

Vs. 15 ἁρπάζειν See Wettstein. The phrase is used widely see Tacitus, *Hist.*
1.26, 27—*raptus fuent*—of Otho.

εἰς τὸ ὄρος i.e. further back in a remote part of the mountain country.

Comparison of St. John's miracle with that in the Synoptics: 1) it is an
independent account; 2) it has a greater definiteness and vividness. The part
taken by Andrew and Philip is peculiar to it.[2] Again Ἔστιν παιδάριον; 3) the

---

[2]Here, as elsewhere, Lightfoot does not mean "strange"; rather, he employs *peculiar* to mean
"distinctive, unique."

season in which it happened throws considerable light on the incident; 4) the irreconcilableness of any theory of innate verbal inspiration with the facts. See the arguments given by Alford, p. 711.

Vs. 16 The walking on the sea is given by St. Matt 14:22 and St. Mark 6:45 but not by St. Luke. These two Evangelists describe it as happening εὐθέως after the feeding of the 5,000.

ὀψία a wide term, late in the day. There was the early and the late evening, the πρωΐα and the δείλη (afternoon and nightfall). See *Dictionary of Ant.* p. 339. Hence St. Matthew can speak of the miracle itself as taking place ὀψίας δὲ γενομένης (14:23), and then of our Lord's solitude after the embarkation of the disciples. Vs. 23 is likewise taking place ὀψίας δὲ γενομένης. The corresponding first ὀψία is described by St. Mark (6:35) as ἤδη ὥρας πολλῆς γενομένης, and by St. Luke (9:12) as Ἡ δὲ ἡμέρα ἤρξατο κλίνειν. St. Mark 6:47 describes the voyage as ὀψίας γενομένης ἦν. Thus the time described here, as by St. Matthew and St. Mark, was the δείλη ὀψία.

Vs. 17 ἤρχοντο The imperfect here prepares for the incidents which follow. Πέραν from the Northeast of the lake.

Vs. 19 Now St. Matthew (14:24) says they were πλοῖον ἤδη σταδίους πολλοὺς ἀπὸ τῆς γῆς, Mark ἐν μέσῳ τῆς θαλάσσης. This is a sight estimate. Josephus says the lake was forty stadia wide (*Bell. Jud.* iii.10.7), but like all of the lakes its width varies at different points; and 2) their course would not be directly across but transversely (?).

Vs. 20 They gladly took him on board. Comp. 1:44; vs. 35; 8:49.

Vs. 21 ἤθελον οὖν λαβεῖν αὐτὸν They were eager to do so.

Hence θελείν in modern Greek is an auxiliary of the future as in English. Thus there is no contradiction with the Synoptic account.

εὐθέως The other Evangelists explain the reason—καὶ ἐκόπασεν ὁ ἄνεμος (Mark 6:51). St. Matthew adds the incident of St. Peter walking on the water.

Vs. 22 The naturalness of the narrative, natural in its very limitation (?). T.R. adds ἐκεῖνο εἰς ὃ ἐνέβησαν οἱ μαθηταὶ αὐτοῦ to explain.

Vs. 23 ἐκ Τιβεριάδος the town, mentioned only by St. John. In 6:1; 21:1 it may be a question whether we should take ἡ θάλασσα . . . ἡ Τιβεριάς or ἡ θαλάσσης τῆς Τιβεριάδος perhaps for the sake of uniformity with the present passage. It is indicative of the later date of St. John's Gospel that the sea should be so named. The city was only built by Herod Antipas, and it gradually gave its name to the lake. The lake however is so called by Josephus before St. John wrote.

Vs. 24 εἰς Καφαρναούμ They probably thought he had gone round by land, as he might (easily) have done.

Vs. 26 σημεῖα The force of the word here is brought out in the discourse which follows.

ἐχορτάσθητε See Phil 4:12, means 'work out,' not as A.V. See the references in Meyer.

Vs. 31 This is the equivalent to asking him to rain down manna from heaven. See the Judaic belief to which allusion here has already been made in vs. 14 above. Ἄρτον ἐκ τοῦ οὐρανοῦ see Psalm 77(78):24.

Vs. 42 See above 1:46. Comp. Luke 4:22; Matt 8:55.

οἴδαμεν Does not imply that Joseph was living at the time.

Vs. 44 ὁ Πατὴρ ὁ πέμψας με Our Lord indirectly corrects the false conception involved in οἴδαμεν τὸν πατέρα καὶ τὴν μητέρα (vs. 42). So also Luke 2:49.

Vs. 45 ἐν τοῖς προφήταις Perhaps a general form of citation as in Acts 13:40. The other citations in Alford will not do because in Mark 1:2, the correct reading is probably ἐν . . . τῷ προφήτῃ and in Acts 7:42 ἐν βίβλῳ τῶν προφητῶν. ἐν τῷ νόμῳ Μωϋσέως καὶ τοῖς προφήταις καὶ ψαλμοῖς (Lk 24:44), notice that the Law and the Prophets comprise two sections but the Psalms and the rest are excluded from either. This quote however is not from the LXX. Here we have a loose citation of Is. 54:13—καὶ πάντας τοὺς υἱούς σου διδακτοὺς Θεοῦ καὶ ἐν πολλῇ εἰρήνῃ τὰ τέκνα σου. Comp. Jer 31:34 and 1 Thess 4:9. See the rabbinical quotation in John Lightfoot, p. 553.

Vs. 46 οὐχ ὅτι τὸν Πατέρα ἑώρακέν τις explains the somewhat difficult parenthesis in vs. 37.

Vs. 51 δώσω must refer to our Lord's death.

Vs. 53 ἐὰν μὴ φάγητε τὴν σάρκα τοῦ Υἱοῦ τοῦ ἀνθρώπου καὶ πίητε αὐτοῦ τὸ αἷμα, οὐκ ἔχετε ζωὴν ἐν ἑαυτοῖς. It is obvious there is a reference to the sacrament here again, not solely to the Eucharist, but chiefly to that which the Eucharist gives expression to and is a means to obtaining. Comp. especially 1 Cor 10:16, comp. vss. 3, 4. One finds repeatedly with St. John various means to convey the same idea as St. Paul, but using other words to convey it—the communion of the body, the communion of the blood. The first idea is explained by St. Paul, the second from Matt 26:28; comp. with Heb 9:22. Cf. Mark 14:24; Luke 22:20; 1 Cor 11:25, where however the idea is not so distinctly expressed. The communion of the body is therefore the realization of the membership in the body of Christ, the communion of the blood is the appropriation of the atoning sacrifice of Christ, confirming the consummating act of the new covenant. This realization, this appropriation is extended over the whole Christian life.

But it is intensified, it is concentrated so to speak in the faithful receiving of the holy Eucharist. Because this is the one specially ordained means, the one vivid representative act, whereby we may realize, may appropriate by faith the spiritual truths which it brings before our minds, which it offers for our acceptance.

This is the most remarkable instance of the sacramental teaching of St. John's Gospel, the presentation of the unseen through the seen. But even here, though the lesson is conveyed through the outward ceremonial of the holy Eucharist, prophetically anticipated here, it does not stop with this. The Eucharistic Supper only intensifies the truth, which is the daily and normal food of the Christian life.

Vs. 55 ἀληθής If the reading be correct, 'not deceiving.' ℵ and others have ἀληθῶς (so B.M.T., T.R.) which is simpler. But perhaps the former reading is more probable. Even the ἀληθής is not to be taken as = to ἀληθινή. Still we should expect ἀληθινή here.

Vs. 58 οὐ καθώς Comp. 1 John 3:12; 2 Cor 8:15; the same loose construction as in οὐχ ὅτι (vs. 46).

ὁ τρώγων As φαγεῖν has no present, some other word was necessary. ὁ ἐσθιών might have been used, but ὁ τρώγων is more expressive as it implies eating with satisfaction. Hence τράρηματα, see Philotus esp. in Steph. *Thess.* s.v. τρώγω. Besides this passage (vss. 54-58) the word occurs in the New Testament only at Matt 24:38 πρὸ τοῦ κατακλυσμοῦ τρώγοντες καὶ πίνοντες. Here the idea of living delicately is implied, and in John 8:18 where (in a quotation from Ps 41 (40):10) St. John has Ὁ τρώγων μου τὸν ἄρτον ἐπῆρεν ἐπ᾿ ἐμὲ τὴν πτέρναν αὐτοῦ, from the LXX, καὶ γὰρ ὁ ἄνθρωπος τῆς εἰρήνης μου, ἐφ᾿ ὃν ἤλπισα, ὁ ἐσθίων ἄρτους μου, ἐμεγάλυνεν ἐπ᾿ ἐμὲ. The Hebrew (of Ps 41:9) has אוֹכֵל לַחְמִי. See references in Steph. Anti. Bekk. p. 114, 115.

Vs. 59 ἐν συναγωγῇ as we would say 'in church.' Comp. 18:20. Here however it might be translated 'a synagogue.' There was probably more than one synagogue at Capernaum? But possibly just one because it is afterwards referred to as the one ἐν Καφαρναούμ. Our Lord teaches in a synagogue in Capernaum in Mark 1:21; Luke 4:33, 38, in all such passages the definite article is used. This synagogue (or some synagogue) was built by the centurion, Luke 7:8 (comp. Matt 8:8). Capernaum has recently been identified with Tel Huum where a synagogue has been found, but the synagogue is probably later (?).

Vs. 60 Σκληρός Not difficult to understand (this it might or might not be), but rather difficult to receive. See Meyer. See below on σκανδαλίζει (next verse). It involved the death of Messiah.

ἀκούειν to listen to, as Gal 4:21 τὸν νόμον οὐκ ἀκούετε.

Vs. 62 ἐὰν οὖν θεωρῆτε an allusion obviously to the Ascension. It may mean something else besides, it may carry also with it a spiritual significance, but it means this primarily. Yet the Ascension, like the institution of the Lord's Supper is not recorded by St. John. Thus in this Gospel the spiritual is always taught through the visible and external.

'I have spoken of my death, of conformity to my death, what if I tell you of my ascension and thereafter of all the spiritual consequences that follow upon that?' But reconsider—is ἀναβαίνοντα correlative to καταβάς in vs. 58, so that vs. 62 gives the answer to their doubt?

Vs. 63 τὸ πνεῦμά etc. This applies to the present and to the previous topic. It is not the sensible eating and drinking, not the sensible ascending in the clouds, which is important, but the spiritual effects, the spiritual bearing in both cases.

τὰ ῥήματα My words have a spiritual significance, and in this spiritual significance it is life which is truly apprehended.

Vs. 67 τοῖς δώδεκα [a rare reference in this Gospel].

Vs. 69 ὁ Ἅγιος τοῦ Θεοῦ This very expression is used by the unclean spirit in the synagogue in Capernaum, Mark 1:24; comp. Luke 4:34. There may possibly be an allusion to this in ἐγνώκαμεν. The Received Reading is an interpolation from Matt. 16:16.

Vs. 70 τοῖς δώδεκα, emphasizing the completeness of the number. This completeness shall be outraged (?).

διάβολός a strong mode of expression, like πνεῦμά ἐστιν καὶ ζωή in vs. 63.

Ἰσκαριώτου attached to the name of Simon, his father, here as 13:26 (so the best manuscripts). On Judas' own name see 12:4; 13:2 (comp. 14:22 though there as v.l.), and in the Synoptic Gospels. Hence the term is obviously geographical. And this might also be inferred from the definite article before Ἰσκαριώτης.

Ἰσκαριώτης D here has 'from Kerioth' and see 14:22. Comp. Josephus, *Ant.* vii.6.1. See Winer, s.v. Judas. Thus such interpretations as John Lightfoot offers (from scartea—a leather bag, in rabbinical writers) fall to the ground. Comp. on Kerioth, Merx, *Aichn. fur Wissen. Enfasch. Des Alten Test.*, p. 320.

Jesus the Temple at the Feast of Tabernacles (John 7)

Vs. 1 μετὰ ταῦτα All the events recorded in John 6 take place in Galilee or the neighborhood and not in Judaea. But the notice is inserted here because it explains what follows.

περιεπάτει ὁ Ἰησοῦς ἐν τῇ Γαλιλαίᾳ The greater part of the Galilean ministry of our Lord as recorded in the Synoptic Gospels should probably be inserted here. περιεπάτει implies a lengthy ministry, and as there is no sufficient reason for assuming that the Passover mentioned in 6:4 was the one immediately preceding that of 11:55, we may assume as long an interval as the facts seem to demand. St. John and the Synoptists dovetail incidents together. He recognized the ministry in Galilee which he does not relate, and they recognize the ministry in Jerusalem (e.g. Matt 23:37; Luke 13:34).

οἱ Ἰουδαῖοι in St. John: 1) distinguished from the Galileans; 2) points especially to the ruling powers of Judaism and ὁ ὀχλός, the crowd (see 7:32).

Vs. 2 ἡ ἑορτὴ τῶν Ἰουδαίων This was not in itself an unnatural way of expressing 'the Feast of the Tabernacles' because it was called *the festival par excellence* (so Smith's *Dictionary*, s.v.), see Josephus, *Ant.* viii.4.1: 'The feast of tabernacles happened to fall at the same time, which was celebrated by the Hebrews as a most holy and most eminent feast.' But the expression in Philo, *Sept.* no. 23 refers to the Feast Day of Atonement, and not (as in Smith's *Dictionary* s.v. Tabernacles, p. 1423) the Feast of the Tabernacles. This occurred five days before the Feast of the Tabernacles on the 10th of Tishri.

It was sufficiently prominent to attract the notice of the heathen—see Plato, *Sympos.* iv.16 (*Op. Moral.* p. 672 sq.), who regards it as a sort of Dionysian Festival. Still if ἡ ἑορτὴ τῶν Ἰουδαίων alone had been used it might have referred to the Passover.

Hence, ἡ σκηνοπηγία is added. It is called this in the LXX frequently and in Josephus, and Philo, *Sept.* no. 24. Our Lord is present here at Tabernacles, 10:22 at the Dedication, and 5:1 at some other festival (ἑορτή, without the definite article), perhaps Purim.

Vs. 3 οἱ ἀδελφοὶ αὐτοῦ Observe: 1) not 'some of his brethren'?; 2) nor 'had not a true and perfect belief.' This is therefore fatal to James' theory. Contrast his language here with his language to the Apostles (15:19, see Godet). There are two hypotheses remaining: 1) sons of Joseph and Mary; 2) sons of just Joseph. I prefer the latter view because 1) the charge of our Lord to St. John; and 2) tradition. His brethren here not disiples but in Acts 1:14 they are gathered with the disciples and James especially becomes a very prominent person in the Christian Church. Here apparently an historical incongruity but not a contradiction. But 1 Cor 15:7 links the two notices together strengthened by the Gospel of the Hebrews in Jerome, *Vir. Ill.* 2. See my *Galatians*, p. 260, first edition.

καὶ οἱ μαθηταί σου Some perhaps resident in Jerusalem, but it may be others going to the Festival (4:45). It would be a great opportunity to manifest himself. What is the force of καί here? I would not take καί with οἱ μαθηταί but keep it separate i.e. besides participating in the festival you may also manifest yourself to your disciples.

Θεωρήσουσιν See Winer, sec. xli p. 304. Comp. e.g. John 17:2 denoting continuity.

Vs. 4 γάρ τι ἐν κρυπτῷ ποιεῖ καὶ ζητεῖ αὐτὸς ἐν παρρησίᾳ εἶναι (the correct order). The contrast then is between τι and αὐτός. If he wishes *himself* to be known, he should not conceal *his work*. Note the reading αὐτό B, D, Memph, Theb. (not א).

ἐν παρρησίᾳ in public. See Col 2:15. Generally used in its stricter sense with εἶναι.

Vs. 5 ἐπίστευον εἰς αὐτόν Note their embarrassment, but also their familiarity. Their hesitation appears from the context. See Godet. The εἰ of vs. 4 does not imply disbelief, but simply suspension of belief.

Vs. 6 Ὁ καιρὸς ὁ ἐμὸς οὔπω πάρεστιν, ὁ δὲ καιρὸς ὁ ὑμέτερος πάντοτέ ἐστιν ἕτοιμος. 'I will manifest myself when the time for manifesting myself comes. As for you one time is as safe as another. You have no persecution to fear, and no glory to gain.' To be compared with 2:3—Jesus' response to his mother. The same desire, to make our Lord manifest Himself, and in both cases a similar rebuke is administered and in similar language. Comp. οὔπω ἥκει ἡ ὥρα μου in 2:4, and yet here as there, the Lord apparently complies. We must look for the same implication (?).

'You ask me to go up and take part in the great festivity of the year, to manifest myself to the world and to claim the glory which is mine. My hour is not yet come. This is no time of festivity for me. The great feast in which I shall take part is yet distant. The season of triumph has not arrived. I go not up to take part in *this* feast.'

Vs. 8 Various readings to be noticed.

εἰς τὴν ἑορτήν T.R. adds ταύτην which must be omitted.

οὐκ T.R. has οὔπω.

And in vs. 10 εἰς τὴν ἑορτήν, τότε καὶ αὐτὸς ἀνέβη B.M.T. and T.R. have τότε καὶ αὐτὸς ἀνέβη εἰς τὴν ἑορτήν. All these changes must be made in deference to the MSS, irrespective of the sense.

ἐγὼ οὔπω ἀναβαίνω εἰς τὴν ἑορτὴν ταύτην The ταύτην becomes emphatic in the correct reading that excludes it from the earlier passage. Comp. Luke 9:51. If this explanation is correct, the οὔπω would be out of place, and in fact originates in an entire misapprehension of the meaning, which misapprehension has created the difficulty. I have remarked on two of the three various readings and now take the third.

The alteration in order seems very slight, but it is very important. They went up *to the feast*. He simply went up. So far as regards the festival his attendance was worthless. He seems not to have arrived until after the festival had begun. He does not appear in public (and the festival was especially a public festival, a man could not keep it without being observed) until the middle of the time. He had therefore not fulfilled the injunction of the Law, had not kept the festival.

This seems to be an adequate explanation of the passage. At all events we must look for some meaning that is hidden beneath the surface, such a meaning being in entire accordance with the general tenor of this Gospel.

On the other hand, the *prima facie* interpretation that exposed our Lord's words to a charge of inconsistency (so Porphyry) or deceit (as some moderns have ventured to say), is clearly not so accordant. If there is one thing that one places above all others, it is that the Evangelist is drawing a portrait of a man in which he is concerned that there is no untruth, and no vacillating or shadow of turning. And the *prima facie* interpretation supposes a blot on this portrait so obvious, so palpable that it is inconceivable that the painter was blind to it (see 11:4).

This remark is equally applicable whether we suppose the Gospel to have been written by St. John, according to the belief of the Church and all antiquity, or to be a forgery. I will only add in conclusion that these very obscurities, these very perplexities (see e.g. 2:8 (?)sq.) are a valuable testimony to the veracity of the witness and therefore to the authenticity of the Gospel.

Vs. 10 Not ἐν κρυπτῷ but ὡς ἐν κρυπτῷ. Not as one of the great processions of pilgrims (comp. 1:14; Luke 2:44), but in the quiet way in which a man might go who wishes to escape observation, and pass unnoticed. ὡς softens the expression. It describes the manner rather than the motive.

Vs. 12 γογγυσμὸς not here denoting complaint. It is indicative of a sound, like murmuring, a suppressed under-current of language, so again vs. 32 ἐγόγγυζον. See 2 Sam 19:10 (not the LXX). The Attic is ζονθορυσμός, here in its primary sense with παρρησία.

Ἀγαθός ἐστιν, not ὁ Χριστός ἐστι. They did not dare to venture so far as this. Notice it is τὸν ὄχλον not τὸν λαόν, the crowd, not 'the people.'

Vs. 13 οὐδεὶς 'We are the ones who were disposed to believe in his claims, for those who disbelieve do not need to suppress their disbelief.'

Vs. 14 τῆς ἑορτῆς μεσούσης The festival lasted seven days or (including the holy convocation at the end) eight days. See below on vs. 37 τῇ μεγάλῃ τῆς ἑορτῆς. The view of Wiesler (*Synops.* pp. 279, 299) that this was a Sabbath day depends on the year A.D. it took place, and he seems to aim at greater definiteness in his chronology than the circumstances allow.

τὸ ἱερόν here but ναός Matt 23:35; Rev 11:1.

Vs. 15 γράμματα The teaching of the schools. So γραμματεύς. See Acts 26:24 τὰ πολλά σε γράμματα, much learning. This is said of St. Paul, but of the Twelve we have Acts 4:13 that they were ἀγράμματοί εἰσιν καὶ ἰδιῶται (compare the common Greek sense of ἰδιῶται). They had attended no rabbinical schools, had no university degree, or as we might say, had no diploma for teaching.

Vs. 17 ἐάν τις θέλη τὸ θέλημα αὐτοῦ ποιεῖν The English translation is inadequate. 'Has a will to do the will, and so is in union with God's will.'

Γνώσεται because he is *en rapport* with Christ's teaching, because he like our Lord is seeking God's will, God's glory, and not his own. Therefore, his spirit reads the Spirit of Christ.

Vs. 18 οὗτος ἀληθής ἐστιν The sense of ἀληθής in the New Testament, and especially in St. John's Gospel. It comprises the whole sphere of moral duty, refers to acts and character, as well as the words and hence the opposite of ἀδικία. See references in Meyer e.g. Rom. 1:18; 2:8.

Vs. 19 This passage is unhindered by an explanation. Its explanation is found in the incidents that occurred preceding his visit to Jerusalem, see 5:16. Note the naturalness of this.

Note vss. 19sq. οὐ Μωϋσῆς ἔδωκεν and again in vss. 22sq. Μωϋσῆς δέδωκεν ὑμῖν. Two different arguments here: 1) You who break the Law are not the persons to complain of a breach of the Law; 2) One ordinance supercedes another. The Sabbath according to the Law itself is made to give way to circumcision.

Μωϋσῆς the form of the name. Hebrew מֹשֶׁה, hence commonly in Greek, especially in profane sources. See Exod. ii.10 וַתִּקְרָא שְׁמוֹ מֹשֶׁה וַתֹּאמֶר כִּי מִן־הַמַּיִם מְשִׁיתִֽהוּ׃. Name related to his being drawn out of water. The form Μωϋσῆς comes from the Alexandrian Jews anxious to give a Coptic derivation. But see Josephus, *Ant.* ii. 9.6. See Gesenius but do not trust his references without investigation.

Vs. 20 Δαιμόνιον ἔχεις 'you are infatuated.' Comp. 10:20. Some evil spirit is persecuting you, placing these strange thoughts into your mind.

Vs. 21 πάντες θαυμάζετε διὰ τοῦτο For the combination καὶ ἐθαύμασεν διὰ τὴν ἀπιστίαν αὐτῶν see Mark 6:6, and see Rev. 17.7 Διὰ τί ἐθαύμασας.

Vs. 22 Here we have διὰ τοῦτο not διὰ τὸ ἔργον, for in this sense we should rather have expected δι' αὐτο. On the other hand, nothing can be made of διὰ τοῦτο if it goes with what follows. There are two ways of taking it: 1) connecting it with οὐχ ὅτι—'for this reason,' not 'because' etc. But though διὰ τοῦτο ὅτι is a common expression διὰ τοῦτο οὐχ ὅτι is not. The negative makes all the difference, and it makes no sense. 2) detaching οὐχ ὅτι . . .' 'I do not say that. . . . etc.' But then διὰ τοῦτο is quite out of place, and has no meaning. It cannot refer to anything. Note that ℵ omits διὰ τοῦτο.

οὐχ ὅτι seems to be inserted in order to anticipate a possible objection. True, circumcision was older than Moses, was inherited from the patriarchs. This only makes the case stronger. The older institution overrides the Mosaic ordinance. *A fortiori* the principle of charity, which is previous to any ordinance, is even more ancient. On οὐχ ὅτι see e.g. Phil 3:12; 4:11, 17.

ἐν σαββάτῳ etc. It was universally allowed that a son of a Hebrew could be circumcised on a Sabbath day, but different teachers decided in different ways as to whether it was right to circumcise the son of a Gentile. See the references in Wettstein and John Lightfoot. 'Circumcision supercedes Sabbath' is the rabbinical way of putting the maxim. The argument of our Lord here is found in some rabbis, e.g. in a saying attributed to Rabbi Eliezer the son of Azariah. See Wettstein.

Vs. 23 ἵνα μὴ λυθῇ etc. The Law was read every seventh year at the Feast of the Tabernacles (Deut 31:10sq.). This might possibly have been a sabbatical year, but there is nothing very distinctive or special in the allusion here, and no such reference is needed. There seems however to have been given a special prominence to the reading of the Law at the Feast of the Tabernacles generally (see e.g. Neh 8:18).

ὅλον ἄνθρωπον ὑγιῆ ἐποίησα Both words are emphatic. Comp. Col 2:11 ἐν τῇ ἀπεκδύσει τοῦ σώματος τῆς σαρκός. See Godet, p. 173.

Vs. 24 κρίνετε do not go on judging; κρίνατε judge once for all; τὴν δικαίαν κρίσιν, which is one.

Vs. 26 μήποτε Can it possibly be that?

Vs. 27 ὁ δὲ Χριστός etc. Perhaps founded on Is 53:8, 'His generation who shall declare. . . .' On the prevailing belief that obscurity should hang over the person of the Messiah until he was manifested in some remarkable way, see Justin Martyr, *Dialog.* sec. 9,110.

Vs. 28 ἐν τῷ ἱερῷ Perhaps added with a tacit allusion to Mal 3:1. The Lord whom they sought had suddenly come to his temple, and they hesitated and questioned.

Κἀμὲ οἴδατε Must be treated as an interrogative, or at least ironical. Comp. 8:14.

καί 'and yet,' as in vs. 30 καὶ οὐδεὶς etc.

ἀληθινός genuine, real, not ἀληθής that is used in 8:26. The two passages point to the difference between the two. ἀληθινός describes the intrinsic passive character possessed in contrast to the counterfeit, ἀληθής the outward active manifestation of the character and so its antonym is lying. Hence ἀληθής may be used for ἀληθινός but not conversely.

Vs. 30 καὶ οὐδεὶς and yet no one. No miracle intended, but the over-ruling providence of God asserted in the natural actions of men.

Vs. 31 μήτι (B.M.T. and T.R.) as μήποτε in vs. 26.

Vs. 35 εἰς τὴν Διασποράν See Franckel, *Morals(?)schrift* 1853, p. 413. The word 'Diaspora' is abstract before it is concrete. In a concrete sense, it is always the Jewish (or Christian) Dispersion. See Judith 5:19; and James 1:1; 1 Pet 1:1. It does not refer to the heathen scattered abroad. It has two nuances: 1) either the dispersed nation itself Ps 146:2 οἰκοδομῶν Ἱερουσαλὴμ ὁ Κύριος, καὶ τὰς διασπορὰς τοῦ Ἰσραὴλ ἐπισυνάξει; Isaiah 49:6 καὶ εἰπέ μοι· μέγα σοί ἐστι τοῦ κληθῆναί σε παῖδά μου τοῦ στῆσαι τὰς φυλὰς Ἰακὼβ καὶ τὴν διασπορὰν τοῦ Ἰσραὴλ ἐπιστρέψαι· ἰδοὺ δέδωκά σε εἰς διαθήκην γένους, εἰς φῶς ἐθνῶν τοῦ εἶναί σε εἰς σωτηρίαν ἕως ἐσχάτου τῆς γῆς. See also 2 Macc 1:27 ἐπισυνάγαγε τὴν διασπορὰν ἡμῶν, ἐλευθέρωσον τοὺς δουλεύοντας ἐν τοῖς ἔθνεσι, τοὺς ἐξουθενημένους καὶ βδελυκτοὺς ἔπιδε, καὶ γνώτωσαν τὰ ἔθνη, ὅτι σὺ εἰ ὁ Θεὸς ἡμῶν. 2) or of the nation among which they are dispersed, 1 Pet 1:1 and here.

τῶν Ἑλλήνων therefore is not = Ἑλληνιστων, a sense which it never has in the New Testament. See the v.l. in Acts 9:29; 11:20. 'Greeks and Grecian' in the A.V. But whether Ἑλλήνων means: 1) Greeks strictly speaking as op-posed to the Babylonian dispersion, or other dispersions (so John Lightfoot, see his remarks), or 2) it means Gentiles e.g. Mark 7:2 ἡ δὲ γυνὴ ἦν Ἑλληνίς, Συροφοινίκισσα τῷ γένει (the Syriac appears to have Aramaean for Ἑλληνίς here, but this may be doubtful). The latter seems more in accord with New Testament usage. The word has lost its sense of nationality and suggests that of religion, thus οὐκ ἔνι Ἰουδαῖος οὐδὲ Ἕλλην (Gal 3:28); τῶν Ἑλληνιστῶν πρὸς τοὺς Ἑβραίους (Acts 6:1).

Three remarks may be made respecting this incident in John: 1) The idea may have had a point of departure in the incident of the festival. The 70 bullocks, see Num 39:17sq. were explained to represent the 70 nations. See John Lightfoot, *Temple Service* I, p. 975; 2) The Evangelist respects this saying, because there was a divine irony over-ruling it. It was an unconscious prophecy said in mockery, like Caiaphas's words in 11:50; 3) St. John, as the head of the Greek (Gentile) church takes special notice of what refers to Gentiles (e.g. 12:20).

Vs. 37 Ἐν δὲ τῇ ἐσχάτῃ ἡμέρᾳ τῇ μεγάλῃ τῆς ἑορτῆς What is meant by this is: 1) the last of the seven days, i.e. strictly speaking the last of the feast; 2) the eighth day, the holy convocation that follows on the seven. There seems however to have been no special sanctity about the seventh day. The first was apparently much more important than the seventh. Though Buxtorf, *Sym. Jud.* xvi, p. 327 gives a pre-eminence to it in his descriptions of the modern Jewish celebrations of the Feast of the Tabernacles, so too Groddeke (?) in *Light* xviii, p. 534. On the other hand, it is supposed that the eighth day did not properly belong to the feast, which later was seven days. But though the festival is sometimes spoken of as a seven day festival, and the eighth day is not named (cf. e.g. Deut 16:13sq; Ezek 45:25), yet elsewhere the eighth day is regarded as part of the festival and a special prominence given to it. See Num 39:35; Zech 8:18. See 2 Macc 10:6 καὶ μετ' εὐφροσύνης ἦγον ἡμέρας ὀκτὼ σκηνωμάτων τρόπον, μνημονεύοντες ὡς πρὸ μικροῦ χρόνου τὴν τῶν σκηνῶν ἑορτὴν ἐν τοῖς ὄρεσι καὶ ἐν τοῖς σπηλαίοις θηρίων τρόπον ἦσαν νεμόμενοι. Cf. Josephus, *Ant.* iii.4; Succah, iv.4, 8, 9; v.6. B.T. Succah 48.1 and on Jewish interest generally, see Meyer and the discussion below.

On the eighth day especially see Ewald, *Altest.* p. 404. On this eighth day the people packed up their tents and repaired to the Temple. Note the symbolism. The living in tents symbolized the wilderness life, itself a deliverance from bondage. But the eighth and last day would be taken to signify the end of these wanderings, when they settled in the land of promise (see Dachs, *Succah* p. 368). See Philo, *Sept.* sec. 24, p. 298M, and the discussion in *Light*, xviii, p. 492. See especially Iken. *In 1rst ed. New Test.* II, p. 377, 379, 380, and *Monuments* p. 377; and John Lightfoot I, p. 979.

Vs. 37 εἱστήκει ὁ Ἰησοῦς, καὶ ἔκραξεν λέγων To be taken with 8:12 Πάλιν οὖν αὐτοῖς ἐλάλησεν, the pericope 8:1-11 being omitted.

Ἐάν τις διψᾷ etc., the ceremonial. Not suggested in the Law but still a *most* important part of this festival. The libation of water (see Lightfoot, I, p. 977; and Succah iv.1,9.10; v.1). Water is taken from the pool of Siloam, in a golden pitcher, through the water gate to its altar, a direct line from the stream. See

Succah v.1. Succah iv.1 speaks of hymns and praise on the 8th day, but see R. Jehuda in iv.9 (see Gem. Hier. *Light*, xviii, p. 472 and p. 466); comp. Tosephta Succah iii.3 (xviii, p. 384). There was a discussion about whether this part of the ceremonial was part of the Law or not (Gem. Hier. p. 468).

As for the *spiritual meaning* Gem. Hier. p. 480 and see Is 12:3. In Tosephta iii.4 (ib. p. 384) the ceremony is connected with the prophecy in Ezek 47. See passages in Wettstein also.

Thus it seems to have a Messianic bearing. It spoke of a stream of running, life-giving water that should issue from the Temple rock, and serve the nations. It recalled and remembered the type of water issuing from the rock smitten by Moses, which rock St. Paul understood to be the Christ (1 Cor 10:4 γὰρ ἐκ πνευματικῆς ἀκολουθούσης πέτρας, ἡ πέτρα δὲ ἦν ὁ Χριστός).

And this is the force of the Lord's declaration here. These ceremonials were σκιά, shadows of the coming things. He was the true antitype, the living rock from which issued the perennial stream, the fountain coming forth from the house of the Lord (Joel 3:18), the fountain opened to the house of David and to the inhabitants of Jerusalem (Zech 13:1), the living water going out from Jerusalem (Zech 14:8), 'the waters going from under the threshold of the house' such that everything should live whither the current cometh (Ezek 47:1, 9).

Vs. 38 ὁ πιστεύων εἰς ἐμέ The common interpretation. The grammar involves 1) an anacoluthon ὁ πιστεύων . . . ἐκ τῆς κοιλίας αὐτοῦ ῥεύσουσιν ὕδατος ζῶντος. This in itself is no serious objection (see e.g. 6:39) if the sense required it, BUT, 2) the correspondence between the type and the antitype clearly requires that the living water should issue from Christ, not from the believer.

It is said indeed that the believer himself becomes a new source of life to others. This is true, but it has nothing to do with this context. For not only does the correspondence of the type and the antitype require it, but the very expressions in the passage itself: 1) πινέτω—drinking; 2) ἔμελλον λαμβάνειν οἱ πιστεύσαντες εἰς αὐτόν (vs. 39); 3) the quotation. There is nothing to which the words ἐκ τῆς κοιλίας αὐτοῦ can well refer. An apocryphal saying is out of the question. Our Lord never quotes such passages as Is 12:3 or 44:3 where the believer is spoken of as the recipient. These texts do not at all meet the case. Is 58:11 is nearer in sense, where the faithful himself is compared to a never-failing well, but this is wide in expression. Alford (following others) seems to have the right idea, referring to the prophetic passage describing the stream issuing from Jerusalem. But he does not see that these sorts of passages almost require that the reference be to the giver, not the receiver. With the corrected punctuation we have πινέτω ὁ πιστεύων εἰς ἐμέ, corresponds with ὃ ἔμελλον λαμβάνειν οἱ πιστεύσαντες εἰς αὐτόν (vs. 39). The Spirit flows from Him, as the living water from the rock, and they drink of the stream and they receive the Spirit.

Origen, *Opus* II, p. 779E refers ῥεύσουσιν etc. to the believer, but Chrysostom (see Tisch.) is evidently aware of different modes of punctuation. Cureton Syriac is wanting. Peshitto and Egyptian seem to defend our punctuation, like the Greek.

αὐτοῦ the rock, or the Temple as prefiguring Christ. He is probably not quoting any one passage (the one that's nearest Zech 14:8) but gives the meaning of several. The Lord might have pointed to the rock, thus making the reference at once intelligible.

κοιλίας Referring primarily to the hollow center of the rock, but secondarily to the Christ. Of κοιλίας as the seat of affections, nothing in the LXX, but ref. to Plutarch, Epictetus, Polybius, etc.

ὕδατος ζῶντος a double meaning; comp. 4:10, 11. On the first meaning see e.g. Gen 26:19 καὶ ὤρυξαν οἱ παῖδες Ισαακ ἐν τῇ φάραγγι Γεραρων καὶ εὗρον ἐκεῖ φρέαρ ὕδατος ζῶντος.

Vs. 39 περὶ τοῦ Πνεύματος The gift of the Spirit is spoken of as ἐξέχεεν 'poured out.' Acts 2:17, 33; 10:45; Tit 3:6. Here again the metaphor is much better perceived by referring αὐτοῦ to the divine source himself. Compare 15:26 ὃ παρὰ τοῦ Πατρὸς ἐκπορεύεται.

οὔπω γὰρ ἦν Πνεῦμα Not the Spirit as the source for this is eternally existent, but the Spirit as manifested, as poured out; comp. Acts 19:2 οἱ δὲ πρὸς αὐτόν Ἀλλ' οὐδ' εἰ Πνεῦμα Ἅγιον ἔστιν ἠκούσαμεν.

Additions: 1) ἅγιον (both B.M.T. and T.R.). It has very considerable support but wanting in some key authorities. Obviously, an interpolation; 2) δεδομένον; 3) επ' αὐτός, both even more obviously interpolations.

Vs. 40 ὁ προφήτης comp. 1:21, 25; 6:14; Deut 18:15. The Apostles *identified* the prophet predicted by Moses with our Lord (Acts 3:22; 7:37). But the national expectation generally seems to have looked on him as a forerunner or a companion of Messiah.

The truthfulness of the narrative here: 1) the mode of expression, ὁ προφήτης. The popular idea has to be supplied to explain it; 2) the fact that the prophet and the Christ are separated, even though to the Christian Apostle himself they would be identified.

Vs. 42 ἡ γραφή Micah 5:2 (Bethlehem); Isaiah 11:1; 23:5, David. It has been strangely argued (de Wette and others), that the birth at Bethlehem was unknown to St. John. This admits of direct refutation: 1) if the inference is good for one clause, it must be good for the other. Therefore, the Evangelist must also have been ignorant of the descent from David. No one would venture to assert this. Thus the argument proves nothing, because it proves too much; 2) the fallacy of the argument is shown by parallel instances e.g. Luke 4:22 Οὐχὶ υἱός ἐστιν Ἰωσὴφ οὗτος; though Luke himself knows Joseph is not his father. The parallel is exact.

On the other hand, I should argue for the passage itself (independently of other considerations) that the Evangelist did know of the birth in Bethlehem, for he puts very prominently forward the prophecies about Bethlehem, prophecies generally believed to point to the Messiah. For this reason alone, it is very awkward to dispose of, if they were not fulfilled in the birthplace of our Lord, and yet he says not a word in refutation of this interpretation. It is clear, therefore, that he considered these questioners had got hold of a truth, though they were at a loss because they did not know how it was fulfilled in Jesus.

ἔρχεται 'Is destined to come.' The present tense denotes the certainty. It is used especially of Christ's advent (1 Thess 5:2 and where he is called ὁ ἐρχόμενος Matt 11:3; John 1:15, 27; 3:31; 6:14?) and of his attendants e.g. Elijah (Matt 17:10 ὅτι Ἠλείαν δεῖ ἐλθεῖν πρῶτον).

Vs. 45 Ἦλθον etc. When? Probably synchronous with and not subsequent to the event related in the last paragraph as e.g. John 18:25-27. The case before us is an exact parallel. The sending of the attendants is related (see vs. 32). The Evangelist is relating two synchronous chains of incidents, and he takes one link of each in succession.

Thus then 8:12 Πάλιν οὖν αὐτοῖς ἐλάλησεν etc. is part of the links as continuous with 7:44.

πρὸς τοὺς ἀρχιερεῖς καὶ Φαρισαίους also vs. 32 οἱ ἀρχιερεῖς καὶ οἱ Φαρισαῖοι (not as T.R. which reverses the order of the two nouns). They were two distinct classes, but in this case they have made common cause, and are accordingly regarded as a combined body in the two passages.

Vs. 47 Here again as above in vs. 32. The Pharisees are the active turbulent people, the prime movers. The 'rulers' are diligent to follow their dictation and put themselves at the head of the opposition to our Lord. Comp. 11:46, 47.[1]

ὁ ὄχλος οὗτος The rabbinical phrase is *am ha'aretz* of the uninstructed multitude, as opposed to the wise, the educated few. See the references in Wettstein and Lampe. Targum Euma (?) on Hos 4:14.

ἐπικατάρατοί i.e. they came under the curses of Deut 27 etc. (Ewald). See the interpolation in D after Luke 6:4.

Vs. 50 πρότερον 3:1sq.

νυκτός Must be omitted here (against T.R. and B.M.T.).

Vs. 51 ἐὰν μὴ ἀκούσῃ See Deut 1:16sq.

τὸν ἄνθρωπον Comp. 2:25.

Vs. 52 Μὴ καὶ σύ etc. Said contemptuously, 'We did not know that God sent a Galilean; for a Galilean too you must be, for no one but a Galilean could be favorably disposed towards this Jesus.' The Galileans, a tumultuous people, were constantly intrigued with rumors of false Messiahs.

ἐραύνησον See Tischendorf, *Prob.* pp. xliv, xlix (ed. 7). This is the general reading of ℵ as well as A, B, C.

ἐγείρεται ℵ, B, D, T, Lact., Syr. Peshit., Arm. have this reading which is undoubtedly right, but T.R., B.M.T. have ἐγήγερται.

It is said that the Evangelist has erred because: 1) several ancient prophets were from Galilee (at all events Elijah and Jonah were from Galilee); 2) But this is answered by saying the mistake is not the Evangelist's but the speakers.' In their indignity they were either forgetful or unscrupulous. But the objection and the answer are beside the text. They apply to ἐγήγερται but not to ἐγείρεται. And it is surprising that critics reading ἐγείρεται should entertain such a view. There is no presumption from Scripture, and there is the very contrary of a presumption from the ignorance of the Galilean people, that we are to expect a prophet from Galilee (see the Talmudic writers). It is the Galilee of the present, not the Galilee of the past with which the speakers are concerned. We are not however to take προφήτης as ὁ προφήτης.

---

[1] See his discussion of the internal evidence in the introduction above (pp. 41-76).

[Lightfoot, with the vast majority of New Testament scholars in the last 150 years, realized that John 7:53–8:11 was not an original part of this Gospel, and therefore he skips to 8:12 at this point, but first gives his rationale for doing so. Even though the material in this excursus comes later in the John manuscript, it is better to put it here, maintaining the numerical order, since searchers will look here for his comments. (BW3)]

EXCURSUS: THE QUESTION OF THE AUTHENTICITY OF JOHN 7:53–8:11

The pericope about the woman caught in adultery, found most often at John 7:53–8:11, cannot be genuine, both on grounds of external and internal evidence.

External Evidence: 1) it is wanting in the following important witnesses—‏ℵ‎, A, B, C, T, L, X, Δ, 33. Of these there is a gap in A, C, but the space is insufficient for the pericope. In L and Δ there is more than enough space; 2) it is also wanting in various versions—Peshitto, Harcleon Syr., Memphis, Theb., Goth. Arm. On this see Tregelles; 3) Origen in his John Commentary (iv, p. 299) runs on continuously from 7:52 to 8:12. Tertullian, *de pud.* 6 would not have made the statement he did if he had this passage in his text. Of the other Greek Fathers, while Chrysostom betrays knowledge of the existence of this story (viii, p. 306), neither he nor Eusebius, Theodosius of Mop., Cyril of Alex. (see *Cramer's Catena*), nor Apollin. recognize it as part of the text of the Fourth Gospel. The testimony of Eusebius is especially important, as a collector and sifter of manuscripts. Yet the natural influence from his discussion of Papias is that he himself had not seen this pericope in any manuscript. On the possible exception of Euthymius, *Sac.* XII, see Tregelles, but it is quite clear from the evidence that it was not generally known or recognized by the Greek Fathers for many centuries after Papias. *In short there is no evidence that it appeared in St. John's text before the fourth century. When it finally does occur, it appears in three or four different places and with numberless lexical variants, which is always a suspicious sign, especially when it cannot be explained by any known text critical means or interpretations of how it could have been omitted or moved.*

Internal Evidence. The awkwardness of the connection between 7:52 and 53, and 8:11 and 12. On the fact that it interrupts the discussion of the elements of the Feast of Tabernacles, specifically the water and light images, see the commentary below. The phrase at the beginning of the pericope is very awkward in connection with what went before Καὶ ἐπορεύθη ἕκαστος εἰς τὸν οἶκον αὐτοῦ (7:53), and 8:12 hardly fits with what has just been said in 8:11. One would have to ask—To whom is vs. 12 addressed (the woman, the crowd) when it says Πάλιν οὖν αὐτοῖς ἐλάλησεν ὁ Ἰησοῦς? But at this juncture, the crowd, the elders, the woman had left. There was no one there. Furthermore, John 7:53–8:11 has no bearing on the leading ideas of St. John's Gospel. Every incident, every comment in this Gospel tends to bring out the Person of Christ.

Then too we must consider the style of 7:53–8:11. St. John very often omits all connecting particles. When he inserts one, it is most frequently οὖν, as here in 8:12, 13, 19 etc. But in 7:53–8:11 all the sentences are strung together, οὖν is not once used, and the common connecting particle is δέ. Individual expressions in 7:53–8:11 are not often St. John's language e.g. πᾶς ὁ λαὸς, καθίσας ἐδίδασκεν αὐτούς, οἱ γραμματεῖς καί etc. and many individual words e.g. ἐπέμενον, ἀναμάρτητος, κατελείφθη etc. These specific examples are however much less conclusive than the general different structure of the sentences.

But though not part of St. John's Gospel, it appears to be an authentic narrative. Note its affinity to the Synoptic Gospels and their thrust. For example, the attempt of the scribes and the Pharisees to entangle our Lord in a question related to the Mosaic Law. His mode of dealing with their machinations, not by a direct reply, but by turning the problem back on themselves e.g. his moral treatment of the subject: 1) his declining to judge the case as an earthly judge; 2) his conviction of the moral hypocrisy of the woman's accusers; 3) his holding out the hope, even there, of forgiveness.

But whence, how, and when was it interpolated into this Gospel?

WHENCE? It appeared in Papias and in the Hebrew Gospel (see Eusebius, *Hist. Eccles.* iii.39).

HOW AND WHERE? Perhaps it was added in the margins as a comment on 8:15, 'But I judge no one' (as suggested by Ewald, p. 271). The older manuscripts were written in single columns. Hence it was slipped into the text here in most manuscripts, but in at least two (see 225) after vs. 36 and in another at the end of the Gospel, set apart. In 69 and others (see Tisch.) it occurs at the end of Luke 21. The link of connection is different in the two

cases. In St. Luke the connection is historical/chronological—the time and
scene, and doctrinal—the function of Christ not to condemn. It is recognized by Jerome, who says, '*In Evangel. . . . in multi et Graeci et Latinis co-
diatus* etc.' The Apostl. Constit. (perhaps the beginning of the fourth century)
also recognizes it but it is by no means clear that they did not take it from
Papias or from the Hebrew Gospel. It is commented on, at length, by St.
Ambrose, *Ep.* xxv.II, p. 892 and though he does not mention St. John's Gospel
he would hardly have assumed it was from elsewhere. He does not seem to
be aware of its doubtful provenance. This then may be regarded as the first
distinct reference to the passage as in St. John's Gospel. It seems however to
have been received in the West prior to in the East, for D is connected with
Western contexts. Eventually it was accepted in: 1) Greek; 2) Latin; 3) Syrian;
4) Armenian; 5) Egyptian Churches. Afterwards it got into Syrian Testaments in different form (see *Bible and Orient*, ii.53, p. 169). It appears in the
Jerusalem Syriac lectionary and is read on the day of St. Pelagia (see Adler,
p. 190). Augustine's comment (*de conj. adult.* ii.7), plausible in itself, does
not at all meet the circumstances of the case. In particular it does not satisfy
either: 1) the external evidence (its absence in the early authorities), or 2) the
internal evidence. Nor does it account for the difference in style or the confusion of sense.

The first extant manuscript in which it appears is D (sixth century). This
accords with the character of D. It inserts traditions, some apparently authentic. For example, compare its rendering of Matt 20:28; Luke 6:4 (on the
Sabbath); John 7:56; Acts 5:15, 39; 10:25; 11:1, 26; 12:10. Some of these traditions reflect local knowledge, so one infers Palestinian tradition. One must
also consider the connection of D with the Latin manuscripts. The distinc-
tives in these different texts may be explained either by different translations
from the Hebrew Gospel or by interpolation from the version of the story
given by Papias. The mistake of *ecce homo* being the motive of Christ
stooping down and writing on the ground. His character was above feeling
shame whereas other men were beneath feeling shame. On the motif of Jesus
refusing to interfere compare Matt 15:22 and Luke 12:14 ('who made me a
judge'). The whole lesson is a contrast between God's pure abhorrence of sin
and man's hypocritical allowance, between the depth of God's mercy and the
hardness of man's judgment.

[In view of the great popularity and Christian use of the story, and because he thinks it may be an authentic story about Jesus, just not a canonical one, Lightfoot proceeds to comment on the passage and its textual criticism at some length. (BW3)]

Commentary on John 7:53–8:11

The question about the two textual traditions of the story is do they represent Papias and the Hebrew Gospel? I will take D as the basis for the exposition.

Vs. 53 Καὶ ἐπορεύθη ἕκαστος εἰς τὸν οἶκον αὐτοῦ A notice not explained by anything that went before it in this Gospel. Who went? The people gathered in the Temple for the Festival (7:37-44)? The chief priests and the Pharisees (7:45–8:52)? It should be the latter, but the contrast with Jesus is thus greater, and out of place here. Seemingly, in the original context, it was the dispersion of the multitude, perhaps after some discussion held, or some miracle wrought.

Vs. 1 εἰς τὸ ὄρος τῶν ἐλαιῶν the only mention of it in St. John, but no argument can be founded on this fact. E.g. look at 18:1, though certainly it has no place there. Comp. Luke 21:37, 38. *Historically*, this is doubtless the right place for the incident. The narrative from which the interpolator took the story must have stood so.

Vs. 5 ἐν δὲ τῷ νόμῳ Μωσῆς etc. There is some difficulty with this. In Deut 22:22, the punishment of stoning is ordered in the case of a betrothed virgin. Vs. 22 also says that an adulteress (purposely so called) is *to be put to death*. Perhaps the proximity of the latter story to the former and the similarity of the offense suggests the same punishment, but the rabbinical influence [here] is not the natural inference from Deut. discussions. And later (at all events) it is said to be a rabbinical maxim, but where no special mode of death was named, hanging (*strangalato*) can be understood. Lücke quotes Mamonides Sanhedr. vii.1 on this, but this I cannot verify. Alford got his reference to Mish. Sanhed. x from Lücke, and it responds to something, but the quote is different. See Lightfoot II, p. 563—if a daughter of Israel commits adultery after she is married, she must be strangled; if she is only betrothed, she must be stoned. The ordinances in the Mishnah however seem to make the distinction that stoning is the punishment for the one offense, strangling for the other. The references in the Mishnah are Sanhedr. vii.9; x.1, 6.

But: 1) our authority is probably older, on any showing, and as well informed as these rabbinical writers. And we find in other cases the authorities
disputing among themselves and most agreed as to what the penalty was in
other special crimes; 2) but this case may be an example of an act by a betrothed woman and not a married woman (see Philo, *de Spec. Leg.* sec. 12, II,
p. 311M).

The Koran (see Sale, *Koran I*, p. 54, 88). Mohammed may have gotten the
idea from this incident, but it does not follow that he had before him the
Gospel of St. John, because he made large use of the Apocryphal Gospels.

Vs. 6 τοῦτο δὲ ἔλεγον πειράζοντες αὐτόν etc. Omitted by D here, but it
has a similar notice in vs. 4. In what did the tempting or trial consist? 1) The
word πειράζοντες is used in Matt 16:1; Mark 8:11; Luke 4:16, tempt him to
work a sign; 2) Matt 19:3; Mark 10:2 tempt him to pronounce on divorce in
cases of adultery; 3) Matt 22:18; Mark 12:15; Luke 20:23, the tribute money;
4) Matt 22:35, which is the great commandment. In the first case there is no
malice or treachery. It is simply an attempt to elicit his Messiahship (our
Lord himself is said to test John 6:6). In the other cases, there is evil intent
to entangle Him either with the Mosaic Law 2) and 4), or to entangle him
with the civil government 3). Any entanglement with the civil government
seems out of the question. It seems clear then that in John 7:53–8:11 we are
talking about an attempt to entangle him with the Mosaic Law.

What then? He must either confirm the Law or abrogate it. The former
would be contrary to his mission of mercy. The latter would condemn Him
in the eyes of all who are zealous for the Law. The 'testers' doubtless reckoned
on the former and at all events hoped, somehow or other (perhaps with no
very definite view as to the result) 'to entangle Him in his talk' as in the case
with the Law of divorce (see Ambrose, *Epist.* xxv who, unlike Augustine, is
substantially correct in his interpretation).

Vs. 6 κάτω κύψας To what purpose? Not that of the conjecture of the *ecce
homo* manuscript. As not wishing to be interrupted but preoccupied with
his own thoughts. It is a sign to them, a sign that they do not take that the
subject is intrusive, is alien to His work, alien to the purpose of His ministry.
He refuses to be a judge. He came not to condemn sinners, but to save
sinners. The supposed parallel passages in Wettstein (Aelian 31; Orest. 631)
are not good. Meyer quotes Diogenes Laertius ii.127.

μὴ προσποιούμενος 'as though he heard not' A.V. which is correct. Only found in E, G, H, K (also B.M.T. and T.R.). It is however absent in D, which is probably the earliest manuscript with this narrative. The word means either: 1) to pretend not to, to dissemble, or 2) not to heed. Here it would have the latter sense. See Diogenes Laertius ix.29 and Menander in Steph. *Thess.* VI, p. 1990 (edition H+D). The other readings such as καὶ προσποιούμενος are from transcribers who do not understand the meaning of the phrase.

Vs. 7 Ὁ ἀναμάρτητος There are two possible interpretations: 1) Comprehensive—'guiltless of breaking the Law in any respect'; 2) Special—'free from all stain of impurity.' Comp. 5:14 and vs. 11 below. No doubt it is the latter. It is not however referring to adultery, but to any slight violation of the sexual laws. It is an appeal to their consciences. His look aided the word. He pierced their hearts, read their thoughts, and they were conscious of this. See John 2:25.

τὸν λίθον E etc. (omitted in D). The first stone cast was to be by the principal witness (Deut 17:7; Acts 7:58).

Vs. 8 ἔγραφεν εἰς τὴν γῆν It is vain to enquire what was written. Probably something unconnected with the scene before Him, if the view of the *motive* of the action is correct. One mss. adds at this point 'and each one of them, their sins' and so also in a Syriac version—Assem., *Bible. Or.* II, p. 170. St. Ambrose, *Epistl.* xxv conjectures it was their names. He quotes Jer 22:29—'Is not my word like fire?' says the Lord, 'It breaks the rocks in pieces.'

Vs. 9 ἀρξάμενοι ἀπὸ τῶν πρεσβυτέρων ἕως τῶν ἐσχάτων When there was a movement among them, the younger would naturally make way for their elders to leave first, seniority being greatly regarded among the rabbis. The explanations which account for the notice by suggesting: 1) greater accumulation of the evidence of his mercy; 2) quicker presentation of our Lord's meaning, are all out of place. κατέκρινεν (vs. 10) refers to judicially, for morally he does condemn her actions as μηκέτι ἁμάρτανε (vs. 11) makes clear. He does not say she does not deserve to be judged . . . ,[2] [but then so do her accusers, particularly the elders, who were responsible for maintaining the moral fabric of their community].

---

[2]What follows is illegible, but the drift of it seems to be as I have reconstructed in square brackets.
  (BW3)

Jesus the Light and
Abraham the Forefather
(John 8)

Vs. 12 Πάλιν οὖν, connected with 7:12. This connection is all the more obvious when: 1) 7:53–8:11 is struck out as an interpolation; 2) 7:45-52 is recognized as a synchronous and not continuous incident, thus a *chronological* narrative. John 8:12 follows immediately on 7:44, and πάλιν connects the two images, the living water and light. I find the same connection of images in reference to the Feast of Tabernacles in Philo, *Sept.* sec. 24 (not in the ordinary texts but in Tischendorf, *Philomea*). There is the ceremonial of the lighting of the great candelabras in the Court of the Women (so John Lightfoot, but Succah v does not give the number of the candelabras but apparently there were four sockets to each candelabra). First was the drawing of the water, then the lighting of the candelabras. The festivities included dancing and music, the torches and the fifteen Psalms of degrees (see Lightfoot I, p. 977sq.; Succah v. 2, 3 cf. with Gem. Hier. Ugol.??, p. 484sq). Philo connects the Festival with the idea of light in another way (see *Philomea* p. 67).

Points to be observed: 1) the lighting was part of the festivities of the pouring of water, initially connected therewith; 2) it was in the *Court of the Women* where the γαζοφυλακίον was and where our Lord was speaking. He would point to the candelabras. The duration of the ceremonial is not clear. It must have continued as many days as the libations continued. It must have lasted more than the first day. The account in Succah suggests, based on the continuing to light the candelabras, that libations continued several successive days. The lighting was absolutely necessary because the festivities continued well into the night. Even if the libations concluded on the seventh day, the lighting continued into the eighth day. But suppose both ceased on the seventh day. The significance of our Lord's comparison would even be advanced. The trickling stream of water has ceased, but the perennial fountain of living water is ever present. The σῶμα takes the place of the σκιά. The light that lit up Jerusalem with a natural grace is quenched. But the light, not of Jerusalem only but of the whole world, still abides.

All this is in strict accordance with our Lord's mode of teaching, e.g. with the Samaritan woman at the well, or with the Galileans after the feeding of the 5,000. Was Is 42 read at the Feast of the Tabernacles? If so, it was probably chosen with reference to the ceremonial of the lights, and thus the light would be directly connected with the Messiah coming. And the significance of the Lord's words, and the claims therein, would be all the more appreciated.

περιπατήσῃ the right reading.

Vs. 14 Κἂν ἐγὼ μαρτυρῶ περὶ ἐμαυτοῦ 'Supposing I bear witness concerning myself.' The hypothesis is neither affirmed nor denied.

ὅτι οἶδα πόθεν ἦλθον 'I cannot be false, I cannot be mistaken, for I know I came from the Father, and that I return to Him.'

ἔρχομαι below (rather than ἦλθον) because it refers to his continuous presence as God's Messiah.

Vs. 15 κατὰ τὴν σάρκα 'You can see in me nothing but an unaccredited adventurer, a poor Galilean.'

ἐγὼ οὐ κρίνω οὐδένα 'I do not judge you, nay I do not judge any man at all. It is not my mission to judge' (cf. 3:17; 12:47, 48). Yet in another sense, he will judge every man (5:22). This statement seems to have been the occasion of the insertion of 7:53–8:11.

Vs. 16 καὶ ἐὰν κρίνω δὲ ἐγώ Observe the δέ. If, by an exceptional circumstance, the ἐγώ is emphatic, then we have 'I, whose mission it is *not* . . .'

ἀληθινή Genuine. But ℵ, E (B.M.T. and T.R.) etc. have ἀληθής, probably from vss. 13, 14.

Vs. 17 τῷ ὑμετέρῳ 'The Law, behind which you are always shielding yourself, which you are always using as a weapon against me.' See John 10:34.

δύο ἀνθρώπων etc. Deut 17:6; 19:15. See Matt 18:16; 2 Cor 13:2; Heb 10:28; perhaps 1 John 5:5-7.

Vs. 20 ἐν τῷ γαζοφυλακίῳ In the Court of the Women. See Josephus, *Bell Jud.* v.14; John Lightfoot, I, p. 1094.

καὶ οὐδεὶς ἐπίασεν αὐτόν etc. A sort of refrain, see 7:30; 8:45; and here. In these two latter cases, closing the account; here the account of our Lord's application of the two images of the Feast.

Vs. 21 ζητήσετέ με ['seek me'] and shall not find me, and this in a double sense: 1) you shall not be able to find me in the body: 2) you shall lose me spiritually. The corporal image suggests the spiritual sense.

Hence, ἐν τῇ ἁμαρτίᾳ ὑμῶν ἀποθανεῖσθε. Similarly, the double sense of ὑψωθῆναι and the context e.g. 12:32, 34 comp. 3:14; 8:28. So again a double sense in ὅπου ἐγὼ ὑπάγω ὑμεῖς οὐ δύνασθε ἐλθεῖν.

Vs. 22 Said in mockery.

Vs. 23 ἐκ τῶν κάτω The interpretation adopted by Alford is too strained. Obviously ἐκ τῶν κάτω is to be interpreted by ἐκ τούτου τοῦ κόσμου ἐστέ. E.g. Acts 2:19 quoted by Meyer. They were of the earth, earthy.

Vs. 24 ἐγώ εἰμι 'I am he' i.e. the expected One, the Messiah, the hope of Israel comp. vs. 28 and 12:19. Also Mark 13:6 (comp. 14:62); Luke 21:8 and 22:70. Three points: 1) here the predicate is understood; 2) but with no predicate, the verb denotes absolute existence (as in vs. 58 here); 3) ἐγώ is the predicate! 'It is I.' In Matt 14:27 and elsewhere it is different still, for there too ἐγώ is the predicate.

Vs. 25 Τὴν ἀρχὴν ὅ τι καὶ λαλῶ ὑμῖν; Two questions to be decided: 1) Is it ὅτι or ὅ τι? Certainly, the latter. 2) Is it interrogative or affirmative? 'Do you ask me that which I have been telling you all along?' Comp. Matt 26:50 Ἑταῖρε, ἐφ' ὅ πάρει.

ἀρχὴν or Τὴν ἀρχὴν? Originally a cognate accusative. Many adverbs have arisen in this way. All (?) those end in -ήν, e.g. ἀνεδήν etc. 'As a beginning,' 'to begin with,' 'and so from first to last.' Hence, it is used most frequently with a negative, and signifies *ominum* = 'at all.' But it occasionally, as here, stands without the negative. The question here is not so much one of difference of meaning (as Dean Alford seems to make it) 'altogether' or 'throughout,' but whether it is to be taken with εἰμι understood, 'I am altogether that, etc.' or 'all along . . .' or instead with the following λαλῶ 'that which I have been telling you all along.' The latter seems to me more simple. Alford (after de Wette) seems to go wrong about the present, not understanding that the present tense can refer to an action begun in the distant past and continued into the present. Thus Πάλαι λέγω is as good Greek and much more pregnant than Πάλαι ἔλεγον or ἔλεξα.

Vs. 26 πολλὰ ἔχω περὶ ὑμῶν 'I might say much about you also, I might pronounce many judgments on you. But this would interrupt my message, would interfere with the work. I came not to judge or discuss men, I am the bearer of my Father's message and into it I must delve.'

εἰς τὸν κόσμον as 1 Cor 14:9, quoted by Alford.

Vs. 28 ὑψώσητε See on vs. 24. To the natural eye, they raised Him on a cross of ignominy and shame. But in the sight of God he was raised to be adored by all. Comp. Phil 2:9 διὸ καὶ ὁ Θεὸς αὐτὸν ὑπερύψωσεν. They exalted Him to shame, but God through their act exalted Him to honor.

Vs. 31 πρὸς τοὺς πεπιστευκότας αὐτῷ Πιστεύω used of the initiative act not the continuous state. Not πεπιστευκότας εἰς αὐτῷ. See my notes on Gal 2:16. It is evident that our Lord, though speaking to those Jews who in some sense believed Him, yet in speaking through them to their fellow countrymen we must suppose that though the believing Jews about Him were more immediately addressed, the greater part of his word was focused on the unbelieving and *they* take up the condemnation in vs. 48, if not before.

μείνητε here is emphatic.

Vs. 33 σπέρμα Ἀβραάμ ἐσμεν and therefore the destined rulers of the world. See Gen 17:16; comp. Rom 4:13.

οὐδενὶ δεδουλεύκαμεν πώποτε This was not strictly true, and can only be understood of the freedom of spirit which had never acquiesced in the external bondage whether to Egypt, or to Babylon, or to Syria, or to Rome. The boast of *liberty* was strong amongst the Jews. The selling of an Israelite into slavery was looked upon with the highest disfavor. See John Lightfoot here. But perhaps here it refers to the present generation. Titus, addressing the Jews, stresses that they were allowed the free exercise of their laws and customs (in Josephus, *Bell Jud.* vi.6.2).

Vs. 34 δοῦλός, a favorite Stoic term, perhaps derived from the East by the Stoics.

Vs. 35 ὁ δὲ δοῦλος οὐ μένει ἐν τῇ οἰκίᾳ εἰς τὸν αἰῶνα. Note the reference to Ishmael and Isaac; see Gal 4:30.

εἰς τὸν αἰῶνα not the preferred phrase but it = 'always' here.

Vs. 36 ἐὰν οὖν ὁ Υἱὸς ὑμᾶς ἐλευθερώσῃ, ὄντως ἐλεύθεροι ἔσεσθε. Will be free indeed, will be co-heirs with Him (Rom 8:17), will abide in His house forever, as He abides forever.

Vs. 37 οὐ χωρεῖ ἐν ὑμῖν 'Does not advance in, does not make any progress in your hearts.' See Plutarch, *Pomp.* 54. See the references in Wettstein and Meyer. The A.V. 'hath no place' seems erroneous and perhaps a confusion with the other sense of χωρεῖν—'to contain,' 'to have a place for,' but not *in*.

Vs. 38 An important v.l. Meyer IV, p. 317 is very explicit about the reading. And it should be: 1) ἠκούσατε not ἑωράκατε (B.M.T. and T.R.); 2) παρὰ τοῦ Πατρός, not παρὰ τῷ Πατρί. For ἑωράκα comp. 1:34; 3:11; 19:35; 1 John 1:1 etc. ἃ ἑωράκα παρὰ τῷ Πατρί implies absolute truth, but ἃ ἠκούσατε παρὰ τοῦ Πατρος may involve falsehood; hearing is not seeing. This distinction of hearing and seeing is carried out in the distinction of cases dative and genitive.

Vs. 39 They are σπέρμα Ἀβραάμ (vs. 37) but it still remains a question whether they are τέκνα. See Rom 9:7 οὐδ' ὅτι εἰσὶν σπέρμα Ἀβραάμ, πάντες τέκνα, ἀλλ' Ἐν Ἰσαὰκ κληθήσεταί σοι σπέρμα.

ἐποιεῖτε T.R. adds ἄν. Comp. Winer, p. 321. Not ποιήσετε the natural apodosis of εἰ τέκνα τοῦ Ἀβραάμ ἐστε. The apodosis indirectly negatives the statement in the protasis. I do not understand Tregelles punctuation here.

Vs. 40 ἄνθρωπον ὃς 'the One who . . .'; comp. 4:29 v.l.; 7:22 etc.

οὐκ ἐποίησεν On the contrary, Abraham even interceded for the Sodomites facing judgment. Gen 18:23sq.

ἐκ πορνείας They begin to discuss that our Lord's mention of Abraham has a spiritual bearing. See especially Is 57:3, where idolatry is described as immorality. Comp. Hos 2:4; Ezek 16 and 23. The spiritual mother has been true to her allegiance to her divine spouse, not like the Samaritan mother who had committed spiritual fornication. Comp. Philo, *de. Confus. Ling.* Sec. 28 p. 426M; *de Migra. Abr.* 12 p. 447 where the image is manipulated.

Vs. 42 καὶ ἥκω 'and as such I present myself to you.'

ἐξῆλθον καὶ ἥκω The former verb refers to the origin, the latter the destination.

Vs. 43 λαλιά the form, my way of speaking, my language. The λαλιά should have declared to them his parentage, his race. λόγος, the substance (of dialect see Matt 26:73; Mark 14:7sq.).

οὐ δύνασθε They had disabled, incapacitated themselves.

Vs. 44 ἀνθρωποκτόνος . . . ἀπ' ἀρχῆς He refers to the first murder, of Abel by Cain. Comp. 1 John 3:12-15; See my notes on Clement of Rome 6. See Gospel of Nicodemus 23 where the devil is called the origin of death and the root of sin. The reference is to their intent to kill him (vs. 40).

ὅταν λαλῇ (i.e. τίς or ἄνθρωπος)? See Telf. *Gramm.* sec. 373.6 where are several references e.g. Plato, *Gorg.* 456D, and see the Strabo note. This was common in Plato. And possibly John 7:51. But generally in the New Testament there is something explaining the τίς e.g. John 16:17. The sense however seems absolutely to require it.

The common interpretations are: 1) ὅτι οὐκ ἔστιν ἀλήθεια ἐν αὐτῷ. ὅταν λαλῇ τὸ ψεῦδος 'for he is a liar and the father of it' (i.e. the Lie). And if λαλῇ must refer to ὁ διαβόλος, this is the best. I see no objection to the expression 'father of falsehood.' Comp. Clement of Rome ii.2, 'the father of truth.' It is so taken by all the Greek Fathers (e.g. Chrysostom who takes λαλεί to refer to ὁ διαβόλος). But still the αὐτῷ is awkward and the ὁ before 'father' slightly so. 2) 'for he is a liar, and the father of him' (i.e. the ψεύστης). This is still more objectionable. αὐτῶν would be intelligible, but ψεύστης has been specialized, individualized, and he cannot be the father of the same liar that he is himself! Yet this interpretation has found great favor.

The interpretation which I have given seems certainly to be that of Origen (see *Opus* iv, p. 345sq. and investigate). So too Pseudo-Ignatius, *Philadel.* 6—'the liar is just as also his father, the devil.'

Some manuscripts read ὡς and others καθώς for καί. The transcribers of these manuscripts must have referred λαλῇ to someone other than the devil. See Epiphanius xxxvi.4; xl.5 and other references to the Fathers in Tisch. In some cases it is as if their text had ὅς ἄν, which would make excellent sense and Lactant. II, p. viii disposed to adopt it (see on the other hand Lücke II, p. 829). But the authority is quite insufficient.

Meyer, p. 308 refers to some early heretics who referred the αὐτῷ to the devil, but on what authority? Nothing in Irenaeus or Hippolytus refers the word to ὁ διαβόλος. Rather the Father is the Demiurge, and he is the father of the devil. See Plotinus, *Quaest. Amphil.* 88. (See Ewald, *Jahrbuch* v. p. 198 from Meyer). Hilgenfelds(?) has taken up this monstrous notion, taking the phrase to mean 'the father of the devil'!!

Vs. 45 ἐγὼ δέ 'but unlike your father the devil, unlike your own lying proposition, I . . .'

Vs. 46 ἁμαρτίας this is not = to ψεῦδος, but including this and much more. 'If I am free from sin, I am free from falsehood, I speak the truth.'

Vs. 47 This verse contains the answer to the question posed in the previous verse διὰ τί? The fault is not in the speaker who speaks the truth and how he claims to be heard, but rather in the hearers who have a repugnance to the truth, and refuse to listen. With this verse comp. 1 John 4:6. And on καὶ διὰ τοῦτο together see John 5:16, 18; 10:17; 12:18, 39 etc.

Vs. 48 Οὐ καλῶς λέγομεν ἡμεῖς ὅτι Σαμαρείτης εἶ σὺ καὶ δαιμόνιον ἔχεις; The assumption is Samaritans are both heretics and foes to Israel. These two seem to be the main ideas in using the term 'Samaritan' pejoratively. See Sirach 50:26 οἱ καθήμενοι ἐν ὄρει Σαμαρείας καὶ Φυλιστιεὶμ καὶ ὁ λαὸς μωρὸς ὁ κατοικῶν ἐν Σικίμοις. Comp. the saying in Wettstein of R. Shammai. Perhaps there is an allusion here to the dialogue of Jesus with the Samaritans (John 4) assuming something which has not been narrated, which is common in St. John. The δαιμόνιον ἔχεις might be explained by Matt 12:24; Luke 11:15, and there is no mention elsewhere of the charge. Cutheans (Samaritans) was a term that later Jews used to denigrate the followers of Christ.

Vs. 49 He makes no reply to the charge that 'you are a Samaritan.' In the parable of the Good Samaritan, he speaks of himself under the image of one of that nation. Augustine connects these facts together comp. *Sermo.* 171.a.2; *Evan.* in Ps. cxxxvi.3. See Tisch. *Parables*, p. 317.

ἀτιμάζετέ με dishonors me, and Him in me.

Vs. 50 ἐγὼ δὲ οὐ ζητῶ τὴν δόξαν μου 'Not that *I* seek my own however, so that I shall notice this dishonor paid to me.'

ἔστιν ὁ ζητῶν See vs. 45.

καὶ κρίνων This introduces the subject of the next issue.

Vs. 54 ἡμῶν T.R. wrongly has ὑμῶν.

Vs. 55 ἐγνώκατε The process of acquiring knowledge, whereas οἶδα, the absolute possession John 21:17; Eph 5:6; Gal 4:8; 1 John 2:29; 5:20.

Vs. 56 Ἀβραὰμ ὁ πατὴρ ὑμῶν ἠγαλλιάσατο ἵνα. ἵνα here is not final but denotes the object etc. See Matt 5:29, 30; John 4:34;17:3; 18:39 etc.

'Rejoiced at the thought of seeing . . .' But in what sense and with what closeness the idea of Messiah's day was present before in Abraham's mind, we are not told. Perhaps it was nothing more than a firm faith in the promise in Gen. 16, 17, 22 (on the reference to the laughing see Meyer). See John 13:41.

εἶδεν i.e. he saw this in Paradise. On the rabbinical fantasies about what Abraham knew in Paradise see Falina (?) *Cod. Pseud.* I, p. 423; Beer, *Leben Abraham*, p. 90sq. and 205sq. These absurdities need not prejudice the interpretation here.

Vs. 57 Πεντήκοντα ἔτη οὔπω ἔχεις καὶ Ἀβραὰμ ἑώρακας; What was our Lord's age at this time? 1) Our Lord was born before Herod's death (St. Matthew) and Herod died before the Passover in 750 A.U.C. His ministry began in the fifteenth year of Tiberius, or at least the Baptist began preaching in that year. The fifteenth year of Tiberius began 19th August 781. Thus our Lord must have been in his thirty-second year at the point of St. Luke's notice (3:23), though that notice is intended to be vague. One must ask about the length of his life before he began his ministry. 2) As to the length of the ministry, the better part of three years. It must have ended before Pilate's recall, i.e. before the death of Tiberius (A.D. 37; A.U.C. 790); therefore the Passion was not later than A.U.C. 789. The notice in John 2:20 agrees with this calculation. Unwarranted inference from it mentioned by St. Augustine. See Irenaeus ii.22.5 with the v.l. here of 40.

Vs. 58 Note the opposition of γενέσθαι and εἰμί. Absolute eternal being is in view here, not merely priority in time that could be expressed by ἐγὼ ἦν. Observe St. Paul in Col 1:17 καὶ αὐτός ἐστιν πρὸ πάντων καὶ τὰ πάντα ἐν αὐτῷ συνέστηκεν. The sense is drained in the A.V. 'He is before all things.' No, 'He *is*, prior to all things.' A reference to Exod 3:14; see Rev 1:4.

Vs. 59 ἦραν οὖν λίθους The Temple was still unfinished (see 2:20) so that loose stones would be lying about. See the rabbinical story in John Lightfoot about R. Gamaliel, about the mountain used in building the Temple.

Jesus and the Man Born Blind
(John 9)

Vs. 1 Notice no note of time here, just Καὶ παράγων. The narrative may be continuous with the preceding one, but there is nothing to indicate that it is. The incident happens on a Sabbath day (vs. 14) and therefore the time seems to have been after the Festival, for it can hardly be the end of the Festival Sabbath mentioned in 7:37 as Ἐν δὲ τῇ ἐσχάτῃ ἡμέρᾳ τῇ μεγάλῃ τῆς ἑορτῆς, else it would have been otherwise than we find described in John 9. A brief outline of what follows will be useful:

1) John 9:1–10:21—The healing of the blind man on the Sabbath day, the ensuing discourse, the door of the sheepfold

2) John 10:22-39—Jesus at Jerusalem at the Feast of Dedication (Chislev-December) in Solomon's Porch

3) John 10:40-42—He returns beyond Jordan.

4) John 11:1-44—The death and raising of Lazarus

5) John 11:45-57—The Conspiracy of the 'Jews'

With the Twelfth Chapter begins the history of the Paschal Week.

Vs. 2 οὗτος ἢ οἱ γονεῖς αὐτοῦ, ἵνα τυφλὸς γεννηθῇ; I do not know that it is necessary to ask how the man's being born blind was caused by his own sin. This is the sort of expression that might rise to the lips of anyone, speaking carelessly and off-hand. If any explanation be necessary, it is perhaps that this text refers to sin foreseen by God and punished at the birth, rather than to: 1) the pre-existence of souls, or 2) sin in the embryo. Of these two, the latter is more probable. On rabbis that at least considered that sin began before birth, see John Lightfoot.

ἵνα τυφλός Not a final ἵνα.

Vs. 3 ἀλλ' ἵνα φανερωθῇ There is an ellipsis between ἀλλ' and ἵνα. See 11:52; 13:18; 14:31; 15:25; 18:28; 1 John 2:19; 2 Thess 3:9.

Vs. 4 Ἐμὲ δεῖ ἐργάζεσθαι (B.M.T. and T.R. reading) A reference to the fact of it being a Sabbath day, not mentioned until vs. 14. Comp. vs. 17. 'Six days in the week are too little to do deeds of mercy. My time is short, and I must work. The day closes in, and the night comes too soon.'

But observe how naturally these words flow. The Evangelist has not told us that it is the Sabbath day. He has the whole scene before him, and assumes that his readers have as well. He proceeds with the narrative accordingly. Comp. 9:9, 10.

Vs. 5 The day, the night. The time for working and the time for resting. This suggests another application of the image. The daytime—the light. 'I am the light of the world. My presence, my work, in the daytime, in the light.'

Vs. 6 The action is familiar and would be understood. There is a large collection of passages both from classical writers and rabbinical ones quoted at this point in Wettstein, showing that it was customary to anoint some eyes with saliva and clay. So Vespasian heals the blind man in Alexandria—Tacitus, *Hist.* iv.81. Alford has copied the false reference (iv.8) from Trench.

The rabbinical passages are especially interesting inasmuch as they discuss whether it is lawful to perform this process on a Sabbath day. One would almost infer that the discussion had arisen out of our Lord's action in the first instance. See Sabbath folio 10 col. 2, the discussion begins with R. Samuel.

But whatever they might have thought of the anointing with saliva, the making of clay would have been a violation of the Sabbath in their eyes. See John Lightfoot and Wettstein. Our Lord uses this common instrumentality, but uses it to work a great, a miraculous result.

Vs. 7 Σιλωάμ as in the LXX and Luke 13:4, and in Josephus frequently. In the Hebrew usually with the definite article—הַשִּׁלֹחַ. Aquila, Theodotion, Symach. have Σιλωά. The modern name is Silwan. Probably the same place as in Neh. iii.15—שֶׁלַח. See Buxtorf, p. 2412sq. As for the verbal form comp. Job 5:10; Ezek 36:4; one reference seems to use the term to refer to a field artificially irrigated.

The Situation Alford's statement is incorrect. The situation (unlike that with Bethesda) can hardly be considered doubtful. This place is frequently mentioned and described in Josephus. And the tradition is tolerably continuous. The place bears the same name now. At the north of the Tyropaeon valley, close to its juncture with the valley of Hinnom. Fed with a stream issuing somewhere from the heart of the rock of Jerusalem, within proximity of the Temple. Remember the libations at the Feast of the Tabernacle, and the Water Gate. So here.

We are talking about both a fountain and a pool. On the fountains, see Josephus; on the pool, see Neh 3:15. Its symbolism existed already. See 1) Isaiah 8:6 (just mentions 'the water'); comp. Ps. 46:4 and perhaps Is 33:21; 2) the libation of the Feast of Tabernacles. Our Lord has adopted these as a type of Himself, see 7:37. And doubtless this washing in Siloam was intended as a symbol of the healing water of Life. Rightly explained by the commentators on Isaiah 8. See Epiphanius, *Hom.* xxxv.3, p. 261 (Petan ?).

Hence the Evangelist sees a significance in the name which signifies 'sent.' On the passage's sense see Ewald, *Lehrbuch* sec. 156a. The Siloah, therefore properly called, seems not to be the pool but the streams that feed it or issue from it.

Ἀπεσταλμένος This refers here not to the man sent thither to be healed. That would be senseless, but to our Lord Himself as the messenger, the Sent One of the Father. Of this, the water of Siloam is a symbol, as we have seen before.

ἀποστέλλω In this Gospel at 3:17; 5:36, 38; 6:29, 57; 7:29; 8:42; 10:36; 11:42; 17:3, 8, 18, 21, 23, 25; 20:21; comp. Luke 4:18. The Messiah is called the Sent in rabbinical literature, in passages cited by Wettstein.

νίψαι εἰς A.V. 'go wash in the pool of Siloam.' This leaves a false impression. νίψαι—'wash your eyes'; 'wash off the clay.' See Trench, *New Testament Synon.* sec. 178 for εἰς meaning 'at.' See *Test. Twelve. Pat. Levi*, 9. Compare this to the relevant passages in Exodus LXX.

Vs. 11 ἀνέβλεψα There are two senses to this word: 1) to look up as in Matt 14:19 'to look up into heaven'; 2) to see again, recover sight, as in Matt 11:5. Here 'recovery of sight' is not strictly correct, but the expression is very intelligible. See Pausanias iv.12, p.310, quoted by Lücke.

Vs. 16 ὁ ἄνθρωπος 'this fellow' asserted contemptuously. See Mark 14:21; Luke 14:30, and so perhaps the words since consecrated in all Christian hearts. See John 19:5. In the proper order it becomes very emphatic οὐκ ἔστιν οὗτος παρὰ Θεοῦ ὁ ἄνθρωπος, א, B,D, etc. There is however no opposition of ἄνθρωπος and Θεός here, as some have suggested.

ἄλλοι Nicodemus, Joseph of Arimathea, perhaps Gamaliel.

ἄνθρωπος ἁμαρτωλός See Luke 7:34, ἄνθρωπος φάγος; Luke 19:21-22, ἄνθρωπος αὐστηρός; Acts 22:25, ἄνθρωπον Ῥωμαῖον. This is a Hebraism.

Vs. 17 ὅτι ἠνέῳξέν 'bearing of the fact that he opened' i.e. 'to explain his opening.' The same elliptical use of ὅτι is seen in 2:19 and 11:47.

Προφήτης ἐστίν comp. 6:14. Hitherto, the truth had only partially dawned on him. The further revelation only came afterwards, vss. 36-37.

Vs. 18 οἱ Ἰουδαῖοι St. John uses the word to signify the party opposed to Jesus. Here he has substituted the word for οἱ Φαρισαῖοι. The Pharisees are mixed, some opposed, some half-believing. So vss. 22-23 and again the 'Jews' sought to kill Him—5:16, 18; 7:1 etc. The mode of speaking in Rev 2:9; 3:9 is an earlier stage, but it is a stage on the same road.

αὐτοῦ τοῦ ἀναβλέψαντος A.V. wrong has 'of him.' That lad received his sight. Some texts leave out αὐτοῦ.

Vs. 21 ἡλικίαν ἔχει Just as we say 'to come of age' we say 'mature age.' The αὐτός from its position is emphatic. Ask *himself* (A.V. has 'ask him'). ἡλικίαν is 1) stature, or 2) age, this being measured by stature.

Vs. 22 ἀποσυνάγωγος comp. 16:2. Mentioning here an expression for a limited period or little repentance. Thirty days seems to have been the mildest form of this penalty. Comp. Luke 6:22, and see Trench, *Miracles*, p. 300 and references there.

Vs. 24 δὸς δόξαν τῷ Θεῷ· A.V. wrongly has 'give God the praise' which implies admitting the fact of a miracle. Rather it is a solemn prefatory injunction. See Josh 7:19; Exod 9:8 (quoted by Meyer); 1 Sam 6:5 (quoted by Godet). See especially Ewald p. 296. Speak not lies or blasphemies. Do not dishonor God.

ὁ ἄνθρωπος ἁμαρτωλός ἐστιν and therefore he can't have worked a miracle. In other words, they indirectly deny the fact. So he understands them, and replies accordingly.

Vs. 25 τυφλὸς ὢν ἄρτι βλέπω Not as the A.V. has it 'whereas I was blind,' but much more expressive 'being a blind man, now (at this moment) I see.' An oxymoron, a verbal paradox.

Vs. 27 καὶ οὐκ ἠκούσατε· 'And you did not hear, did not take it in.'

τί πάλιν θέλετε ἀκούειν 'Why do you wish me to repeat it a second time, so that the second time you may take it in?'

μὴ καὶ ὑμεῖς θέλετε αὐτοῦ μαθηταὶ γενέσθαι; There is a shrewd move in this. John Lightfoot says he asks them 'in gentle and persuasive terms' and that they answer 'ruggedly.' But this is not consistent with the μὴ καὶ ὑμεῖς comp. 6:67; 7:47, 52; 18:17, 25 and below vs. 40. They understood his irony, and resent it accordingly.

Vs. 30 ἐν τούτῳ γάρ Comp 4:37; 13:35; 15:8; 16:30; 1 John 2:3 etc.

ὑμεῖς οὐκ οἴδατε 'We the ruler, the leaders, the teachers of Israel.'

Vs. 34 ἐν ἁμαρτίαις σὺ etc. As their blindness showed. See the note by Alford.

Vs. 39 εἰς κρίμα ἐγὼ εἰς τὸν κόσμον τοῦτον There is a double idea here: 1) discrimination; 2) allotment of reward or punishment. There is no discernment at present between those who are blind and those who see, the one are mistaken for the other. But in Christ's judgment, the first shall be last and the last shall be first. This separation of the sheep from the goats, this winnowing of the chaff from the grain is Christ's work.

οἱ μὴ βλέποντες A double meaning as is so frequently the case in St. John's Gospel: 1) the physical, as in the case of the blind man; 2) the spiritual, as symbolized by the physical. Whether in service to Him to say 'thy sins are forgiven' or to say 'take up your bed and walk.'

THE GOOD SHEPHERD
AND HIS LOST SHEEP
(JOHN 10)

THE CONNECTION OF THIS CHAPTER with what has gone before is not very obvious, but it exists. The subject of the opening of the tenth chapter is the contrast between the true and false shepherds or guides. Thus τυφλοί (9:40) is the link of connection. The term 'blind' is the link, with the suppressed thought which may be supplied from Matt 15:14: τυφλοί εἰσιν ὁδηγοί τυφλῶν· τυφλὸς δὲ τυφλὸν ἐὰν ὁδηγῇ, ἀμφότεροι εἰς βόθυνον πεσοῦνται. Or Matt 23:16-26. Comp. Luke 6:39.

This is not the only place where St. John's narrative receives its explanation from the deeds or the words of our Lord as reported by the Synoptists. He frequently presupposes these. And this passage, with its repeated denunciations of the Pharisees (repeated as we find from St. Matthew) as blind *guides* seems to be assumed as known. This is, if we may say so, a commonplace of our Lord's teaching.

The image of the shepherd in Palestine is naturally very common. For the Old Testament see especially Jerm 23:1sq.; 31:10; Ezek 34; 37:24; Zech 11:4-17; 13:7; Ps 23:7sq.; 81:1sq. The point to be observed about all these passages is that there is a reference to the *one* good shepherd who was to displace all these bad ones. See Jer 33:5; Ezek 24:23; Zech 11:16. God himself in such passages is represented as the shepherd of his people. Again bear in mind the parable of the lost sheep in St. Matthew and St. Luke.

Vs. 1 διὰ τῆς θύρας What is meant by the door is explained in vs. 7. But how can the good leaders, the prophets, be said to have come through the door? We must remember here, as we must remember always, that our Lord's words here apply not only to the Word Incarnate, but also to the Word pre-Incarnate. The Word of God was from the beginning, and has inspired all the servants of God in all ages. They have entered the fold through Him as the door.

αὐλήν as e.g. in the *Odyssey* sec. 5, though there the reference is to swine. A sheep pen was built with high walls as protection against: 1) the weather; 2) the wild beasts; and 3) thieves.

ἀλλὰ ἀναβαίνων ἀλλαχόθεν The last word, either doctrinally or ecclesiastically approach the sheep, otherwise, he'll be making his own road.

κλέπτης ἐστὶν καὶ λῃστής The idea is: 1) κλέπτης, stealth; 2) λῃστής, violence and thus plunder. A thief is a 'robber' correctly translated here, but not so always, e.g. Matt 21:13, a den of thieves, correctly here, though later robbers in Jer 7:11. For λῃστής see John 18:40; Matt 27:16 δέσμιον ἐπίσημον (see Trench, *Syn.* sec. xliv. p. 176). For κλέπτης see John 12:6; so a thief in the night. The rabbis make the same distinction between these sorts of terms. See John Lightfoot here.

Vs. 2 ποιμήν a shepherd.

Vs. 3 ὁ θυρωρός i.e. when spiritually applied it is God (or the Spirit of God). See Acts 14:2 (a favorite metaphor of St. Peter); Col 4:3 (references selected from Alford). But we must remember that hitherto there is no spiritual application, at least no direct application, to Christ.

τὰ ἴδια πρόβατα there is a plain distinction here between τὰ πρόβατα and τὰ ἴδια πρόβατα. There are many inferior shepherds, many ministers, many preachers of the Gospel, each of whom has his own sheep, all included in the same αὐλή. The distinction of τὰ πρόβατα and τὰ ἴδια πρόβατα would not apply to Christ, as all the sheep in the αὐλή are His.

φωνεῖ κατ' ὄνομα i.e. spiritually applied, he appeals to them according to their several capacities, several tempers, several opportunities.[1] He has a distinct word to address to each.

ἐξάγει i.e. to pasture and to drink. Ps 23:2—'thou shalt feed me in a green pasture, and lead me by the waters of comfort.'

---

[1] By "tempers" here Lightfoot means temperaments, not emotional volatility or the lack thereof.

Vs. 4 ἐκβάλῃ More forceful than ἐξάγει (to lead out). A little pressure must be put upon the lostness, the unwillingness, the sluggishness. '*Curva trahit, quos virga regit, pars ultima pungit.*'

Vs. 5 ἀλλοτρίος A stranger, the false shepherd, the thief who tries to lead them.

ἀκολουθήσουσιν The correct reading.

Vs. 6 τὴν παροιμίαν a wayside, popular, trite saying. Herzel (?) recognizes as a πάροιμος. It is used of: 1) short pithy sentences, proverbs, as of Solomon; 2) more extended metaphors or figures which have a moral meaning, as here. In the latter case, παροιμία also differs from παραβολή, in that while the παραβολή put the image and the thing side by side, gives the story, and then applies it, the παροιμία the thing signified is contained implicitly but not explained by the speaker. Both are 'similitudes.' There is a distinct comparison. The most perfect instance, of the seed sown by the wayside, but the comparison is always brought out more or less previously in a parable, e.g. comparison with the Kingdom of Heaven (see St. Luke).

Our Lord's discussions in the other Gospels are, and are called, παραβολαί. The word παροιμία is not found in the Synoptics. In St. John as here and in John 15 they are, and are called παροιμία. Comp. 16:25, 29. Neither the name nor the long παραβολή occur in the Fourth Gospel. But the words are closely aligned and sometimes interchanged. They are both renderings of the same Hebrew word מָשָׁל, similitude. In Ezek 12:22 and 16:44 Symach. has παροιμία, but the LXX has παραβολή (see Trench, *Parables*, p. 65sq.), e.g. Solomon's proverbs in 1 Kngs 4:32 are called παραβολή comp. Luke 4:23. In Sirach 47:17 we have ἐν ᾠδαῖς καὶ παροιμίαις καὶ παραβολαῖς καὶ ἐν ἑρμηνείαις ἀπεθαύμασάν σε χῶραι. We do not know what the original Hebrew was.

Vs. 7 ἡ θύρα τῶν προβάτων The door of the sheep, and not the sheep only but also of the shepherds. See vss. 1, 2, 8. There is a twofold application to Jesus: 1) he is the door, but 2) he is also the good shepherd. This is like he is the victim, but also the priest. This is characteristic of Christianity, as distinguished from Buddhism or Islam. Jesus is at once the preacher of the Gospel and the subject of the Gospel. See Ignatius, *Phil.* 9.

Vs. 8 πάντες ὅσοι ἦλθον. πάντες ὅσοι over-rendered here by the A.V. 'all that come,' 'must come.' The translation is important—it refers to a particular coming. Two variant readings here: 1) omission of πάντες—Origen and others; 2) omission of πρὸ ἐμοῦ by very considerable authorities including א, Theb. Lat., Cureton Syr. The second certainly, the first due to a particular cause. On the use made of the text by the Gnostics e.g. Valentinius see Hippolytus, *Haer.* vi.35 (p. 194). On the Manicheans use of it, see Augustine and Theophylact; so recently writers of the Tübingen school. This is contrary to the language of the Gospel throughout—see 1:46; 3:14; 5:45 and reference to the prophets e.g. 12:38sq. and the constant authoritative quotations from the Old Testament. I will reserve consideration of its meaning until vss. 10, 11. The πρὸ ἐμοῦ is the first indication of his other application of his imagery where our Lord is no longer the door, but the good shepherd.

Vs. 9 δι᾽ ἐμοῦ ἐάν τις εἰσέλθῃ, σωθήσεται, καὶ εἰσελεύσεται καὶ ἐξελεύσεται καὶ νομὴν εὑρήσει. εἰσελεύσεται καὶ ἐξελεύσεται is perhaps a reference to Num 27:17 ὅστις ἐξελεύσεται πρὸ προσώπου αὐτῶν καὶ ὅστις εἰσελεύσεται πρὸ προσώπου αὐτῶν καὶ ὅστις ἐξάξει αὐτοὺς καὶ ὅστις εἰσάξει αὐτούς, καὶ οὐκ ἔσται ἡ συναγωγὴ Κυρίου ὡσεὶ πρόβατα οἷς οὐκ ἔστι ποιμήν.

νομὴν εὑρήσει see Ps 33:2. Implying safety, liberty, support. 'He shall feed us in a green pasture.' It is difficult to say whether it is the shepherd or the sheep intended in this sense. The passage in Numbers points to the former and so also the immediate context here in vss. 8, 10. Yet probably the sheep are meant.

Vss. 10-11 He is the Good Shepherd, whereas before him have been thieves and robbers. They have come only to kill and slay. There is a reference to the prophetic passages that observe, in the same order: 1) the bad shepherds who destroy and scatter the sheep; 2) the good shepherd who shall supplant the bad ones and shall feed the sheep. The good shepherd carries a distinctively messianic reference. See Jerm 23:1, 5; Ezek 24:1, 23; 37:24; Zech 11:7.

The πάντες ὅσοι πρὸ ἐμοῦ are these blind guides, these false teachers, the scribes and the Pharisees of whom it might truly be said that they came to kill and to plunder. He is also referring to false teachers of false messianic ideas. See Matt 23:34; Mark 12:40. The πάντες must be limited by the sphere of vision which is contemplated in the context.

θύσῃ 'slay' a reference again to the prophetic imagery Ezek 34:3; Zech 11:17.

περισσὸν ἔχωσιν περισσόν is used substantively. περισσόν with αὐτῷ, as e.g. Xenophon, *Anab.* vii.6.31. As in ἐκ περισσόν.

ὁ ποιμὴν ὁ καλός Not the ἀγαθός 'the beneficent,' the good, the beautiful, the ideal. A reference to the prophetic passages. As appears from the emphasis and the repetition, *the* shepherd, *the* good one. Heb 13:20 where the effect is the same τὸν ποιμένα τῶν προβάτων τὸν μέγαν.

Vs. 11 τὴν ψυχὴν αὐτοῦ τίθησιν prophetic, layeth down.

Vs. 12 ὁ μισθωτός He who, for selfish ends, tends the sheep, will for selfish ends desert them. He is not a shepherd.

τὸν λύκον the enemy to the truth, to God, e.g. a persecutor of the faith, or a teacher of wrong (moral or doctrinal), not as Alford. See Matt 10:16 (Luke 10:3); comp. Acts 20:29. For the image see 1 Sam 17:34; Amos 3:12; Is 31:4; Jer 5:6. No passage in itself is quoted, but obviously things are taken from them. See also the rabbinical quotations in John Lightfoot, II, p. 576; how far is a minder, a keeper, honor bound to watch the flock, etc.

Vs. 15 A.V. has 'As the Father knoweth me, even so, know I the Father, and I lay down my life for the sheep.' This is wrong.

καθὼς γινώσκει 'just as the Father knows me, and I know the Father. . . .' Comp. 15:10; 17:21. The union of the believer with Christ is at once a consequence of, and a reproduction of the union of Christ with the Father.

Vs. 16 καὶ ἄλλα πρόβατα Remember St. John's position at Ephesus, and the comprehension of the Gentiles elsewhere in this Gospel. See 7:35 and 12:20 (comp. 11:51). It is worth remarking that Ἕλλην does not occur in the other Gospels, not even in St. Luke (though we have Ἑλληνίς in St. Mark 7:26).

ἔχω '*Hoc verbum habet magnum potestatem*'—Bengel.

αὐλῆς See Alford's note: 'Observe that they are not in these folds, but scattered, see xi.52.' The idea is in Bengel and Meyer.

ἀγαγεῖν 'lead' not 'bring.'

γενήσεται See Ezek 34:11sq. 'There shall come to pass . . .' i.e. this slate of things, this proverb 'One flock, One Shepherd.' The fulfillment of the Messianic prophecy in Ezek 34:23. See Bengel. Comp. Ephes 4:4-6 to εἰς ποιμήν here. A.V. has 'one fold' confusing the term used here with αὐλή. The Stoics used a similar image—see Plutarch, *Moral.* p. 439 (*de Alex.* i.6). See Meyer on this quote.

Vs. 17 ἵνα πάλιν λάβω i.e. to earn the victory by the humiliation. Alford points to the διό in Phil 2:8sqq.

Vs. 18 ἀπ᾽ ἐμαυτοῦ as 5:19; 16:13 etc. The ἀπ᾽ ἐμαυτοῦ is not to be taken in the same sense as ἀπ' ἐμέ, as the apparent parallelism of the clauses might suggest.

τὴν ἐντολήν This is the complemental aspect to the ἐξουσία.

Vs. 20 Δαιμόνιον ἔχει See 7:20 and 8:48.

Vs. 22 τὰ ἐγκαίνια (following T.R., B.M.T.) This word and its modifiers are used in the LXX of: 1) the rededication of the first Temple by Solomon (1 Kngs 8:64; 2 Chron 7:5, 9); and 2) the dedication of the second Temple under Ezra (Ezra 4:16, 17); 3) the purification and dedication of the altar and Temple after the pollution by Antiochus Epiphanes in 167 B.C. It is to this last ἐγκαίνια that this text refers. This was kept as an annual Festival. See 1 Macc 4:36sqq. (54-59). There is a full description of the initiation of this Festival, see especially 2 Macc 10:5. See Josephus, *Ant.* xii.7.7. Chislev, Nov./ Dec. coinciding more often with December. There is no reference to the discourse that follows, and the ceremonial of the Festival.

ἐν τοῖς Ἱεροσολύμοις—The Dedication (unlike the three great festivals) might (as would appear from the passages given in John Lightfoot) be celebrated elsewhere besides Jerusalem, hence the additions. But do these passages cited by John Lightfoot refer to the time before the destruction of Jerusalem? If not the celebration might be no different than those of the other festivals, which since the destruction it has been the custom to hold elsewhere.

Between Tabernacles and Dedication is an interval of two months. Where was our Lord meanwhile? Probably in Jerusalem and its neighborhood. The one incident related as occurring between the two is the healing of the man born blind in John 9. At first sight, we might suppose that this took place at or immediately after the Feast of Tabernacles. There is however no expressions in the narrative that require or suggest this. And the connection of subject in 10:26sq. seems to bring it close upon the Feast of the Dedication. But this will depend much on the rejection or retention of καθὼς εἶπον ὑμῖν.

χειμὼν ἦν as it would be at the Feast of the Dedication. This is added however to explain how our Lord should be walking in Solomon's Porch. Solomon's Porch is described in Josephus, *Ant.* xx.9.7. It was a part of Solomon's original construction, involving enormous stones. It was left to the last and was not ever repaired or completed. Its aspect is noticeable in connection with χειμών.

Vs. 24 τὴν ψυχὴν ἡμῶν αἴρεις This last word in the phrase may be used of any emotion—fear, uncertainty, hope, etc. which disturbs the calm, the repose of the soul which uplifts it. See references in Meyer.

Vs. 25 εἶπον ὑμῖν. καθώς εἶπον ὑμῖν if genuine may be explained in two ways: 1) referring to utterances such as found in vss. 3, 14. I told you implicitly; 2) take καθώς εἶπον ὑμῖν with what follows. Comp. 7:38; 13:33. The latter explanation is much better. The reading however is more than questionable. The omission is support by ℵ, B, L, K, M*, Vulg., Memph., Theb., Origen, i.e. better authorities than those to retain it. But see Tregelles. Both the omission and the insertion can be explained, and about equally well. This being so, the authority of the oldest copies must prevail.

Vs. 29 The correct reading is ὁ Πατήρ μου ὃ δέδωκέν μοι πάντων μεῖζόν ἐστιν. This is to be retained for two reasons: 1) as being better supported by ℵ, A, B, Latt. Memph. Goth.; 2) as being slightly harder, and so more likely to be altered.

Vs. 30 ἕν ἐσμεν See Hippolytus, c. *Noet.* 7; see other references in Tregelles.

Vs. 31 πάλιν λίθους as they had done before at the Feast of the Tabernacles, 7:59. Does Ἐβάστασαν here imply that they got there from a distance, from the part of the Temple that was being rebuilt?

Vs. 34 ἐν τῷ νόμῳ ὑμῶν See Ps 82:6. See Perowne on this passage.

Vs. 35 ὁ λόγος τοῦ Θεοῦ ἐγένετο The last word has a certain emphasis, at least to the Evangelist himself. We can scarcely doubt that in the Evangelist's mind the contrast was present between those to whom the Word of God came, and He himself who is the Word of God.

λυθῆναι 'explained away,' 'set at nought,' 'made light of,' 'got rid of.' See Matt 5:19; John 5:18; 7:23 (see Meyer).

Vs. 36 Υἱὸς τοῦ Θεοῦ See the expression in Ps 82:6. 'I have said, you are gods, and you are all children of the Most High.'

Vs. 38 καὶ γινώσκητε Two v.l. 1) καὶ πιστεύσητε A, Δ, 69, Vulg., Peshit., Goth. and [al]so ℵ except it has the present tense of the verb 'believe'; 2) omit καὶ γινώσκητε D, A, B, C, Tertull., Cyprian. 'That you may discern and continue to discern. . . .' Meyer quotes Plato, *Leg.* 8, p. 849B.

Vs. 40 Καὶ ἀπῆλθεν πάλιν See Matt 19:1; Mark 10:1sq.

ἦν Ἰωάνης τὸ πρῶτον βαπτίζων It is a question whether this refers to: 1) Beltabara (or Beltany) referred to in 1:29 or; 2) to an earlier place of baptizing mentioned previously, near Jericho. If St. John wrote of Beltabara (or Beltany), comp. Matt 3:5; Mark 1:5. The latter seems more probable, see Smith's *Dictionary* I, p. 1127.

Vs. 41 Ἰωάνης μὲν σημεῖον ἐποίησεν οὐδέν etc. The scene reminds them of the Baptist.

The Raising of Lazarus and
the Plotting of the Foes
(John 11)

Vs. 1 Λάζαρος, a contraction of Ελεάζαρος. This contraction is found frequently in the Talmud, see Smith's *Dictionary* III, p. 78. The article by E.H.P is full of the wildest suggestions. He was less well known than Mary and Martha. Perhaps a younger brother.

ἀπὸ Βηθανίας etc. Bethany i.e. 'house of dates' like Bethphage, 'olives.' On the palm branches, [see] 12:13. It is now called El Azariyeh. The words ἐκ τῆς κώμης Μαρίας etc. are added to distinguish this village from the one in 1:29.

ἀπό, ἐκ perhaps the simple desire to distinguish the place he came from accounts for the change of prepositions.

It would appear that Martha was the elder sister, but Mary the more famous in the Church. 1) Of Martha, see vs. 5, τὴν Μάρθαν καὶ τὴν ἀδελφὴν αὐτῆς; vs. 19; 12:2; Luke 10:38.; 2) Mary's greater fame may explain the prominence of Mary's name here, comp. Matt 26:13; Mark 14:9. On the character of the two sisters see the discussion in the Introduction above on the 'Internal Evidence.'

Vs. 2 ἦν δὲ Μαριὰμ ἡ ἀλείψασα τὸν Κύριον μύρῳ St. John himself afterwards relates the incident, see 12:2. But here he assumes his readers know it already. This accords with the language of the other Evangelists— Matt 26:13; Mark 14:9. The forms Μαριὰμ and Μαρία seem to be used indifferently by St. John. Hence the reading is doubtful.[1]

---

[1] It is notable that Lightfoot passes over v. 3 in silence even though it is the only place in the Fourth Gospel where a personal name is given to "the one whom Jesus loved."

Vs. 4 οὐκ ἔστιν πρὸς θάνατον Not to be taken in its *prima facie* meaning. For a parallel see above on 78.

τῆς δόξης τοῦ Θεοῦ For the glory of the Son is the glory of the Father, see 13:3sq.; 14:13; 17:1sq.

Vs. 5 ἠγάπα The notice seems to be interjected here quite as much to correct any misunderstanding (as though his remaining case of indifference), as to explain vs. 11. On ἀγαπᾶν and φίλειν, see Trench *New Testament Synonyms*, p. 45. D substitutes ἐφίλει here, doubtless for uniformity. This shows that *the change of word is not without a meaning*.

Vs. 6 τότε μέν In the time *indeed*. The μέν is added to keep the attention on the alert for some account which showed that Jesus ἠγάπα them.

Vs. 7 εἰς τὴν Ἰουδαίαν πάλιν He was in Peraea.

Vs. 8 νῦν Here it means 'just now, only the other day.'

Vs. 9 'There is a proper time for working. He that avails himself of this time performs his task faithfully, successfully. The daylight is for work, and he avails Himself of this work.' Comp. ix.4.

Οὐχὶ δώδεκα ὧραί εἰσιν τῆς ἡμέρας i.e. twelve hours of daylight. A rough reckoning, though at this time of the year (the vernal equinox) it would be very nearly true. Alford's note is quite beside the point. See 19:14.

τὸ φῶς τοῦ κόσμου τούτου βλέπει i.e. the sunlight, light in its primary physical sense. The words τοῦ κόσμου τούτου are added to show that our Lord is here using a *figure*, and to suggest the spiritual and moral application. As in the natural world, so in the spiritual world. The word τούτου suggests the analogy.

Vs. 10 But if instead of following God's Spirit, instead of choosing God's times, man will choose his own. Instead of walking in the daylight, he will walk at night, then his work must be a failure, he must be brought to ruin.

ὅτι τὸ φῶς οὐκ ἔστιν ἐν αὐτῷ If the figure had still been preserved, the words should here run τὸ φῶς and βλέπει or words to the same effect. But the type, the figure, has gradually dissolved into the thing typified. For the physical light, the moral light has been substituted. And this spiritual light is an internal light. 'The light of the gods is the eye' (quoted by Alford). See Matt 6:22.

Vs. 11 ἐξυπνίσω On this word see Lobeck, *Phrygn.* p. 224.

Vs. 12 σωθήσεται Aramaic.

Vs. 13 εἰρήκει 'had spoken' not as A.V.

Vs. 16 Θωμᾶς On his character, see in the Introduction above on 'The Internal Evidence.' On his name, see my *Galatians*, p. 257 (2nd ed., 251 1rst). See also Clement, *Hom.* ii.1. The writer did not seem to know that Thomas = Didymus.

Vs. 17 τέσσαρας... ἡμέρας Supposing that Jesus were at the place suggested above (see 10:40) i.e. in the neighborhood of the Jordan, where the river is the least distance from Jerusalem, one day's journey would be sufficient to bring him to Bethany. Lazarus therefore must have died (see vs. 6) on the same day when the message was dispatched, and been buried the same evening.

Vs. 18 ἀπὸ σταδίων δεκαπέντε See my notes on Acts 1:12.[2]

ἦν δὲ Βηθανία Comp. 3:23; 4:6; 18:1; 19:41, 42. See Kinglaki's(?) *Crume.* III, pp. 38, 117, 118, 122, 286. This is the narrative of a person who was an eye-witness of the events he relates, and who writes not half a century later, but within a very few years of the occurrence. No inference therefore can be safely drawn. On the other hand, the present is used in 4:11 and 5:2 and the present and past are used together in 4:6, 11. Comp. Luke 4:29 ᾠκοδόμητο. Therefore, it is not strictly true that St. John alone uses this mode of speaking (as Alford states).

Vs. 19 πρὸς τὰς περί (T.R. and B.M.T., A) This reading, it seems, must be adopted, as it's not likely to have been substituted for the simpler one. On the other hand πρὸς τὴν Μάρθαν καὶ Μαριάμ is better supported by ℵ, B, C, L, X, Peshit., Memph, Theb., Goth., Arm. The πρὸς τὰς περί reading refers to Mary, Martha, and the mourners with them. These are the friends of the family, though sometimes hired mourners were employed (Jer 9:7; Amos v.16). On the rationale for seven days of mourning see Smith's *Dictionary* s.v. on 'Mourning' and John Lightfoot here.

Vs. 20 On the contrast of the demeanor of the two sisters see Luke 10:39; John 12:2, 3.

Vs. 22 αἰτήσῃ The feebleness and inadequacy of the confession is shown not only in the whole tenor of the sentence but in this individual word. See Trench, *New Testament Synon.* sec. xl, p. 161.

---

[2]See J. B. Lightfoot, *The Acts of the Apostles: A Newly Discovered Commentary*, ed. Ben Witherington III and Todd D. Still, assisted by Jeanette M. Hagen, The Lightfoot Legacy Set 1 (Downers Grove, IL: IVP Academic, 2014), p. 78.

Vs. 23 Ἀναστήσεται ὁ ἀδελφός σου A reproof is implied in our Lord's answer. He does not say αἰτήσω (or for that matter even ερωτήσω) τόν Θεόν etc. but ἀναστήσεται . . .

Vs. 25 ἡ ἀνάστασις καὶ ἡ ζωή both the quickening power and the sustaining power. 'I bring to life and I preserve in life.' The two words correspond to the two claims that follow. The words of our Lord imply physical death and physical life (in the first instance) i.e. they refer to the case of Lazarus, but they refer secondarily and chiefly to the moral life and death.

Vs. 27 πεπίστευκα 'have accepted the belief once for all.' See Acts 11:17; 14:23; 1 Cor 15:2; (Rom 13:11) etc.

ὁ εἰς τὸν κόσμον ἐρχόμενος A title of Messiah like ὁ ἀπεστόμενος. E.g. Matt 11:13; and frequently especially in St. John.

Vs. 28 λάθρᾳ εἰποῦσα It might possibly have been 'for fear of the Jews,' and if so, as Alford says, 'their fears were realized' (vs. 46). But this mode of communication was natural under the circumstances without such a motive. He was a dear friend, a good master with two sisters, but he was not living, and all were present to see what happened.

Vs. 30 He would approach by the long and narrow ascent from Jericho, the same that we find in the parable of the Good Samaritan. See Stanley, *S+P*, p. 416. Perhaps he sat down to rest or he was unwilling that his presence should be widely known, before the miracle was wrought.

Vs. 31 ὑπάγει εἰς τὸ μνημεῖον With us, it might be the spontaneous outburst of a passionate affection for the lost one, but with the Jews and with Jewish women especially it was a common custom, almost a necessary ceremonial (as it is now in the East) to go from time to time and mourn at the grave. See *Smith's Dictionary* II s.v. 'Mourning,' p. 437. See the references to the 'Arabian night'; see also Steph. *Thess.*

Vs. 33 ἐνεβριμήσατο 'To chide,' properly of horses chomping at the bit. See Aeschylus, *Sept.* 461. Hence in the New Testament Matt 9:30; Mark 1:43; 14:6, always with the idea of suppression, prohibition.

τῷ πνεύματι in spirit, with the spirit, i.e. within himself as in vs. 38. Suppressing the inner conflict. See Gundert, *Stud. und Krit.* 1852, pp. 260-69. Comp. Mark 8:12; Luke 10:21; John 13:21.

ἐτάραξεν A gesture denoting the effort to suppress his feelings.

Vs. 37 Said in mockery? See vs. 46. But there is no idea of rebuke in ἐμβριμώμενος in vs. 38.

Vs. 38 ἦν δὲ σπήλαιον, καὶ λίθος ἐπέκειτο ἐπ' αὐτῷ There were tombs of two kinds: 1) sunk in the ground, Luke 11:44; 2) caves, as here. Comp. Mark 15:46 (Matt. xxvii.60)—καὶ προσεκύλισεν λίθον ἐπὶ τὴν θύραν τοῦ μνημείου. See Mark 16:3, 4 (Luke 24:2). See Buxtorf s.v., Smith's *Dictionary* s.v. 'Burial.'

Vs. 39 τεταρταῖος γάρ ἐστιν 'He is in his fourth day' i.e. since his burial, i.e. four days dead. See Xenophon, *Anab.* vi.4.9. There may be a reference to the rabbinical belief (quoted by Meyer) that the soul hovered about the corpse for three days only, and then left when corruption began. See the passages in John Lightfoot, and Wettstein.

Vs. 41 ἤκουσάς μου 'thou heedest me' foreknowing and foretelling the result. Not 'will hear' or 'thou hearest' but 'thou heedest.'

Vs. 44 κειρίαις Only here in the New Testament. In the LXX once only— Prov. 7:16, where it is used of a quilt on a couch, as generally in classical sources.

σουδαρίῳ περιεδέδετο a kerchief. Comp. 19:40 and 20:7. On σουδαρίῳ adopted as a rabbinical word see Buxtorf, p.1442; Lenz, II, p. 149. Is it the word used in Nicidian (?) *Tulum.* xvi.2?

Vs. 45 οἱ ἐλθόντες πρὸς τὴν Μαριάμ as she was the most afflicted mourner.

Vs. 47 οἱ ἀρχιερεῖς καὶ οἱ Φαρισαῖοι See on them in the Introduction above under the heading 'Internal Evidence.'

Τί ποιοῦμεν What are we about? ὅτι to be connected with these two words as in 2:19; 9:17.

Vs. 48 οὕτως As he is, comp. John 4:6; 13:25 (v.l. probably correct).

καὶ ἐλεύσονται οἱ Ῥωμαῖοι i.e. they will seize the occasion of the tumult thus excited to destroy our national existence.

τὸν τόπον Perhaps the city generally, but with a special reference to the Temple.

τὸ ἔθνος our national existence.

Vs. 49 Καϊάφας on his relationship to Annas see Introduction, 'Internal Evidence,' above, and also on the phrase Ὑμεῖς οὐκ οἴδατε οὐδέν.

Vs. 50 λογίζεσθε ℵ, A, B, D, Origen. Doubtless therefore the right reading.

τὸ ἔθνος the national and political term; λαός = theocratic term. On the latter see Acts 4:25; Rom 9:26. See also Acts 15:14. So vs. 52. St. John substitutes ἔθνος for λαός because 'the people' is no longer the Jewish nation. Comp. 1 Pet 2:10.

Vs. 52 τὰ τέκνα τοῦ Θεοῦ τὰ διεσκορπισμένα They also belong to the people, though not to the nation, and not to *the people* as Caiaphas used the term. Comp. 10:16. For the Old Testament analogy, see Ezek 34:11, 12, 13.

εἰς τὴν χώραν not the country as opposed to the city, the metropolis. See vs. 55. Rather a region ἐγγὺς τῆς ἐρήμου.

Ἐφραίμ See the Introduction above 'Internal Evidence' section.

Vs. 55 τὸ πάσχα τῶν Ἰουδαίων 2:13; 6:4; 11:55 i.e. in every place where it is not distinctly defined by the context. St. John must distinguish it from the Christian πάσχα which he and his Asiatic disciples kept.

ἵνα ἁγνίσωσιν ἑαυτούς See 2 Chron 30:17sq. Rosh Hashannah folio 16.2. R. Issac says, 'Every man is bound to purify himself for the Feast.' Part of the ceremonial was washing and scrubbing themselves (quoted by John Lightfoot). See Mold.(?). Katon. fol. 13.1. Among those who are required to purify themselves are enumerated such as 'come from a heathen country.' The near impossibility of avoiding contact with heathen in any other place than Jerusalem and its neighborhood would lead the more scrupulous to repair thither in time.

An Annoying Anointing
(John 12)

The same incident is recorded in Matt 26:6-13; Mark 14:3-9. Whatever may be the real or apparent contradiction as regards time, the narrative so closely resembles that of St. John that we must suppose them to be the same.

There is another anointing in Luke 7:36. On the same grounds on which we are obliged to accept the identity of the narrative in the former case, we are obliged to reject it in the latter case. The place and time are different, the woman is different (here a faithful and devout disciple, in Luke 7 a sinner), the host is different (here a leper, there a Pharisee), the objection itself is different (there on the waste of a pound of nard, wasting money, but in Luke 7, it is that the woman would defile our Lord with her touch). Furthermore, bearing the point of the parallel must be considered in evidence when comparing Luke 7 with these other narratives. And lastly as the objection is different, so also is the answer. Here our Lord replies with reference to His burial, there with a parable about the debtors.

Anointing must have been common (see Beeler's *Clement of Rome* pp. 71, 75, 79, 111). It is the fact of Mary's prodigality, the costliness of her gift, which is brought into prominence here. In St. Luke's narrative it is not the act of the woman but the sufferance of the Lord that is remarkable. Thus, these are two different anointings. But what of the name Simon, the name of the person in whose presence the Lord was anointed? This has been alleged to show that we have two different versions of the same story. And even some who consider the differences striking, think that the name has crept into St. Luke's account from some confusion.

But the name Simon is extremely common, the name of the person in whose house he was anointed (as common as the name John with ourselves). For example, Josephus (*Ant.* 38) mentions a Simon the Pharisee in the same sentence he mentions another Simon. Simon Peter is a fellow disciple of Simon the Zealot, Peter refutes Simon Magus, and lodges at the house of Simon the Tanner. There are *eight people of this name besides Simon Peter (10 counting the two Symeons) just in the New Testament.*

COMPARISON OF ST. JOHN'S ACCOUNT WITH THAT IN MATTHEW AND MARK

The time. πρὸ ἓξ ἡμερῶν τοῦ πάσχα (John 12:1), six days before the Passover. St. John's chronological notice, as usual, is precise, not so those of the Synoptic Evangelists e.g. Matt 26:2, 6—after two days and the Ἰησοῦ γενομένου ἐν Βηθανίᾳ etc. (vs. 6), but there is no suggestion that the sequence is chronological. The events are suggested by our Lord's declaration that 'after two days the Son of Man is betrayed.' This suggests to the Evangelist to relate: 1) that at that time the chief priests etc. conspired against Him, and 2) that Jesus was anointed before and for his burial (Alford's idea that there may have been a reference in the original account to Judas' part). In St. Mark's narrative the events follow in the same order, but the links of connection are different. It is possible that he did not know that this was the chronological order. This is in accordance with an account given not by an eyewitness or an Apostle but a close disciple of an Apostle. So Papias in Eusebius, *Hist. Eccles.* iii.39.13sqq. This is given on the authority of John the Elder. Whether John the Elder was John the Apostle or not, it may be regarded as substantially the testimony of John the Apostle. I have already remarked that this notice in Eusebius compares and contrasts St. John with St. Mark.

Now this exactly agrees with the panorama here. While the chronology is different, the coincidence of language and fact is striking e.g. vs. 3, νάρδου πιστικῆς πολυτίμου; vs. 5, τριακοσίων δηναρίων, whereas St. Matthew has simply πολλοῦ (26:9). So again in a former narrative compare John 6:7 with Mark 6:37.

The house and the entertainers. St. John has ἐποίησαν οὖν αὐτῷ δεῖπνον ἐκεῖ. In St. Matthew and St. Mark the meal is said to take place in the house of Simon the leper. There is no contradiction here. There is nothing (as some have assumed) implying that it took place in the house of the two sisters or was given by them. To my mind ἐποίησαν ('they made') is impersonal and excludes this idea, for Mary, Martha, and Lazarus are not mentioned until afterwards. It would be at least a strange mode of expression if this were the meaning. Some have supposed that Simon was the father, or the husband of Mary (see Smith's *Dictionary* s.v. 'Lazarus,' 'Mary Magdalene' etc.). There is nothing in the narrative to indicate this. Lazarus appears to be one of the guests. Martha is just the sort of person to make herself useful anywhere. We have often and again seen the same ourselves, and in Palestine where social conventions were less tyrannous, such a part might well be taken by one who was not even a member of the family. I should gather from ἐποίησαν that it was a feast given by several of the villagers who would thus do the feast for Lazarus and friends.

The persons. We have the usual particularity of St. John as e.g. John 6:5, 7, 8 or again John 18:10, 11, so here Mary, Judas. The common idea representing Mary Magadalene here arises from two combinations: 1) Luke 7:36sqq. with Luke 8:1-3. Everything is against this combination: a) the form of the narrative; b) the description of Mary Magadalene in Luke 8, her association with other women, the description of the malady; 2) the identification of the anointing in Luke 7 with the one in John 7 and parallels. We thus get a Mary as an anointer. But, a) we have shown that the narratives are quite different, and b) neither Luke (10:38-42) nor St. John is aware that Mary Magdalene and Mary of Bethany are the same person. They would not have so spoken, had they intended to suggest that Mary Magadalene = Mary of Bethany. See Prescott, *Journal of Sacred Literature* (Oct.) 1867, p. 123, and Plumptre in Smith's *Dictionary* s.v. (though in the Lazarus article he dallies with the idea).

[THE MANUSCRIPT ON THE FOURTH GOSPEL BREAKS OFF HERE. (BW3)]

Appendix A

EXTERNAL EVIDENCE
FOR THE AUTHENTICITY OF
THE FOURTH GOSPEL

This appendix, originally transcribed from Lightfoot's lecture notes, was first published in the posthumous volume titled Biblical Essays *(London: Macmillan, 1904). The lecture-like nature of the material will be evident in what follows with the references to this academic term or that. This study was reprinted in 1979 by Baker Books, but has since passed out of print again. It presently appears on the Project Canterbury website (anglicanhistory.org) under the heading of Lightfoot's name. However, as the website indicates, it is no longer in print. We are pleased that InterVarsity Press has once again made it available. (BW3)*

THE GENUINENESS OF ST. JOHN'S GOSPEL is the centre of the position of those who uphold the historical truth of the record of our Lord Jesus Christ given us in the New Testament. Hence the attacks of the opponents of revealed religion are concentrated upon it. So long however as it holds its ground, these assaults must inevitably prove ineffective. The assailants are of two kinds: (1) those who deny the miraculous element in Christianity—Rationalists, (2) those who deny the distinctive character of Christian doctrine—Unitarians. The Gospel confronts both. It relates the most stupendous miracle in the history of our Lord (short of the Incarnation and the Resurrection), the raising of Lazarus. Again, it enunciates in the most express terms the Divinity, the Deity, of our Lord. And yet at the same time it professes to have been written by the one man, of all others, who had the greatest opportunities of knowing the truth. The testimony of St. Paul might conceivably be set aside, as of one who was not an eye-witness. But here we have, not an ἐκτρῶμα (1 Cor 15:8), not a personal disciple merely, not one of the Twelve only, but the one of the Twelve—the Apostle who leaned on his Master's bosom, who stood by his Master's cross, who entered his Master's empty grave. If therefore the claim of this Gospel to be the work of John the son of Zebedee be true, if in other words the Fourth Gospel be genuine, the most formidable, not to say an insuperable, obstacle stands in the way of both classes of antagonists. Hence the persistence and the ingenuity of the attacks; and hence also the necessity of a thoroughness in the defence. No apology therefore is needed, if the subject should seem dry and uninviting.

And details too are necessary. For the nature of the proof is cumulative. Some points which I shall have to urge may seem weak. The allusions to the Gospel in many cases are uncertain or anonymous. But they must be taken *pro tanto*. To borrow a mechanical simile, evidence for the authenticity of a document is not like a chain, where the strength of the whole is the strength of its weakest link. It is like the supports of a building, where the strength is in the aggregate. One pillar may be weak, or may fall; but the superstructure will still remain, for each instance is independent of the others.

Consequently, considerable mental effort is necessary in order to keep in view all the elements of a cumulative proof. We are apt to concentrate our attention on that which is last, or that which is exceptional. If then the last argument stated is weak, or if anywhere there is one argument exceptionally weak, we may leap to the conclusion that the whole is weak. This is manifestly a false mode of arguing, and we must constantly be on our guard against its subtle influence.

Hence the necessity of keeping the whole in view. We shall be occupied during the present term with the external evidence. But the external evidence is not all. And in summing up in our own minds the results that we shall obtain, we must not forget what lies beyond—what will occupy us probably next term—the reinforcement of the internal evidence. For the present however we shall confine ourselves to the former. And we cannot help being struck at the outset by the inadequacy of treatment which the question has met with in the prolegomena of the majority of commentators. An allusion to Theophilus, to Irenaeus, to Eusebius, an apology, somewhat lame, for the silence of Papias, and the whole subject is briefly and summarily dismissed. Now the injury done to the cause of revealed truth by this method of treatment is very serious, and has resulted in an undue disparagement of the external evidence for the Fourth Gospel.

On this point I cannot do better than quote so temperate and judicious a writer as Mr. Sanday, who, in his introduction to his work on *The Authorship and Historical Character of the Fourth Gospel*, when stating his reasons for confining himself to the internal evidence, writes as follows:

> Several reasons seem to make this limitation of treatment desirable. The subject of the external evidence has been pretty well fought out. The opposing parties are probably as near to an agreement as they ever will be. It will hardly be an unfair statement of the case for those who reject the Johannean authorship of the Gospel to say that the external evidence is compatible with that supposition. And on the other hand, we may equally say for those who accept the Johannean authorship, that the external evidence would not be sufficient alone to prove it. As it at present stands, the controversy may be regarded as drawn; and it is not likely that the position of parties will be materially altered (p. 3).

Now I hope to show that there is no deficiency of testimony (considering the nature of the subject), that on the contrary there is a vast body of evidence of various kinds, which cannot be set aside; that the result is a very powerful argument in favor of the genuineness; and that therefore, when we enter upon the question of internal evidence, we shall enter upon it with a very strong weight of evidence in support of St. John's authorship, which can only be counterbalanced by powerful considerations on the other side.

But, before commencing the investigation, let us first see what is the nature of the antagonism with which we have to deal. The history of the controversy may be seen in Bleek, *Beitrage zur Evangelien-Kritik* (1846). Briefly stated, the position of affairs is this. The universal reception of the Gospel as the work of St. John (with the exception of an obscure sect, the Alogi) up to the close of the last century has been assailed since the early

years of the present century by a series of writers, who unite in denying the
Johannine authorship, and place the date somewhere in the middle or latter
half of the second century.

I give the names of the principal exponents of the new view, with the
dates which they respectively assign for the authorship :—Bretschneider,
Probabilia de Evangelii et Epistolarum Joannis Apostoli indole et origine
(Leipzig 1820). He expressed himself vaguely as to the date, but apparently
placed it at the beginning or middle of the second century. After two years,
in the preface to his *Handbuch der Dogmatik* (1822), he withdrew his conclusions, and declared his conviction that the Johannine authorship was finally
established. Lutzelberger, *Die kirchliche Tradition über den Apostel Johannes
und seine Schriften in ihrer Grundlosigkeit nachgewiesen* (Leipzig 1840). He
considers that the Gospel was written near Edessa, about 135–140. Baur first
expressed his views on the Johannine question in the *Theologische Jahrbucher* (Tübingen 1844). He fixes the date somewhere about 160–170, and
this is the view of the older Tubingen School. Hilgenfeld, *Das Evangelium
und die Briefe Johannis nach ihrem Lehrbegriff* (1849). He considers that the
Fourth Gospel took its rise in the middle of the second century owing to the
prevalence of the Valentinian Gnosis. Scholten, professor at Leyden, and
head of the modern Dutch negative school, in his work entitled *Het Evan-
gelie naar Johannes* (1864–6) places the writing of the Fourth Gospel in 150,
but considers that it was interpolated subsequently. In a later work *De oudste
getuigenissen* (1867) he throws the date back later still to 170. Tayler, J. J. *An
attempt to ascertain the character of the Fourth Gospel, especially in its relation to the Three First* (London 1867). In reading this work we cannot fail
to be struck with its evident sincerity; at the same time it exhibits singular
deficiency in the enumeration of facts, and looseness in the treatment of
them. Tayler's conclusion is that the Fourth Gospel was written after 135 and
before 163 (p. 151). And yet (p. 155) he suggests that 'John the Presbyter' is the
author of the book—John the Presbyter, of whom we only know that he was
a personal disciple of our Lord. Keim, *Geschichte Jesu von Nazara* (1867)
ascribes the Fourth Gospel to the reign of Trajan, A.D. 98–117. Renan in the
first edition of his *Vie de Jesus* (1863) considers that our Fourth Gospel is
based upon the genuine work of St. John, but edited by his disciples at the
end of the first century. M. Renan's view has fluctuated in subsequent edi-

tions of his book. In reviewing this list of writers, we cannot fail to be struck with two facts: (1) the variety of their opinions; (2) their gradual retrogression from the extreme position taken up at first. The pressure of facts has compelled them to abandon one position after another, and to approximate more and more closely to the traditional view.

I. *The Churches of Asia Minor.* Unless we are prepared to reject without a hearing all the traditions of Christianity, we cannot refuse to believe that the latest years of the Apostle St. John were spent in the Roman province of Asia and chiefly in Ephesus its capital. This tradition is singularly full, consistent and well-authenticated.[1] Here he gathered disciples about him, organized churches, appointed bishops and presbyters. A whole chorus of voices unite in bearing testimony to its truth. One who passed his earlier life in these parts and had heard his aged master, a disciple of St. John himself, recount his personal reminiscences of the great Apostle (i.e. Irenaeus); another, who held this very see of Ephesus and writing less than a century after the Apostle's death was linked with the past by a chain of relatives all bishops in the Christian Church (Polycrates); a third who also flourished about the close of the century and numbered among his teachers an old man from this very district (Clement of Alexandria)[2]—are the principal, because the most distinct, witnesses to a fact which is implied in several other notices of earlier or contemporary writers.

As to the time at which St. John left his original home and settled in this new abode no direct account is preserved; but a very probable conjecture may be hazarded. The impending fall of the Holy City was the signal for the dispersion of the followers of Christ. About this same time the three other great Apostles, St. Peter, St. Paul and St. James, died a martyr's death; and on St. John, the last surviving of the four great pillars of the Church, devolved the work of developing the theology of the Gospel and completing the organisation of the Church. It was not unnatural that at such a crisis he should fix his residence in the centre of a large and growing Christian com-

---

[1]Papias in Eusebius, *Hist. Eccles.* iii. 39; Irenaeus ii. 22. 5, Fragm. 2 (p. 822 Stieren) etc; Polycrates in Eusebius, *Hist. Eccles.* v. 24; Apollonius in Eusebius, *Hist. Eccles.* v. 18; Clement of Alex. *Quis div. salv.* 42 (p. 958); cf. Can. Mur. (p. 17 ed. Tregelles), Tertullian, *adv. Marc.* iv. 5, *Praescr. Haer.* 32; *Ancient Syriac Documents*, pp. 32, 34 (ed. Cureton). The variety of the sources of these quotations—Gaul, Asia Minor, Alexandria, Rome, Carthage, Syria—is worth noticing.

[2]One of his teachers was an Ionian Greek (*Strom.* i.1 sec. 11, p. 322). See below.

munity, which had been planted by the Apostle of the Gentiles, and watered
by the Apostle of the Circumcision.[3] The missionary labours of St. Paul and
St. Peter in Asia Minor were confirmed and extended by the prolonged
residence of their younger contemporary. At all events such evidence as we
possess is favorable to this view of the date of St. John's settlement at
Ephesus. Assuming that the Apocalypse is the work of the beloved Apostle,[4]
and accepting the view that assigns it to the close of Nero's reign or thereabouts, we find him now for the first time in the immediate neighbourhood
of Asia Minor and in direct communication with Ephesus and the neighbouring Churches.

St. John however was not alone. Whether drawn thither by the attraction
of his presence or acting in pursuance of some common agreement, the few
surviving personal disciples of the Lord would seem to have chosen Asia
Minor as their permanent abode, or at all events as their recognised headquarters. Here at least we meet with the friend of St. John's youth and
perhaps his fellow-townsman, Andrew of Bethsaida,[5] who with him had
first listened to John the Baptist and with him also had been the earliest to
recognise Jesus as the Christ.[6] Here too we encounter Philip the Evangelist[7]
with his daughters, and perhaps also Philip of Bethsaida, the Apostle.[8] Here
also was settled the Apostle's namesake, John the Presbyter, also a personal
disciple of Jesus, and one Aristion, not otherwise known to us (see Papias
l.c.), who likewise had heard the Lord. And possibly also other Apostles
whose traditions Papias recorded, Matthew and Thomas and James, may
have had some connection, temporary or permanent, with this district.

Thus surrounded by the surviving disciples of the Lord, by bishops and
presbyters of his own appointment, and by the pupils who gathered about
him and looked to him for instruction, St. John was the focus of a large and

---

[3]On the relation of the Apostles to the Ephesian Church see Theodore of Mopsuestia, *praef. in Epist. ad Ephesos.*
[4]If the Apocalypse be conceded, the testimony is decisive. And as opponents with very few exceptions (Scholten is one) allow the genuineness, and indeed use it against the Gospel, it may be
urged.
[5]See the account in *Anc. Syr. Documents*, p. 25.
[6]Canon. Mur. (*revelatum Andreae ex apostolic*), p. 17 ed. Tregelles, *Anc. Syr. Documents*, pp. 32, 34.
[7]Papias in Eusebius, *Hist. Eccles.* iii. 39; Polycrates in Eusebius, *Hist. Eccles.* iii. 31; Caius in Eusebius, *Hist. Eccles.* iii. 31; cf. Clement Alex. in Eusebius, *Hist. Eccles.* iii. 30.
[8]See my *Colossians*, p. 45sq.

active society of believers.[9] In this respect he holds a unique position among the great teachers of the new faith. St. Peter and St. Paul converted disciples and organized congregations; St. John alone was the centre of a school. His life prolonged till the close of the century, when the Church was firmly rooted and widely extended, combined with his fixed abode in the centre of an established community to give a certain definiteness to his personal influence which would be wanting to the wider labors of these strictly missionary preachers. Hence the notices of St. John have a more solid basis and claim greater attention than stories relating to the other Apostles.

This fact is significant for the preservation of a tradition, especially one so important as that of the authorship of the Gospel. But there is another point, which increases the value of the tradition itself, viz., the longevity of the principal witnesses. Of St. John himself we are told that he 'lived to the times of Trajan.'[10] His pupil Polycarp, who suffered martyrdom A.D. 155 or 156[11] speaks of himself at the time of his death as having 'served Christ fourscore and six years.'[12] The expression in the original may leave some doubt whether these eighty-six years should be reckoned from his birth or from his conversion, though the former would be the more natural interpretation. But in any case he must have been born not later than A.D. 70. And as Polycarp was the disciple of St. John, so Irenaeus was the disciple of Polycarp. Again, of Pothinus bishop of Lyons we are told (Eusebius, *Hist. Eccles.* v.1) that he was more than ninety years old when he suffered in the persecution of the Churches of Vienne and Lyons (A.D. 177). The date of his birth therefore cannot be later than A.D. 87. A later tradition[13] makes him a native of Asia Minor; and this would be a highly probable supposition, even if unsupported by direct evidence. But whether an Asiatic Greek or not, he must have been a lad when St. John died. And Irenaeus was the successor of Pothinus in the see of Lyons. Thus one link only, and that a double one, connects the life of

---

[9]Irenaeus ii.22.5; Clement Alex. *Quis div. salv.* 42 (p. 958); Canon Mur. l.c. (*condiscipulis et episcopis suis*); Epiphanius li.6 (pp. 427-28).

[10]Irenaeus ii. 22.5. The date of Trajan's accession is A.D. 98. According to the *Chronicon Paschale* St. John survived until A.D. 104; see Clinton, *Fast. Rom.* I, p. 87.

[11]On the question of the date of Polycarp's martyrdom, see my *Apostolic Fathers* (Part ii.), vol. i, pp. 646sq. [2nd ed.].

[12]*Mart. Polyc.* 9. See the note on this passage in *Apostolic Fathers* (Part ii.), vol. iii, p. 379 (cf. Irenaeus iii.3.4).

[13]See the references in Tillemont, *Memoires*, p. 343.

the traditional author of the Fourth Gospel with Irenaeus who preserves the tradition in writing; and two long lives, St. John and Polycarp, link the personal ministry of our Lord with the latter half of the second century.[14]

Of the traditions of this school, Irenaeus, who had been educated in Asia Minor, though his later life was spent in Gaul, is the principal witness. He was a pupil of St. John's personal disciple Polycarp, whom he mentions more than once. He set great store on these traditions as representing most truly the primitive teaching of the Church, and appeals to them again and again with confidence. On one occasion, writing to Florinus, whom he had known in youth as a fellow-pupil of Polycarp, but who in after years had taken up heretical views, he urges that these are not the doctrines delivered to him, by the Elders, who were before them, who also associated with the Apostles, and he appeals to his reminiscences of their common master in this language:

> I distinctly remember (διαμνημονεύω) the incidents of that time better than events of recent occurrence; for the lessons received in childhood, growing with the growth of the soul, become identified with it; so that I can describe the very place in which the blessed Polycarp used to sit when he discoursed, and his goings out and his comings in, and his manner of life (τὸν χαρακτῆρα τοῦ βίου) and his personal appearance, and the discourses which he held before the people; and how he would describe his intercourse with John and with the rest who had seen the Lord, and how he would relate their words. And what were the accounts he had heard from them about the Lord, and about His miracles, and about His teaching, how Polycarp, as having received them from eyewitnesses of the life of the Word . . . used to give an account harmonizing on all points with the Scriptures. . . . To these (discourses) I used to listen at the time with attention by God's mercy which was bestowed upon me, noting them down, not on paper, but in my heart; and by the grace of God, I constantly ruminate upon them faithfully (Eusebius, *Hist. Eccles.* v.20).

---

[14]There was doubtless a tendency to exaggeration in this matter e.g. in the Christian Essene sources, where the age of Symeon, bishop of Jerusalem, is given as 120 years. But the instances in the text are thoroughly substantiated, and can easily be paralleled. Thus three Lord Chancellors since the Reform Bill (Brougham, Lyndhurst and St. Leonards) have lived to be 90. The longevity of the most distinguished German professors has been remarkable. Boeckh died at eighty-one, Humboldt at eighty-nine, Ranke (and Dollinger) at ninety. For the great age of the Jewish rabbi Hillel see Etheridge, *Jerus. and Tiber,* p. 33. The simple life of the early Christians had probably a great deal to do with this; see Southey, e.g. in *Life of Wesley* ii. pp. 273sq., 284 (1858), and compare Josephus, *Bell. Jud.* ii. 8. 10, who states that the Essenes often lived to a great age.

As regards this whole extract it will suffice to notice: (1) the opportunities of the witness, (2) the thoroughness of the evidence ('harmonizing on all points with the Scripture'). In more than one passage also of his great work he refers to the 'Church of Ephesus' (Irenaeus v.33.4) or to the Elders who associated with John in Asia. It was not the object of Irenaeus to defend the authorship of the Fourth Gospel, for his Valentinian antagonists not only accepted it as genuine, but even set an exclusive value on it; and therefore any testimony to its authorship from the earlier school of Asia Minor which may be gathered from his writings is incidental. But any such testimony must have the highest value.

1. It can hardly be doubted that *the Elders* whom Irenaeus quotes, and quotes for the most part anonymously, belonged to this school. Of Polycarp and Papias, of whom the former is mentioned several times by him and the latter once casually, this is certain. I shall endeavor immediately to discriminate the several persons whom he thus quotes by the topics on which they write or speak; but, before doing so, one reference to such anonymous authority deserves attention, where Irenaeus refers not to individual opinion, but to the collective testimony of all the Elders who associated with St. John (Irenaeus ii.22). It relates to a question of chronology. His Valentinian adversaries laid great stress on the number 'thirty.' Their celestial hierarchy comprised thirty aeons, and they appealed to the thirty years' duration of our Lord's life. This computation of the Gospel chronology they derived from the notices in St. Luke, interpreted by themselves.[15] At the commencement of His ministry, they contended, He was entering upon His thirtieth year, and His ministry itself lasted a twelvemonth, the 'acceptable year of the Lord' foretold by the Prophet. Irenaeus in reply expresses his 'great astonishment' that persons professing to understand the deep things of God should have overlooked the commonest facts of the Gospel narrative, and points to the three passovers recorded in St. John's Gospel during the term of our Lord's life (§3). Independently of the chronology of the Fourth Gospel, Irenaeus has an a priori reason why the Savior must have lived more than thirty years. He came to sanctify every time of life, infancy, childhood, youth, declining age. It was therefore necessary that He should have passed

---

[15]On the chronology of the Valentinians, whom Irenaeus here opposes, see Epiphanius, *Haer.* li. 20 (p. 450).

the turn of middle life. 'From thirty to forty,' he argues, 'a man is reckoned young, but from his fortieth and fiftieth year he is already declining into older age, which was the case with our Lord when He taught, as the Gospel and all the Elders who associated with John the disciple of the Lord testify that John delivered his account. For he 'remained with them' . . . till the times of Trajan. Some of them saw not only John but other disciples also, and heard these very things from their own lips (*ab ipsis*), and bear testimony to such an account (*de huiusmodi relatione*)' (§4). Irenaeus goes on to argue that the same may be inferred from the language of our Lord's Jewish opponents, who asked, 'Thou art not yet fifty years old, and hast Thou seen Abraham?' (John 8:57). This, he contends, is properly said to one who had already lived more than forty years, but had not yet reached his fiftieth year, though not far off his fiftieth year (§6).

On this passage three points are to be remarked. (1) The Valentinian chronology was derived from an obvious, though not a necessary, interpretation of the synoptic narrative, more especially of St. Luke (3:1, 23; 4:19) while, on the other hand, the Asiatic reckoning, which Irenaeus maintains, was, or might have been, founded on the Fourth Gospel, whereas it could not possibly have been suggested or elicited from the first three independently of the fourth, whether reconcilable with them or not.[16] (2) Irenaeus does not commit the Elders of the Asiatic School to his own interpretation of the passage quoted from St. John's Gospel, nor to his own view that our Lord was close upon fifty years old. He only asserts that the Gospel and the testimony of all the Elders together support the view that our Lord was past middle life; and the vagueness of his language at this point may suggest the inference that he had their testimony distinctly on his side as against the Valentinian chronology, but that it did not go beyond this;[17] (3) So far as the chronology of the

---

[16]St. John is our authority for the chronology of our Lord's ministry. In the Synoptic Gospels it is highly probable that the sequence of events is not strictly chronological, but that in places incidents are grouped according to subject and treatment. But still, though the Synoptic Gospels are consistent with a more lengthened ministry, they do not suggest it, and thus the argument given above, that a knowledge by the Elders of the Fourth may be assumed, is justified.

[17]The argument from John 8:57 is clearly Irenaeus' own, and is not justified by the passage itself. And this suggests the probability that much besides is his. We cannot safely assume that the *a priori* argument is taken from the Elders, or that the term of years was extended by them beyond forty. Irenaeus classes together *evangelium et omnes seniores*. It is a legitimate assumption that the testimony of the Elders went as far as the *evangelium* and no further.

Asiatic School is known from other sources, the statement of Irenaeus is confirmed; for the Asiatic reckoning was distinctly based on the narrative of the Fourth Gospel. This is the case with the duration of our Lord's ministry[18] as given by Melito, and the time of the Crucifixion as given by Claudius Apollinaris, to both which writers I shall have to refer hereafter.[19]

From this general notice of the Asiatic Elders I turn to the opinions of individuals belonging to this school, as reported by Irenaeus. As these opinions are given anonymously and scattered throughout his work, we can only separate one authority from another by considering the subject-matter and treatment. This criterion of course may be fallacious; and allowance must be made for the possibility of separating one authority into two or more, or again of counting two or more authorities as one. But the argument will not be materially affected by allowance made for errors which may occur on either side. Judging then by the subject-matter, I find that the following authorities are referred to: (1) A person quoted with great respect as 'one better than us . . .' [(*i. praef.* i.13.3), *superior nobis* (iii.17.4)], in another as 'the divine old man and herald of the truth, the old man beloved of God' (i.15.6). Anyone who will compare these references together cannot hesitate, I think, to see that they allude to one and the same person. He is a writer, as may be inferred both from the manner and from the subject of the references. His style is epigrammatic and telling, full of quaint metaphors and pointed sayings, and on one occasion he runs off into iambic verse which is more vigorous than rhythmical. The work which Irenaeus quotes is di-

---

[18]It may be interesting to consider what was the term of our Lord's life. The chief data are as follows: (a) Matt 2:16, 22—the death of Herod, which occurred March 4 B.C., see Clinton, *Fast. Hell, sub anno.* Thus the Nativity might have taken place in the year 5 B.C. or 6 B.C. (b) Luke 3:1, 23—our Lord's Baptism, and the commencement of His ministry, stated to have been 'in the fifteenth year of the reign of Tiberius Caesar' when our Lord was 'about thirty years old (ὡσεὶ ἐτῶν τριάκοντα).' As Sept. A.D. 28 was the beginning of the fifteenth year of Tiberius, our Lord would be 32 or 33 years old, which does not conflict with St Luke's statement, (c) Matt 27:2—the Passion under Pontius Pilate. We learn from Josephus, *Ant.* xviii. 4. 3 that Pilate was sent to Rome by Vitellius to answer charges made against him, and that before he arrived Tiberius had died, and Gaius (Caligula) had succeeded. Now Tiberius died March A.D. 37. Therefore the Passover of the Passion might have been as late as Easter A.D. 36, but could not be later. Thus it is possible that our Lord did live to be over forty years of age; for we have no right to assume that St. John gives all the Passovers that occurred during the ministry. On the whole, however, a ministry of not more than three or four years seems the more probable view.

[19]See below. For the references to Melito and Claudius Apollinaris see Routh, *Reliq. Sacr.* i. pp. 124, 160.

rected against heresies of the magico-gnostic school, and more especially against Marcus.

(2) An 'Elder of a bygone generation' (*de antiquis presbyter*), a 'primitive character' (iv.31.1), an 'elder and disciple of the Apostles' (iv.32.1), or, as he is elsewhere more precisely described, 'an elder who had heard from those who had seen the Apostles and from those who had learnt' [*ab his qui didicerunt*, i.e. from personal disciples of the Lord (iv.27.1)]. Irenaeus quotes at some length the opinion of this presbyter. From the form of quotation it appears that he is relating oral discourses (perhaps from his own lecture-notes), and not any written treatise of this elder (*audivi a quodam presbytero. Huiusmodi quoque disputabat*). The subject of these discourses is the relation of the two covenants, and the Elder defends the Old Testament Saints, describing the office of the patriarchs as witnesses of Christ.

(3) A single saying is quoted as from 'one of the ancients' (*quidam ex veterihus ait*), apparently from a written treatise, that God cursed not Adam but the earth in (or through) his works (iii.23.3).

(4) Irenaeus, in explaining the expression 'sons of God,' 'sons of the devil,' refers to a distinction made by one of these Elders. 'A son, as also one before us said (*dixit*, or 'has said'), is understood in two senses: one is a son according to nature, because he is born a son, another is reputed a son according to what he has been made, though there is a difference between the one who is born such, and the one who is made such' (iv.41.2).

(5) Irenaeus twice refers to some writing or writings, in which the opinions of 'the Elders, the disciples of the Apostles,' on eschatological subjects are given. In one passage it is declared that the Old Testament saints have been transferred to Paradise and there await the coming of the Lord (v.5.1). The second, which is of considerable importance, runs as follows:

> As the Elders say, then also shall they which have been deemed worthy of the abode in heaven go thither, while others shall enjoy 'the delight of Paradise,' and others again shall possess the brightness of the city (i.e. the New Jerusalem); for in every place the Savior shall be seen, according as they shall be worthy who see Him. (They say) moreover that this is the meaning of the distinction between the habitation of them that bring forth a hundred-fold, and them that bring forth sixty-fold, and them that bring forth thirty-fold; of whom the first shall be taken up into the heavens, and the second shall dwell

in paradise, and the third shall inherit the city; and that therefore our Lord has said, 'In My Father's abode are many mansions' (St. John 14:2); for all things are of God, Who giveth to all their appropriate dwelling, according as His Word saith that allotment is made unto all by the Father, according as each man is, or shall be, worthy. And this is the banqueting-table, at which those are seated who are called to the marriage and take part in the feast. The Elders, the disciples of the Apostles, say that this is the arrangement and disposal of them that are saved, and that they advance by such stages, and ascend through the Spirit to the Son, and through the Son to the Father, the Son at length yielding His work to the Father, as it is said also by the Apostle, 'For He must reign until He putteth all enemies under His feet,' etc (v.36.1-2).[20]

Of these five Elders (assuming them to be distinct persons) no coincidence with St. John's Gospel can be traced in notices of the first and third. Of the first, indeed, though he is appealed to four times, only epigrammatic sentences against his heretical antagonists are adduced, and these naturally do not give room for any quotations from either the Old Testament or the New. The third is represented by a single short sentence relating to Adam's transgression, which from its brevity admits of no such reference. The remaining three, the second, fourth and fifth, all present more or less distinct coincidences with St. John's Gospel. Of the second Irenaeus reports that he was wont to say that the patriarchs and prophets gave thanks and gloried in our salvation, where there is an obscure parallel to our Lord's words in the Fourth Gospel, 'Your father Abraham rejoiced to see My day, and he saw it and was glad' (John 8:56). The fourth is adduced to explain an expression especially characteristic of St. John 'sons of the devil.' It is not certain indeed from the language of Irenaeus that this Elder actually used this expression; but it is at least more probable than not that the distinction, which Irenaeus quotes, was quoted by this father i.e. to explain the words 'sons of the devil.'[21] I shall presently suggest a probable source from which this reference is taken. And, lastly, the fifth Elder distinctly quotes and explains a saying of our Lord

---

[20]The references in Irenaeus to the five Elders are as follows : (1) Iren. *i. praef.* i.13.3; i.15.6; ill. 17. 4 (written . . . *dixit*); (2) iv.27.1sq.; iv.30.1sq., iv.31.1; iv.32.1; v.17.4 (oral: *audivi, dicebat, reficiebat nos et dicebat, disputabat* . . .); (3) iii.23.3 (written *ait*); (4) iv.41.2 (doubtful: *dixit* . . .); (5) v.5.1; v.36.1-2 (written . . .).
[21]See John 8:44, 1 John 3:8, 10; cf. Acts 8:10. The expression is peculiar to St. John among the Evangelists.

peculiar to the Fourth Gospel (14:2). I shall have something to say shortly
about the name of this Elder also. At present it is sufficient to remark two
things: first, the form of the sentence shows that the quotation is given as
part of the Elder's own saying, and not of an after-comment of Irenaeus; and,
secondly, as Irenaeus uses the present tense 'the elders say' and yet the
persons referred to belonged to a past generation and were no longer living
when he wrote, he must be quoting from some written record, and therefore
we cannot suppose that he has unconsciously fused his own after-thought
with the original saying. These references are anonymous. But Irenaeus
likewise mentions by name two of these Asiatic Elders who had conversed
with Apostles or personal disciples of the Lord, and of whom something is
also known from other sources, Polycarp and Papias.

3. Of *Polycarp* and his reminiscences of St. John, as recounted by his own
pupil Irenaeus, I have already spoken. It is worthwhile to observe in passing
that in the single sentence in which he describes the conversation of Polycarp,
he represents him as retelling lessons which he professed to have learnt
'from eyewitnesses of the life of the Word . . .'[22] an expression characteristic
of the writings of St. John and suggesting that Irenaeus' recollections of
Polycarp were intimately connected with those writings. Of the many letters
which Polycarp himself wrote, as Irenaeus (in Eusebius *Hist. Eccles.* v. 20)
tells us, 'either to the neighboring Churches to confirm them, or to individual brethren, to admonish or encourage them,' only one remains. The
extant *Epistle to the Philippians* was written after the death of Ignatius, but
so soon after that Polycarp had not yet heard the particulars. It may therefore
be placed about the year A.D. 110. The Epistle is not long and contains very
few direct references to the New Testament writings; but numerous passages,
more or less exactly quoted, are embedded in it. For the most part they are
taken from the Epistles, as more suited to the hortatory and didactic character of the letter, and the references to the Gospels are very few. With the

---

[22]We might be tempted to translate the passage 'from the eyewitnesses of the Word of Life' (cf.
1 John 1:1), but the Greek order makes this impossible. Moreover the phrase αὐτόπται τοῦ
λόγου, occurs in Luke 1:2. On the other hand the rendering 'from the eyewitnesses the life (the
earthly career) of the Word' would require τοῦ βίου for τῆς ζωῆς. Possibly there is an accidental transposition in the text of Irenaeus; cf. Ign. *Polyc.* 5. But it matters little for our immediate
purpose. The personal use of ὁ λόγος is Johannine in either case. The Syriac translator has
'those who saw with their eyes the living Word.'

Fourth Gospel no distinct coincidence is found; but Polycarp was evidently well acquainted with the First Epistle of St. John, for he writes (§7): 'Every one that confesseth not that Jesus Christ has come in the flesh, is Antichrist';[23] and 'whosoever confesseth not the testimony of the Cross, is of the devil' (1 John 4:3, compare 2 John 7, and shortly after (§8)), 'but He endured all for our sakes, that we might live through Him' (1 John 4:9). It will be shown hereafter that this First Epistle was in all likelihood written at the same time with and attached to the Gospel. At present I will assume that it proceeds from the same author. There is a presumption therefore that the Gospel also was known to this writer. At all events, the quotations show that the writer of the Gospel flourished before Polycarp wrote. And he is cited by this father, in the same way in which our canonical writings, more especially the Epistles of St. Paul and St. Peter, are cited.

2. *Papias* of Hierapolis was a contemporary and a friend of Polycarp. Whether he was a personal disciple of the Apostle St. John, as asserted by Irenaeus, or only of a namesake of the Apostle, the presbyter John, as Eusebius supposes, I will not stop to enquire.[24] It is certain that he lived in the confines of the apostolic age, that he was acquainted with the daughters of Philip, and that he conversed with two personal disciples of the Lord, Aristion and John. He wrote an 'Exposition of our Lord's Oracles' in five books, which he illustrated by oral traditions. Its date is somewhat uncertain, but on the whole it would appear to have been written in his old age, towards the middle of the second century, not before 130 to 140. Of this work only the most meagre fragments remain; but it is distinctly stated by Eusebius, that he 'made use of testimonies from the First (πρώτερος) Epistle of John' (*Hist. Eccles.* iii. 39). We cannot indeed assume from this notice that he mentioned the Apostle by name as the author, or that the quotations were given as quotations (for Eusebius uses this same expression of the quotations from St. Peter in

---

[23]On the genuineness of Polycarp's Epistle see my *Apostolic Fathers* (Part II.), I. p. 578sq. (ed. 2).

[24]Irenaeus speaks of Papias as a hearer of John (v.33.4). On the other hand Eusebius, who mentions this statement of Ireneus remarks, 'Yet Papias himself, in the preface to his discourses certainly does not declare that he himself was a hearer and an eyewitness of the holy Apostles, but he shows, by the language which he uses, that he received the matters of the faith from those who were his friends' (*Hist. Eccles.* iii.39). It is, however, not stated by Irenaeus that he derived his knowledge from this preface, and from his frequent intercourse with Polycarp, Irenaeus doubtless had sources of information that were closed to Eusebius. Still Eusebius may have been right (see *Essays on Supernatural Religion*, p. 142sq.).

Polycarp, where St. Peter is not so mentioned and the passages are indirectly quoted); but it is a fair inference from the procedure of Eusebius elsewhere that the passages were obvious quotations (otherwise he would not have noticed them), and that the coincidence was not so slight as to be accidental, but clearer than the quotation from St. John in Polycarp's epistle, which Eusebius does not mention. In carrying over the evidence from the Epistle to the Gospel, the same remark will apply, as in Polycarp's case.

But great stress has been laid on the silence of Eusebius, as though it were inconsistent with the supposition that Papias was acquainted with the Gospel. The historian quotes a few lines from Papias, preserving some traditions respecting the Gospels of St. Matthew and St. Mark which he related on the authority of John the presbyter, but says nothing about the Fourth Gospel. And the negative argument appears stronger, when it is remembered that Eusebius elsewhere (*Hist. Eccles.* iii.39) declares his intention of extracting from early writers such notices as bear on the formation of the Canon.

Before accepting this hasty conclusion however, we must answer two preliminary questions, the one following from the other: (1) What is the practice of Eusebius elsewhere? Does he, or does he not, fulfill to the letter the intention thus expressed relative to the Canon? (2) If he does not, what principle of selection, if any, does he follow here or elsewhere in omitting or recording such notices?

To the first of these questions the answer is decisive. The Epistle of Clement besides many embedded quotations from St. Peter, St. James, and St. Paul, and a few from the Gospels and Acts, refers by name to St. Paul's First Epistle to the Corinthians. Yet Eusebius says nothing of all this. He mentions only its coincidences with the Epistle to the Hebrews (*Hist. Eccles.* iii. 38). The Epistle of Polycarp again, besides the references to the Gospels mentioned above, is replete with the most obvious quotations from St. Paul, and in two passages refers to his Epistles by name (sec. 3, 11). But Eusebius omits all mention of these and simply says 'he employs some testimonies from the First Epistle of Peter,' not mentioning even the coincidences with St John's First Epistle (*Hist. Eccles.* iv. 14). His account of Irenaeus is equally defective. Excepting one or two of the Catholic Epistles, Irenaeus, as is well known, quotes by name all the canonical books of the New Testament, and most of them repeatedly; yet Eusebius, after giving one passage containing an account of the origin of the four Gospels, and another referring to the Apocalypse, adds 'he makes mention also of the First Epistle of John, adducing very many testimonies from it, and in like manner of the First Epistle of Peter' (*Hist. Eccles.* v. 8). If Irenaeus had been known to us only from the account of Eusebius, it would doubtless have been inferred of him (as even cautious writers have drawn this inference respecting Papias), that he ignored or repudiated the Acts of the Apostles and all St. Paul's Epistles.

It will then be seen that the mere silence of Eusebius justifies no such inference. And, when we come to enquire the grounds on which he has omitted or recorded notices, I think it is impossible altogether to acquit him of a certain carelessness or caprice. Yet, so far as he is guided by any principle, it appears to be this. The four Gospels, the Acts of the Apostles, the thirteen Epistles of St. Paul were universally allowed as canonical. He therefore records no references to, or quotations from, these, except such as contain some interesting traditions respecting their origin or history, as e.g. in Papias the account of the Hebrew original of St. Matthew or the Petrine authority of St. Mark. On the other hand the authority of the Apocalypse and of the Epistle to the Hebrews was doubted; and the limits of the Catholic Epistles also (e.g. how many Epistles of St. John or St. Peter should be received) were an open question. On these points therefore he is more full; and, though the First Epistle of St. John and the First Epistle of St. Peter were not themselves questioned, yet their relation to the others leads him to note where they are quoted as authoritative.[25] There is no reason therefore to suppose that, though Papias might have quoted the Gospel of St. John a score of times, Eusebius would have cared to note the fact, unless the notices contained some interesting particulars respecting its origin and history. And in his account of Papias there is less completeness than usual in repeating the traditions of his author. The five books of the *Expositions* were largely interspersed with such traditions, which it would have been tedious to reproduce in full. The millennarian views of Papias were repulsive to Eusebius; and the historian's impatience is very evident when he is dealing with this author. He mentions the fact that Papias records 'other narratives of the aforesaid Aristion of our Lord's discourses, and also traditions of the Elder

---

[25]But even this rule he fails to observe strictly e.g. we know that Papias commented on the Apocalypse, yet in his account of Papias Eusebius, does not mention the Apocalypse at all.

John' which he does not repeat, and he contents himself with 'referring . . .
the studious readers' to the book itself, professing to give what the exigencies
of the case demand and nothing more on this head (*Hist. Eccles.* iii.39).[26]

But there is also positive evidence very strong, though not absolutely conclusive, that Papias did quote from this Gospel. I have already mentioned
the reference in the Asiatic Elder cited by Irenaeus to our Lord saying 'In My
Father's house are many mansions.' If anyone will take the pains to read with
care from the thirty-third to the thirty-sixth chapter of the fifth book of
Irenaeus continuously, he can hardly fail (I think) to arrive at the conclusion
that the Elder in question is none other than Papias. In the thirty-third
chapter he gives a passage from Papias, and in the thirty-fifth comes this
passage from 'the Elders,' with which we are immediately concerned. That
they are taken from the same book, appears in the highest degree probable
from the following considerations. (1) Both passages treat of the future
kingdom of Christ, and both regard it from the same point of view, as a
visible and external kingdom, in which the enjoyments are enjoyments of
the senses. (2) The subject is continuous, the matter which intervenes between the two quotations extending over some pages but all having reference
to the same topic. (3) The authority in the first quotation is 'the Elders who
saw John the disciple of the Lord' (33§3); in the second 'the Elders' (36§1)
simply, at the end 'the Elders, the disciples of the Apostles' (36§2). At the
close of the first quotation Irenaeus adds, 'But these things Papias also . . .
testifies in writing in the fourth of his books, for there are five books composed by him.' Papias therefore reports the statements of these Elders as we
know from Eusebius that he did on several occasions, and there is no difficulty about the authority in the first passage. But in the second passage
Irenaeus fails to explain whom he meant by 'the Elders,' unless they are the
same who have been mentioned shortly before. Only on this supposition is
the reference plain. (4) I have pointed out before that the manner of quo-

---

[26]But why should he mention St. Matthew and St. Mark, without St. John? The answer is probably
as follows. Papias related curious facts of the two former. These are retailed. If Papias simply
quoted the Gospel of St. John (whether he mentioned St. John's name or not) or if he only related
what was known to everyone, there is no reason why Eusebius should state it. Early references
to a Gospel that was universally acknowledged had no interest for anyone, unless they contained
some curious or important fact. If we are at a loss to say why Eusebius singled out 1 Peter and
1 John in the case of Papias, we are equally at a loss to say why he should single out 1 Peter in
the case of Polycarp, except on the theory given above.

tation obliges us to suppose that Irenaeus refers to a written document, and not a mere oral tradition. This limits the possibilities of the case: for (so far as we know) Polycarp and Papias are the only writers who could satisfy the description. (5) The tenor of the passage accords entirely with the known subject of Papias' work, as described by its title *Expositions of Oracles of the Lord*. We have here one of these explanations.[27]

It seems fairly probable too, that not only our fifth Elder, but the fourth also, must be identified with Papias. His explanation of 'sonship' would be framed to explain our Lord's words addressed to the Jews: 'ye are of your father the devil.' Gnostic dualists would interpret these words to mean that the old covenant was directly opposed to the new, and was the work of the evil principle. To meet this argument the Elder makes the distinction between sons by nature and sons by habit. In the latter sense only the Jews were sons of the devil. The explanation at all events is a close parallel to an extant fragment of Papias, where he explains that 'those who practiced a godly innocence were called children' by the early Christians.[28]

Lastly, in the few lines which Eusebius quotes from the preface of Papias, it is worth observing, first, that the names which he places at the head of the list of authorities are those of the Apostles known to us from the Fourth Gospel and from this alone, Andrew, Philip, Thomas[29] and secondly, that he speaks of 'the truth itself'[30] meaning our Lord, in accordance with the characteristic phraseology of this Gospel.[31]

---

[27]It is curious that Eusebius (*Hist. Eccles.* v. 8), describing the work of the Elder, whom Irenaeus quotes, calls it ἐξηγήσεις θεῖον γραφῶν unconsciously an expression almost identical with the title of Papias' work.

[28]The extract is preserved in Maximus Confessor's scholia to the work of Dionysius Areopagiticus, *de eccles. hierarch.* c.2 and is given in Routh, *Reliq. Sac.* I, p. 8, Fragm. 2.

[29]Papias in Eusebius, *Hist. Eccles.* iii.29. Andrew, Peter and Philip are mentioned together in St. John's Gospel as belonging to the same place (John 1:44). Of Philip nothing is recorded except in the Fourth Gospel. The last remark applies also to Thomas.

[30]Eusebius l.c. Comp. John 5:33; 8:32; 14:6.

[31]The story of the woman taken in adultery (John 7:53–8:11) may also be an extract from Papias' work. It is certain that it is an interpolation where it stands. It is wanting in all Greek mss. before the sixth century; it was originally absent from all the oldest versions—Latin, Syriac, Egyptian, Gothic. It is not referred to, as part of St. John's Gospel, before the latter half of the fourth century. It is expressed in language quite foreign to St. John's style, and it interrupts the tenor of his narrative. Eusebius tells us that Papias 'relates also another story concerning a woman accused of many sins before the Lord' and adds that it is 'contained in the Gospel according to the Hebrews.' It may very well be an illustration given by Papias of our Lord's saying in John 8:15, 'I judge no man.' See *Essays on Supernatural Religion*, p. 203.

But indeed, though the evidence is late and confused, we are not without direct testimony that Papias was acquainted with this Gospel. 'The Gospel of John was revealed (*manifestatum*) and given to the Churches,' says an old Latin argument to this Gospel,[32] 'by John while he still remained in the body as one named Papias, of Hierapolis, a beloved disciple of John, related in his five books (or in his fifth book) of *Expositions*.'[33] If the corruption of the context and the uncertainty of the source of the statement forbid us to lay much stress upon it, we are nevertheless not justified in setting it aside as wholly valueless.

4. About the year 165 *Polycarp* suffered martyrdom at a very advanced age. An account of the death of Polycarp is extant in the *Letter of Christians at Smyrna* addressed to a neighboring Church at the time. In this document the brethren draw a parallel between the sufferings of their martyred friend and the Passion of the Lord, which is suggested to them by some remarkable coincidences. 'Nearly all the incidents which happened before his death,' it is said at the outset, 'came to pass, that the Lord from heaven might exhibit to us a martyrdom after the pattern of the Gospel; for Polycarp remained that he might be betrayed, just as the Lord did' (§1). This account is the earliest instance of the type of hagiology that sees the sufferings of Christ visibly reflected and imaged in detail in the servants of Christ, of which in the middle ages the lives of the great monastic founders St. Francis and St. Dominic, of Anselm and of Becket, are an example, and which has been unconsciously reproduced in more or less distinct lineaments in the biographies of the Wesleyan heroes in very recent times. This idea of literal conformity to the sufferings of Christ runs through the letter. Some of the coincidences are really striking, but in other cases the parallelism is more or less artificial. The name of the convicting magistrate is Herod (§6); the time of the martyrdom is the passover, 'the great Sabbath' (§21); Polycarp's conviction is obtained by a confession elicited by torture from a youth in his

---

[32]The argument is contained in a Vatican ms. of the ninth century first published by Cardinal Thomasius (Op. I. p. 344).

[33]The MS. has *in exotericis, id est, in extremis quinque libris.* Overbeck in Hilgenfeld's *Zeitschr. f. Wissensch. Theol.* X. p. 68sq. (1867), contends that someone had forged five additional works in the name of Papias, and had entitled them *Exoterica*, attaching them to the genuine books. Hilgenfeld adopts this view. But it is simpler to suppose that *exegeticis* should be read for *exotericis*, and *extemis* (a gloss on *exotericis*) for *extremis*. The passage then presents no difficulties. (See *Essays on Supernatural Religion*, p. 210sq.)

employ, and thus he is 'betrayed by them of his own household' (§6); he is put upon an ass and so carried before the magistrate, and of course this is a parallel to the triumphal entry at Jerusalem (§8); his pursuers come on horseback and in arms as 'against a robber' (§7); when he is apprehended, he prays, 'The will of God be done' (§7), and so forth.

Most of these incidents have their parallels in the circumstances of the Passion as recorded in the Synoptic Gospels, or recorded by these in common with St. John. This is natural; for they refer mainly to external incidents, in which the Synoptic account is rich. But there are one or two exceptions. Thus we are told, at the crisis of Polycarp's trial, that a voice came from heaven, 'Be strong and play the man, Polycarp.'[34] 'And the speaker no one saw, but the voice those of our company that were present heard' (§9). This corresponds to the voice that St. John records as speaking from heaven to our Lord, and as imperfectly apprehended by the bystanders (John 12:28, 29). In §§5, 12 a change of circumstances brings with it the fulfilment of his prophecy as to the manner of his death (cf. John 12:33; 18:32). Again we are told, when the fire would not consume the body of the Saint, his persecutors 'ordered an executioner (*confector*) to go up to him and thrust a dagger into him. And when he had done this, there came forth a dove and[35] a quantity of blood, so that it extinguished the fire; and all the multitude marvelled that there was so great a difference between the unbelievers and the elect' (§16). The parallel to the incident recorded in St. John's account (19:34) of the crucifixion alone is obvious; and just as the Evangelist lays stress on his own presence as an eyewitness of the scenes (19:35) so also have these hagiologers done; 'We saw a great marvel,' they say, 'we to whom it was given to see; and we were preserved that we might relate it to the rest' (§15). And, lastly, as St. John emphasizes the fact that everything was fulfilled in the death of Jesus (19:28, 30), so also they declare of Polycarp that 'every word which he uttered out of his mouth hath been, and shall be, accomplished' (§16). To these facts it should be added that the dying prayer of Polycarp contains one or two coincidences with the characteristic phraseology of the Fourth Gospel, as 'the resurrection of life,' 'the true God' (§14; cf. John 5:29; 17:3).[36]

---

[34]The expression itself is probably from Deut 31:7, 23; Josh 1:6, 7, 9.
[35]The parallel is not affected by the question whether the words περιστερά καί are genuine or not.
[36]Perhaps too the closing words of §16 are a reminiscence of John 19:30—'It is finished.'

5. Of all the Asiatic school, exclusive of its great Gallic representative, *Melito of Sardis* appears to have been the ablest. He possessed some slight knowledge at least of Oriental tongues; he had travelled to the East to obtain certain information about the Old Testament canon; he was at once learned, thoughtful and eloquent. He moreover won deep respect by his ascetic earnestness. His writings were very various, embracing alike questions of speculative theology, of scriptural exegesis, of practical duty, of ecclesiastical order. Those works, of whose date any record is preserved, appear to have been written between the years 165–175. When Polycrates of Ephesus wrote in the last decade of the century he was no longer living; and it may perhaps be inferred, from the language there used of him[37] that his death was not very recent.[38] These facts will fix his epoch approximately. Though he is not likely to have conversed with St. John or other personal disciples of the Lord, he belonged to the generation immediately following, and must have had large opportunities of intercourse with men like Polycarp and Papias; for he was a flourishing and apparently an influential and prolific writer about the time of their death.

Of his numerous works only a few fragments remain; but these are quite sufficient to attest the influence of the Fourth Gospel on his teaching and language. It has been already mentioned that the chronology of the Savior's life, adopted in the Asiatic School, was derived from this Gospel. Of this fact Melito is an illustration. Of our Lord he thus writes: 'Being at the same time both perfect God and perfect Man, He convinced us of His two natures, of His Godhead through His miracles in the three years after His baptism, and of His manhood in the thirty years which passed before His baptism.'[39] If the thirty years before the baptism are taken from St. Luke, the three years after the baptism cannot be derived from any other canonical Gospel but St. John.

The largest extant fragment is taken from his apology to M. Antoninus. In a treatise of this kind direct quotation is not usual; and accordingly we find

---

[37]See Polycrates in Eusebius, *Hist. Eccles.* v. 24.

[38]His treatise *On the Paschal Festival*, he himself tells us, was written while Sergius Paulus was proconsul of Asia (A.D. 164–166; see Waddington's *Fastes des Provinces Asiatiques*, p. 731 in Le Bas and Waddington's *Voyage Archiologique* etc.). Again we are informed that he addressed his Apology to M. Antoninus (A.D. 161–180). From an extant fragment we learn that L. Verus, the colleague of M. Antoninus was no longer living: this places the date after the spring of A.D. 169.

[39]Quoted by Anastatius of Sinai (Migne, *Pat. Graec.* xxxix. p. 228sq.).

no passage of either the Old or the New Testament cited in Melito's work. But the language and ideas are throughout colored by the influence of the Fourth Gospel. 'Neither can any sight see Him, nor any thought comprehend Him, nor any word express Him' (p. xxxix).[40] 'Behold a light is given to us all, that in it we may see. They dare to make an image of God, Whom they have not seen' (p. xl). 'What is God? He that is Truth, and His Word is Truth' (p. lxv; cf. John 17:17). 'What then is Truth?' (cf. John 18:38). 'If then a man adoreth that which is made by hands, he adoreth not the Truth nor the Word of Truth. But I have many things to say concerning this matter' (p. xlv; cf. John 8:26; 16:12). 'Wherefore I give thee counsel, that thou know thyself and know God' (p. xlvii; cf. John 17:3). 'Worship Him with thy whole heart; then will He grant thee to know His will' (p. xlvii; cf. John 7:17). 'To know God is Truth' (p. xlix). 'To know the true God' (ib.; cf. John 17:3). 'The word of Truth reproacheth thee' (p. l). 'If thou canst not know God, at least think that He is' (p. li). 'It is impossible for a mutable creature to see the immutable' (p. lii; cf. John 1:18; 1 John 4:12). 'Then shall they who know not God, vanish away' (p. lii). 'According as thou shalt have known God here, so will He know thee there' (p. liii). 'We worship the only God, Who is before all and above all; and we worship also His Christ, being God the Word from eternity' (p. lvi).

In like manner in one of the homiletic fragments which remain[41] he speaks of our Lord as the 'Word of God and begotten before the light, the Creator with the Father the fashioner of man; all things in all, the Son in the Father, God in God, King unto all eternity' (p. lix);[42] and in another using the images of St John he says: 'He appeared as a lamb, but He abode as a shepherd. He wanted food, in so far as He was man, yet He ceaseth not, in so far as He is God, to give food wherewith He feedeth the world' (p. lviii).[43]

---

[40]The references are to Pitra's *Spicileg. Solesm.* I.

[41]The fragment is extant in a Syriac version; it is given in Pitra's *Spicileg.* II. p. lixsq., in Cureton's *Spicileg. Syr.* p. 53sq., and in Otto *Corp. Apol. Christ*, p. 420.

[42]There is an Armenian extract (*Spicileg. Solesm.* i. p. 4) which give this passage with some alterations and a different commencement, assigning it to Irenaeus. There is also a Syriac abridgment of the Armenian. It is probable that Irenaeus introduced this passage from Melito either anonymously or otherwise, into one of his writings. Another Armenian fragment (*Spicileg. Solesm.* i. p. 1), gives as Irenaeus what is really an extract. (See *Essays on Supernatural Religion*, p. 232sq., 236sq.)

[43]Cf. John 1:36; 10:1sq. The so-called Clavis of Melito may contain a residuum of genuine matter, but as the amount of this is not ascertainable with any degree of certainty, its evidence must be left out of the question.

6. *Claudius Apollinaris* was a contemporary of Melito; the two being coupled together by Eusebius, Jerome and others. He was a successor, if not the immediate successor, of Papias, as bishop of Hierapolis. The ascertainable dates of his life are: (1) He presented an apology to M. Antoninus, who died in A.D. 180. (2) He mentioned the incident of the thundering legion, which occurred A.D. 174. (3) Eusebius in his *Chronicle* seems to place his accession to the episcopate A.D. 171.[44] (4) He is no longer living in the last decade of the century, when Serapion[45] alludes to him (Eusebius, *Hist. Eccles.* v. 19).

Of several works known to have been written by this father, the scanty fragments which remain occupy something less than half an octavo page. They contain however two or three undeniable references to the narrative of the Fourth Gospel. Thus Claudius speaks of our Lord as 'pierced in His holy side' and 'pouring forth from His side the two purifying elements, water and blood, word and spirit' (Routh *Reliq. Sac.* I. p. 160; cf. John 19:34). Thus too, he says, that the 14th was the true Passover of the Lord, the day on which He suffered, finding fault with those who maintain He ate the Paschal lamb with His disciples on the 14th and was crucified on the 15th, on the ground that 'according to their view the Gospels appear to be at variance.' Thus he himself takes the Fourth Gospel as the chronological standard, and interprets the others by it; and here again, as in the case of Melito, we have a confirmation of the statement of Irenaeus, that the reckoning of the Asiatic School was founded thereupon or accorded therewith. It is only necessary to add that his allusions to the Gospels seem to imply that they had long been received as authoritative, but that the discussions on the Paschal question had at length awakened criticism, and started difficulties in harmonizing them which hitherto had not been perceived.

7. *Polycrates of Ephesus* closes the list of authorities belonging to the Asiatic School. In the last decade of the second century he writes to Victor, Bishop of Rome (A.D. 190–202), on the Paschal question: and having occasion to mention the practice of St. John describes him in the language of

---

[44]See Clinton, *Fast. Rom* I, p. 167.
[45]Eusebius, *Chron.* and Jerome place the accession of Serapion to the episcopate in the eleventh year of Commodus, i.e. A.D. 190–91 (Clinton, I, p. 187) and he died apparently about A.D. 203 (Clement of Alex. in Eusebius, *Hist. Eccles.* vi.11), though Eusebius himself says A.D. 212. See Clinton I, p. 211.

the Fourth Gospel, as the disciple that 'reclined on the bosom of the Lord.'[46] Nothing like this occurs in the other Gospels. It must be borne in mind also that Polycrates states that seven of his relatives before him had been bishops; that he carefully observes their traditions; and that he has 'gone diligently through every holy scripture' (Polycrates in Eusebius, *Hist. Eccles.* v. 24).

8. But to complete the evidence, before passing away from the Asiatic Church to her Gallic colony, let me direct attention to one fact. *Montanism*, which took its rise about or soon after the middle of the second century, was strictly an offspring of the Christianity of Asia Minor. As might have been expected, the two main props on which it relied for support were the two great writings ascribed to the Apostle St. John. As its picture of the earthly metropolis of Christ's kingdom, the New Jerusalem, was drawn from the Apocalypse, so also the prophetic mission of its founder was held to be the realization of the promise recorded in the Fourth Gospel of the Paraclete, who should lead the faithful into all truth. On this subject I shall have more to say when I come to discuss the extreme view, into which the more extravagant opponents of Montanism were driven, of rejecting the writings of St. John wholly.

II. *The Churches of Gaul.* Intimately connected with the Churches of Asia Minor were the Christian brotherhoods established in the south of Gaul. The close alliance existing between these communities as early as the middle of the second century of the Christian era is a striking testimony to the power of the new faith in cementing the bonds of union between far-distant peoples. As, centuries before, the districts of Gaul lying on the seashore and along the banks of the Rhone had been civilised by colonists from the Greek peoples of Asia Minor, so now it would appear that these regions were indebted to the same country for the higher knowledge of the Gospel. However this may be, the intercourse between the two Churches during the second century was close and uninterrupted. More than one instance is recorded in which they corresponded with each other on matters of common or individual interest. On one occasion the Christians of Vienne and Lyons write to their brethren in Phrygia and Asia, giving them an account of the last

---

[46]Polycrates in Eusebius, *Hist. Eccles.* v. 24 offers the very expression which occurs in John 13:25. Comp. Irenaeus iii.1 where this resemblance is important, when coupled with the fact that Irenaeus and Polycrates were allied on the question of the Paschal controversy.

hours of the martyrs who had suffered under M. Aurelius, and among these are mentioned at least two who were Asiatics by birth, Alexander, a physician from Phrygia (§13), and Attains of Pergamum (§17). On another, the Gallican brotherhoods write to the same communities to express their opinion on the recent heresies of Montanus, Alcibiades, Theodotus, and others, an opinion which Eusebius describes as 'circumspect and most orthodox' (Eusebius, *Hist. Eccles.* v. 3). This opinion was appended, he tells us, to a collection of letters written severally by the martyrs from their prisons, and addressed to the brethren in Phrygia and Asia (Eusebius l.c.).

Though all these documents were known to Eusebius, he has only preserved fragments (though very considerable fragments) of the first mentioned (*Hist. Eccles.* v. 1). Its date is fixed as A.D. 177. In this letter the Gospel of St. John is once distinctly quoted (§4), 'So was fulfilled the saying of our Lord, 'The time shall come, in which every one that killeth you shall think to do service to God' (John 16:2), while elsewhere its language is indirectly borrowed. Thus one of the martyrs is described as 'having the Comforter in himself, the Spirit, which he showed in the fullness . . . of love, having been well-pleased to lay down even his own life in defense of the brethren (§3; cf. John 16:26; 15:13): for he was and is indeed a genuine disciple of Christ, following the Lamb whithersoever He goeth' (ib.; Rev 14:4); and another as being 'sprinkled and strengthened from the heavenly fountain of the water of life, that goeth forth from the body . . . of Christ' (§22; cf. John 4:14; 7:38).

The persecution which was fatal to these martyrs placed *Irenaeus* in the vacant see of Lyons. His testimony is important, not only because a close connection existed between the Churches of Gaul and Asia generally, but because he was himself by birth and education an Asiatic. It is important also for another reason. He was directly connected with the Apostolic age by two remarkable instances of longevity. Polycarp, his early instructor in his Asiatic home, declared himself to have been 'eighty-six years in the Lord' at the time of his martyrdom. Pothinus, his immediate predecessor in the see of Lyons, his late abode, was close upon ninety when he too died under the hands of the persecutor. Polycarp was a disciple of St. John, and is said to have been placed by him in the see of Smyrna. Pothinus was a growing boy when the Apostle died, and it seems probable (though of this there is no direct evidence) that he, like his successor at Lyons, was of Asiatic birth and parentage. Irenaeus, as we have seen, lays great stress on the teaching of the former, which he professes to follow implicitly; and we may suppose with much probability that among the anonymous presbyters whose authority he quotes as having associated with the Apostles and their immediate successors the latter held a prominent place. We are therefore greatly interested in enquiring what language Irenaeus holds with respect to the Fourth Gospel.

The answer is decisive. He not only mentions or quotes it many times, as the work of the beloved disciple, but gives many particulars respecting it. He states in one place that it was written at Ephesus (iii.1.1), in another that its object was to counteract the heresies of the Nicolaitans and Cerinthians (iii.11.1). He uses it freely (quoting it between 70 and 80 times), not only to establish his own position, but also to confute his Gnostic opponents. To them and to him alike, as to the universal Church, it is a recognised authority. In short, a Fourth Gospel is to Irenaeus not only a historical fact, but a foreordained necessity. He ransacks heaven and earth for reasons why the evangelical record should thus be foursquared. In analogies from the physical world, in types from Old Testament prophecy, in the successive developments of God's revelation to men, he finds evidence that this number alone is consonant with the Divine order of things (iii.11.8).

The extant work of Irenaeus on heresies, from which these references are taken, was written during the episcopate of Eleutherus[47] who held the see of Rome from about A.D. 175 to A.D. 190. The exact date is of little or no importance. The point to be kept in view is this; that in youth he had lived in familiar intercourse with Polycarp, and had heard his aged master speak again and again of the Apostle St. John, that he professed to have a very vivid remembrance of those early days, and that on every occasion he appealed to the traditions of the Asiatic School as authoritative in matters of Christian faith and history.

Of his honesty and good faith I think no reasonable doubt can be entertained. Eager partisanship may occasionally have blinded his judgment

---

[47]Eleutherus is mentioned as still living (Iren. iii.3.3). On the other hand, a reference occurs to Theodotion's version of the LXX (iii.21.1), and Theodotion's version is stated not to have been published until the reign of Commodus (A.D. 182–190). But Epiphanius, our authority for Theodotion's date, is guilty of such startling confusions in the passage (*De mens. et pond.* 16, 17) that his trustworthiness is much discredited. (See *Essays on Supernatural Religion*, p. 260.)

as to the value of the evidence before him. Close and searching criticism
was not the characteristic either of his age or of his class. A tradition may
here and there have been confused or exaggerated in the course of transmission; a metaphor translated into a fact; a categorical statement substituted for an individual opinion; an early date replaced by a later or conversely. Let all reasonable allowance be made for these possibilities. The
fact still remains, that he firmly believed himself, and received as the tradition of St. John's personal disciples, that the Fourth Gospel was written
by none other than the beloved Apostle himself. On this point he does not
betray a shadow of a misgiving.

On reviewing the evidence of the Asiatic school, which thus culminates
in Irenaeus, we cannot fail to be struck with the solidarity of the body
through which it is transmitted. Polycarp and Papias, Melito and Claudius
Apollinaris, Polycrates and Irenaeus, the martyrs of Asia and the martyrs of
Gaul, are not isolated individuals, nor is church-membership their only
bond of union; but within the Church itself they belong to a more or less
compact community, of which the members are in constant mutual intercourse, and consult and advise each other on very diverse matters of interest.
This fact is a strong safeguard for the continuity of transmission where a
tradition so important is concerned, but in the case before us the disputes
of the age and country afford an additional security. As soon as we bring the
original theory of the Tübingen school, which dated the Fourth Gospel
about A.D. 170, or even the modified hypothesis of some recent antagonists,
which places it close upon the middle of the second century, face to face with
these controversies, we at once see what enormous improbabilities are involved in either supposition. The forgery (for professing, as it evidently does,
to emanate from the beloved disciple, the Fourth Gospel must be called by
this hard name, unless it be genuine), the forgery is almost contemporary
with, or even subsequent to, the rise of Montanism and the first outburst of
the Quartodeciman controversy. It has a very direct bearing on Montanism,
for it supplies a basis for the prophetic theory of this sect; and yet it is received by Catholics and Montanists alike. It raises questions connected with
the celebration of Easter (though it does not touch the main subject of
dispute); and yet it is accepted without misgiving equally by the Quarto-
decimans and their opponents. Yet, if the hypothesis were true, that it first

saw the light during the lifetime of the very generation which was most actively engaged in both these controversies, must we not believe that its authenticity would have been most fiercely contested, and that the clearest traces of this contest would have been stamped on the extant literature of the period?

III. *The Church of Antioch.*

1. From the Churches of Asia Minor and their Gallic colonies it is natural to turn to the neighbouring and allied Church of Antioch; and here the apostolical father Ignatius first claims attention. His testimony is the more important, because he is historically connected with the two principal Churches in which the influence of St. John prevailed, Ephesus and Smyrna. The genuine Epistles of Ignatius were written A.D. 110, very few years after the probable date of St. John's Gospel. They are brief, abrupt and epigrammatic, being chiefly occupied with personal explanations and instructions. An aged disciple on his way to martyrdom writes a few hurried lines to the Christian congregations with whom he has been brought into contact on his journey. Though they reflect the teaching, and in many places echo the language, of the New Testament—especially of St. Paul—the letters contain only two direct quotations, as such, from Holy Scripture.[48]

Under these circumstances it is sufficient if we are able to trace the influence of the Fourth Gospel in individual thoughts and phrases. Nor are such traces wanting. When in his *Epistle to the Philadelphians* Ignatius writes (§7), 'The Spirit is not deceived, being from God; for it knoweth whence it cometh and whither it goeth ... and it searcheth out the hidden things' we recognise at once our Lord's description of the Spirit in His conversation with Nicodemus as related in John 3:8. Other reminiscences, not so obvious but equally real, of Johannine language are traceable elsewhere. Thus the sentence, 'The prince of this world is abolished' (*Trall.* 4) is an echo, almost a repetition, of our Lord's language (John 7:31; 16:11). Again, the contrast of

---

[48]*Magn.* 12, *Eph.* 5. In *Eph.* 5 the quote may have been taken direct from Prov 3:34, but the substitution of θεός, for κύριος inclines me to suppose that Ignatius got it through 1 Pet 5:5 or James 4:6. The same substitution is found in Clement, *Rom.* 30. The following are the most striking coincidences in the Ignatian Epistles (1) with the Gospel [of Matthew]: *Ephes.* 14 (cf. Matt 12:33); *Smyrn.* 1 (of our Lord's baptism; cf. Matt 3:15) *Smyrn.* 6 (cf. Matt 19:12); *Polyc.* 2 (cf. Matt 10:16); (2) with the Pauline Epistles: *Eph.* 10 (cf. Col 1:23), *Eph.* 16 (cf. 1 Cor 6:9); and *Eph.* 18 (cf. 1 Cor 1:20); *Rom.* 5 (cf. 1 Cor 4:4); *Polyc.* 5 (cf. Eph 5:29).

the 'corruptible food' with the 'bread of God, which is the flesh of Christ and the draught of His blood' (*Rom.* 7), is an adaptation of the characteristic discourse related in the sixth chapter of the same Gospel. So too in other passages he echoes the same expressions, 'the flesh of the Lord,' 'the blood of Jesus Christ' (*Trall.* 8; cf *Philad.* 4), 'the bread of God' (*Eph.* 5). And elsewhere the coincidences with St. John are equally patent; 'we ought so to receive him (the bishop), as Him that sent him' (*Eph.* 6; cf. John 13:20); 'where the shepherd is, there follow ye, as sheep, for many fair-seeming wolves make captive those that run the race of God' (*Philad.* 2; cf. John 10:4, 12); 'to Him alone (Christ) are committed the hidden things of God, He Himself being the door of the Father' (*Philad.* 9; cf. John 10:7); 'Jesus Christ, His Son, Who is His Word, coming forth from silence. Who in all things pleased Him that sent Him' (*Magn.* 8; cf. John 6:38).[49]

2. Following the succession of the Antiochene bishops we arrive at *Theophilus*—the sixth bishop according to Eusebius (*Hist. Eccles.* iv. 20), the seventh according to Jerome (*Ep. ad Algas. quaest.* 6), who commences his list of Antiochene bishops with St. Peter. In his extant *Apologia ad Autolycum*, an undoubtedly genuine work, Theophilus quotes the beginning of the Fourth Gospel and mentions St. John as its author. The passage runs as follows: 'Whence the Holy Scriptures and all the inspired men (πνευματοφόροι) teach us, one of whom, John, says, "In the beginning was the Word, and the Word was with God," showing that at the first God was alone, and the Word in Him. Then he says, "And the Word was God. All things were made through Him, and without Him was not anything made"' (*ad Autol.* ii.22). This direct and precise reference is the more conspicuous, because it is the solitary instance in which Theophilus quotes directly and by name any book of the New Testament. To this undoubted quotation

---

[49]The silence of Ignatius respecting St. John has been urged on the other side, especially in *Rom.* 4 where, it is contended, the introduction of the names of St. Peter and St. Paul makes the omission of St. John's name more remarkable. But there is a good reason for this omission. Ignatius is addressing the Roman Church, and therefore appeals to the two Apostles to whose precepts that Church had listened. Again in *Eph.* 12, where St Paul is again mentioned, reference has been already made in the previous section to other Apostles with whom the Ephesian Church was in harmony. Moreover, Ignatius singles out St. Paul on account of the parallel to himself. The Ephesian converts had sheltered St. Paul as he passed through; and now passing through Ephesus on his way to martyrdom. Besides these two passages, no Apostle is mentioned by name in the Ignatian Epistles, except St. Peter in *Smyrn.* 3, where there is a reference to an incident in our Lord's life.

should be added the following coincidences: 'How can one fail to notice the pangs which women suffer in child-bearing, and after that they forget their trouble?' (*ad Autol.* ii.23; cf. John 16:21); 'A corn of wheat, or of the other seeds, when it is cast into the earth, first dieth and is dissolved, then it riseth and becometh an ear . . .' (*ad Autol.* i.13). Here the language of Theophilus combines expressions in John 12:24 and 1 Cor 15:36, 37. Lastly, in *ad Autol.* i.14 occurs the following expression, 'Do not therefore disbelieve, but believe,' a reminiscence of John 20:27, 'Be not faithless, but believing.'

The date of these notices may be fixed with tolerable accuracy. Eusebius in his *Chronicon* gives A.D. 177 as the year of Theophilus's death. But it is almost certain that he has antedated the event by six or more years at the lowest computation. For in his *Apology*, Theophilus mentions the death of M. Aurelius, and he carries his chronological calculations down to this epoch (iii.28). These calculations indeed are confessedly taken from Chryseros 'the *nomenclator*' (ii.27), a freedman of Aurelius, who stopped at this point; but as the object of Theophilus is to calculate the age of the world at the time when he writes, it is a tolerably safe conclusion that the third book, in which these calculations occur, must date not long after the death of the Stoic emperor, i.e. not long after A.D. 180. The three books were written and despatched separately, so that the first and second, in which the quotations are found, may be placed a little earlier than the third book. Besides the direct evidence which the *Apologia ad Autolycum* supplies to the authorship of the Fourth Gospel, Theophilus is in another way an indirect witness to the wide acceptance of four Gospels in the Canon of the New Testament. Jerome speaks in more than one passage of a work of Theophilus, now lost, which he calls his 'commentaries.'[50] In one reference indeed he appears to throw doubt upon the authenticity of this work. Speaking of Theophilus in *Vir. Illustr.* 25 he says, 'I have read commentaries written in his name on the Gospel and on the Proverbs of Solomon, which in my opinion do not appear

---

[50]The four books of *commentarii*, extant in Latin and ascribed to Theophilus, cannot represent the genuine work alluded to by Jerome. The theology is evidently post-Nicene; passages are found nearly word for word in St. Ambrose (i. §120, p. 295, ed. Otto; cf. Ambrose *Comm. in Luc.* iii. §2) in Cyprian (i. §153, p. 301; cf. Cyprian, *Epist.* lviii. §5), and in Jerome (i. §4, p. 280; cf. Jerome, *Comm. in Matt.* i. Op. vii. p. 12); and the work is evidently not a translation from the Greek, but originally written in Latin, see e.g. i. p. 283: '*apex autem; quatuor literas habens per evangelium in quadruplex testamentum indicat novum.*'

to agree with the elegance and style of the volumes mentioned above' (i.e. the *ad Autolycum* and other works). But elsewhere he quotes the work without the slightest misgiving. In the preface to his own commentary on St. Matthew's Gospel (in *Matth. Praef.* Op. vii. p. 7) he confesses 'to have read many years before the commentaries on Matthew . . . of Theophilus, bishop of the city of Antioch.' In his *Epistle to Algasia* (Ep. cxxi. Op. I. p. 866), written in A.D. 407, he throws further light upon the character of this lost writing. He speaks of it as a harmony of the four Gospels and as a lasting monument of the writer's genius ('*Theophilus . . . qui quattuor Evangelistarum in imum opus dicta compingens ingenii sui nobis monumenta dimisit*'). It is needless to point out the importance and significance of a harmony of the four Gospels constructed in the second century, in its relation to the genuineness of St. John's Gospel, and to the Diatessaron of Tatian.

IV. *The Churches of Palestine.*

Contemporaneously with the Ignatian Epistles and the treatise of Theophilus, we have the evidence of writers in the neighboring region of Palestine.

1. The date of the writings of Justin Martyr is of some importance. The two *Apologies* were written in the reign of Antoninus Pius, i.e. between July, 138 and March, 161. If we can trust the present text, the first (the longer) *Apology* was composed before M. Aurelius became Caesar, i.e. before A.D. 140. Against this early date, however, it is urged (1) that L. Verus, who is there styled ἐραστὴς παιδείας, was only ten years old at this time; (2) that Justin (*Apol.* i.46) speaks of our Lord as born 150 years before; (3) that Marcion is mentioned as already influential (*Apol.* i. 26). I do not think that much stress can be laid on these arguments. The expression ἐραστὴς παιδείας was a very fit one to apply to an imperial boy, who was, or was presumed to be, studious and intelligent, and to whom owing to his youth no other compliment could be paid. As regards the question of the chronology of our Lord's life, if Justin followed the ordinary computation (which is probably the case), he would place the Crucifixion in A.D. 29; and, allowing about thirty-three years for the interval between the Nativity and the Crucifixion, Justin's 150 years would bring the date of the work to A.D. 146. The third objection, the allusion to Marcion, is more difficult to meet, but the dates of his life are very uncertain. Happily, however, we can escape these difficulties altogether. By a

very plausible emendation (see Hort in the *Journal of Philology*, iii., 1857, pp. 163, 165), which reads Καὶ Καίσαρι for Καίσαρι Καὶ in the opening words of the *Apology*, M. Aurelius has already become Caesar before the date of the work.[51] If we accept this conjecture, the passage itself affords no posterior limit except the martyrdom of Justin, and the death of Antoninus Pius in A.D. 161. The second *Apology* is a sort of appendix or postscript to the first, written at the same time or soon after.

The *Dialogue with Trypho* was written after the longer *Apology* to which it contains a clear allusion[52] and therefore probably after both *Apologies*. It is represented as held at Ephesus, where Justin had stayed (Eusebius *Hist. Eccles.* iv.18). Justin's testimony therefore becomes in some sense the testimony of the Asiatic school. The time of the *Dialogue* is stated to be during the war of Barcochba[53] A.D. 132–135, i.e. when Polycarp and Papias were scarcely advanced beyond middle age, and while Melito and Apollinaris were yet young men. From the allusion to the first *Apology* given above, it is evident that if we accept the later date for the *Apology*, the dialogue cannot have been published until several years after it actually took place.

Eusebius and others after him place Justin's martyrdom in the reign of M. Aurelius, and the *Paschal Chronicle* fixes it at A.D. 165.[54] On the other hand, Epiphanius[55] apparently and others place it in the reign of Antoninus Pius, and, as far as we can judge, before A.D. 150. If we adopt with Hort A.D. 149 as the date, and leave time for the *Dialogue*, we may place the extant works of our author between A.D. 145–149.

We now turn to the evidence which Justin affords as to the Fourth Gospel.

---

[51]The *Apology* opens as follows: 'To the Emperor Titus Ælius Adrianus Antoninus Pius Augustus Cæsar, and to his son Verissimus the Philosopher, and to Lucius the Philosopher, the natural son of Cæsar, and the adopted son of Pius, a lover of learning, and to the sacred Senate, with the whole People of the Romans.' Over and above the question of date involved, it is unnatural to describe Antoninus' title in a descending scale from Imperator to Caesar.

[52]See *Dialog.* §120.

[53]*Dialog.* §1.

[54]Eusebius, *Hist. Eccles.* iv. 15; *Chron. Pasch.* 481sq. (ed. Bonn).

[55]Epiphanius (391 a; ii. p. 411 ed. Dindorf) makes Justin thirty years at the time of his martyrdom, which he places at the time of Rusticus. The name Rusticus is too common at this period to give us much assistance, and the text of Epiphanius is so corrupt that we may without hesitation read 'Antiniou' for 'Adrianou' in this passage, especially as a few lines lower down Epiphanius speaks of Tatian as setting up his heretical school about the twelfth year of Antoninus. He had already described Tatian as a contemporary of Justin who lapsed into heresy after Justin's death.

238

He does not quote it by name, but he shows more than one striking coincidence with its language. Thus speaking of the sacrament of baptism he says (*Apol.* I.61), 'For Christ also said, "Unless ye be born again (ἀναγεγεννήθητε), ye cannot enter into the kingdom of heaven, for that it is quite impossible for those that are once born to enter into their mother's womb is manifest to all" (cf. John 3:3-5).' If any doubt could be entertained whence this saying was derived, it will appear from a passage in the chapter immediately preceding (§60) that the Fourth Gospel was present to his mind. Applying the incident of the brazen serpent as an image of the Crucifixion, he reports Moses as erecting the serpent and saying, 'If ye look on this image . . . and believe, ye shall be saved in Him.' This is a very wide departure from the account in Numbers (21:7-9), where there is nothing about a type or about the necessity of belief; but the writer obviously had in his mind John 3:14, 15, 'as Moses lifted up the serpent in the wilderness, even so must the Son of man be lifted up, that whosoever believeth in Him . . . should have eternal life.'[56] Again, in the sixth chapter of the same *Apology*, Justin says: 'The prophetic spirit we reverence and worship, honouring (it) in reason and in truth,' where we are reminded of John 4:24. Speaking of the holy eucharist, 'We have been (or were) taught (ἐδιδάχθημεν),' he writes (§66), 'that the bread and wine are both the flesh and the blood of that Jesus Who became flesh,' an expression founded upon John 6:54. 'For,' he adds, 'the Apostles, in the memoirs left by them, which are called Gospels, have recorded that it was so enjoined on them' etc. This passage alone however would be far from conclusive. It can only be taken to strengthen a position already established. One other coincidence from the same work will suffice. Speaking of the prophecy in Isaiah of the miraculous conception of the Messiah, Justin remarks that God by the Spirit of prophecy foretold what was incredible, 'so that, when it came to pass, it might not be disbelieved, but might be believed from its having been foretold' (*Apol.* I.33), where we are at once reminded of John 14:29.

Turning now to the *Dialogue with Trypho* we find numerous expressions, which cannot well be explained except on the supposition that Justin had the Fourth Gospel before him. Our Lord is described as 'the only spotless

---

[56]Compare the treatment of this incident in *Dial.* §94.

and righteous light, that was sent from God to men' (*Dial.* 17; cf. John 1:9); He is the 'only-begotten of the Father of the universe, His Word and Power sprung in a special way from Him, as we have learnt from the memoirs' (*Dial.* 105; cf. John 1:14). An allusion to the imagery of Genesis xlix.11 is explained of Christ because 'His blood sprung not of man's seed, but of the will of God' (*Dial.* 63; cf. John i.13). We are informed (*Dial.* 69) that the Jews 'dared to call Him a magician and a deceiver of the people (λαοπλάνον),' where the last word seems to have been suggested by John 7:12, 'Nay, but He deceiveth the people.' Speaking of himself and of his brother Christians, Justin says, 'We are called, and are, the true children of God, who keep His commandments' (*Dial.* 123; cf. John 1:12; 1 John 3:1, 2); 'to us it is given both to hear, and to be with, and to be saved through this Christ, and to know all the things of the Father' (*Dial.* 121; cf. John 14:7); 'who are instructed in all the truth' (*Dial.* 39; cf. John 16:13). 'He that knoweth not Him (i.e. Christ), knoweth not the counsel of God, and he that insulteth and hateth Him, manifestly hateth and insulteth Him that sent Him; and if any man believeth not on Him, he believeth not the preaching of the prophets, who announced the glad tidings of Him, and preached them unto all' (*Dial.* 136, a reminiscence of John 5:23, 45, 46). Again, in the description of John the Baptist given in *Dial.* 88, an account which is chiefly taken from the Synoptic Gospels, unmistakeable proofs are given of Justin's acquaintance with the Fourth Gospel also. Thus the repudiation of the Baptist's own claim to the Messiahship is closely associated with the announcement of the presence of the 'one stronger,' whose shoes John proclaims himself unworthy to bear, in a way which presupposes Justin's knowledge of John 1:19-27. Lastly, in *Dial.* 57 occurs an expression which reminds us very forcibly of John 6:31, 'Of the manna, on which your fathers were nourished in the wilderness, the Scripture saith, that they ate angels' food.'

A work of Justin earlier than any extant is his treatise against Marcion. A few lines of this lost work are preserved in Irenaeus (iv.6.2). The passage is very short, not more than half a dozen lines, and does not give much scope for quotations from the New Testament, but in it occurs an expression suggested by St. John, 'The only-begotten Son came to us, gathering up His own creation in Himself.' The latter part of the clause is based on Eph 1:10, the former on John 1:18.

2. We now turn from the master to the scholar, from Justin Martyr to *Tatian*. The facts of Tatian's life are soon told. An Assyrian by birth, as he himself distinctly says, and a heathen, he exercised the profession of a sophist, in which capacity he travelled far and wide. His mind was first turned towards Christianity by reading the Scriptures, which impressed him greatly. He was converted, and became a disciple of Justin Martyr, doubtless at Rome, and after the death of his master appears to have remained some time in the metropolis teaching. Subsequently he left Rome, and seems to have spent the remainder of his life in the East, more especially in Syria and the neighboring countries. After Justin's death—how soon after we do not know—his opinions underwent a change. He separated himself from the Church, and espoused views closely allied to those of the Encratites. When Irenaeus wrote his first book, Tatian was no longer living, as may be inferred from the language of this father (Iren. i.28.1); and this book must have been written before A.D. 190, and may have been written as early as A.D. 178.[57] On the whole, we shall perhaps not be far wrong if we place the period of his literary activity at about A.D. 155–170.[58]

Of several writings of Tatian mentioned by the ancients, only one has come down to us,[59] his *Address to the Greeks*, a work composed before Tatian's separation from the Church, apparently not long after the death of Justin. This *Oratio ad Graecos* is an *Apology*, addressed to Gentiles. We do not therefore expect to find in it quotations from the sacred books, with which Gentile readers would as a matter of course have no acquaintance, and to which they would attribute no authority. But the following passages place beyond the reach of any reasonable doubt what was at least an *a priori*

---

[57]Clement of Alexandria, *Strom.* i.1.11 (p. 322) mentions an 'Assyrian' as one of his earlier teachers, and the identification of this Assyrian with Tatian is highly probable; see below.

[58]On the whole subject of Tatian see *Essays on Supernatural Religion* p. 272sq.

[59][The discovery and publication in 1888 by Ciasca of Tatian's *Diatessaron* in an Arabic version has set at rest forever the question whether Tatian knew the Fourth Gospel. The *Diatessaron* is, as its name implies, a harmony of the four Gospels; and as Dr. Lightfoot had surmised, it consists of our four canonical Gospels, and commences with the opening words of St. John's Gospel.] This note, and the previous citations of *Essays on Supernatural Religion* in earlier notes we owe to Professor Hort, who in July of 1893 went over Lightfoot's notes for this and several other lectures and prepared them for publication by Macmillan. The last edition of the volume of *Biblical Essays*, which includes this essay, appeared in 1904. There is something of an irony in Hort's adding references to *Essays on Supernatural Religion* to this lengthy essay; Lightfoot spent no little time deconstructing in print the many errors and critical misjudgments in that volume. It is unlikely that Lightfoot would have approved of these additions.

presumption, that the pupil of Justin knew and accepted the Fourth Gospel, to which his master's extant writings have been shown to give testimony.

§4. 'God is a Spirit' (cf. John 4:24).

§13. 'And this then is the saying, "The darkness comprehendeth not the light"' (cf. John 1:5).

§19. 'Follow ye the only God. All things have been made by Him, and apart from Him hath been made no thing' (cf. John 1:3).

These passages are conclusive, for they are characteristic passages of the Fourth Gospel. There are other coincidences with Johannine language, such as §5 'God was in the beginning,' which, taken by themselves, cannot be pressed, but in the light of the extracts given above are probably derived from the same source.

V. *The Church of Alexandria.*

1. In all probability, the *Epistle of Barnabas* is to be considered the earliest piece of extant Christian literature, outside the Canon, which emanates from Alexandria. Whoever is its author—and it is noticeable that he nowhere claims to be the Apostle Barnabas—in his general style and his interpretation of the Old Testament, he represents Alexandrian thought. He gives us moreover a picture of feuds between Jews and Christians, which is in keeping with what we know from other sources of the character of the population of that great city. For reasons which cannot be entered into here, but which bear upon the interpretation of a passage in §4, I am inclined to place the date of the Epistle in the reign of Vespasian, after that Emperor's association with himself of his sons Titus and Domitian in the supreme power (A.D. 70–79). In this case, it was written before the Fourth Gospel; we must therefore look elsewhere for the evidence of which we are in search. We shall find, if I mistake not, that the earliest quotations from the Fourth Gospel (and these very important) which proceed from Alexandria, are contained in the works of Gnostic writers, such as Basilides, Valentinus etc.; and these will be considered later on. At present we will confine ourselves to orthodox writings.

With one possible exception there is no orthodox literature extant which comes from the Alexandrian Church between the *Epistle of Barnabas* and the writings of Clement of Alexandria. That exception is the latter part (§§11, 12) of the *Epistle to Diognetus*. In our solitary authority for this epistle, the Strassburg MS., now no longer extant, the beginning of one treatise and the conclusion of another have been accidentally attached together so as to form in appearance one work. The writer of the latter part is clearly an Alexandrian, and indulges in the allegorical interpretations of the Old Testament which are characteristic of that school. He calls himself 'a disciple of the Apostles and a teacher of the Gentiles.' The whole tone of thought of the fragment is second-century. These indications appear to point to Pantaenus, the master of Clement, and the Apostle of the Indies (c. A.D. 180–210), as the author of the treatise. The account given of him in Eusebius (*Hist. Eccles.* v. 10) would seem to imply that his journey to India[60] preceded his appointment as head of the Catechetical school of Alexandria; and Anastatius of Sinai speaks of him as one of those early exegetes, who understood all the narrative of the Hexaemeron as referring to Christ and the Church, a view which harmonizes in a remarkable degree with the allegorical interpretation of the garden of Eden preserved in this fragment.

The influence of St. John is very manifest in this treatise, though there is no direct quotation from his Gospel. The Word who is called 'the Life' (§12; cf. John 1:4), 'who was from the beginning' (§11 cf. John 1:2), 'through whom the Father is glorified' (§12; cf. John 13:31; 14:13), 'has revealed Himself to His disciples' (§11; cf. John 2:11). These and other coincidences with the Fourth Gospel, occurring in a fragment which occupies less than two octavo pages, are sufficient to indicate that the writer's mind was imbued with Johannine teaching and phraseology.

2. *Clement of Alexandria* in his *Stromateis* (i.1.11)[61] describes one of his instructors in Greece as 'the Ionian' and places him first on the list of his teachers, as though he were the earliest. Thus he is connected with Asia Minor, and probably with the school of St. John. Consequently his testimony is of great importance for our purpose. To Clement we owe several tradi-

---

[60]Jerome, *Vir. Ill.* 36; *Ep.* 70 (p. 428) states that he was sent to India by Demetrius (bishop of Alexandria 189–231). But Eusebius (l.c.) represents him as head of the catechetical school ten years before the accession of Demetrius. We must conclude that Jerome places the visit to India too late.

[61]The *Stromateis* was written A.D. 194 or 195 under Severus. Clement's other extant works are earlier. He enumerates his teachers as follows, by giving the country in which he was their pupil: (1) in *Greece*, 'the Ionian'; (2) in *Magna Graecia*, (a) one from *Coelo-Syria*, (b) another from Egypt; (3) *in the East*, (a) one from Assyria, (b) another, in Palestine, a Hebrew; (4) in *Alexandria*, the last and greatest, i.e. Pantaenus. I am inclined to identify 'the Ionian' with Melito.

tions of St. John.[62] He speaks of a certain statement[63] as 'not occurring in the four Gospels handed down to us but only in the Gospel according to the Egyptians,' thus showing that in his time the number of the Gospels was definitely fixed at four. In another passage[64] he appeals to the tradition of the presbyters of a former generation as to the order in which the Gospels were written, saying that after the other Gospels had been written, 'John, last of all, observing that the external (bodily) facts (τά σωματικά) had been set forth in the existing Gospels, at the urgent request of his friends and by the divine guidance of the Spirit, composed a spiritual Gospel (πνευματικόν ... εὐαγγέλιον).' The value of this tradition may be great or it may be small; but his whole language bears testimony to the fact that the Gospel of St. John had long been recognised as authoritative, and that traditions had grown up about it.[65]

3. *Origen* was born in A.D. 185, and began to teach at eighteen. Of him it is sufficient to say that he wrote a commentary on St. John's Gospel, and that he betrays no knowledge that the authenticity of the Gospel had ever been called in question.[66]

VI. *The Churches of Greece and Macedonia.*

1. The extant remains belonging to this branch of the Church in the second century are very slight indeed. In the few lines of Dionysius of Corinth that survive, no quotation could have been introduced naturally. Perhaps however the *Epistle to Diognetus* §§1-10 may belong to this Church. It certainly shows evidence of Hellenic culture both in diction and matter. This however is a very slight presumption in favor of its ascription to Greece proper; and I only include it here because some place must be found for a document which is undoubtedly very early, and cannot well be assigned to

---

[62]E.g. the story of St John and the young robber (*Quis div. salv.* 42, p. 958) quoted in Eusebius, *Hist. Eccles.* iii. 23.

[63]*Strom.* iii. 13, p. 553.

[64]Cited in Eusebius, *Hist. Eccles.* vi. 14.

[65]In his book of the Paschal Festival, Clement makes the 14th the day of the crucifixion (*Fragm.* p. 1017; ed. Potter), thus following out the tradition of the Asiatic school. Of this work only two short fragments survive, but Eusebius informs us (*Hist. Eccles.* vi.13) that in it he mentioned 'the traditions which he had heard from the elders.' This is another indirect link with the School of St. John.

[66]See Lücke, p. 78. His Commentary on St. John was written about the year 222. In it he controverts Heracleon.

a later date than the middle of the second century.[67] The Epistle is full of indications of the influence of St. John's writings. 'Christians dwell in the world but are not of the world' (§6; cf. John 17:11, 14, 16). The doctrine of the Word is drawn out fully in §7. He is described as 'the artificer and creator of the universe, by Whom God made the heavens, by Whom He enclosed the sea in its proper bounds' (cf. John 1:3; Heb 1:2); 'God sent Him as saving . . . He sent Him as loving and not as judging' (cf. John 3:17). In a later passage (§10), in language which is an echo of John 3:16, we are told, 'For God loved men . . . to whom He sent His only-begotten Son, to whom He promised the kingdom in heaven and will give it to those that love Him' (cf. 1 John 4:9). 'How then,' the writer goes on, 'shalt thou (worthily) love Him, that before loved thee so' (cf. 1 John 4:10, 11)?

2. That *Athenagoras* should be considered a representative of the Church of Greece is evident from the heading of extant *Apology*, in which he describes himself as an 'Athenian.' Thus the account of him given by Philippus Sidetes and preserved by Nicephorus Callistus[68] which makes him the first leader of the Catechetical school at Alexandria, must be inaccurate. But Philip of Side, who lived in the fifth century and was ordained deacon by Chrysostom, was a notoriously pretentious and careless writer. For instance, in his short account of Athenagoras he makes Pantaenus the pupil of Clement, and asserts that Athenagoras' *Apology* was addressed to Hadrian and Antoninus, whereas its title shows it to have been dedicated to the emperors Aurelius and Commodus, and therefore written after Commodus was associated in the government (autumn of A.D. 176). From other indications it seems possible to fix the date more precisely between the end of A.D. 176 and the end of A.D. 177.[69]

---

[67]Westcott, *Canon of the New Testament*, p. 88 (ed. 4), places it c. A.D. 117, Bunsen *Hippolytus* i. p. 170, A.D. 135. I am inclined to date it somewhat later. The Diognetus addressed is not improbably the tutor of Marcus Aurelius, and the reference to 'a King sending his son as a King' (§7), as illustrating the Incarnation, may very well have been suggested by the adoption of M. Aurelius by Antoninus Pius in A.D. 147. On the other hand the simplicity of the theological teaching will not allow us to bring the date down much later.

[68]See Dodwell, *Dissert. In Irenaeus*.

[69]The βάθεια εἰρήνη (§2) is only applicable to the years 176–178 in the reign of M. Aurelius. This peace intervened between the insurrection of Avidius Crassus and the outbreak of the Marcomannic War. On the other hand to place the *Apology* after the outbreak of the persecution of the Christians of Vienna and Lyons (A.D. 177) raises a difficulty. Athenagoras declares (§§35) that no slaves had ever accused their Christian masters of the infamous crimes attributed to them. This statement ceased to be true after the commencement of the persecution in question.

The absence of all appeal to Holy Scripture, which is characteristic of apologies addressed to the heathen, is noticeable in Athenagoras also. But this does not prevent him from exhibiting correspondences with the thought and teaching of the Fourth Gospel. Thus God the Father 'hath made all things by the Word that proceedeth from Him' (§4; cf. John 1:3). Again, 'the Son of God is (the) Word of the Father in form and in energy; for of Him and by Him were all things made, the Father and the Son being one, the Son being in the Father, and the Father in the Son' (§10; cf. John 1:3; 17:21sq.). 'To know God and the Word that proceedeth from Him, what is the union of the Son with the Father, what the communion (κοινωνία) of the Father with the Son' is the Christian's life (§12; cf. John 17:3). The later Church of Greece proper is almost a blank as regards any literary activity.

VII. *The Church of Rome.*

The genuine *Epistle of Clement* has been assigned with great probability to A.D. 95 or 96, during the reign of Domitian, when St. John was still in banishment in the island of Patmos. It was almost certainly composed before St. John wrote his Gospel. Accordingly, in this, the first contribution to Christian extra-canonical literature which emanated from Rome, no quotation from the Fourth Gospel is possible.

1. We therefore pass on to the *Shepherd of Hermas*, the author of which is described in the Muratorian Canon, in a well-known passage, to have composed his work during the episcopate of his brother Pius (c. A.D. 141–156) in Rome.[70] It is the earliest Christian allegory, written probably by a slave[71] and is noticeable for its lack of quotations from Holy Scripture. This applies not merely to the New Testament but to the Old Testament likewise. There are numerous passages which recall the language of the psalms and prophetical books in the one case, and of the Synoptic Gospels and Epistles—especially the Epistle of St. James—in the other, but the coincidences are embedded in the narrative itself, and have to be carefully disentangled from it. The only quotation which is avowedly such is taken from an apocryphal work, the book of Eldad and Modad (*Vis.* ii.3). In spite however of this characteristic feature, the treatise contains indications that the author was influenced by

---

[70]'*Sedente cathedra urbis Romae ecclesiae Pio episcopo fratre eius*' *Can. Murator.* p. 58sq. (ed. Tregelles).
[71]*Vis.* i.1, unless indeed he is assuming a fictitious character. His mention of Arcadia (*Sim.* ix.) makes it probable that he came originally from Southern Greece.

the writings of St. John. The very title *The Shepherd* recalls the parable of the Good Shepherd in John 10, and the sixth *Similitude* is an elaboration of the metaphor employed in that parable. The same chapter in the Fourth Gospel affords a more remarkable coincidence. In the ninth *Similitude* the Son of God is called 'the Gate'[72] and it is added that 'no man can enter into the kingdom of God otherwise than through the name of His Son Who is beloved by Him' (*Sim.* ix.12; cf. John 10:9; 14:6). In the same section the Son of God is said to be 'begotten prior to all His Creation, so that He became His Father's adviser in His Creation.' These correspondences occurring together seem to indicate the influence of the Fourth Gospel. Elsewhere St. John's teaching on 'the Truth' underlies Hermas' words as in *Mand.* iii., 'Love the truth, and let nothing but truth proceed out of your mouth . . . and thus shall the Lord, Who dwelleth in thee, be glorified, for the Lord is true in every word, and with Him is no lie,' a clear allusion to 1 John 2:27. Lastly, another passage recalls expressions in John 10:18, the Son 'having Himself cleansed the sins of His people, showed them the paths of life, giving them the law which He received from His Father' (*Sim.* v.6).

2. The reasons for assigning the *Muratorian Canon* to Rome are briefly as follows: (1) the mention of *urbs*, implying that the writer was familiar with Rome and probably wrote at Rome; (2) the translation of the work into Latin and its preservation in the Western Church; (3) the fact that the Canon which it presents is substantially the Canon of the Western Church;[73] (4) the knowledge which the writer displays of the Roman authorship of the *Pastor of Hermas*; (5) the prominent position assigned to the Epistle to the Romans, which he explains more fully than usual, promising an exposition of the Epistle itself.[74] I will not discuss the question of the authorship of this interesting fragment. It has been assigned to Gaius, the Roman presbyter, to Hegesippus, to Hippolytus. It was obviously written in Greek originally, and Greek was for the first two centuries the language of the Roman Church. The

---

[72]The word is θύρα in St. John, πύλη in Hermas; but the passage in St. John is loosely quoted at least three times by the early heretics given in Hippolytus with πύλη instead of θύρα, and so also in the *Clementine Homilies*, see below.

[73]There is however an obscure allusion to some (*quidam ex nostris*) who refuse to allow the public reading of the Apocalypse of Peter, as though implying that the majority accepted this work as canonical.

[74]'*Romanis autem ordine (?ordinem) scripturarum sed et principium earum esse Christum intimans prolixius scripsit, de quibus singulis necesse est a nobis disputari.*'

data for ascertaining the age of the writing are two: (1) the notice of an event occurring in the episcopate of Pius (A.D. 141–156) as having taken place '*nuperrime temporibus nostris*'; (2) the mention in a passage manifestly corrupt of Arsinous, Valentinus, Miltiades, Basilides and the founder of the Montanists.[75] We have thus the inferior and the superior limits within which the work is to be assigned; and, though the problem presents considerable difficulties, we may provisionally place the date at A.D. 170 or thereabouts.

The fragment opens with an account of the Four Gospels. It is mutilated at the beginning, and the description of St. Matthew's Gospel is wanting. This is the case too with the notice of St. Mark's Gospel, which is lost all but the conclusion of the last sentence—'at which however he was present and so he set them down.'[76] But the account given of St. Luke throws light upon the writer's meaning. St. Luke, he tells us, was a physician who after the Ascension became a follower of St. Paul and compiled his Gospel in his own name. 'But neither did he (*nec ipse*, i.e. any more than St. Mark) see the Lord in the flesh,' that is to say, he was not an eyewitness. 'He wrote from hearsay (*ex opinione*).' The writer then continues, 'The Fourth Gospel is (the work) of John one of the (personal) disciples (of Christ) (*ex discipulis*).' This expression is significant. St. John's position is here contrasted with that of St. Mark and St. Luke, who were not eyewitnesses. The word μαθητής implies a personal disciple of the Lord, and it is so used in Papias and Irenaeus.[77] Moreover in this place it is peculiarly appropriate, inasmuch as St. John uses this expression of himself (John 18:15-16; 19:26-27; 21:20, 23-24);[78] and his example doubtless fixed the usage of the Asiatic School. A little lower down, after quoting 1 John 1:1, he draws attention to the fact that St. John 'not only claimed to have seen and heard' the Lord (read *non solum visorem se esse et auditorem*), 'but to have written all the marvels of the Lord in order (*sed et scriptorem omnium mirabilium Domini per ordinem profitetur*).' This statement is emphatic. As distinct from the arrangement of events in the second and third (perhaps also in the first) Gospel, the eyewitness is declared to preserve the true chronology.

---

[75]For speculations as to Arsinous and Miltiades see Bunsen, *Anal. Anten.* I. p. 134 sq., and Credner, *Canon*, p. 82.

[76]'*Quibus tamen interfuit et ita posuit.*'

[77]Irenaeus always calls John 'the disciple of the Lord.'

[78]See Westcott, *Canon of the New Testament*, p. 211 (ed. 4).

The references to the writings of St. John in the Muratorian Canon are full and explicit. (1) The circumstances under which the Gospel was written are first described; (2) incidentally the opening words in the first Epistle are quoted, 'What wonder then if John so boldly puts forward each statement in his Epistle (*in epistolis suis*)[79] also saying of himself, "What we have seen with our eyes and heard with our ears and our hands have handled, these things we have written unto you"'; (3) The mention of the number of St. Paul's Epistles introduces an allusion to the Apocalypse, 'for John likewise in the Apocalypse, although he writes to seven Churches, yet speaks to all'; (4) Next the Catholic Epistles are discussed,[80] and we are told that 'two Epistles of the before-mentioned John are considered canonical';[81] (5) lastly, the Apocalypse is mentioned again in conjunction with the Apocalypse of St. Peter, and an unqualified testimony is given to its acceptance in the Church. Thus there is a continuous chain of notices, and the absence of the faintest hint to the contrary renders it unquestionable that the same John is meant from beginning to end as the author of the Gospel, of the First Epistle, of the two shorter Epistles, and of the Apocalypse.

But is not the account of the Gospels in this fragment founded upon Papias? And if so, what account did Papias give? We have found that the Muratorian writer lays stress on the secondary character of St. Mark's account, with apparent reference to his chronology. Papias also[82] informs us concerning St. Mark, that, though strictly accurate, he 'did not write in order (οὐ μέντοι τάξει), for he was not himself a hearer or follower of the Lord.' Again, we notice that the Muratorian writer quotes from the First Epistle of St. John in evidence. Papias likewise does the same. We are not told with what object Papias adduced this testimony from the Epistles; but it is at least a plausible hypothesis that he had the same end in view as the Muratorian

<hr>

[79]The plural is here probably used to describe one epistle. This is not uncommon, cf. the Epistle of Polycarp (§3); Eusebius, *Hist. Eccles.* vi. 1; vi. 43; Joseph. *Ant.* xii. 4.10; and in classical writers Thucydides i. 132; iv. 50; viii. 51; Polybius v. 43. 5 etc. It is common in the LXX. Cf. Esth 3:14; 1 Macc 5:14, etc. See my *Philippians*, p. 140sq.

[80]There is evidently a lacuna in the MS. hereabouts, for the First Epistle of St. Peter is not mentioned.

[81]'*Superscripti Iohannis duas* (l. *duae*) *in catholica* (l. *catholicis*) *habentur.*' The two Epistles meant are probably the Second and Third Epistles, the first being considered as a kind of prologue to the Gospel, detached from the shorter pair, and treated with the Gospel.

[82]In Eusebius, *Hist. Eccles.* iii.39.

writer. May it not then be inferred with some degree of probability that the writer of the Muratorian Canon borrowed in some degree from Papias? The use of the term *ex discipulis* seems to point to such a source of information.

3. It might have been unnecessary to carry the history of the Canon in the Roman Church further; but doubts have been thrown of the view of Hippolytus upon this question.[83] It has been maintained that he shows no knowledge of the Gospel as the work of St. John. It would indeed have been marvellous if Hippolytus, the pupil of Irenaeus, and the friend of Origen, both of whom bear such unmistakeable testimony to the reception of the Fourth Gospel, had entertained any doubts on this subject. But the answer to the objection is evident: (1) When Hippolytus expounds his own views, he is addressing heathens. He therefore does not appeal to any Scripture, because it would not carry authority with his hearers. (2) It is perfectly evident when he refers to the quotations from St. John in Gnostic writings that he and they alike received as authoritative the documents which are quoted. (3) He does not mention by name St. Matthew or St. Luke. He mentions St. Peter and St. James indeed, but without any connection with their writings in the New Testament. The only Pauline Epistles which he connects with the name of St. Paul are Romans, 2 Corinthians, 1 Timothy and perhaps Galatians though he quotes these and most of the other Epistles of St. Paul repeatedly.[84] In the work against Noetus (§§12, 14, 15 etc.) and in a fragment preserved by Lagarde (p. 52) he distinctly quotes the Fourth Gospel and attributes it to 'John, the beloved disciple.'[85] (4) Among the list of works ascribed to him on his statue is a 'Defence of the Gospel and Apocalypse of St John.' The work is lost, but there is reason to suppose that it was known to, and used by, Epiphanius. These reasons seem to me amply to justify our claim to reckon Hippolytus among the witnesses for the Johannine authorship. Hippolytus is the last and most famous representative of the Greek Church of Rome. Henceforward Rome becomes the focus of Latin Christendom.

VIII. *The Churches of Africa.*

Meanwhile Latin Christianity has had its headquarters in Africa and es-

---

[83]Tayler, *An Attempt to Ascertain the Character of the Fourth Gospel*, pp. 57, 77, 87.

[84]Romans, 2 Corinthians, Galatians once only, 1 Timothy twice.

[85]The quotations are as follows: John 1:1 (by name), 1-3 (by name), 10, 14, 18, 20, 29 (twice, once by name), 30; 2:19; 3:6, 13 (twice by name), 31; 4:34; 5:25 (twice) 36; 6:27, 35, 45; 8:12; 10:18, 30; 11:35, 52; 14:6, 8sq., 12; 16:28; 19:14, 37; 20:1, 17.

pecially at Carthage. And it is here that we must seek the opinion of the early Latin Church on the question of the Canon. The Roman Church, Greek in nation and Latin in soil, was the natural link between Greek and Latin Christendom. Carthage and Africa were converted from Rome. The Canon of the African Church therefore may be supposed, in all the more important points, to reproduce the Canon of the Church of Rome.

1. *Tertullian* is the first known writer of the African Church; as to his own individual opinion on the authority of the Fourth Gospel no doubt can be entertained. He quotes it some two hundred times or more without the slightest misgiving. It is more important to trace the evidence, which his language affords, to the traditional testimony to its use. Thus in his treatise against Marcion (iv.2.5), after mentioning the four Evangelists together by name, he appeals to the Churches founded by St John and the succession of bishops derived from St. John, as evidence for the reception of the Gospels by the Catholic Church. Making all allowance for his rhetoric, such an appeal cannot be considered unmeaning. Of the Gospel of St. John especially he speaks (*adv. Prax.* §5) as though it had long worked itself into the phraseology and the teaching of Christianity.

2. Another document, contemporary with, or rather earlier than, Tertullian, the Acts of Martyrdom of SS. Perpetua and Felicitas (Ruinart, p. 80sq.) shows what a deep hold the writings of St. John had taken on the African Church at this time. At the outset, we meet in the preface with two obvious coincidences with Johannine phraseology. The courage of the martyrs is instanced as a proof of the power of God, 'Who worketh always the works which He hath promised, for a testimony to them that believe not, for a support to them that believe' (*quae repromisit non credentibus in testimonium, credentibus in beneficium*, a reference to John 10:38). The passage then proceeds, 'accordingly in our case too, that which we have heard and handled declare we unto you also, brothers and sons, that ye also may . . . recount the glory of God (*et nos itaque quod audivimus et contrectavimus annuntiamus et vobis, fratres et filioli, ut et vos . . . rememoremini gloriae Domini*),' an expression based upon the opening words of St. John's First Epistle.[86] Less stress can be laid on the fact that in her vision Perpetua sees

---

[86]The passage quoted is probably verse 3. Notice however the variation '*quod audivimus et contrectavimus*' for '*quod vidimus et audivimus.*'

(§4) sitting in the midst of a garden '*hominem canum in habitu Pastoris,*' for this favorite idea of Christ as the Good Shepherd may have been derived from the Pastor of Hermas, though its original source was doubtless John x. But towards the close of the document occurs an allusion to the Fourth Gospel, which is interesting because it is not apparent on the surface. The only direct quotation from the New Testament found in this martyrology runs as follows: 'But He who had said, "Ask and ye shall receive" (*qui dixerat Petite et accipietis*), gave (to the martyrs) at their prayer that form of death which each had desired' (§19). Now, though the passage quoted occurs in three of the four Gospels (Matt 7:7; Luke 11:9; John 16:24), yet the exact form in which it is couched shows that it was derived, not from the Synoptic narrative, but from the Fourth Gospel.[87] In short, with the exception of the Apocalypse (e.g. especially §12), there are no such coincidences with any other part of the New Testament as are afforded to the language of the Fourth Evangelist.

The Montanist, or rather Montanizing tendencies of this martyrology bear testimony to its early date.[88] Indeed, there is every reason to believe that it was contemporary with the events which it records. Tertullian refers to the document in his *de anima* §55, and the date usually assigned to this treatise is c. A.D. 208. The date of the martyrdom of St. Perpetua and her companions is fixed by a reference in the martyrology itself to the birthday of Geta Caesar,[89] thus placing it between A.D. 198, when Geta became Caesar, and A.D. 209, when he was created Augustus. It is highly probable that the actual year was A.D. 202, during the persecution of Severus.

IX. *The Churches of Syria.*

There is no early Syrian writer of importance until Bardesanes. He flourished at the close of the second century, or at the beginning of the third century, according as we consider the Emperor Antoninus mentioned in connection with him (Epiph. i.477 A, Eusebius, *Hist. Eccles.* iv.20, Jerome *Vir. Ill.* etc.) to have been M. Aurelius or Caracalla. Bardesanes was a voluminous writer, but of the various works assigned to him only one has sur-

---

[87]St. Matthew and St. Luke have Αἰτεῖτε, καὶ δοθήσεται ὑμῖν. St. John alone αἰτεῖτε, καὶ λήμψεσθε.
[88]The allusion to 'cheese' in §4 can, I think, hardly be taken to show that the writer or the martyrs were Artotyrites.
[89]*Natale tunc Getae Caesaris* §7.

vived, *The Book of the Laws of Countries*, which was discovered by Cureton among the Nitrian MSS., and published by him in his *Spicilegium Syriacum* in 1855. When examined, however, this treatise appears to have emanated from the disciples of Bardesanes rather than from Bardesanes himself, and its date is too late to be of assistance in determining the tradition of the Syrian Church on the question of the Fourth Gospel. Among the ancient Syriac documents discovered by Cureton in 1848 and published in 1864, is one entitled *The Doctrine of the Apostles*, in which Simon Peter is represented (Cureton l.c. p. 25) as quoting the promise of the Comforter in the language of John 14:26; and in another document. *The Doctrine of Simon Cephas*, the same quotation in a shorter form is again put into St. Peter's mouth (Cureton l.c. p. 36). But here again, the value of this evidence is lessened by the uncertainty of the date which is to be assigned to these ancient documents.

X. *The Testimony of Heretical Writers.*

We now pass from the evidence of orthodox writers to the testimony of heretics, and when we begin to look into it we are surprised at its extent and at its early date. The numerous controversies which the early fathers held with the multiform systems to which Christianity gave rise, has resulted in our possessing, embedded in the works of the defenders of the faith, large extracts from the writers who assailed it. This mine of unorthodox literature has been largely increased by the acquisition in recent years of Hippolytus' great work the *Refutation of All Heresies*. From this newly-discovered work I shall draw the greater part of the evidence which I hope to bring before you. The evidence itself I shall state as briefly as I can. We will begin with the Gnostics.

A. *The Gnostics.*

1. *Simon Magus* is credited with a work called *The Great Revelation* of which Hippolytus has preserved considerable extracts (*Refut.* vi.9-18). There is however reason to believe that the treatise was mainly written by his disciples. In a quotation from this book given by Hippolytus (l.c. vi.9), where man is described as 'born of blood,' some have found an allusion to John 1:13 (ἐξ αἱμάτων). This seems to me very doubtful. Indeed the book was probably composed somewhere about the close of the first century, perhaps before the Gospel of St. John was written, or at least circulated.

2. *The Ophites or Naassenes.* This was a very early sect, almost pre-Christian in its origin, which broke up into several distinct branches, as it adopted diverse extraneous elements. But its assimilative character makes it next to impossible for us to separate the more ancient features of its teaching from the more recent developments. Thus we have no means of ascertaining the exact date of the writings quoted by Hippolytus. But Hippolytus himself composed his *Refutation* some time early in the third century,[90] and he intimates that when he wrote the Ophite system was already on the wane. There is good reason therefore for assigning an early period in the second century for the document which he had before him. It abounds with quotations from the Fourth Gospel. I will not weary you by detailing them at length, but will content myself with giving the references to the Gospel and to the pages in Duncker and Schneidewin's edition (1859) of the *Refutatio*, merely premising that the quotations are clear and explicit.

John 1:3	*Refutatio* v. 8 (p. 150); v. 9 (166)
1:9	v. 9 (p. 172)
3:5	v. 8 (p. 162)
4:6	v. 7 (p. 148)
4:10, 14	v. 9 (p. 172)
4:21	v. 9 (p. 166)
5:37	v. 8 (p. 154)
6:44	v. 8 (p. 158)
6:53	v. 8 (p. 152)
8:21	v. 8 (p. 154)
10:9	v. 8 (p. 156)
13:33	v. 8 (p. 152)

There are also undoubted allusions to the marriage of Cana in Galilee (John 2:1-11; cf. *Refut.* v. 8 p. 152) and to the man born blind (John 9:1; cf. *Refut.* v. 9, p. 172), which are evidently taken from the same source. And this list might be enlarged without difficulty.

---

[90]The limits of date for the composition are the death of Callistus A.D. 220, of whom an account is given (*Haer.* ix. 11sq.), and Hippolytus' own death, which took place somewhere between A.D. 235 and 238 (*Liber Pontificalis* i. pp. 64, 145, Duchesne).

3. The distinction between the Peratae and the Naassenes is not very clearly defined, and the two bodies seem to have held many tenets in common; but Hippolytus treats them as separate sects, and it is evident therefore that he considered the Peratae, as a body, to have a real and independent existence. I tabulate as before the obvious quotations from the Fourth Gospel, which occur in the account of them taken by Hippolytus from one of their own documents.

John 1:1-4	*Refutatio* v. 16 (p. 194)
3:14	v. 16 (p. 192)
3:17	v. 12 (p. 178)
8:44	v. 17 (p. 196)
10:7	v. 17 (p. 198)

4. We pass on to another *Ophite sect*, which is treated next in order in the *Refutatio*—the *Sethiani*. As far as we can judge from the extracts which Hippolytus gives us, the formularies of this sect do not indulge in scriptural phraseology to any great extent. But here again we meet with traces of the use of St. John's language, e.g. *Refut.* v. 19 (p. 206), where the Logos is said to have 'drunk the cup of the living water which springeth up,' an expression which recalls John 4:10, 14; and *Refut.* v. 21 (p. 212), where true believers are spoken of as those 'who are born again of the Spirit, not of the flesh,' words which remind us of John 3:6.

5. *Justinus*, whom Hippolytus quotes as another Ophite heresiarch, elaborated a system which combined heathen mythology and the book of Genesis into a fantastic theory of the universe. The *Book of Baruch*, from which Hippolytus quotes, presents few correspondences with the New Testament, but the same coincidence is found with John 4:10, 14, which we have noticed already; and Jesus, as he leaves his body on the cross, says to his mother Eden, 'Woman, thou hast to the full thy son' words which, though with a wholly different application, betray an acquaintance with John 19:26.

6. The evidence which the Ophite system affords can be supplemented from the *Pistis Sophia*, one of the few remains of the old Gnostic literature which have come down to us. This work is preserved in a Coptic version. It is in four books, the fourth probably by a different author, and containing a simpler form of teaching than the other three. The date usually assigned to

the composition is the middle of the third century. I give from Petermann's edition the correspondences which it presents with the Fourth Gospel.

John 1:20	*Pistis Sophia* p. 9
7:33	p. 11
7:35	p. 11
14:3	p. 145
15:15	p. 145
15:19	pp. 8, 145
17:14, 16	pp. 8, 145
17:23	p. 145
17:25	pp. 120, 175

The Johannine expression 'Verily, verily' (ἀμήν, ἀμήν) occurs very frequently (pp. 23, 55, 117, 197) in this treatise.

7. *Basilides*, Gnostic teacher of Alexandria, flourished in the reign of Hadrian (A.D. 117–138). He professed to have been instructed by Glaucias, a follower of St. Peter. Clement of Alexandria, to whom we owe this information (*Strom.* vii.17, p. 898), classes him in a loose way with those heretics 'who arose about the times of Hadrian, and who reached until the period of the elder Antoninus.'[91] Though Clement was interested in placing his date as low as possible, there is no serious difference of opinion in this respect. Within a few years the limit must lie. Now Hippolytus gives an abstract of a work, or portion of a work, by Basilides; and in it one or two passages of St. John are quoted and gnostically explained: 'And this,' says he, 'is what is called in the Gospels, "That was the true light that lighteth every man who cometh (or coming) into the world"' (cf. *Refut.* vii.22, p. 360; cf. John 1:9). And again: 'But that everything,' says he, 'has its own proper times the Savior states explicitly, saying, "My time is not yet come"' (*Refut.* vii.27, p. 376; cf. John 2:4). It is said, however, that these quotations are taken not from Basilides himself, but from some other Basilidean writer. But what are the facts? The general form in which the quotations are introduced—the word φησίν—

---

[91]Our chief authorities for the life of Basilides are Clement, l.c. (he is contending that the Catholic Church is older than the sects); Irenaeus i.24.3sq.; Eusebius, *Hist. Eccles.* iv. 7; Epiph. *Haer.* xxiv. 1. (p. 68 e); Theodoret, *H.F.* i.2.9.

cannot be urged as an argument one way or the other; for the expression is often used impersonally, and may mean 'he says' or 'they say.' The question must be decided by an examination of the passages themselves. Hippolytus begins by stating (p. 356, l.64), that Basilides and Isidore his son and disciple declare that Matthew delivered to them certain secret truths which he had heard from the Savior. Then follows a series of quotations, extending over many pages and ushered in (p. 356, l.69) by φησίν. This connecting particle is repeated again and again, but it links together a continuous argument from which it is patent that Hippolytus is quoting some one book and some one representative of the school. When he comments on the statements made, he occasionally speaks of his opponents in the plurals but the narrative quoted exhibits more than once the writer's personality, e.g. 'I do not admit,' says he (with φησίν, p. 356, l.79); 'By willed, I mean,' says he (with φησι p. 358, l.97), clearly showing that the writer was a single individual who delivered his opinions with authority. Who then was this writer? The answer is obvious. None other than Basilides himself. No other name is mentioned by Hippolytus. After the first introduction Isidore is tacitly dropped, and Basilides is treated as the solitary antagonist. But it may be contended that this was a later work written by a disciple in the name of Basilides. To this contention we may reply: (1) that no such work was ever heard of; (2) that Basilides differed herein from other heresiarchs, as Simon Magus for example, in that his followers had no interest in forging documents in his name. For unlike the Ophites and the Valentinians, the Basilideans were not a large and spreading sect. They soon dwindled away, leaving by a natural selection the Ophites and Valentinians masters of the Gnostic field. On the other hand, the abstract which Hippolytus gives shows the influence of a master mind. Now it is known that Basilides wrote twenty-four books upon the Gospel[92]—a work which is quoted by Clement of Alexandria (*Strom.* iv.12.83sq., p. 599sq.) and which therefore was very likely to be in the hands of Hippolytus. And part of the abstract in Hippolytus is taken up with explaining what is meant by the term 'the Gospel'; while the whole is closed with the significant sentence, 'These then are the fables which Basilides utters, who taught throughout Egypt, and such were the fruits which he

---

[92]See Agrippa Castor in Eusebius, *Hist. Eccles.* iv.7.

produced who was instructed in so great wisdom' (p. 378, 1.40 sq.). And then Basilides is dismissed, and Hippolytus goes on to combat his contemporary Saturninus (*Refut.* vii.27, p. 378, l.40sq.). The extreme probability therefore that we have in the *Refutation* the very words of Basilides himself falls little short of demonstration; and thus we have a passage from St. John quoted, as contained 'in the Gospels', by one outside the Church who ranks in antiquity between Clement of Rome and Polycarp.[93]

8. *Valentinus* came to Rome, we are told, in the episcopate of Hyginus (A.D. 138–141) and was in his full vigour in the episcopate of Pius (c. A.D. 141–156).[94] He professed to have received his instruction from Theodas, a disciple of St Paul.[95] Tertullian informs us[96] that he adopted the Canon of the New Testament complete, and the fact that the whole phraseology of the Valentinian system is built upon the opening verses of St. John's Gospel is conclusive evidence that he recognised our Fourth Evangelist.[97] Indeed, we have Irenaeus' authority (iii.11.7) for saying that the Valentinians especially affected the Gospel of St John. But the matter is set at rest once for all by a distinct quotation from St John (10:8) which Hippolytus records of him (*Refut.* vi.35, p. 284, 1.77sq.).

9. The *Valentinians* were divided into two schools: (1) Western and (2) Eastern (Hipp. *Refut.* vi.35, p. 286). Of the Western Valentinians the most noticeable names are Heracleon, Ptolemaeus and Marcus. Now Heracleon[98] wrote a commentary on St. John, which is quoted frequently by Origen.[99] Origen informs us that Heracleon was reported to have been a familiar friend of Valentinus (*Comm. in John. Tom.* ii. §8). The rise of commentaries shows an advanced stage in the history of the text of the Fourth Gospel. Ptolemaeus, like Heracleon, was a direct disciple of Valentinus. His letter to his sister Flora is preserved in Epiphanius (*Haer.* xxxiii.3, p. 216 sq.); and in it John 1:3 is quoted (§3) as the statement of ὁ ἀπόστολος. Again, in Irenaeus

---

[93]See Westcott, *Canon of the New Testament*, p. 290, ed. 4.

[94]Irenaeus iii.4.3.

[95]Clement Alex. *Strom.* vii.17, p. 898.

[96]*de praescr.* 381: '*si Valentinus integro instrumento uti videtur, non callidiore ingenio quam Marcion manus intulit veritati.*' Cf. *de carn Chr.* 19; Iren. iii.14.4.

[97]Πλήρωμα, ζωή, φῶς, σκοτία, λόγος, ἀλήθεία μονογενής are Valentinian terms, and so is παράκλητος.

[98]For his date see Hilgenfeld *Zeitschr.* x. p. 75, and Westcott, *Canon*, p. 299 sq. ed. 4.

[99]He is also quoted by Clem. Alex. *Strom.* iv. 73, p. 595.

i.8.2 a Valentinian writer quotes John 12:27, and a little later on (§5) follows a direct quotation from the same or another writer, commencing, 'John the disciple of the Lord,' and explaining from a Valentinian standpoint the prologue of the Fourth Gospel. From the clause added at the end of the section in the Latin version (*et Ptolemaeus quidem* etc.) it appears that the anonymous writer was Ptolemaeus. *Marcus* himself must have been of early date, inasmuch as 'the Elder who lived before' Irenaeus wrote against him (Iren. i.15.6). From the account which Irenaeus preserves of him, he appears to have used our Four Gospels, and the extracts from his teaching which survive in the works of this father contain an illustration of the mystical number ten, founded on a reference to the appearance of our Lord after His resurrection 'when Thomas was not present' (Iren. i.18.3; cf. John 20:24).

It is doubtful whether Marcus should be included among the Western, and not rather among the Eastern Valentinians. Our information as regards these last is very scanty, but a ray of light is thrown upon them by a collection of extracts appended to the works of Clement of Alexandria and according to Bunsen (*Analect Antenic.* p. 203) taken from the first book of the *Hypotyposeis*. The collection is entitled *From the Teachings of Theodotus*. It abounds in quotations from the Fourth Gospel, explained in a Valentinian sense. I tabulate the most striking, giving the pages from Potter's edition of Clement:

John 1:1	Clem. Alex. §§6, 18, pp. 968, 973
1:3	§45, p. 979
1:4	§§6, 18, pp. 968, 973
1:9	§41, p. 979
1:14, 18	§6, p. 968
2:16	§9, p. 969
3:8	§17, p. 972
4:4	§17, p. 972
8:12	§35, p. 978
8:56	§18, p. 973
10:7	§26, p. 975
11:25	§6, p. 968
14:6	§6, p. 968

10. *Marcion* elaborated his system about A.D. 150. At first he accepted all the Four Gospels (Tertullian, *de carne Chr.* §§2, 3), but afterwards he became 'ultra-Pauline', rejecting all but mutilations of the writings of St. Luke and St. Paul. The ground on which he would reject the authority of the three 'pillar Apostles' (Gal 2:9) is evident from Tertullian (*adv. Marcion.* v.3), who tells us that he appealed to St. Paul's references in the Epistle to the Galatians to certain false apostles who had perverted the Gospel of Christ, and especially to St. Peter, as not walking uprightly after the truth of the Gospel. Thus he would consider them plunged in the blackness of intellectual darkness and incapable of imparting any teaching to a Gnostic like himself, while his condemnation of the Fourth Gospel would be pointed by the consideration that St. John was an Apostle of the circumcision. His silence therefore with respect to the Fourth Gospel becomes an argument in favour of its genuineness; had Marcion quoted it with approval, the fact would have been, so far as it went, evidence against the Johannine authorship. Apelles, his disciple, was certainly aware of its existence, for he tells us (in Hippol. *Refut.* vii.38, p. 410) that after His resurrection our Lord showed His disciples 'the marks of the nails and in/of His side', an incident which is mentioned by St. John alone (20:25).

11. The *Docetae* doubted the reality of the Incarnation, saying that our Lord's humanity was an appearance and nothing more. Their language was founded upon St. John's phraseology—λόγος, μονογενής, πλήρωμα occurring constantly in their formularies (Hipp. *Refut.* viii.9, 10, pp. 416, 418, 420). John 3:5, 6 is adduced in support of their opinions in a Docetic document given us by Hippolytus (*Refut.* viii.10, p. 422).

12. The *Judaizing Christians* in the primitive Church separated off into two main divisions, according to the view that they adopted of the obligation of the Mosaic Law. The Nazarenes, while recognizing the binding nature of the law upon themselves, were in the main orthodox. On the other hand the Ebionites considered the old dispensation permanent and for everyone, and repudiated the authority and Apostleship of St Paul. In considering the testimony which these two early Judaizing sects afford to the Fourth Gospel, we are fortunate in being able to appeal at first hand to extant works emanating from representatives of both schools of thought.

The *Clementine Homilies* represent the views of Gnostic Ebionism.[100]
The exact date of the work is uncertain, but it may be placed with confidence between A.D. 100–180. I am myself inclined to fix it at c. A.D. 150.
Formerly our knowledge of the treatise was derived from a manuscript
mutilated at the end, and some alleged correspondences with the Fourth
Gospel, which it contained, were hotly disputed by the Tubingen school,
who made this document the keystone of their elaborate theory of the alleged antagonism between St. Paul and St. Peter in the early Church. In
1853, however, Dressel published the missing conclusion from a Vatican
MS., and it was found to contain an obvious allusion to the story of the
man born blind.[101] From that time the acquaintance of the Clementine
writer with the Fourth Gospel has not been denied. Though this passage
in the 19th homily is decisive, it may be of interest to give other coincidences from the earlier portions of this work; e.g. *Clem. Hom.* iii.25 'He
was a murderer and a liar' (cf. John 8:44); *Clem. Hom.* iii.52 'I am the gate
(πύλη) of life, he that entereth through me entereth into life' (cf. John
10:27); ib. 'My sheep hear my voice' (cf. John 10:9); *Clem. Hom.* xi.26 'Verily
I say unto you, except ye be born again of living water in the name of the
Father, Son and Holy Spirit, ye shall not enter into the kingdom of heaven'
(cf. John 3:5).

The book entitled *The Testaments of the Twelve Patriarchs* is a product of
a Nazarene, as the *Clementine Homilies* of Ebionite, Judaism. It was written
after the capture of Jerusalem by Titus, and probably before the rebellion of
Barcochba (A.D. 132–135).[102] It professes to be a prophecy of the Messiah, and
it could not therefore without loss of dramatic propriety quote from the
evangelical record, but it contains many expressions which are characteristic
of the Fourth Gospel, as μονογενής (*Test. Benj.* 9), 'lamb of God' (*Test. Jos.*
19; *Benj.* 3), 'the Savior of the world' (*Test. Levi* 14; *Benj.* 3; only in John 4:42

---

[100]On the Clementine Literature see my *Galatians*, pp. 327sq; 340sq. and *Dissertations*, pp. 83sq;
98sq.
[101]*Clement. Hom.* xix §22; cf. John 9:2, 3.
[102]For the various dates assigned to this work see my *Galatians*, p. 320 (*Dissertations*, p. 76). It is
directly named by Origen (*Hom. in Jos.* xv.6) and probably was known to Tertullian (*c. Marc.*
v.1; *Scorpiace* 13) and (as I believe) even earlier to Irenaeus (*Fragm.* 17, p. 836sq., Stieren). Had
it been written after the suppression of the Barcochba's rebellion, it is next to impossible that
no mention should have been made of an event so important to the Judaizing Christians as the
second destruction of Jerusalem by Hadrian.

and 1 John 4:14 in the New Testament), 'the gate into life for all flesh' (*Test. Jud.* 24). Other longer sentences are apparently due to the same source; thus *Test. Levi* 14 'the light of the world given unto you which enlightens all mankind' (cf. John 1:9; 8:12); ib. § 'he himself makes judgments of truth upon the earth' (cf. John 5:27); 'then Abraham rejoiced' (cf. John 8:56); *Test. Jud.* 20 'the Spirit of truth witnesses to all . . .' (cf. John 15:26); *Test. Benj.* 9 'he shall be lifted up upon the cross, and is ascending from earth to heaven' (cf. John 3:13, 14; 6:62).

Hitherto the voice of antiquity, whether uttered by the early fathers of the Church or by those who stood outside her pale, has been unanimous, as far as we can follow it, in testifying to the genuineness and authenticity of the Fourth Gospel. To this universal tradition, however, there is one exception, and one only, and we will conclude our examination of the external evidence by a consideration of this solitary exception to the chorus of universal attestation.

After speaking of Marcion's mutilation of the Canon, Irenaeus (iii.11, 9) goes on to mention others also, who, in order that they may frustrate the gift of the Spirit, do not admit that type of Church teaching (*illam speciem*), which is in accordance with St. John's Gospel, in which the Lord promised that He would send the Paraclete; but at one and the same time reject both the Gospel and the spirit of prophecy. 'Unhappy men in very truth, who desire false prophets to exist (*pseudo-prophetae*—read *pseudo-prophetas*— quidem esse volunt*), but yet banish from the Church the grace of prophecy. . . . Accordingly they ought not to acknowledge the Apostle Paul either . . . because he testifies to men and women prophesying in the Church' (a reference to 1 Cor 11:4, 5).

Now from Irenaeus' argument, of which I have given only a part, it is clear: (1) that these objectors repudiate the Gospel of St. John, because it contains a special promise of spiritual gifts; (2) that they confess the existence of false prophets, and yet deny the existence of a true prophecy; (3) hence, Irenaeus argues, they are as unreasonable as those who refuse to associate with the brethren for fear there should be hypocrites among them; (4) on this ground they ought not only to reject the Gospel of St. John, but also the Epistles of St. Paul, for St. Paul has spoken very emphatically about spiritual gifts, and recognises both men and women as prophesying in the

Church.[103] Irenaeus goes on in the next chapter to show at great length that there is a Spirit.

It is evident therefore that the persons spoken of are strong anti-Montanists; they took offence at the claims of the Montanists to spiritual gifts, more especially at the prophesyings of women. We must therefore read *pseudo-prophetas* in the passage given above.[104] For Montanism was spiritualism considered as a reaction against formalism and intellectualism. The Montanists laid great stress upon the writings of St. John, especially the Apocalypse, hence these opponents of Montanism cut the knot by denying the authority of the Fourth Gospel.[105] And they did more than this. Irenaeus speaks only of their rejection of the Gospel of St John. He is dwelling only on the Gospels; and therefore he would naturally not say anything about their position with respect to other canonical books. It appears however from other sources that they rejected also the Apocalypse. For Epiphanius (who wrote after A.D. 350) describes a sect of heretics, whom he dubs ἄλογοι, or irrationalists. It is a play on the word, for they rejected the testimony of John, who taught the doctrine of the Logos. He says, 'I put upon them this nickname; from henceforth they shall be so called, and therefore, my beloved, let us give them this name' (Epiph. *Haer.* li.3). He seems to have succeeded in affixing this opprobrious title upon them, for Augustine so calls them afterwards (*Haer.* 30, Oehler i. p. 202). Of these Alogi, Epiphanius relates that they sprang up after the Cataphrygians, and he evidently considers that they originated in the same neighborhood (l.c. esp. §33). He begins by describing them (§1) as 'material,' 'sensual,' in their views, and as gainsaying the Holy Spirit and the wonderful sequence of the Gospels (§16). He closes a full account of them with a passage commencing (§35) 'And these

---

[103]See a similar argument used against these same persons by Epiphanius (li.32, p. 106, ed. Oehler).

[104]The alternative correction of Lücke (p. 65) *nolunt* for *volunt* seems to interfere with the sense.

[105]Considerable light is thrown on Irenaeus' attitude upon this matter the letter of the Galilean Churches to the Asiatic Churches quoted in Eusebius, *Hist. Eccles.* v.3 on this very subject Montanism. The letter is an attempt at mediation; it was written avowedly εἰρήνης ἕνεκεν, and it was penned by the martyrs 'while yet in bonds' to the brethren in Asia and Phrygia. At the same time the martyrs sent Irenaeus then a presbyter, as their delegate with letters of recommendation to Eleutherus, bishop of Rome (Eusebius, *Hist. Eccles.* v.4) for the sake of conferring with him on this same question. Irenaeus therefore is not a strong Montanist. He mentions the *pseudo-prophetae* in another passage (*Haer.* iv.33.6) with, again, a probable reference to Montanism.

not receiving the Holy Spirit are convicted by the Spirit etc.' Thus his account begins and ends with an allusion to their attitude towards the doctrine of the Holy Spirit, and his expressions are meaningless unless he is describing an anti-Spiritualist, anti-Montanist movement. We may therefore take it for granted that Irenaeus and Epiphanius are referring to one and the same body of people. Epiphanius goes on to say that they rejected the Gospel and the Apocalypse, and attributed these writings to Cerinthus. He supposes that they also rejected the Epistles of St. John likewise, 'for these,' he says, 'agree in character with the Gospel and the Apocalypse' (§34), but he evidently knows nothing definite about this last point.

In every other respect the *Alogi* seem to have been orthodox (Epiph. li.1.4; Compare *Praedestinatrus Haer.* i.30 '*omnia nobiscum sapient*' Oehler I. p. 243). It does not appear that they rejected the doctrine of St John's Gospel. The silence of Epiphanius on this point is speaking. Certainly this energetic champion of orthodoxy does not detect any mark of Ebionism in them. They may, however, have repudiated the Johannine form under which the Divinity of our Lord was taught, though even this is doubtful.

Very similar is the brief notice of the *Alogi* in Philastrius (Oehler I. p. 61). He mentions those who reject both the Gospel and the Apocalypse; but he seems to restrict to the Apocalypse their attribution of the authorship to Cerinthus. And this was perhaps really the case. For Dionysius of Alexandria (Eusebius, *Hist. Eccles.* vii.25; comp. iii.28) speaks of some before him who attributed this book to Cerinthus and the Cerinthians, because they thought that they saw in it a gross and material picture of an earthly kingdom of Christ. This ascription would suit very well the fragment of Gaius written against the Montanists and preserved in Eusebius (*Hist. Eccles.* iii.28), and it is possible that Dionysius alludes to Gaius; but it is strange that, if this was the view of Gaius, Eusebius should not have told us so distinctly. Certainly Theodoret interpreted it differently (*Haer. Fab.* ii.3; see Routh E. S. ii.139).

But whence did Epiphanius draw his information? We can make a shrewd guess. Hippolytus of Portus wrote a book *Concerning the Gospel of John and the Apocalypse*. This fact is recorded on his statue (*Fabricius Hippol.* pp. 36sq., Bunsen Hippol. I. p. 460). That this book was known in the East appears from the *Catalogue of Ebed-Jesu* (Assemani *Bibl. Or.* III. p. 15), where it occurs in the list of Hippolytus' works as *Apologia pro Apocalypsi et Evan-*

gelio Ioannis Apostoli et Evangelistae. It is probable also that this is the same
work of which the title is given by other writers, e.g. *de Apocalypsi* (Jerome
Vir. Ill. 61), περί ἀποκάλυψεως (Andreas of Caesarea in *Apocal. Synops.*; Syncellus, *Chron.* p. 674 ed. Bonn). At all events, Epiphanius is borrowing largely
from some earlier writer.[106] Here then and elsewhere Epiphanius may have
consulted Hippolytus. Now twice in the immediate context (li. §§6, 7) is an
allusion to a Merinthus who is mentioned side by side with Cerinthus; and
from another passage (Epiph. *Haer.* xxviii, 8, p. 1150) it is clear that Epiphanius was uncertain whether they were not after all one and the same
person. The passage is interesting. 'Whether the same Cerinthus was afterwards called Merinthus, or there was a separate person by name Merinthus,
a fellow-worker of his, is known to God (alone).' Now Merinthos means a
'noose,' and was doubtless, as Fabricius shrewdly suggested (*Cod. Apoc. N. T.*
344), nothing more nor less than an opprobrious nickname given by an
earlier writer, whose work was in Epiphanius' hands, and who may have
written thus 'Cerinthus, or had we not better say Merinthus,' and in this way
misled his copyist. Such pleasantries were by no means uncommon as applied to antagonists. Thus Democritus is called by Epicurus Lenocritus
(Zeller *Stoics* iii.1 p. 429), Photinus of Pirmium in the *Macrostich* Skotinus,[107]
'Manes' by Eusebius[108] and others Maneis. This habit of playing upon names
is quite characteristic of Hippolytus. Thus in his treatise against Noetus, he
turns his antagonist's name to ridicule, (*c. Noet.* 8), and in his *Refutation*,
when dealing with the *Docetae*, he plays upon the words δοκεῖν 'to seem' and
δοκός 'a beam,' contending that they are so named (Hippolytus *Refut.* viii.11),
not because they 'seemed to be of importance' (Gal 2:6), but because of 'the
beam in their eye' (Matt vii.3). For these reasons we are tempted to infer that,
though Epiphanius claims for himself the invention of the term *Alogi*, he
may have borrowed the name and the account which he gives from his more
fanciful predecessor.[109]

---

[106]The common source underlying the works of Epiphanius, Philastrius and the pseudo-Tertullian
on heresies is an interesting problem, which cannot be entered upon here.

[107]See Bright, *Church History*, (1860), p. 52 who gives instances from Eusebius, *Hist. Eccles.* v.23,
vi.41, vii.10, 31.

[108]See Bright l.c. and Cotelier, *Patr. Apost.* I. p. 543.

[109]Two additional sources of testimony have been omitted in the above account, viz. that (1) of
heathen writers, (2) of Apocryphal documents. In the former class, Celsus (c. A.D. 150) treats
the Gospel of St. John as a record considered authoritative by the the Christians (Origen, *c.*

In looking back over the subject which has been occupying us, we cannot fail to be struck with the variety and the fullness of the evidence which has been adduced. Within the Catholic Church that evidence springs in the first instance direct from the fountain-head, the band of disciples which in Asia Minor gathered round the person of the aged Apostle of Love. From Polycarp and Papias it is handed down to the next link in the chain in Irenaeus, the great scholar and traveller, whose life is associated with three distinct and important Churches—Churches in constant intercommunication—Asia Minor, Rome, and Gaul. These three great centres we are able to test by independent extant documents, the *Apology of Theophilus, Muratorian Canon, the Letter of the Gallican Churches*, and we find an unhesitating response to our enquiry. We pass over to other Churches of the East, to Palestine and Alexandria, to Greece and Macedonia, with equally satisfactory results. We cross the Mediterranean southwards to Carthage, and the earliest extant writings of the Latin Church of Africa show unmistakeable acquaintance with St. John. And now we take a new departure. We leave the apologists and fathers of the orthodox Church, and we turn to the representatives of those multifarious heresies whose rank growth seemed likely to stifle the infant Church of the second century. And here we are startled at once by the

---

Celsum i.67, ii.18, x.24). He speaks of Christians calling our Lord αὐτολόγον (*c. Celsum* ii.31), he refers to our Lord sitting thirsty by Jacob's well (*c. Celsum* i.70; cf. John 4:6), and to the piercing of His side and the result (*c. Celsum* ii.36; cf. John 19:34). Therefore we conclude that by the middle of the second century this Gospel was so well known amongst Christians that Celsus could appeal to it as an accredited witness. Again Lucian (c. A.D. 165–170), in his account of Peregrinus Proteus (§11), gives indications of acquaintanceship with the Fourth Evangelist (see Zahn, *Ignatius*, p. 593), and so does Amelius in Eusebius, *Praep. Evang.* xi.19. The last-named was a disciple of Plotinus, and flourished c. A.D. 250. Prominent in the latter class are the *Acta Pilati* (given in Tischendorf, *Evangelia Apocrypha*), which form the first sixteen chapters of the *Evangelium Nicodemi*, and appear not only in Greek but in Coptic and in Latin. This is a very early work, and in its Latin form exists in a Vienna palimpsest of the 5th or 6th century. There is little doubt that it is the composition referred to by Justin Martyr (*Apol.* i.35, 48) and Tertullian (*Apologeticus* 21), for it answers in all particulars to the books described by these writers. Apocryphal Gospels are notoriously liable to interpolations; we cannot therefore lay much stress upon the evidence in this case, but as the document stands, with whatever uncertainty hanging over it, the incidents are again and again taken from St. John's Gospel. Lastly the Sibyllist lends her voice to the general attestation. The eighth book of the *Oracula Sibyllina* is the work of a Christian who wrote during the reign of Antoninus Pius (A.D. 138–161). Speaking of the resurrection, the poet declares that those shall rise with the risen Lord 'who have washed away their former sins in the waters of the eternal fount having been born again from above. For the Lord will exhibit Himself first to His own, in bodily shape as He was before, and will show them His hands and His feet and the marks printed upon His limbs, four in number, east and west, south and north' (*Orac. Sib.* viii.316 sq.; cf. John 3:3; 20:20).

variety and the unanimity of the evidence presented. Differing in almost every other particular, heterodoxy unites in bearing testimony to St. John's Gospel. Gnosticism, the outcome of Gentile license of speculation and practice, Ebionism, the offspring of Judaizing tendencies, Montanism, the expression of spiritual excitement—they all presuppose, and to some extent build upon, the Fourth Gospel. Fresh discoveries, which have added considerably to our stock of heretical treatises, have only served to give new weight and force to this testimony. Making every allowance for the possibility that in some cases zealous disciples may have interpolated documents already existing, or have perpetrated forgeries in their masters' names, yet more than enough of unorthodox literature can be tested to throw back the date of the general acceptance outside the Church of St. John's Gospel as genuine to a very early period in the second century. The solitary exception to this chorus of attestation is found to proceed from an insignificant sect, which, having a special doctrine to inculcate, seeks to effect its end by impugning the documents which strike at the root of its theory. When we pass to the consideration of heathen writers in the opponents of Christianity, or of Apocryphal literature, the supplementary evidence which we are able to collect, though necessarily scanty, still bears out the results to which our previous investigations have already pointed us.

Lastly, so far from considering that the general subject is in any way exhausted, we rise from our review with the consciousness that it has been most inadequately treated, and with the confident persuasion, that a little more patient investigation bestowed on the literature of the first two centuries of the Christian era, as it has come down to us, would enable us to add very materially indeed to the weight of external evidence which with fresh force from year to year tends to the conviction that this most divine of all divine books was indeed the work of 'the disciple whom Jesus loved.' [1867–1872.]

Appendix B

More Internal Evidence for the Authenticity and Genuineness of St. John's Gospel

In considering this question three points will be taken in succession. I shall endeavour to show: I. That the writer was intimately acquainted with the language, customs, ideas, geography and history of Palestine at the time which he describes. Inference: He was not only a Jew, but a Palestinian Jew; not a Hellenist, but a Hebrew. And most probably too he was a contemporary. For the double destruction of Jerusalem—by Titus and by Hadrian—had caused a dislocation, a discontinuity, in the history of the Jews, which it would be difficult to bridge over by one writing after the occurrence of the second of these events. II. That the narrative bears on its face the credentials of its authenticity. It is precise, circumstantial, natural in the highest degree. Inference: It is the work of an eyewitness. III. That it contains indications—the more convincing because they are unobtrusive—(a) that the author was the Apostle St. John; (b) that the book was written at the time and under the circumstances, under which tradition reports it to have been written, i.e. at Ephesus, towards the close of the first century after Christ.

These, then, are the three stages in the argument: (1) The writer was a

---

This material also came from Lightfoot's lecture notes. Originally appearing in *Biblical Essays*, it has long been out of print, until now.

Hebrew, probably a contemporary. (2) The writer was an eyewitness. (3) The writer was St. John (and as a subsidiary matter, St. John writing under peculiar circumstances).

I. The writer was a Hebrew, probably a contemporary. The main heads of this division of the argument are as follows: 1. His knowledge of the Jewish language. 2. His knowledge of Jewish ideas, traditions, expectations, modes of thought, etc. 3. His knowledge of external facts, the history, geography, names and customs of the Jewish people.

I. THE WRITER'S KNOWLEDGE OF THE JEWISH LANGUAGE. This is shown (i) indirectly, by his own Greek style; (ii) directly, by his interpretation of Hebrew words and his quotations from Hebrew Scriptures. (i) The writer's indirect knowledge of Hebrew shown by his Greek style. I spoke of the Jewish language; but what is meant by this? There are two languages with which a Palestinian Jew might be familiar: (1) The Hebrew—the sacred language, the language of the Old Testament. (2) The Aramaic—the colloquial language, the language of common life. He would necessarily know the second, not necessarily know the first. The Hebrew of the New Testament is Aramaic. This is the meaning of Ἑβραϊστί in such passages as John 5:2; 19:13, 17; 20:16. The forms quoted as Hebrew ('Talitha cumi,' 'Maranatha') are Aramaic. This is no doubt the language of the inscription on the cross (John 19:20), and of St. Paul's speech on the temple stairs (Acts 21:40). It is a common error to suppose that Aramaic is a corrupt form of Hebrew. This is quite wrong. The Semitic family of languages has three main languages, one of which—Arabic—may be neglected for our purpose, leaving Hebrew and Aramaic. Of these, Aramaic, the language of Aram (Syria) [the highland ?], has, as its dialects, Syriac, Chaldee, Assyrian (the cuneiform inscriptions). On the other hand, Hebrew, the language of Canaan [the low-lands ?], was originally the language of Phoenicians and Canaanites, the people on the coast.

Which then was the language of the Jewish nation at the beginning of the Christian era? Abraham comes from Ur of the Chaldees, and therefore would naturally speak an Aramaic language. But he settles in Palestine among the Canaanites, adopts a Canaanite language, and speaks what we call Hebrew. Hence the incident in Gen 31:47, 48. The 'heap of witness' is called by Laban 'Jegar-sahadutha,' by Jacob 'Galeed.' Thus the descendants of Terah in the third generation speak two languages. The grandson of Nahor retains his Aramaic, while the grandson of Abraham has adopted Hebrew. This is what we should expect, and is an incidental testimony to the credibility of the Mosaic narrative. After the return from the Babylonian captivity the Jews gradually merged their own Hebrew language in Aramaic but the name *Hebrew* was transferred to the adopted language. Thus the Jews returned apparently to what was the language of their ancestors. How they came by this Aramaic—whether it was the dialect of their Chaldean masters, or the dialect of the people who overran their land during their absence, or a mixture of both—we need not stop to enquire. At the time of our Lord the natives of Palestine were bilingual; they spoke Greek and Aramaic. At least this was the case in a great part of the country, more especially in the towns and populous districts, the centres of commerce such as the lake of Galilee and Jerusalem.[1] In this respect the Palestinian Jew resembled a Welshman on the border-land, a Fleming in the neighborhood of the half-French towns of Flanders, a Bohemian in Prague.

Now apply this to the case of the Apostle St. John. John was not a man of the lowest class socially. He was a native of Bethsaida, and had connections or friends in high quarters at Jerusalem (18:16). He would be able to understand and speak Greek from his boyhood, possibly even to write it. But he would think in Aramaic. Aramaic would mould the form of his thoughts.[2]

Take the case of a person writing in a language which was not the common language of his daily life, not his mother-tongue. What would be the phenomena, which his style would present? The two parts of a language, in which a person writing in a foreign tongue is apt to be at fault, are the vocabulary and the syntax. As regards vocabulary, we should not expect great luxuriance of words, a copious command of synonyms for instance. In the matter of syntax, we should not look for a mastery of complex and involved syntax, or of sustained and elaborate periods. Now apply this to the Fourth Gospel.

1. *The Vocabulary*. The words in this Gospel are very few; probably

---

[1]See Roberts, *Dissertations on Gospels*, whose view however is perhaps somewhat exaggerated.
[2]The incident given in John 12:20-22, relating to his friends and the fellow townsmen Andrew and Philip is strictly in accordance with probabilities. It is a significant fact that they both bear Greek names.

much fewer than in any other portion of the New Testament of the same length. (a) We meet with constant repetition of the same words: e.g. γινώσκειν (57 times); κόσμος (79 times); πίστις/πιστεύειν (99 times); ζωή/ ζῆν/ζωοποιεῖν (55 times); μαρτυρία/μαρτυρεῖν (47 times); πρόβατον occurs in the tenth chapter alone 15 times; κόσμος occurs in the seventeenth chapter alone 18 times.[3]

(b) We find not only the same words, but the same phrases: e.g. ἔρχεσθαι, ὁ πέμψας με, ἀποστέλλειν, καταβαίνειν ἐκ τῶν οὐρανῶν—all used of Christ's Incarnation, etc.[4]

2. *The Syntax.* On the extreme simplicity of the Fourth Gospel in this respect, I shall have to speak later. This characteristic of the writer is well expressed by Heinsius, who describes him thus: 'In sermone ἀφελεία in sensibus est ὕψος.'[5] The absence of periods is particularly noticeable, and is without a parallel in the New Testament. Thus much, generally, of one writing in another language than his mother tongue. Now to come to the special case of one accustomed to speak in a Semitic tongue, and obliged to write in an Aryan; of one familiar with (say) Aramaic, the conversational, spoken language, and Hebrew, the sacred language; but writing in Greek. Both these languages present striking contrasts with Greek. In these Semitic tongues there is little or no syntax. This is due partly to (1) The absence of moods, inflexions, etc. (2) The paucity of connecting particles. On this last point, which is of special importance, one example will suffice.

(1) *Paucity of connecting particles.* The וֹ is used equally for opposition and for simple connection; in Hebrew and Aramaic it stands for 'but' as well as 'and.' The extent of this use is best shown by the variety of particles which are employed to render it in the Authorised Version of the Old Testament. Thus in Deut 1 (taken at haphazard) וֹ is translated 'so' vv. 15, 43, 46; 'then' v. 29; 'yet' v. 32; 'but' v. 40; and with לֹא, 'notwithstanding' v. 26. Again in 1 Kings 12 (again taken at haphazard) it is rendered 'but' vv. 8, 17, 22; 'so' vv. 12, 33; 'so when' v. 16; 'wherefore' vv. 15, 19 ; 'then' vv. 18, 25; 'whereupon' v. 28; 'that' v. 3. There are thirty-three verses in this chapter, and all the verses but vv. 4, 23, 27 (i.e. thirty verses out of thirty-three), begin with וֹ. Of the remaining

---

[3]These calculations are based upon Luthardt, *Das Johanneische Evangelium*, I, p. 27 (1852).
[4]See Luthardt, I, p.31sq.
[5]Quoted by Luthardt, I, p. 28.

three, two are beginnings of speeches, and therefore necessarily are asyndeta. Indeed in the later Aramaic, Greek particles (ἀλλά, δέ and afterwards μέν) were deliberately introduced to supply the deficiency.[6]

Consequently, in these languages sentences are not subordinated, but co-ordinated. 'Hence,' as Winer describes it, 'the very limited use of conjunctions (in which classical Greek is so rich), the uniformity in the use of the tenses, the want of the periodic compactness which results from the fusion of several sentences into one principal sentence, and along with this the sparing use of participial constructions, so numerous and diversified in classical Greek.'[7] The result is an entire absence of periods, producing a monotony of expression, which however is most impressive.

The character of the Greek language was quite different. Greek writers distinguished two styles: (1) The periodic (κατεστραμένη); (2) The disjointed (διηρημένη) or 'jointed' (εἰρομένη). (See Aristot. Rhet. iii.9.)

In the infancy of the language the earlier prose writers Hecataeus and Herodotus exhibit the εἰρομένη; the later, when a mastery over the language had been attained, the κατεστραμένη. Now, Hebrew and Aramaic do not lend themselves to κατεστραμένη, the genius of the languages necessitating the εἰρομένη. Hence, as a rule, the general simplicity of the New Testament writers, who either spoke Aramaic, or derived their materials from Aramaic sources. The exceptions are the cases of those who commonly spoke Greek, and did not speak Aramaic at all, as St. Luke in the prologue to his Gospel (for where he is using documents, the case is different), and the author of the Epistle to the Hebrews.

This simple, jointed style, is seen in its extreme form in St. John. In fact, no greater contrast can be exhibited in this respect than the prologue of St. John when compared with the prologue of St. Luke. The sentences are strung together, where they are not altogether *asyndeta*. There is no attempt at periodicity. The καί takes the place of the ן, and has almost as wide a range, connecting together not only independent, but dependent, and even opposite and contrasted clauses.[8] I give a few examples of this:

---

[6]This strange lack of particles, which seem to us indispensable to express our simplest thoughts, is illustrated likewise by Coptic.

[7]Winer, *Grammar of New Testament Greek*, p. 33 (Moulton's translation).

[8]See the references in Wilkii, *Clavis New Testament* (ed. Grimm, 1868, s. v. καί p. 215).

John 1:1, 4, 5, 10, 14, 19, 20, 21, 24, 25, 34; 2:1, 3, 4, 8, 12-16; 3:11, 12, 13, 14; 4:11, 40, 41; 6:17; 7:26, 28, 33, 34; 9:18, 19; 10:3, 9, 12, 14-16, 22, 27, 28, 39-41; 14:23, 24; 15:6; 16:22, 32; 17:1, 8, 10, 11 (six times in three lines); 19:34, 35.

For instances where καί introduces an opposition, with the meaning of 'and yet,' 'nevertheless,' see John 1:5, 10; 3:10, 11, 19, 32; 4:20; 5:40; 6:70; 7:4, 19, 26, 30; 8:49, 55; 9:30, 34 etc.

A single instance would occur here and there in classical Greek as in any other language; but it is the frequency of occurrence in the Fourth Gospel which betrays the Hebraeo-Aramaic mould in which the diction is cast.

(2) *Hebraic parallelism of sentences.* Instances of this characteristic can be found in almost every part of the Fourth Gospel. The prologue especially presents a succession of parallel clauses. I content myself with drawing attention to some special phenomena of this parallelism. (a) Repetition of words and phrases in parallel and opposed clauses, e.g. 3:6 (τὸ γεγεννημένον ἐκ τῆς σαρκὸς σάρξ ἐστιν, καὶ τὸ γεγεννημένον ἐκ τοῦ Πνεύματος πνεῦμά ἐστιν.); 3:31 (ὁ ὢν ἐκ τῆς γῆς ἐκ τῆς γῆς ἐστιν καὶ ἐκ τῆς γῆς λαλεῖ. ὁ ἐκ τοῦ οὐρανοῦ ἐρχόμενος ἐπάνω πάντων ἐστίν·). Cf. 7:6, 7, 8; 8:14, 23; 10:18; 11:9, 10 etc., etc.

(b) Repetition of words and phrases in parallel, but not opposed clauses, e.g. 9:21, 22 (πῶς δὲ νῦν βλέπει οὐκ οἴδαμεν, ἢ τίς ἤνοιξεν αὐτοῦ τοὺς ὀφθαλμοὺς ἡμεῖς οὐκ οἴδαμεν); 17:16 (ἐκ τοῦ κόσμου οὐκ εἰσὶν καθὼς ἐγὼ οὐκ εἰμὶ ἐκ τοῦ κόσμου). Cf. 18:18; 19:10 etc., etc.

(c) Strengthening of a statement by the negation of its opposite, e.g. 1:3 (πάντα δι᾽ αὐτοῦ ἐγένετο, καὶ χωρὶς αὐτοῦ ἐγένετο οὐδὲ ἕν); 1:20 (καὶ ὡμολόγησεν καὶ οὐκ ἠρνήσατο). Cf. 3:18; 10:28; 11:25, 26; 20:27 etc., etc.

(3) *Oriental definiteness of expression by the repetition of the same word or phrase.*

(a) Repetition of the name, instead of using a personal pronoun, e.g. 1:43-46 (εὑρίσκει Φίλιππον . . . ἦν δὲ ὁ Φίλιππος . . . εὑρίσκει Φίλιππος τὸν Ναθαναὴλ . . . καὶ εἶπεν αὐτῷ Ναθαναὴλ . . . λέγει αὐτῷ ὁ Φίλιππος). Cf 3:23sq.; 7:21sq. etc., etc.

(b) Repetition of the nominative pronoun, where the Greek does not require it, e.g. 1:42 (Σὺ εἶ Σίμων ὁ υἱὸς Ἰωάνου, σὺ κληθήσῃ Κηφᾶς). Cf. 1:25, 31; 4:10, 19 etc., etc.

(c) Repetition of the noun, e.g. 7:6 (Ὁ καιρὸς ὁ ἐμὸς οὔπω πάρεστιν, ὁ δὲ καιρὸς ὁ ὑμέτερος πάντοτέ ἐστιν ἕτοιμος). Cf. 7:8, 19; 12:43, 47 etc., etc.

(d) Repetition of the verb, e.g. 5:17 (Ὁ Πατήρ μου ἕως ἄρτι ἐργάζεται, κἀγὼ ἐργάζομαι·). Cf. 6:63; 7:24, 28; 8:53; 10:10; 13:43 etc., etc.

(e) Repetition of the same phrase in successive clauses, e.g. 3:31 (ὁ ὢν ἐκ τῆς γῆς ἐκ τῆς γῆς ἐστιν καὶ ἐκ τῆς γῆς λαλεῖ. ὁ ἐκ τοῦ οὐρανοῦ ἐρχόμενος ἐπάνω πάντων ἐστίν). Cf. 8:14, 23, 24; 10:18; 11:9sq. etc., etc.

(f) Taking up a word or expression from the preceding sentence, e.g. 10:11 (ἐγώ εἰμι ὁ ποιμὴν ὁ καλός. ὁ ποιμὴν ὁ καλὸς τὴν ψυχὴν αὐτοῦ τίθησιν ὑπὲρ τῶν προβάτων). Cf. 1:1; 3:32, 33; 17:2, 3 etc., etc.

(4) *Preference of the direct over the oblique narrative in relating the words of another.* In some instances these will be the precise words themselves; in others only an approximation, and in this latter case the direct narrative is only a different way of expressing what we express by the oblique. Thus we find the narrator himself relating the words or surmises of a crowd, where from the nature of the case the exact words cannot be reproduced; or we find persons referring back to their own words or the words of another, and not always reproducing the exact expressions. Examples of all these varieties are very common, see the narrative of the Samaritan woman in ch. 4 (esp. vv. 17, 27, 33); of the sick man healed in ch. 5 (esp. vv. 11, 12); the conversation in ch. 6 (esp. vv. 41, 42); cf. 7:11sq., 35, 36, 40sq.; 8:22; 9:8sq., 23sq., 40sq.; 10:20, 36, 41; 11:31, 36, 37; 12:19sq. etc., etc.

(5) *The arrangement of words in the sentence, especially the precedence of the verb,* e.g. 1:40-47 (Ἦν Ἀνδρέας . . . εὑρίσκει οὗτος . . . ἤγαγεν αὐτὸν . . . ἐμβλέψας αὐτῷ . . . εὑρίσκει Φίλιππον . . . εὑρίσκει Φίλιππος τὸν Ναθαναὴλ καὶ λέγει αὐτῷ . . . λέγει αὐτῷ ὁ Φίλιππος . . . εἶδεν Ἰησοῦς). This is noticeably the case with the expression λέγει αὐτῷ, e.g. 4:7-26; 9:34, 35, 39sq. etc., etc.

(6) *Other grammatical and lexical peculiarities.*

(a) The superfluous pronoun (1) after a relative, representing the Hebrew אֲשֶׁר which is indeclinable, e.g. 1:12 (ὅσοι δὲ ἔλαβον αὐτόν, ἔδωκεν αὐτοῖς); v. 38 (ὃν ἀπέστειλεν ἐκεῖνος, τούτῳ ὑμεῖς οὐ πιστεύετε). Cf. 1:33; 7:38; 17:2; 18:9, 11 etc., etc.; (2) after nouns or participles, e.g. 1:18 (μονογενὴς Θεὸς ὁ ὢν εἰς τὸν κόλπον τοῦ Πατρὸς, ἐκεῖνος ἐξηγήσατο.); 5:11 (Ὁ ποιήσας με ὑγιῆ, ἐκεῖνός μοι εἶπεν Ἆρον τὸν κράβαττόν σου). Cf. 6:46; 7:18, 38; 10:1; 14:21, 26; 15:5, etc., etc. This construction, it is true, occurs in classical Greek, but the point to be noticed is the extreme frequency of the usage in the Fourth Gospel.

(b) The characteristic Hebraism πᾶς . . . οὐ occurs three times in this Gospel 3:16; 6:39; 12:6.

(c) The frequent use of ἵνα in St. John, especially as the complement of a demonstrative pronoun, is probably to be explained by the flexibility of the Aramaic בְּ. Instances are 1:2; 4:34; 6:29, 40; 8:56; 11:50; 13:34; 15:8, 12, 13, 17; 16:7, 33; 17:3, 24 (see Winer §xliv. p. 425 ed. Moulton). In every one of these passages a Greek would probably have expressed himself differently.

(d) The use of ἄνθρωπος for τις, e.g. 5:7 (Κύριε, ἄνθρωπον οὐκ ἔχω); 7:22, 23 (ἐν σαββάτῳ περιτέμνετε ἄνθρωπον. εἰ περιτομὴν λαμβάνει ἄνθρωπος etc.). Cf. 8:40; 9:16 etc. This represents a thoroughly characteristic use of אִישׁ. See Gesenius s. v.

(e) The transition from the dependent to the independent clause, e.g. 1:32 (Τεθέαμαι τὸ Πνεῦμα καταβαῖνον ὡς περιστερὰν ἐξ οὐρανοῦ, καὶ ἔμεινεν ἐπ᾽ αὐτόν.) Cf. 11:44 (Winer §Ixiii. p. 717 ed. Moulton). This transition however appears in other New Testament writers also, and cannot be pressed into an argument.

(f) The frequent recurrence of the expression εἰς τὸν αἰῶνα especially with a negative, e.g. 4:14; 6:51, 58; 8:35, 51, 52; 10:26; 11:28; 12:34; 13:8, 14:16; and the use of ἐκ τοῦ αἰῶνος 9:32.

(g) Other Hebraisms are: 1:13 (αἱμάτων), 15, 30 (πρῶτός μου cf. 15:18); 3:29 (χαρᾷ χαίρει); 7:33; 12:35; 14:19 (ἔτι μικρόν cf. 16:16, 17, 19); 4:23 (ἔρχεται ὥρα καὶ νῦν ἐστιν); 11:4 (οὐκ ἔστιν πρὸς θάνατον cf. 16:20); 4:26; 8:24, 28; 13:19; 18:5, 6 (Ἐγώ εἰμι); 10:24 (Ἕως πότε); 18:37 (Σὺ λέγεις).

(7) *Imagery, secondary senses of words etc.*

This displays a thoroughly Hebrew, or at least Oriental, coloring. The simple facts in life are used to convey deep spiritual truths. Nature and history become signs (σημεῖα) of the heavenly and the eternal. Instances of this figurative treatment are to be found in the Evangelist's use of the following words and phrases ἀλήθεια 1:14, 17; 3:21; δόξα 1:14; 2:11; 12:41; ὕδωρ ζῶν 4:10, 13; κοιλία 7:38; ζωή 5:24; τὸ μάννα 6:31; ἄρτος 6:32; ὑψωθῶ . . . ἑλκύσω 12:32; τὸ ποτήριον 18:11.

If the special Hebraisms or Aramaisms, are few, this is unimportant, for the whole casting of the sentences, the whole coloring of the language, is Hebrew. In short, it is the most Hebraic book in the New Testament, except perhaps the Apocalypse. The Greek is not ungrammatical Greek, but it is cast in a Hebrew mould. It is what no native Greek would have written. As Grotius puts it: '*Sermo Graecus quidem, sed plane adumbratus ex Syriaco illius saeculi.*'[9] On the general accord of recent writers on this point, see Sanday.[10]

On the other hand, there are no classicisms, not a single sentence, I believe, from first to last which suggests in the smallest degree acquaintance with classical literature. In this respect the writer presents a great contrast to St. Luke, and even to St. Paul, e.g. Luke 1:1sq.; 2 Cor 4:14sq.

(ii) *The writer's direct knowledge of Hebrew.*

1. The quotations from the Old Testament. The quotations are a valuable criterion of the position of a writer. The quotations in St. Paul show a knowledge of the Old Testament in Hebrew. He frequently quotes the LXX, but in other passages he is as plainly indebted to the original. On the other hand, the quotations in the Epistle to the Hebrews are all derived from the LXX. There are no distinct traces of a knowledge of the original.

What are the facts in St. John's case? The quotations in St. John are not very numerous. Moreover they are often free quotations; so free that we cannot say whether they were taken from the Hebrew or the Greek. But there is a residuum of passages, which are decisive, and certainly cannot have been borrowed from the Greek.

(a) *Passages certainly taken from the Hebrew.*

(1) Zech 9:9 quoted in John 12:14, 15 (see Turpie, p. 222). The quotation is loose. Two points are noticeable. St. John has ὁ Βασιλεύς σου ἔρχεται. The LXX ὁ βασιλεὺς σου ἔρχεταί σοι (but some eds. insert σου). The Hebrew represents ὁ Βασιλεύς σου ἔρχεταί σοι as in Matt 21:5. The other point is more important. St. John has πῶλον ὄνου, which comes from the Hebrew, the LXX having πῶλον νέον, while St. Matthew quotes the Hebrew still more literally, ἐπὶ πῶλον υἱὸν ὑποζυγίου.

(2) Zech 12:10 quoted in John 19:37, Ὄψονται εἰς ὃν ἐξεκέντησαν (Turpie, p. 131). This agrees with the Heb. 'They shall look upon me whom they have pierced.' But the LXX is quite different, καὶ ἐπιβλέψονται πρός με ἀνθ᾽ ὧν κατωρχήσαντο, i.e. 'they shall look on me, because they have derided.' The LXX evidently read the same radical but not with the pointing דָּקָרוּ, and this

---

[9]Quoted in Lücke, *Commentar uber das Evangelium des Johannes* (1840), i. p. 172.
[10]*Authorship of the Fourth Gospel*, p. 28. Mr. Sanday says 'The Greek is purer than that of the Synoptists. If purer in one sense, yet it is more Hebraic.'

reading is actually found in some MSS. of Kennicott and de Rossi. The LXX has not a single word in common with St. John.[11]

On the reading of the Hebrew as 'unto me' rather than 'unto him' which is read by many MSS., see de Rossi ill. p. 217. Aquila, at least, of the other versions, seems to point to this reading. The Evangelist, however, if he had אֵלַי, would not unnaturally change the person from the first to the third to suit the connection. Comp. Apoc 1:7.

(3) Ps 40:10 quoted in John 13:18 (Turpie, p. 55). St. John has Ὁ τρώγων μου τὸν ἄρτον ἐπῆρεν ἐπ᾽ ἐμὲ τὴν πτέρναν αὐτοῦ. The LXX ὁ ἐσθίων ἄρτους μου, ἐμεγάλυνεν ἐπ᾽ ἐμὲ πτερνισμόν. Here again there is hardly a word the same in the two translations. St. John's is evidently a loose quotation taken from the Hebrew. The LXX translation has lost the meaning in endeavouring to render הִגְדִּיל. St. John gives the more correct, though free, rendering. So Gesenius takes it (p. 266, ed. 1829); but Perowne ad loc. seems to think either interpretation admissible.

(4) Is 6:10 quoted in John 12:40 (Turpie, p. 233). It is a very free quotation. The LXX is quite different. The point to be observed is the use of the active in St. John. Τετύφλωκεν αὐτῶν τοὺς ὀφθαλμοὺς καὶ ἐπώρωσεν αὐτῶν τὴν καρδίαν. God Himself is represented as blinding, as hardening. This points to the Hebrew, which has also the active. But there it is imperative, and the change to the indicative is intelligible. As Symmachus translates וְעֵינָיו הָשַׁע, it is quite possible that St. John translated the same words Τετύφλωκεν αὐτῶν, perhaps from a mixture of Aramaic with Hebrew forms. In the Syriac the imperative and 3rd pers. pret. are the same. On the other hand, the LXX has adopted a passive form of the sentence, ἐπαχύνθη γὰρ ἡ καρδία τοῦ λαοῦ τούτου, καὶ τοῖς ὠσὶν αὐτῶν βαρέως ἤκουσαν καὶ τοὺς ὀφθαλμοὺς αὐτῶν ἐκάμμυσαν μήποτε ἴδωσι τοῖς ὀφθαλμοῖς καὶ τοῖς ὠσὶν ἀκούσωσι καὶ τῇ καρδίᾳ συνῶσι, καὶ ἐπιστρέψωσι, καὶ ἰάσομαι αὐτούς, evidently to get rid of a doctrine which was a stumbling-block. Symmachus seems likewise to have surmounted the difficulty, though in another way. He takes הָעָם הַזֶּה as the nominative, 'This people . . . etc.' Now it is quite inconceivable that the writer of the Fourth Gospel, having only the LXX before him, should accidentally have reconverted it, and thus reintroduced the perplexity. The chances are

---

[11]My investigation was made before I saw Bleek's *Beitrage*, and it agrees almost entirely with his results (p. 244sq). I have derived much help from Turpie, *The Old Testament in the New* (1868).

a thousand-fold against it; and he would surely have shrunk from it. It is noticeable too, that the other New Testament writers who quote the sentence (Matt 13:14, 15; Acts 28:26, 27), quote it from the LXX. In Mark 4:12, Luke 8:10, this part of the quotation is omitted.

(5) Is 54:13 quoted in John 6:45 (Turpie, p. 198). This is a doubtful case. The Hebrew has 'And all thy sons (are) disciples of God.' St. John [reads] Καὶ ἔσονται πάντες διδακτοὶ Θεοῦ. The LXX however attaches the sentence to what goes before, καὶ πάντας τοὺς υἱούς σου διδακτοὺς Θεοῦ. St. John treats it as independent—so do the Targum, Ewald, Gesenius, in interpreting the Hebrew.

These passages then, except perhaps the last (5), are decisive. In no case could they be derived from the LXX. But, it may be said, they came perhaps not from the original Hebrew, but from a Targum. This admission is sufficient for my purpose, which is to show the direct acquaintance of the Evangelist with Hebrew writings.

(b) *Passages which may have come from either the Hebrew or the Septuagint.* In many cases it is doubtful whether a quotation was taken from the LXX or the Hebrew. These instances divide themselves into three classes:

(1) *Where the Greek and Hebrew differ,* but the quotation is too loose to allow of any inference. Examples of this are: (a) Deut 19:15 quoted in John 8:17 (Turpie, p. 49). Here the LXX inserts πάν; but St. John paraphrases the whole sentence δύο ἀνθρώπων ἡ μαρτυρία. Thus the crucial point of difference is evaded.

(b) Exo 12:46 (Num 9:12) quoted in John 19:36 (Turpie, p. 31). Here St. John follows neither the Hebrew nor the LXX. But the passage intended to be quoted may be Ps 33:21; in which case the Hebrew and LXX agree, and no inference can be drawn. Or St. John may have had all three passages in his mind, and combined them in a loose way.

(2) *Where the Greek and Hebrew agree,* but the Greek is the obvious, or an obvious, rendering of the Hebrew; and no conclusion can be drawn. Examples:

(a) Ps 34 (35):19; 68 (69):5 οἱ μισοῦντές με δωρεάν. Comp. Ps 108 (109):3, in John 15:25 (Turpie, p. 30).

(b) Ps 69 (68):10 quoted in John 2:17 (Turpie, p. 29), where the Evangelist substitutes καταφάγεται, for καταφάγεν.

(c) Ps 82 (81):6 quoted in John 10:34 (Turpie, p. 4).

Or again, (3) *The Greek and Hebrew agree,* but the Greek is not an obvious rendering. Yet the Evangelist's quotation is not exact enough to warrant an inference. Examples:

(a) Ps 78 (77):24 quoted in John 6:31 (Turpie, p. 60). The use of ἄρτον however here in St. John seems to show that he had the LXX rendering in mind, for this is apparently the only passage in the Old Testament where דָּגָן is rendered ἄρτος.

(c) Is 40:3 quoted in John 1:23 (Turpie, p. 219). Yet εὐθύνατε (St. John) for εὐθείας ποιεῖτε (LXX) looks like a direct derivation from the Hebrew, which has one word יַשְּׁרוּ, not two, in the original. All the other Evangelists have εὐθείας ποιεῖτε (Matt 3:3; Mark 1:3; Luke 3:4); and this makes the probability stronger.

(c) *Passages almost certainly, or most probably, taken from the LXX.*

(1) Ps 21:19 quoted in John 19:24 (Turpie, p. 4). The LXX is a literal translation of the Hebrew; but the probabilities are greatly against the Evangelist stumbling upon the same rendering word for word, more especially the opposition of ἱμάτια and ἱματισμός.

(2) Is 53:1 quoted in John 12:38 (Turpie, p. 106). Again the LXX is a literal rendering of the Hebrew, for τίνι as a rendering of עַל־מִי can hardly be regarded as an exception. But the probabilities are against the whole combination of words being the same.

These are all the quotations from the Old Testament in St. John, and the result at which we arrive is as follows: The writer certainly derived several of his quotations from the Hebrew, or from an Aramaic Targum, not from the LXX. On the other hand, he most probably took one or two from the LXX, though the evidence for the LXX is not so decisive as for the Hebrew. The majority of the passages prove nothing either way.

2. *The writer's interpretation of Hebrew words.* (a) Rabbi, Rabbouni, 1:38 Ῥαββεί (ὃ λέγεται μεθερμηνευόμενον Διδάσκαλε); 20:16 Ῥαββουνεί (ὃ λέγεται Διδάσκαλε). The longer form is the more impressive, the higher title; hence it is peculiarly adapted to the solemnity of the circumstances of Mary's recognition of the risen Lord. In this respect compare Mark 10:51, where again the circumstances are exceptional. These are the only two passages in the New Testament in which the form occurs.[12] The omission by St. John of

---

[12]See Keim iii. p. 560; Buxtorf p. 217sq.; Levy II. p. 401.

the interpretation of the pronoun 'my master' is to be explained by the fact that it had got attached to the word, as in Rabbi, and had ceased to have any distinct force: just as, by the reverse principle, ὁ κύριος is rendered in Syriac 'our Lord.'

(6) Messias, 1:41 Εὑρήκαμεν τὸν Μεσσίαν (ὅ ἐστιν μεθερμηνευόμενον Χριστός); 4:25. The word does not occur in the New Testament save in these two places.

(c) Cephas, 1:42 Κηφᾶς (ὃ ἑρμηνεύεται Πέτρος). This title is only used by John and St. Paul. Elsewhere, when the appellation is employed, the Greek form is preferred.

(d) Thomas, 20:24; 21:2 Θωμᾶς ὁ λεγόμενος Δίδυμος. Thus St. John takes care to let us know that the familiar name of this Apostle was merely a surname, 'twin.' There was an early tradition in the Syrian Church that Thomas' real name was Judas (e.g. Eusebius, *Hist. Eccles.* i.18; *Acta Thomae* I ed. Tisch. p. 190).[13] In the Curetonian Syriac of John 14:22 'Judas Thomas' is substituted for 'Judas, not Iscariot.' As there were two other Apostles of this same name, some distinction would be necessary; and this we find was the case, one being called Lebbaeus, another Thomas, the third Iscariot.

(e) Siloam, 9:7 εἰς τὴν κολυμβήθραν τοῦ Σιλωάμ ὃ ἑρμηνεύεται Ἀπεσταλμένος. The word occurs in Isaiah 9:6 שִׁלֹחַ (A. V. Shiloah), and signifies a 'conduit,' 'emissary,' 'aqueduct,' from the root שלח 'send,' which is used of water in Ps 94:10; Ezek 31:4 (Gesenius, p. 1415). הַשִּׁלֹחַ־בַּיִת occurs in the Talmud, meaning either 'a conduit for irrigation' or 'field needing artificial irrigation' (Buxtorf, p. 2412sq). Another form שִׁלֹּו (A. V. Siloah) is found as a proper name in Neh 3:15, if indeed the Masoretic pointing may be trusted. That two forms should exist side by side is very conceivable, for the word is not strictly speaking a proper name. In Greek the forms vary: Σιλωάμ (LXX Luke 13:4; Josephus frequently); Σιλωάς (Josephus elsewhere); Σιλωά (Aquila, Symmachus, Theodotion). The geographical and symbolical bearing of the notice will be considered hereafter. At present I am only concerned with the etymology. This the Evangelist has explained rightly. Two further points deserve attention. He has given the correct meaning, notwithstanding that it is somewhat obscured by the Greek form. Again he has

---

[13]See Assemani, *Bibl. Orient.* I. pp. 100, 318; Cureton's *Syriac Gospels*, p. 1; *Anc. Syr. Documents*, p. 32.

added the definite article 'the Siloam.' This is in accordance with Jewish usage. In the Old Testament, and generally in the Targums and the Rabbinic passages, as well as in St Luke l.c. the definite article occurs. With this compare Acts 9:35 'the Sharon' (τὸν Σαρῶνα).

(f) *Golgotha*, 19:17 εἰς τὸν λεγόμενον Κρανίου τόπον, ὃ λέγεται Ἑβραϊστὶ Γολγοθᾶ. Cf. Matt 17:33; Mark 15:22 (Luke 23:33). As the interpretation occurs in the Synoptic narrative also, no argument can be drawn from it.

(g) *Gabbatha*, 19:13 εἰς τόπον λεγόμενον Λιθόστρωτον, Ἑβραϊστὶ δὲ Γαββαθα. Pliny (*H. N.* xxxvi.28) tells us that the pavements called *lithostrota* were first introduced by Sulla, and that in the temple of Fortune at Praeneste one could be seen in his day which Sulla had placed there. Again, Suetonius (*Jul.* 46) states that Julius Caesar was accustomed to carry tesselated pavements about with him for his own use in his expeditions ('*in expeditionibus tesselata et sectilia pavimenta circumtulisse*'). This last notice however does not help us much, for evidently St. John's account speaks of some fixed locality. It shows, however, that such a flooring would seem necessary for a Roman magistrate's tribunal. A fixed place at Amathus was so called.[14]

But what is the meaning of the Hebrew Gabbatha? It is commonly connected with the Hebrew for 'to be high,' meaning a 'prominence' or 'hill' (גִּבְעָה). Cf. *gibbus*. The word would then represent the Hebrew radical גבעה.[15] This theory receives further support from the fact that Josephus (*Ant.* v.1.29; vi.4.2 and elsewhere) uses Γαβάθα for Gibeah, 'a hill.' And it is a very possible solution, for the Evangelist does not say that the Hebrew represents the meaning of the Greek equivalent. But this interpretation labours under the disadvantage that it does not account for the doubling of the β. Accordingly Ewald (*Johan. Schr.* I. p. 408) suggests as the derivation גְּבַע קָבַץ 'to collect together' and thus the word would imply 'a mosaic.' This appears to me highly probable, for I find this word קָבַץ used of studding or inlaying with jewels or precious stones, e.g. Ex. 25:7, of the jewels of the high-priest's ephod, and Deut 33:21, where the Targum Ben Uzziel has 'a place inlaid (קְבִיעִם) with precious stones and jewels'; see Levy s.v. ii. p. 342. Thus here again St. John shows his intimate knowledge of the derivation of an obscure Hebrew term.

---

[14]Boeckh *C. I. G.* 2643 notes the use of the word Λιθόστρωτον, here.
[15]See Levy, i. p. 123; Lücke; Hengstenberg ad loc; Keim iii. p. 365.

(h) *Iscariot.* The phenomena which St. John's Gospel presents in the use of this name are somewhat remarkable. As soon as the false readings are swept away which obscure the true text, we find (1) that the designation is attached to the father's name (6:71; 13:26) as well as to the son's (12:4; 13:2; 14:22); (2) that in more than one place (12:4; 14:22) the definite article should precede the name. We gather therefore that the word is not strictly speaking a proper name at all, but merely describes the native place of the traitor. This solution is suggested by St. John's Gospel, but there is no hint of it given by the Synoptists. Yet it is rendered highly probable by other considerations also. The word Ἰσκαριώτης is 'the man of Kerioth.' Now in 2 Sam 10:6, 8 among the mercenaries hired by the children of Ammon to attack David are mentioned 'of Ishtob twelve thousand men,' or, as it almost certainly should be rendered, 'of the men of Tob twelve thousand men,' Tob being a district mentioned in Judges 11:3-5. This word becomes in Josephus, *Ant.* vii.6.1 a proper name, Ἴστβος. The interpretation of Josephus may be right or wrong; but we are only concerned with the representation of the Hebrew form in Greek; and, so far as it goes, it is an adequate illustration of the way in which 'man of Kerioth' would appear in a Greek dress. Again, the tradition of Judas' birthplace is preserved in some MSS. of the New Testament. Thus in Matt 10:4; 26:14 some old Latin MSS. have Karioth, while other authorities have intermediate readings, Scarioth, Σκαριώτης; in Mark 3:19 the correct reading (ℵ, B, C, L) is Ἰσκαριώθ, the termination not having been interfered with, e has Cariotha, and there are other variations. In Mark 14:10 ℵ, B, L, C* have Ἰσκαριώθ, while Ἰσκαριώτης is found in A and the majority of authorities. Here again Scarioth is read by some Latin MSS. On the whole it seems probable that Ἰσκαριώθ is consistently St. Mark's form of the appellation. In Luke 4:16 Ἰσκαριώθ is the right reading (ℵ, B, L); on the other hand in 22:3 Ἰσκαριώτην seems to be correct, though here again the alternative form has supporters. St. Luke therefore appears to vary, and this we might expect from the manner in which his Gospel was composed. Turning now to St. John's Gospel we find that D has ἀπό Καρυωτου in four out of the five verses in which the name occurs, and (followed by three Latin MSS.). Σκαριώθ in the fifth passage (6:71), where, on the other hand, ἀπό Καρυωτου receives the support of 69, ℵ 124, and of the margin of the Harclean Syriac. Thus the trace of the original meaning of the word seems to linger in the Western text of the Fourth Gospel.

Καριώθ is the LXX rendering of קריות. The word signifies 'cities,' i.e. a conjunction of small towns. Hence it is of frequent occurrence. Thus a place of the name was situated in Moab (Jer 48:24, 41; Amos 2:2; see Merx, *Arch. fur Wissensch. Erf. des Alt. Test.*, p. 320), another in Judah (Joshua 15:25). This latter is perhaps the birth-place of Judas who, like Perugino, Correggio, Veronese and others, has merged his personal name in that of his native town.

2. THE WRITER'S KNOWLEDGE OF JEWISH IDEAS, TRADITIONS, EXPECTATIONS, MODES OF THOUGHT. (i) The Messiah. Occasion has been taken elsewhere to point out that, in the Fourth Gospel, 'the narrative and the discourses alike are thoroughly saturated with the Messianic ideas of the time.' In discussing this subject attention was drawn to two facts as especially worthy of notice: (1) that though the writer's point of view is twofold, the Word as the theological, the subjective, center, no less than the Messiah as the historical, the objective center, yet, with a true insight which is the best evidence for his veracity, he keeps these two points of view separate. The topic of our Lord's discourses with the Jews is not the doctrine of the Logos, for which His auditors would feel neither predilection nor interest, but the Messianic expectation, in which they were thoroughly absorbed. (2) It was shown that the Messianic conceptions are not the ideas as corrected by the facts, but the ideas in their original form, not yet spiritualised, but coarse and materialistic still, reflecting the sentiments not of the second century but of the early years of the first; in a word, Jewish, not Christian. This Messianic idea is turned about on all sides. We learn very much more about it from the Fourth Gospel than from all the other three Gospels together. This is a fact which we do not sufficiently realise, and it is a characteristic, though an accidental, token to this fact that the Hebrew equivalent for Χριστός, the word Μεσσίας, is found only in this Gospel. The prevalence, nay, the ubiquity, of the Messianic idea is the key to the motive of the narrative. Does Jesus work a miracle? It is a sign of His Messianic office. Does He suffer an indignity? It is fatal to His claims as the triumphant King and Avenger of His people. Does He utter an unpalatable truth, or a seemingly unpatriotic sentiment? Such language is inconsistent with the office of the long-expected Savior of the Jewish nation. Does He exhibit in His person the common associations and relationships of life? This again is not compatible with His Messianic character.

Moreover, He is only one in a long line of claimants who have arrogated to themselves this high office. Before Him, many thieves and robbers have entered into the fold by stealth and violence (10:8). This last passage has been attacked as fatal to the authority of the Gospel, and this on two grounds. First, we are told,[16] that it is a thoroughly Gnostic sentiment, directed against the lawgiver and the prophets. They are the thieves and the robbers. Thus it is inconsistent not only with our Lord's own position, but also with the position of St. John as a 'pillar-apostle' of the Circumcision. Secondly, we are informed[17] that the statement is historically incorrect; for as a matter of fact we do not hear of false Messiahs before Christ. I give this as a sample of the attacks which are made in certain quarters upon the genuineness of the Fourth Gospel.

In reply it is sufficient to state (1) that the interpretation, which sees in the thieves and robbers a reference to Moses and the prophets, is quite untenable. It contradicts the whole teaching of the Gospel. Our Lord constantly refers to the Old Testament Scriptures as authoritative, and as foretelling Himself. Thus Abraham rejoiced to see Christ's day, and he saw it and was glad. The Jews are Abraham's seed, yet they seek to kill Him (8:37, 56). Moses will accuse them to the Father; for had they believed Moses, they would have believed Christ, for Moses wrote of Him (5:45sq.). And the Evangelist sees in the persistent unbelief of the Jewish race a fulfilment of a prophecy of Isaiah uttered when he saw Christ's glory and spake of Him (12:37sq.). The interpretation therefore may safely be dismissed. Curiously enough it is a view borrowed from Valentinus, who states that 'all the prophets and the law spake from the Demiurge, a foolish God, and were foolish themselves and ignorant' (Hippol. *Haer.* vi.35, p. 194), and then proceeds to quote this passage and it is echoed by the Manicheans (August, *c. Faust,* xvi.12, vili., p. 288 F., 289 A.) and probably by other dualistic sects. Such at least would appear from Clement Alex. *Strom.* i.17, pp. 366sq. (ed. Potter). Further, the consciousness of the misuse that was made of the text would account for the omission of the words πρὸ ἐμοῦ by some authorities.[18] (2) The expression

---

[16]By Hilgenfeld.
[17]By Baur and Scholten.
[18]The words are omitted in ℵ*, in most Latin mss., in the Syriac, Sahidic, and Gothic versions, and by Cyril, Chrysostom, and Augustine.

need not necessarily be confined to false Messiahs. 'Shepherds' are teachers (Jer 23:1; Ezek 34:2, 3), and thus the Scribes and Pharisees, the leaders of religious thought, would naturally be included in the category. In other passages our Lord refers to them as robbers, as wolves in sheep's clothing (Matt 7:15), as devouring widows' houses (Matt 23:14; Mark 12:40; Luke 20:47). And the beginning of this corrupt state of teaching did not synchronize with the time of our Lord's life upon earth. For some generations past the whole tendency of religious education had been thoroughly vicious.[19]

But after all there is no sufficient reason for denying the appearance of false Messiahs before the Christian era. On the contrary, everything points to the fact of such appearances. And if these earlier false Messiahs do not come forward so prominently in Josephus as those who flourished afterwards, this is only what was to be expected; for they did not fall within his own lifetime. Gamaliel, at all events, in his speech as recorded by St Luke (Acts 5:35sq.), mentions two of these impostors, Theudas and Judas the Galilean, the latter of whom is described as having revolted 'in the days of the taxing.' In the case of the former, there is a well-known chronological difficulty, Josephus (*Ant.* xx. 5. 1) speaking of a Theudas who headed a rebellion in the procuratorship of Cuspius Fadus after A.D. 44; but the occasion of the revolt of Judas the Gaulanite is given by him in detail (*Ant.* xviii.1.1sq.), and his language shows evidently that the rising took a theocratic character.[20] In another place Josephus, referring to the time of the death of Herod the Great (*Ant.* xvii.10.8), tells us that 'Judaea was infested with robbers,' and as the bands of the seditious found anyone to head them, he was created a king at once, in order to do damage to the community. He mentions several of these adventurers by name, beginning (*Ant.* xvii.10.5) with Judas the son of a certain Hezekiah, whom he calls the 'brigand-chief' (ὁ ἀρχιληστής). Now it is quite impossible to separate all these uprisings from Messianic anticipations, even if the contrary was not directly stated in some cases by the historian. For the air was full of rumors, and echoes of the Messianic expectations had penetrated as far as Rome, and found expression in the pages of Suetonius (*Vesp.* 4) and in the Fourth Eclogue of Virgil. By some, the Herod-family was looked to as the embodiment of the national hope, Antipas (Vict.

---

[19]See Ewald, *Jahrb. Der Bibl. Wissenschaft*, ix.43.
[20]See Josephus, *Ant.* xviii.1.6.

Ant. *ap. Cramer Cat. in Marc.* p. 400), Agrippa (Philastrius, *Haer.* xxviii.), and Herod the Great (Epiphanius, *Haer.* xx. p. 45) being at different times regarded as the Messiah by their partisans.[21]

But it is not only the prevalence of the Messianic idea exhibited in this Gospel, it is the minuteness and variety of detail displayed which arrests our attention, and is so powerful a testimony to the authenticity of the narrative. This phenomenon can be conveniently illustrated by the designations which the Evangelist applies to the Messiah. I give some of the most striking.

(a) *The Lamb of God* (1:29, 36). The reference is to Isaiah 53:4, a passage which was commonly interpreted of the Messiah, apparently before the Christian era (see Bishop Harold Browne, *Sermons*, p. 92sq.[22] and cf. Sanday, *Authorship of the Fourth Gospel*, p. 39 sq.), and is interpreted of our Lord directly by Philip the Evangelist (Acts 8:32) and indirectly St. Peter (1 Pet 1:19). This idea of the lamb as typifying the Messiah is not found in the other three Evangelists. It is introduced however by St. John naturally and without comment, the meaning is only explained by recalling the Messianic expectations of the time, and in fact is lost sight of by many commentators. With the substitution of another Greek word (ἀρνίον for ἀμνός) the same metaphor occurs in the Apocalypse nearly thirty times.

(b) *The Son of God, the King of Israel* (1:49). The naturalness of this outburst on the part of Nathanael is deserving of notice. The titles with which he hails the Messiah are introduced in a way which is absolutely free from artificiality. The first designation, the 'Son of God,' is derived from Ps 2:7. It occurs again in the Fourth Gospel, 1:34; 3:18; 9:35 and especially 11:27, in the last passage coupled expressly with the title 'the Christ,' a combination which we find elsewhere (Matt 16:63 in the mouth of the High Priest, and Matt 16:16 in the confession of St. Peter). Even when it stands alone, as in Luke 4:41; 22:70, it is at once recognised as applying to the Christ. The second title, 'the King of Israel,' is a favorite appellation in the Fourth Gospel (12:13; cf. 18:36, 37; 19:3, 5, 12, 14, 19). As Mr. Sanday appositely remarks (*Authorship of the Fourth Gospel*, p. 35), 'the phrase is especially important, because it breathes those politico-theocratic hopes, which, since the taking of Jerusalem, Christians, at least, if not Jews, must have entirely laid aside. It belongs to the

---

[21]See the article Herodians in Smith's *Dictionary of the Bible* and compare Keim, I, p. 244sq.
[22]*Messiah as foretold and expected*, Cambridge (1862).

lowest stratification of Christian ideas, before Christianity was separated from Judaism; and there is but one generation of Christians, to whom it would have any meaning.'

Other Messianic titles which are found in our Evangelist are (c) *He that is coming* (ὁ ἐρχόμενος) 6:14; 11:27; cf. Matt 11:3; Luke 7:19, 20; derived from the well-known Messianic psalm (Ps 118), which is quoted in this sense by all the four Evangelists (Matt 23:39; Mark 11:9; Luke 13:35; John 12:13); (d) *the Holy One of God* (ὁ Ἅγιος τοῦ Θεοῦ) 6:69; cf. Mark 1:24 and other passages; (e) *the Son of Man*, 1:51 etc., the most familiar of all designations of the Christ, especially in St. Luke's Gospel; (f) *the Light*, 1:7, 8; 8:12, 12:46; cf. Luke 2:32; an idea found in Messianic passages like Is 9:2; 42:6, 7; Mal 4:2, 3, and expressly interpreted of Christ by the Talmud: 'Light is the name of Messiah' (see Lightfoot *Hor. Heb.* p. 564 quoted by Sanday, p. 152); (g) He that hath been sent (ὃ . . . Ἀπεσταλμένος) 9:7, where the interpretation of the name Siloam connects the pool with Christ (see 10:36; 17:3, 8, 18, 21, 23, 25 etc; cf. Is 61:1) rather than with the man (see Wettstein *ad loc*), but where the allusion to the title, so far from appearing on the surface, is inserted in the most unobtrusive manner possible. These instances show the perfect ease and familiarity with which the writer of the Fourth Gospel moves among the Messianic expectations and the national feelings of the period which he depicts.

(ii) *The companions of the Messiah.* Attention has been drawn above to the significant references to 'the prophet' which occur in four places in St. John (1:21, 25; 4:14; 7:40). It has been pointed out that the form which the conception takes is strictly Jewish, not Christian. While Christian teachers identified the prophet foretold by Moses (Deut 18:15) with our Lord Himself (Acts 3:22; 7:37; cf. John 1:46)[23] the Jews in St. John's Gospel conceive of 'the Christ' and 'the prophet' as two different persons. If He is not the Christ, they adopt the alternative that He may be 'the prophet' (1:21, 25); if not 'the prophet,' then 'the Christ' (7:40). But this brings us to another point, which is worthy of consideration. Springing out of the phrase employed by Moses in the passage quoted above ('a prophet like unto me') came the Jewish idea of the paral-

---

[23]This identification is a commonplace in patristic writers. See Tertullian, *adv. Marcion*, iv.22; *Apost. Const.* v.20; *Clem. Recogn.* i.43; Origen, *in Johan.* vi. 4; Eusebius, *Demonstr. Evang.* i.7, p. 26 sq. (ed. Paris 1628).

lelism of the lawgiver and the Messiah. In part this idea was justified by the prophecy, and finds its proper place in the language of the New Testament. Thus, as the writer of the Epistle to the Hebrews shows, Moses and Christ are the two mediators of the two covenants (Heb 8:5, 6). Thus again, in a well-known passage (1 Cor 10:1-11), St. Paul works out the parallel in his record of the wanderings of the children of Israel. The crossing of the Red Sea is a baptism by Moses. The rock smitten in the wilderness is Christ. Thus again, St. John in the Apocalypse (15:3) sets in the mouth of the redeemed a twofold song, 'the song of Moses the servant of God, and the song of the Lamb.' And lastly, our Lord Himself instances the action of Moses in lifting up the serpent in the wilderness as emblematic of Himself (John 3:14). But the Rabbis carried out the parallelism into the most minute details, so that the career of the Messiah became in effect a reproduction of the career of Moses. Of this belief adventurers, who wished to pose as the Messiah, were not slow to take advantage. For instance, Theudas, to whom allusion has already been made, undertakes to divide the Jordan (Josephus, *Ant.* xx.5.1), in imitation probably as much of Moses as of Joshua and Elijah. Again, other nameless adventurers, to whom Josephus makes reference a little later on (*Ant.* xx.8.6), 'urged the multitude to follow them into the wilderness, and pretended that they would exhibit manifest wonders and signs that should be performed by the providence of God.' Gfrorer, who has worked out this subject in his *Jahrhundert des Heils* (ii. p. 318sq), tells us that Micah 7:15 was quoted to prove that the Passover was the time in which this manifestation of Messianic power should be exhibited. In fulfilment of the prophecy of Zechariah (9:9), the King should appear riding an ass (Gfrorer, p. 339). The miracles which he was expected to perform were to include the two mighty works of his prototype, the smiting of the waters as suggested by Zechariah (x. 11), and the giving of the manna. We have seen how the first of these symbolical acts was promised by Theudas. To the general expectation of the second miracle rabbinic literature furnishes full and explicit testimony. Thus in *Qoheleth Rabba*, 9 fol. 86.4, we read Dixit P. Berachia nomine R. Isaaci '*qualis fuit redemptor primus, talis erit redemptor ultimus. . . . Sicut redemptor primus fecit descendere manna, ita redemptor posterior faciet descendere manna.*' Again, in *Shir. Rabba*, fol. 16, '*Redemptor posterior revelabitur iis . . . et quonam illos ducet? Sunt qui dicunt in desertum Judae, sunt qui dicunt in desertum Sichoris et Ogi et descendere faciet pro iis manna*' (see Lightfoot *Hor. Heb.* ii. pp. 552, 557; cf. *Shemoth Rabba* xxv.). In the light of these notices we can imagine the ferment which would be occasioned by the feeding of the five thousand, and we can now understand the full significance of the challenge thrown out to Him on the part of the unbelieving crowd, 'What dost thou work? Our fathers did eat manna in the wilderness' (6:30, 31), which in St. John's narrative occurs in so abrupt and unexplained a manner. The key to the understanding of the whole situation is an acquaintance with the national expectation of the greater Moses. But this knowledge is not obtruded upon us by the Evangelist. It is tacitly assumed. In fact, the meaning is unintelligible, except to one who is brought up among the ideas of the time, or to one who, like a modern critic, has made them his special study.

And so we might pass in review the various details of the Messianic conception, and show how marvellously they correspond with the account given so naturally and incidentally by the Evangelist. The birth and generation of the Christ who, in accordance with Micah 5:2, should be a descendant of David, born in Bethlehem (7:42), and yet at the same time the mystery and uncertainty of that birth (7:27) based upon the well-known passage in Isaiah 'who shall declare His generation?' (Is 53:8),[24] the apparent discrepancies of the two accounts being explained by the rabbis on the analogy of Moses who was born and then hidden; His manifestation 'to Israel' (1:31 a passage with which Sanday, p. 33, compares Luke 1:80 spoken of John the Baptist; cf. 14:22; 17:6sq.), an event which Jewish tradition decided would take place at the Passover (*Shemoth Rabb.* xv.150, Jerusalem Targum on Ex 3:42; *Mechilta* on Ex. xii. 42; R. Bechai in *Kad Hakkemach* 49),[25] doubtless another element in the excitement of the crowds after the Feeding of the Five Thousand which took place at Passover-tide (John 6:2); lastly, His eternal continuance (12:34), a point much discussed among the rabbis.[26]

---

[24]See Sanday, p. 146, Gfrorer, pp. 203, 307; Wettstein and Lightfoot on John 4:27.

[25]The Gemarists (*Hieros. Berachoth* fol. 5.1) alleged that the Messiah had been born at Bethlehem a good while before their own times but had been snatched away. The same idea is found in Midrash Sair fol. 1, 16. 4 (on *Canticles* ii.9). '*Caprea apparet et occultatur, apparet et occultatur. Sic redemptor primus (Moses) apparuit et fuit occultatus, et tandem apparuit iterum. . . . Sic redemptor posterior (Messias) revelabitur iis atque iterum abscondetur ab iis. . . . In fine quadraginta quinque dierum revelabitur iterum iis et descendere faciet pro iis manna.*'

[26]See these various speculations given in Gfrorer, pp. 252sq., 296, 315-317. The passages referred

One of the accompaniments of the Messiah in Jewish anticipations was the return of the Shekhinah, the symbol of that visible divine presence, the loss of which after the captivity had been so universally deplored. This confident hope was based on such prophecies as Ezekiel 37:27; 43:7; Zechariah 2:10sq.; 8:3; Isaiah 8:8, and on the language of Ecclesiasticus 14:8sq.: 'He that created me caused my tabernacle to rest, and said, Let thy dwelling be in Jacob . . . in the holy tabernacle I served before him' (τότε ἐνετείλατό μοι ὁ κτίστης ἁπάντων, καὶ ὁ κτίσας με κατέπαυσε τὴν σκηνήν μου καὶ εἶπεν· ἐν Ἰακὼβ κατασκήνωσον καὶ ἐν Ἰσραὴλ κατακληρονομήθητι. πρὸ τοῦ αἰῶνος ἀπ᾿ἀρχῆς ἔκτισέ με, καὶ ἕως αἰῶνος οὐ μὴ ἐκλίπω. ἐν σκηνῇ ἁγίᾳ ἐνώπιον αὐτοῦ ἐλειτούργησα καὶ οὕτως ἐν Σιὼν ἐστηρίχθην). It finds expression in more than one passage in the Apocalypse (7:15; 13:6; 15:5; 21:3). It remains however for St. John in his Gospel, in words which are replete with local coloring, to point with a quiet triumph to the fulfilment of this expectation in the person of Jesus Christ, 'The Word became flesh, and tabernacled (ἐσκήνωσεν) among us, and we beheld His glory (καὶ ἐθεασάμεθα τὴν δόξαν αὐτοῦ), the glory as of the only-begotten from the Father, full of grace and truth' (1:14).

(iii) *The Messianic expectation among the Samaritans.*

It has been denied that the Samaritans had any Messianic anticipations at all.[27] But, firstly, they had the prophecy referred to above (Deut 18:15), which, as forming part of the Pentateuch, they would accept as authoritative. This was sufficient in itself to suggest such expectations, and the fact that they were under the same stimulating influences as the Jews, influences arising from the political troubles of the times, would encourage presentiments of a Deliverer. Secondly, as a matter of fact, there is sufficient evidence to show that Messianic hopes were as rife among them at the time of our Lord, as they are now at the present day. Thus Josephus informs us (*Ant.* xviii.4.1) that in the procuratorship of Pilate a disturbance arose among the Samaritans in consequence of an impostor who 'bade them assemble on Mount Gerizim' under promise that he 'would show them the sacred vessels (τὰ ἱερὰ σκεύη) which were buried there, because Moses had put them

---

to by the multitude were probably Is 9:6; Dan 7:13, 14, and the Targums on these texts will repay study.

[27]E.g. by the author of *The Jesus of History* (1869).

there.' All this is distinctly Messianic in character, and has an obvious reference to the narrative of 2 Maccabees (2:1-8), where Jeremiah is related to
have buried the tabernacle, the ark and the altar of incense on the mountain
'where Moses climbed up and saw the heritage of God,' and to have declared
that the secret of the hiding place should not be revealed 'until the time that
God should gather His people again together, and receive them unto mercy.'
And this view finds confirmation from a passage in the *Yoma Bahl.* (fol. 52*b*,
quoted by Gfrorer, p. 350), and explains the reference in Apoc 2:17 to the
'hidden manna,' which was one of the treasures contained in the ark (Ex
16:33, 34; Heb 9:4). These disturbances among the Samaritans took place
A.D. 34, 35, and are connected by Keim (I. p. 518) with the preaching of John
the Baptist.

Further light is thrown on these Samaritan aspirations in the *Clementine
Recognitions.* Here Simon Magus and Dositheus are both mentioned as Samaritans who professed themselves to be Messiahs[28] and the Samaritans are
described as rightly looking forward to one true Prophet in accordance with
the foretelling of Moses, but prevented by the perverse teaching of Dositheus
from believing that Jesus was He whom they expected (*Recogn.* i.54; cf.
vii.33). All the major authorities agree that the Samaritans found their hopes
upon the appearance of the prophet like unto Moses.[29] All agree too that
they expect the discovery of the furniture of the Sanctuary, e.g. the ark, the
manna and the tables of the commandments, a fact which leaves the interpretation of the passage in Josephus beyond a doubt. With them the Messiah
is represented under two aspects, first as the Hashah or Hathab (הַתָּב) the
Converter, Restorer, Buyer-back (Westcott and Petermann l.c.); secondly as
the El Muhdi the Guide (Robinson, *Biblical Researches* ii.27.8 1867). Thus we
see how the confident aspirations placed by St. John in the mouth of the
Samaritan woman, 'I know that Messias cometh, which is called Christ;
when he is come, he will tell us all things' (4:25; cf. vv. 29, 42), are not the

---

[28]*Recogn.* ii.7, 'Simon hic . . . gente Samaraeus . . . gloriae ac jactantiae supra omne genus hominum
  cupidus ita ut excelsam virtutem . . . credi se velit et Christum putari' (cf. Hom. ii.22). Recogn. i.54
  'magistrum suum (i.e. Dositheum) velut Christum praedicarunt'; cf. Origen, c. Celsus i.57 (i.372).
[29]For the later communications with the Samaritans held by Scaliger, Ludolf, and de Sacy, see
  Westcott, *Introduction to the Study of the Gospels*, p. 148. Petermann likewise, who resided two
  months at Nablus, gives the results of his visit and investigations in Herzog's *Real-Encyklop.* xiii.
  p. 372sq.

invention of a later generation, but reflect the contemporary national feelings of this interesting people.

(iv) *Jewish beliefs, and sentiments on other points.*

(a) The relation of the Jews to Abraham exemplified in John 8:33sq. is worthy of notice, as illustrating the writer's acquaintance with the Jewish ideas of his time. The boast, 'We are Abraham's seed' is an evidence of a justifiable pride of birth (cf. v. 53), but the latter part of the sentence 'and we have never been in bondage to any man' has given much difficulty to the commentators. Certainly it is not what a stranger would have said of the Jewish people. The opinion felt by the Romans for the Jews is well expressed by Cicero, who contemptuously classes together the Jews and the Syrians as nations born to slavery ('*Judaeis et Syris nationibus natis servituti*' Cicero, *Prov. Cons.* 5). And Apion casts in the teeth of Josephus the fact that, so far from ruling the Gentiles, the chosen people were as a fact subject to them (Josephus, *c. Apion.* ii.11). Yet this proud assertion of liberty is exactly what the Jews would make on their own behalf, whatever wresting of facts might be necessary to maintain it. The answer of Josephus to Apion at the end of the section is quite characteristic. 'At a time when even the Egyptians,' he contends, 'were servants to the Persians and the Macedonians, we (the Jews) enjoyed liberty, and moreover had the dominion of the cities round about us for about a hundred and twenty years, until Pompey the Great. And when all nations were conquered by the Romans, who are kings everywhere, our ancestors were the only people who continued to be esteemed their allies and friends because of their fidelity.' And in a certain sense the claim was true. The national spirit of the Jews had never been thoroughly enslaved. But externally it would appear to be the reverse of the truth, and it is difficult to conceive how words such as the Evangelist records could have found a place in a narrative written in the middle of the second century, after the twofold destruction of Jerusalem by Titus and by Hadrian had stamped out the last spark of national liberty.

(b) The authority assigned to Moses is another graphic touch which shows a minute acquaintance with Jewish thought. The assertion 'We are Moses' disciples' (9:28) is illustrated by John Lightfoot (*Hor. Heb.* ii. p. 572) from *Yoma* fol. 4. 1, where the same expression occurs, and the favourite title of Moses in vogue among the Jews was 'Moses, our master' (quoted by Scholtz on this verse). Associated with this idea is the prestige which attached to the rabbinical schools. The surprise expressed that our Lord should set up for a teacher (8:15), the contemptuous disregard for the opinion of the people (7:49), the very form of address (Σὺ εἶ ὁ διδάσκαλος τοῦ Ἰσραὴλ, 3:10), which was apparently a formula of remonstrance among the Jews[30]—all these features can be readily illustrated from rabbinical literature.

(c) The jealousy and contempt with which the Palestinian Jews viewed the Greek dispersion is strikingly evidenced by the sarcastic comment of the Jews: 'Will he go unto the dispersed among the Gentiles (μὴ εἰς τὴν Διασπορὰν τῶν Ἑλλήνων μέλλει πορεύεσθαι καὶ διδάσκειν τοὺς Ἕλληνας), and teach the Gentiles?' (7:35). Contemporary Jewish opinion drew a hard and fast line between their brethren of the Babylonian dispersion, i.e. those who preferred to remain in the land of their captivity, and the Greek dispersion in Asia Minor, the result of the wholesale deportations of Seleucus Nicator and Antiochus Epiphanes. The former were held in high honour. The land of Babylon was considered to be as holy as that of Palestine (Rabbi Solomon in *Gittin* fol. 2.1), and the descendants of the Jews there even purer than those in Judaea itself (*Kiddush* fol. 69.2). Even Gamaliel deigned to hold correspondence with the 'sons of the Dispersion of Babylonia' (Frankel, *Monatsschrift*, p. 413, 1853). Hence, as John Lightfoot remarks (*Hor. Heb.* ad loc), 'for a Palestine Jew to go to the Babylonish dispersion was to go to a people and country equal, if not superior, to his own: but to go to the dispersion among the Greeks was to go into unclean regions, to an inferior race of Jews, and into nations most heathenized.'

(d) Lastly (to confine ourselves to one further instance), the question put to our Lord concerning the man born blind, 'Master, who did sin, this man, or his parents, that he was born blind' (John 9:2) reflects with a faithful accuracy the popular teaching of the day as regards the consequences of sin. It was a received doctrine in the Jewish schools that physical defect in children was the punishment of sin committed by their parents; and though the Jewish doctrine of metempsychosis was confined to the souls of the righteous (Josephus, *Bell. Jud.* ii.12), and thus a man brought no taint of sins

---

[30]See the story told in Lightfoot, from *Echah Babbathi*, fol. 66.2, *Hor. Heb.* ii. p. 534, of Rabbi Joshua.

with him from his previous existence, yet it is clear from many curious Rabbinic passages which Lightfoot quotes (ad loc) that even in the womb the infant, from the moment of his first quickening, was considered capable of incurring stain of sin.

3. THE WRITER'S KNOWLEDGE OF EXTERNAL FACTS, THE HISTORY, GEOGRAPHY, NAMES AND CUSTOMS OF THE JEWISH PEOPLE.

(i) *The relations of the Jews with those around them.*

(a) *The Galileans.* Owing to the fact that St. John lays special stress on the Judean ministry, the references to the Galileans in his Gospel are less numerous than in the Synoptic narrative. But the notices, though few, are highly significant, and the touches with which St. John depicts them, singularly vivid. Thus we cannot fail to observe the contempt which the Jews of the metropolis display for them. 'Shall Christ come out of Galilee?' 'Out of Galilee ariseth no prophet' (7:41, 52) 'Can there any good thing come out of Nazareth?' (1:46) Such is the objection, which rises unpremeditatedly to the lips of speakers, when the northern province is indicated as the home of the Messiah. This disparagement of the Galileans is reflected more than once in the rabbinic literature of the period. 'Foolish Galilean' seems to have been the inevitable form of address when a Galilean appears as a character in a dialogue.[31]

This contempt arose in great measure from the admixture of foreign blood in the Galilean people. The Sea of Galilee was an important commercial center, and as a natural consequence strangers—Phoenicians, Syrians, Greeks and Romans—settled in the district, and intermarried with the Jewish inhabitants, to the prejudice of the race in the eyes of a strict Jew of the capital (see Keim I p. 309). The distinction thus inaugurated by the taint of foreign blood was further emphasized by a difference of pronunciation.

The rough dialect of the northerners, which was a subject of comment in the case of St. Peter (Mark 14:70), is a favorite theme likewise in rabbinical writers.[32] Thus in one story a Judaean professes himself unable to distinguish between אִמְּר 'lamb,' צָמֶר 'wool,' חֲמַר 'wine' and חֲמוֹר 'an ass,' as pronounced by a Galilean when the latter wants to make a purchase, an illus-

[31]John Lightfoot, *Hor. Heb.* 11. pp. 78, 543.
[32]See the instances given by John Lightfoot, n. p. 78sq., and cf. *First Aram. Idiom.* §15.

tration which shows that the divergence consisted largely in a careless confusion of gutturals on the part of the Galileans.[33] The bad name, from which the Galileans suffered generally, seems to have attached itself more particularly to their city Nazareth (John 1:46). Certainly the account which we have of them from other passages in the Gospels (Luke 4:16-29; Matt 13:54-58) conveys the impression that the Nazarenes were a violent, unscrupulous, irreligious people. They may therefore have fully justified their invidious reputation. That this reputation was widespread appears from the irony in the superscription on the cross, '*Jesus of Nazareth*, the King of the Jews' (John 19:19).

We pass on to notice the Evangelist's accurate knowledge of other traits in the Galilean character. In John 4:45 occurs a brief and incidental mention of the welcome accorded to our Lord by the Galileans in consequence of His doings at Jerusalem at the feast, 'for they also went to the feast.' Now it is worthy of record that Josephus (*Ant.* xx.6.1) relates that serious troubles arose owing to collisions between the Samaritans and the Galileans while the latter were on their way to keep the feasts at Jerusalem.[34] The natural turbulence of the Galileans, to which Josephus calls attention was on these occasions aggravated by their intense religious enthusiasm.[35] It is therefore quite what we should expect when we find a reference in St. Luke (13:1) to certain Galileans 'whose blood Pilate had mingled with their sacrifices' and the portrait which St. John gives us of St. Peter is, as Keim truly observes (I. p. 315), of 'a genuine Galilean type.'

(b) *The Romans.* St. John's consummate skill does not fail him as he sketches the relations of the Jews with their Roman masters. We notice on the one hand the cringing political deference exhibited in the words of the chief priests, 'The Romans shall come and take away both our place and nation' (11:48). 'We have no king but Caesar' (19:15). 'If thou let this man go, thou art not Caesar's friend' (19:12). On the other, the religious horror of the pollution attaching to contact with the Romans, which even at the height of their frenzied hatred of their prisoner kept the Jews outside the

[33]See my *Galatians*, p. 197 (ed. 6).
[34]This notice illustrates John 4:4 compared with Luke 9:51sq.
[35]See Josephus, *Bell. Jud.* iii.3.2; cf. *Vit.* 17. Many of the false Messiahs were Galileans, e.g. Judas the Galilean (see Acts 5:3).

judgment hall, 'lest they should be defiled' (18:28). He then proceeds to give us details which reveal an accurate acquaintance with the Roman customs and military arrangements of the time. Twice over is reference made to 'the band' (σπεῖρα, 18:3, 12), once to 'the captain' (ὁ χιλίαρχος, 18:12). Now, we learn from Polybius and Suidas that σπεῖρα and χιλίαρχος were technical terms, the recognised Greek renderings of *cohors* and *tribunus* respectively.[36] Accordingly the use of the definite article by St. John in both cases, '*the* cohort' and '*the* tribune,'[37] shows that he was aware of a fact, which we learn from Josephus also (*Bell. Jud.* ii.12.1), that a Roman cohort was quartered in the Turris Antonia at Jerusalem to prevent disturbances at the great festivals.[38] A few years later we find soldiers from this Roman garrison employed in rescuing St. Paul from the hands of the Jewish mob during the feast of the Passover.[39]

Again, the scene of the Crucifixion furnishes St. John with another opportunity of showing his intimate knowledge of Roman military customs. A quaternion (τετράδιον, Acts 12:4) of soldiers, as we learn from Vegetius and others,[40] was usually employed as a watch on night duty, or for purpose of escort. Now, it is noticeable that, when the other Evangelists speak of the guard which attended at the Crucifixion, no number is given. It is simply stated (Matt 27:35; Mark 15:26; Luke 23:34), that the soldiers divided the Savior's garments among them. St. John however gives the actual number.

[36]Polybius xi.23. Schweighauser in his note (ad loc.) contends that σπεῖρα here means *manipulis* and that the term *cohors* is applied to the complement of three *maniples*, but Livy in the parallel passage (xxviii.14) has *temis peditum cohortibus*, and the expression καλεῖται shows that he is merely giving the Latin equivalent (κοορτις) for the Greek expression. A little later on (xi.33.1) Polybius has again κοορτις = σπεῖρα where Casaubon has struck out the last four words, though they occur in all the manuscripts. Suidas (s.v.) states that χιλίαρχοι came into office at Rome three hundred and fifteen years after the foundation of the city. This coincides with the institution of military tribunes with consular power at the and the close of the Decemvirate.
[37]On the other hand, though 'the band' is mentioned by the Synoptists (Matt 27:27; Mark 15:16) at a later stage in the proceedings, the definite article, as used in the Fourth Evangelist, is more decisive.
[38]When Cumanus was procurator the insolent conduct of a Roman soldier at the Passover resulted in a riot (*Bell. Jud.* l.c., cf. *Ant.* xx.5.3) in which ten thousand (*Bell. Jud.* l.c., twenty thousand) Jews perished. For the disturbances at the great festivals see *Bell. Jud.* i.4.3. Whiston instances the cautious procedure of the chief priests (Matt. 26:5) as evidence to these disturbances.
[39]Acts 21:31sq., where again the same technical terms are used with the definite article. This account, like that in the Fourth Gospel, is probably the narrative of an eyewitness.
[40]'*De singulis centuriis quarterni equites et quarterni pedites excubitum noctibus faciunt*,' Vegetius, *de re military* iii.8; cf. Philo, *Flacc.* 13, II, p. 533; Polybius vi.33.

But observe how incidentally the fact comes out. He makes no mention of a *quaternion*, he merely says, 'Then the soldiers, when they had crucified Jesus, took His garments, and made four parts, to every soldier a part.' The information is not paraded in any way; it is involved in the narrative. One more instance, and I leave this part of the subject. 'The Jews,' we read, 'besought Pilate that their legs might be broken. . . . Then came the soldiers, and brake the legs of the first, and of the other which was crucified with Him' (19:31, 82). This again is a detail added by St. John, which a forger would not have cared to risk. For *crurifragium* formed no part of a crucifixion. It was a separate punishment to which slaves could be subjected at the caprice of their masters, and it was abolished together with crucifixion at the command of Constantine (Lipsius, *de Grace* III.14).[41] But there is some reason to suppose that it was used to hasten death in the case of Jewish criminals (Lactant. *Inst.* iv.26), in order that the ends of justice might not be defeated by the Mosaic enactment which required the bodies to be taken down on the day of execution (Deut 21:23 quoted by Tertullian, *adv. Judaeos* 10).

(ii) *The writer's acquaintance with Jewish Institutions.*

1. The High-Priesthood.

The relative positions of Annas and Caiaphas at the time of the Crucifixion have been a source of some perplexity. Annas the high-priest had been deposed by Gratus the predecessor of Pilate, and after intermediate appointments Gratus had nominated Caiaphas to the office. The date of Caiaphas' succession is probably A.D. 25, one year before Pilate became procurator, and he was deposed apparently about the passover of A.D. 37; whereupon there followed a series of changes, as many as seven high-priests holding office in the next ten years. These facts we learn from a comparison of certain passages in Josephus (esp. *Ant.* xviii.2.2 compared with xviii.4.3). Thus at the time of our Lord's Passion Caiaphas was the actual high-priest, while Annas had been high-priest a few years before. Turning now to the New Testament, we find a certain vagueness in the description of the two by the Synoptists, a vagueness due partly to the wide use of the word ἀρχιερεύς, but not altogether explained thereby. Thus, in his Gospel St. Luke dates the first year of our Lord's ministry ἐπὶ ἀρχιερέως Ἄννα καὶ Καϊάφα (Luke 3:2),

---

[41]See Plautus, *Asinar*. ii.4.68; Suetonius, *Paen. Aug.* 67; *Tib.* 44, passages quoted with iv.2.64; Seneca, *de Ira* iii.32; Suetonius, others by Lipsius, *de Cruce* ii.14.

but in the Acts he mentions as present at the meeting of the Sanhedrin shortly after the day of Pentecost καὶ Ἄννας ὁ ἀρχιερεὺς καὶ Καϊάφας (Acts 4:6). He would seem therefore either to have consulted documents which did not recognise the validity of Caiaphas' appointment, or to have had himself no very clear conception of the relative positions of the two. The account in the Fourth Gospel is much more precise. St. John is aware that Caiaphas is the high-priest (11:49; 18:13, 24), but he assigns an important position to Annas also, whom in some sense he recognizes likewise as ὁ ἀρχιερεύς (18:15, 16, 19, 22).[42]

On these facts we may remark, first that this unguarded, and to us un-intelligible, way of speaking betokens a genuine author, who does not feel the necessity of explaining what to himself is a familiar fact. As was natural with one who was 'known unto the high-priest' (γνωστὸς τῷ ἀρχιερεῖ, 18:15, 16), he evidently has a very clear conception of the relation of the two persons, though he has not definitely put it on paper. Secondly, so far as we are able to test the accuracy of his facts, they satisfy the test, i.e. Caiaphas *is* the actual high-priest. Thirdly, his account serves as a connecting link between scattered and apparently divergent notices in the New Testament.[43] Yet this episode about Annas in the history of the Passion is peculiar to St. John.[44]

The use of ἀρχιερεύς as applied to two different persons in St. John is admirably illustrated by a passage in Josephus (*Ant.* xx.9.2). The high-priest Ananias (the Ananias of the Acts) has been deposed, and Ishmael the son of Phabi has succeeded (*Ant.* xx.8.8). Ishmael again has been set aside, and his place given to Joseph, surnamed Kabi (xx.8.11). Shortly after, Joseph is deposed, and the office conferred upon the younger Annas or Ananus, son of the Annas of the Gospels (xx.9.1). A period of three months however witnesses the fall of Ananus, and Jesus (Joshua) the son of Damnaeus is appointed (ib.). In spite of this, however, after these four changes in the high-priestly office, when Ananias reappears upon the scene, he is still called 'the high-priest' (ὁ ἀρχιερεύς, xx.9.2), and this title is applied to him, even as late as the breaking out of the Judaic war (*Bell. Jud.* ii.17.6, 9), though in the

---

[42]The A.V. has taken unwarrantable liberties with ἀπέστειλεν in John 18:24. It should be 'sent him' not 'had sent.' The events are related in strict chronological order.

[43]E.g. Matt 26:3, 57 compared with Acts 4:6.

[44]Keim's attempt (iii. p. 322) to set this episode of Annas aside is quite futile.

meantime there has been a fifth change in the actual holder of the high-priesthood.[45] And this is not all. Ananias is designated the high-priest in describing his dealings with the actual high-priest even in the same sentence (*Ant.* xx.9.2). This is at least as great an intermingling of the use as in John xviii. and is exactly of the same kind.[46] Again, the passage in Josephus gives an example of the employment of the plural 'the high-priests,' a sufficiently striking phenomenon. All this is perfectly natural in Josephus, a contemporary and eye-witness, perfectly natural also in the Fourth Evangelist, supposing him to be a contemporary and eye-witness; but incredible in a forger, who could not have failed to betray himself by some slip when treading upon such delicate ground. Lastly, the prominence assigned by Josephus to Ananias is a parallel to the case of Annas in the Gospel and the Acts. If we had only a chapter or two of Josephus detached from the sequence of the narrative, and read of 'Ananias the high-priest,' we should certainly suppose him to have been the actual holder of the office at the time. It is conceivable that some such mistaken inference has resulted in the expression 'Annas the high-priest and Caiaphas' in Acts 4:6. Indeed it is quite possible that St. Luke himself did not know the precise facts, but had copied an authentic document, in which an especially leading part had been assigned to Annas.[47]

2. *The Jewish Festivals.*

We cannot fail to notice the large place which religious festivals occupy

---

[45]Jesus the son of Gamaliel appointed in place of Jesus the son of Damnaeus (*Ant.* xx.9.4).

[46]It is evident that the references in vv. 13, 24 are to Caiaphas, those in vv. 19, 22 to Annas, while vv. 15, 16 may be considered doubtful. On the other hand Mr. Sanday (p. 245) considers the title to apply to Caiaphas throughout, a view which compels him to regard the aorist ἀπέστειλεν in v. 24 as a pluperfect.

[47]For the popular idea that the high-priest had a sort of inspiration (John 11:51, 'And this spake he not of himself, but being high-priest that year prophesied') comp. Josephus, *Bell. Jud.* iii.8.3, and Philo, *de Creat. Princ.* §8 (II. p. 367). Other minor references which show St. John's acquaintance with Jewish rites and customs are (1) 8:17, the necessity for two witnesses (cf. Deut 17:6; 19:15, Matt 18:16; 2 Cor 13:1; Heb 10:28; 1 John 5:7sq.); (2) 8:44, the allusion to Cain (cf. 1 John 3:12); the argument appealed to certain ideas prominent at the time which would not have occurred to any writer of a later date; (3) 4:27, talking with a woman, on which see above; (4) 2:6, the purificatory rites on see Lightfoot, *ad loc.*; (5) marriage customs, especially 'the friend of the bridegroom' (3:29), a metaphor instinct with meaning, but it is only when we enter into the Jewish practice that this meaning comes out; (6) funeral ceremonies, especially the form of the grave (11:38, 41), and the mode in both passages of burial (12:7; 19:39, 40; 20:1, 5, 7, 11), on which last point compare, Tacitus *Ann.* xvi.6, where we read of Poppaea, a Jewish proselyte, 'corpus non igni abolitum, ut Romanus mos; sed regum externorum consuetudine differtum odoribus conditur.' Most of these passages are well illustrated from rabbinical sources in John Lightfoot's *Horae Hebraicae.*

in this Gospel. They are much more prominent than in the Synoptic narrative. The main incidents are connected with them, and this applies not merely to the Passover, but to the other feasts likewise.

(a) *The Feast of Tabernacles* is described in John 7. It is introduced by a remarkable expression (δὲ ἐγγὺς ἡ ἑορτὴ τῶν Ἰουδαίων ἡ σκηνοπηγία, v. 2). 'The feast of the Jews' was not in itself an unnatural way of designating the Feast of Tabernacles. For it was called by the rabbis 'the festival par excellence'[48] and Josephus (*Ant.* viii.4.1) speaks of it as 'a feast of the utmost sanctity and importance among the Hebrews.' It was sufficiently prominent to attract the notice of the heathen, such as Plutarch (*Symp.* iv.6; *Op. Mor.* p. 671 sq.), who regards it as a sort of Dionysiac festival. Still, if the words ἡ ἑορτὴ τῶν Ἰουδαίων alone had been used, the Passover would probably have been meant. Hence the words ἡ σκηνοπηγία are added. A little later on (v. 37) St. John speaks of the 'last, the great day of the feast' (Ἐν δὲ τῇ ἐσχάτῃ ἡμέρᾳ τῇ μεγάλῃ τῆς ἑορτῆς), language which may mean either the last of the seven days, i.e. strictly speaking the last of the feast, or the eighth day, the holy convocation, which followed upon the seven. There seems however to have been no special sanctity about the seventh day.[49] The first was apparently much more important than the seventh. On the other hand, it is urged that the eighth day did not properly belong to the feast, which lasted only seven days. But though the feast is sometimes spoken of as a seven days' feast, and the eighth day is not regarded (Deut 16:13sq.; Ezek 45:25), yet elsewhere the eighth day is reckoned as part of the feast, and a special prominence attached to it. This is the case in Num 29:35, in Neh 8:18, in 2 Macc 10:6, in Philo and Josephus,[50] and in Jewish writers generally.[51] I need not dwell upon the fact, to which attention has been frequently drawn, that on this occasion our Lord bases His discourse (7:37sq.; 8:12sq.) upon the two most prominent features in the ceremonial of the day, the pouring out of the water of Siloam upon the altar, and the illumination of the city by flaming

---

[48]See Smith's *Dictionary of the Bible*, s. v.

[49]Buxtorf, *Syn. Jud.* xvi. p. 327, gives a certain prominence to it in his description of the modern Jewish celebrations of the tabernacles; see too Groddeke in Ugol. xviii. p. 534.

[50]Jos. *Ant.* iii.10.4, and Philo, *Septen.* §24, p. 298 M.

[51]Succah iv.4 (*hymnus et gaudium octo dies*), iv.9 (*omnes octo dies*) v.6 (*octavo die redibant ad sortes*); cf. *Gem. Hieros.* in Ugol. xviii. p. 492.

torches lighted in the Temple area.[52] It will be sufficient to notice, first, that as in our Lord's discourse, so in the ceremonial itself, the lighting of the lamps followed the pouring out of the water, and was intimately connected therewith; secondly, that it took place in the court of the women where the treasury (ἐν τῷ γαζοφυλακίῳ) stood, and where our Lord was speaking at the time (8:20). Thus He would be able to point to the candelabra. Thirdly, it is worthy of remark that Philo also incidentally connects the same two images with the Feast of Tabernacles.[53]

(b) *The Feast of Dedication.* This festival (τὰ ἐνκαίνια) is mentioned by St. John alone, and it is remarkable how thorough and confident a knowledge of it is implied in his narrative. Here, again, the mode in which it is introduced deserves notice, 'At that time the feast of dedication was held at Jerusalem' (10:22, Ἐγένετο τότε τὰ ἐνκαίνια ἐν τοῖς Ἱεροσολύμοις). There is no mention made, as in the case of other feasts (e.g. 2:13; 4:45; 5:1; 7:8), of going up to Jerusalem. For the ἐνκαίνια, unlike the Passover, Tabernacles and Pentecost, might be celebrated anywhere (see Lightfoot ad loc). 'It was winter,' we are told. Now the festival was held to commemorate the purification and dedication of the altar and temple after pollution by Antiochus Epiphanes B.C. 167. This event and the institution of the annual festival are described in 1 Macc 4:36sq., where Judas Maccabaeus directs that the commemoration should take place 'from year to year by the space of eight days, from the five and twentieth day of the month Chislev' (v. 59). Now the month Chislev falls in November and December, coinciding more nearly with December, and the Jewish winter is reckoned to commence on the fifteenth of Chislev. Hence the notice of the season of the year in St John is strictly accurate. Yet it is introduced quite incidentally, apparently to explain the fact that Jesus was not teaching in the open air but under cover. 'It was winter, and Jesus was walking in the Temple in Solomon's porch.'

(c) *The Feast of the Passover.* Graphic touches which illustrate St. John's acquaintance with the details of this feast are his references to the paschal victim (19:36), to the danger of ceremonial pollution (18:28), and to the

---

[52]On the ceremonies of the eighth day see esp. Ewald, *Alterth.* i. p. 404. The people broke up their tents and repaired to the Temple. As the dwelling in tents symbolized the wilderness life itself a deliverance from bondage, so the eighth day would be taken to signify the end of their wanderings when they settled in the land of promise.

[53]Philo, *Septen.* §24, not as read in the ordinary texts, but as given in Tisch. *Philonea.*

Preparation (Παρασκευή, 19:14, 31, 42), a term which he employs in common with the Synoptists (Matt 27:62; Mark 15:42; Luke 23:54), but, unlike St Matthew, uses twice without the article, and in one case defines more accurately by the addition of the words τά πάσχα (19:14), implying that the term was not restricted to the Passover.[54] Lastly, the parenthetical remark on 19:31, 'For the day of that sabbath was a high day' (γὰρ μεγάλη ἡ ἡμέρα ἐκείνου τοῦ σαββάτου) points to the special sanctity of the day as a double sabbath, the sabbath alike of the week and of the festival, hebdomadal as well as Paschal.

(iii) *The Topography of Jerusalem.*

From this review of the festivals we pass on to consider the localities mentioned in the Fourth Gospel, merely premising that the complete destruction of Jerusalem by Titus and Hadrian would have gone far to obliterate traces of the actual sites, and would thus have rendered the work of a subsequent forger more than usually exposed to danger of errors.

(a) *The Temple.* We start with the Temple. Observe the familiarity with which the Evangelist moves about among the sacred precincts. He mentions the Porch of Solomon, 'the east portico,' as Josephus describes it to us (*Ant.* xx.9.7), 'on the outer part of the Temple, lying in a deep valley with walls four hundred cubits (long), built of square and very white stones' of enormous size. It was the work of Solomon, and was left untouched in Herod's restoration.[55] A covered portico of so vast an extent was doubtless a favourite place of resort and shelter in winter time, to which its eastern aspect, catching the warmth of the morning sun, would not be a disadvantage, and thus it was a natural scene for our Lord's teaching. Another spot where our Lord is stated to have taught is the treasury (ἐν τῷ γαζοφυλακίῳ, 8:20). This word St. John employs in common with the Synoptists (Mark 12:41sq.; Luke 21:1), but with characteristic exactness, he gives us additional information. The other Evangelists merely speak of casting money 'into the treasury,' confining the term apparently to the corban-chests, and this is probably the use in Josephus also, when he says (*Ant.* xix.6.1) that Herod Agrippa hung up a certain golden chain which Caligula had given him 'within the temple-

---

[54]This was apparently the case (Lightfoot, *Hor. Heb.* on Mark 15:42).

[55]Herod's restoration of the Temple was so complete that it is unlikely that in the second century a distinction would have been preserved between what was and what was not included in it.

precincts over the treasury' (ὑπερ τοῦ γαζοφυλακίου). St. John however
shows that the expression was extended to embrace the chamber in which
the chests were placed. This chamber was situated in the outer front of the
Temple in the court of the women. Thus it would be a frequented spot, since
women could penetrate no further, and St. Mark (l.c.) calls special attention
to the crowd of people which passed to and from (πῶς ὁ ὄχλος βάλλει
χαλκὸν εἰς τὸ γαζοφυλάκιον). How natural to take advantage of this
concourse, and how significant the addition 'and no man laid hands on him'
(8:20) when we recollect that the Sanhedrin held its meetings hard by between the court of the women and the inner court, within a stone's throw of
the speaker.[56]

(6) *The Watercourses of Jerusalem.*

(1) Bethesda, Bethsaida, or Bethzatha (5:2). The Evangelist describes this
as 'a pool near the sheep (gate)' (ἐπὶ τῇ προβατικῇ κολυμβήθρα). The 'sheep
gate' (A.V. 'sheep market') is mentioned more than once by Nehemiah (3:1,
32; 12:39, καὶ ἕως πύλης τῆς προβατικῆς), but it is difficult to fix its exact
position. It was this uncertainty of locality, doubtless which led to the
omission of the words ἐπὶ τῇ προβατικῇ in the Curetonian and Peshitta
Syriac, and to the reading of the Codex Sinaiticus ἐν τοῖς Ἱεροσολύμοις τῇ
προβατικῇ κολυμβήθρα, which understands the two descriptions as
defining one and the same spot. However it is clear that others also, besides
the scribe of ℵ, explained προβατικῇ as an adjective describing κολυμβήθρα.
Thus Eusebius in his *Onomasticon* makes the following statement:
'Bethzatha, the gate in Jerusalem, which is the sheep (one)' and goes on to
derive the name from the animal sacrifices which used to take place there.[57]
And this interpretation may have produced the reading which we find in ℵ.
It is possible however, that Eusebius may have got hold of the rabbinical
word (Buxtorf, p. 1796), which seems to mean 'a bath,' unless indeed this
word has come from προβατικῇ, the bath as well as the gate bearing the

---

[56]In the hall called Gazzith (John Lightfoot, I. p. 2005).

[57]Jerome, *Hier. de situ et nom.* (Op. iii. p. 182 ed. Vallarsi) knowing the locality better, says '*quae
vocabatur* προβατικῇ.' The curious red colour of the waters to which Eusebius draws attention
is mentioned by the Bordeaux Pilgrims in their description: '*Interius vero civitatis sunt piscinae
geraellares, quinque portions habentes, quae appellantur Betsaida. Ibi aegri multorum annorum
sanabautur: aquam autem habent eae piscinae in modum coccini turbatam*' (quoted by Wesseling,
Itineraria [1735], p. 589).

name. But it does not follow that Eusebius and the Bordeaux Pilgrims were right in their locality. Where then must we place the pool? The question would be answered if we could fix the position of the 'sheep gate.' This however is only roughly possible. From the notices in Nehemiah we draw the conclusion that the gate was situated somewhere near the Temple, on the east side of the city. The traditional site identifies it with St. Stephen's gate, north of the Temple area, but there is no sufficient ground for this; and Robinson's conjecture (i. p. 342) that Bethesda is the intermittent spring in the Upper Pool known as the 'Fountain of the Virgin'[58] at all events accords with the uninterpolated account of St. John,[59] which implies nothing miraculous in the water itself, but describes what was evidently an intermittent and medicinal, perhaps (from the allusions quoted above to the redness of the water) a chalybeate spring. However we need not pursue the enquiry further. Enough has been said to show that from early times much uncertainty was felt as to the actual site. What forger then would have ventured to introduce, or if he introduced, to localise, so obscure and contested a spot? Who but one thoroughly familiar with the scene would have been content to describe the position by so elliptical and ambiguous a phrase as ἐπὶ τῇ προβατικῇ employing an adjective without a qualifying noun, a phrase which, as we have seen, has been interpreted to mean 'sheep market,' 'sheep gate,' 'sheep pool'? The naturalness of this vague allusion is the best guarantee for the authenticity of the narrative.

(2) *Siloam* (9:7). Attention has been drawn already to the derivation of this word, and the symbolical use which St. John makes of this derivation. The topographical question however requires a separate treatment. Fortunately the situation, unlike that of Bethesda, can hardly be considered doubtful. Siloam is frequently mentioned and described by Josephus, and the tradition of its position is tolerably continuous. It bears the same name now, Silwan, as in our Lord's time. It lies at the mouth of the Tyropoeon valley, close to its junction with the valley of Hinnom, and is fed by a stream issuing somewhere from the heart of the rocks of Jerusalem. Its proximity to Jerusalem is evidenced by the well-attested tradition that water was

---

[58]It was connected by an underground passage with the pool of Siloam.
[59]Textual criticism compels us to omit the words ἐκδεχομένων . . . νοσήματι (vv. 3, 4), which are found in the Textus Receptus.

brought from it for the libations customary at the Feast of Tabernacles, and
by the name which it gave to one of the gates of Jerusalem, 'the water gate.'
It was both a fountain and a pool. The fountain (πηγή) is mentioned by Josephus (*Bell. Jud.* v.12.2), the pool or tank by Nehemiah (iii.15, בְּרֵכַת) and St.
John (κολυμβήθρα).[60] The derivation of the name, which means an 'aqueduct'
or 'conduit' (from 'to send') seems to imply that the Siloah properly so-called
was not the pool, but the stream which feeds it or which flows from it. The
points on which the Evangelist incidentally displays his exact knowledge are
two: first, he apparently places the pool near the Temple, for it is improbable
that a blind man would be sent on a long journey; secondly, he is aware of,
and draws a lesson from, the Hebrew meaning of the name, in which he sees
a spiritual significance. Long ago these very waters had been invested by
Isaiah (8:6) with a symbolical interpretation. The contrast between the
'waters of Shiloah that go softly' and the 'waters of the River (i.e. the Eu-
phrates), strong and many' typified the contrast between Judah and Assyria,
between the quiet dwelling in Jerusalem under Yahweh and the overwhelming of a foreign conquest. This idea of an indigenous stream, the possession of the favored people, 'the river, the streams whereof shall make glad
the city of God' (Ps 46:4; cf. Isaiah 33:21), bespoke the Messianic hope. It
foretold the stream of running life-giving waters, which should issue from
the temple-rock, and revive the nations. It recalled and renewed the type of
the waters flowing from the rock smitten by Moses, which rock was understood by St. Paul to be the Christ (1 Cor 10:4). Thus St. John seizes upon the
current thought, and extends its application. The Healer who sends the blind
man is Himself 'the sent.'[61]

(3) *Cedron* (18:1). This is undoubtedly the Kidron of the Old Testament
(2 Sam 15:23 etc.), and is mentioned by St. John alone of the Evangelists. The
common text runs χειμάρρου τῶν Κέδρων ('the torrent of the Cedars'), and
the passage has a peculiar interest because it has furnished the text for an
elaborate attack upon the personality of the Evangelist. Baur and Hilgenfeld
after him (see Ewald, *Jahrbuch*, vi. p. 118) have pointed triumphantly to the

---

[60]Isaiah 8:6 has simply הַשִּׁלֹחַ מֵי, and the LXX simply has 'the waters of Siloam.'
[61]Epiphanius, *Haer.* xxxv.3 rightly connects the two passages. After quoting Isaiah 8:6 he adds
'for the waters of Siloam are the teachings of the Sent One.' So the ps.-Basil on Isaiah 8:6 (Basil,
Op. I, p. 536A).

undoubted fact that Κέδρων is the Hebrew word קֵדָר 'dark,' so called probably from its turbid stream (cf. Ps 130:5 'the tents of Kedar,' i.e. the dark skinned folk) and have proceeded to argue that the Evangelist in his ignorance has imagined it to be the genitive plural of κέδρος 'a cedar.' The writer therefore, they conclude, cannot have been the Apostle St. John, who, as a Jew, must have been aware of the true derivation of the name.

Before admitting this conclusion, let us look the facts fairly in the face. In Josephus the form Κέδρων occurs frequently (*Bell. Jud.* v.2.3; v.6.1; v.12.2; *Ant.* vii.1.5; viii.1.5; ix.7.3) used as a declinable noun. This is quite after Josephus' manner in dealing with Hebrew substantives. In the LXX the expression ὁ χειμάρρους Κέδρων is employed without an article, e.g. 2 Sam 15:23 (its second occurrence in this verse); 2 Kings 23:6, 12; 2 Chron 15:16; 29:16; 30:14; Jer 31:40. But in two passages it is found with the plural article—2 Sam 15:23 (on the first occurrence) and 1 Kings 15:13, ἐν τῷ χειμάρρῳ Κέδρων. This is the reading of A.B. in both passages. Now it is quite clear that the LXX translators did not mistake the meaning of the word. Otherwise they could not have written ὁ χειμάρρους Κέδρων, as they generally do, a solecism on this supposition; but we should have had ὁ χειμάρρους τῶν Κέδρων in every case. Therefore either there is a corruption in the best manuscripts of the LXX, or ὁ χειμάρρους τῶν Κέδρων was considered a legitimate Greek rendering of the Hebrew phrase 'the brook Kidron.' Turning now to the passage in St. John, we find that there is great uncertainty as to the actual reading, authorities varying between τῶν Κέδρων, τοῦ Κέδρου and τοῦ Κέδρων, and that the preponderance of evidence is either for τῶν Κέδρων or τοῦ Κέδρου.[62] But the necessity for making a selection suggests another view. What then is the probability? I believe the true account to be that the original reading was τοῦ Κέδρων and this for two reasons. First, it is the intermediate reading, the reading which explains the other two, whereas neither of the other two will explain either this or each other.[63] Secondly, it is much more probable that τοῦ Κέδρων would be changed into τῶν Κέδρων and τοῦ Κέδρου, than conversely. Indeed the converse change in either case is hardly conceivable,

---

[62]B, C, L with the bulk of the Greek manuscripts and the Gothic Version, have τῶν Κέδρων; A, Δ, S, the Vulgate, and certain manuscripts (c, (e) f, g) of the Old Latin, the Peshitto and the Philoxenian Syriac, and the Armenian have τοῦ Κέδρων.

[63]A good instance of the application of this test is the celebrated passage 1 Tim 3:16, where Ὅς is to be preferred as accounting for both the variants Θεός and ὁ.

the tendency being to assimilate terminations. And unless τῶν Κέδρων be a legitimate rendering of 'the brook Kidron,' the corruption has taken place, and has still more completely obliterated the original reading, in the LXX. This solution was adopted by Griesbach and Lachmann, and recommends itself to Renan, Meyer and Sanday. Tregelles gives it as an alternative. On the other hand Tischendorf reads τοῦ Κέδρου.

But suppose τῶν Κέδρων is after all, as Westcott considers, the right reading, what then? The Septuagint shows that it was held to be an adequate rendering of the Hebrew נַחַל : קִדְרוֹן. We must suppose therefore that it was the equivalent familiar to Greek ears, and that St. John writing to Greeks would not hesitate to employ it. In confirmation of this view we may notice the general tendency to assimilate Hebrew terminations to Greek forms, which has coined the Greek plural σάββατα out of the Hebrew noun שַׁבָּתוֹן as though σάββατον. As Κέδρων was only used with χειμάρρους, the change to the genitive would be natural.[64] Again, the temptation to extract a Greek sense out of Hebrew names is exemplified in the derivations given to Jerusalem and Essene.[65] If by an accident there were any cedars in the valley, the adoption of this Grecized form would be facilitated.

(c) *Scenes illustrating our Lord's Passion.*

Bethany is mentioned by the Synoptists in connexion with the triumphal entry into Jerusalem (Mark 11:1; Luke 19:29), with our Lord's retirement during Holy Week (Matt 21:17; Mark 11:11, 12), especially the feast at the house of Simon the leper (Matt 26:6; Mark 14:3; cf. John 12:1), and with the Ascension (Luke 24:50). It occurs in St. John's narrative likewise as the scene of the raising of Lazarus (John 11:1, 18), and he exhibits his acquaintance with the place in a characteristic way by mentioning that it was distant fifteen furlongs from Jerusalem (11:18, δὲ Βηθανία ἐγγὺς τῶν Ἱεροσολύμων ὡς ἀπὸ σταδίων δεκαπέντε.).[66] This statement exactly accords with the account

---

[64]In Ps 82:10, א, A, B read ἐν τῷ χειμάρρῳ Κεισών (A has Κισσών anarthrous), but some inferior manuscripts have τῶν Κισσών.

[65]See Josephus, *Bell. Jud.* vi.10.1; Philo, *quod omn. prob.* 12.11, p. 467; cf. §13, p. 459; and *Fragm.* 11, p. 632 (ed. Mangey). The same tendency is to be seen in English in the forms Charterhouse, Barmouth, etc.

[66]No inference can be drawn as to the date of the composition of the Gospel from the use of the imperfect tense. The Evangelist sometimes uses the imperfect (18:1; 19:41, 42), sometimes the present (5:2), occasionally both tenses together (4:6, 9). Similarly St. Luke uses the imperfect (Luke 4:29), and we may compare Kinglake's *Crimea*, iii. pp. 38, 117, 118, 122, 286, which is

which a modern writer gives of its situation. 'We reached it in three-quarters of an hour from the Damascus gate. This gives a distance of a little less than two Roman miles from the eastern part of the city' (Robinson I. p. 431).

Gethsemane is not named in the Fourth Gospel, but this does not prevent St John from adding to our stock of knowledge regarding the scene of the Agony, which he describes more precisely than the Synoptists, calling it 'a garden,' κῆπος (18:1) instead of simply 'an enclosure' (χωρίον, Matt 26:36; Mark 14:32), and defining its position as 'over the brook Cedron.' Can we wonder if the events of that evening were burnt into the memory of the beloved disciple in letters of fire? Again, he alone of the Evangelists informs us that the Crucifixion took place outside the city-walls (19:20). This statement is thrown out quite naturally, and no point is made of it, but it is borne out by the author of the Epistle to the Hebrews (13:11sq.), who sees in it a deep moral lesson. And no one denies that this Epistle was written at some time or other in the first century after Christ.

(iv) *The Topography of Palestine generally.*

As far therefore as knowledge of the locality of the Holy City is concerned, our author has ably stood the test applied to him. Let us now take a wider sweep and investigate his acquaintance with the geography of Palestine at large.

(a) *Galilee.* As is well known, the Fourth Evangelist directs his attention chiefly to our Lord's ministry in Jerusalem. We do not therefore expect him to give us many fresh details about the topography of Galilee. However he mentions Cana in Galilee (2:1, 11; 4:46; 21:2),[67] and he gives a new designation to the Lake of Gennesareth, which he calls 'the sea of Tiberias' (6:1; 21:1).[68] Again, in describing the events which clustered round the Feeding of the Five Thousand, his varying use of πέραν 'on the other side,' now for

---

unquestionably the narrative of one who was an eyewitness of the events he relates, and who writes not half a century later, but within a very few years of the occurrences.

[67]Cana is named several times by Josephus (*Vit.* 16; *Bell. Jud.* i.17.5, *Ant.* xiii.15.1), but the references do not throw much light on its position. The traditional site is *Kefr Kenna*, about four miles northeast of Nazareth, and this identification is as old as S. Willibald in the eighth century. Robinson however prefers a village, *Kana el-Jelil*, some five miles further north, and the spelling of the name (with a *Koph* instead of a *Caph*) is more closely allied to the representative in the Curetonian and Peshitto *Katna*, though the *t* is not represented.

[68]The city of Tiberias also occurs (6:23). As it was built by Herod Antipas (Jos. *Ant.* xviii.2.3; *Bell. Jud.* ii.9.1), it could hardly have given its name to the lake as early as the date of our Lord's ministry. The designation however 'sea of Tiberias' is found in Josephus (*Bell. Jud.* iii.3.6), before St John wrote his Gospel.

the west, now again for the east shore of the lake, bespeaks the eyewitness, who, as he records the miracle, fancies himself enacting the scene once more, and speaks as if he were himself first here, then there.

(6) *Judaea.*

(1) *Ephraim.* In 11:54 St. John describes our Lord's retirement 'into the country near the desert, into a city called Ephraim' (εἰς τὴν χώραν ἐγγὺς τῆς ἐρήμου, εἰς Ἐφραὶμ). This 'desert of Judah' seems to mean the broad mountain pasture lands near Jerusalem, which were sparsely inhabited, for in the Gospel narrative 'the desert' (ἡ ἔρημος) is generally associated with 'the mountain district' (τὸ ὄρος). This city Ephraim (or Ephrem) is noticed here only in the New Testament. But it is mentioned by Josephus (*Bell. Jud.* iv.9.9) in connection with the mountain district north of Judaea, as a small fort (πόλιχνιον) captured and garrisoned by Vespasian when on his way westward to fight against Vitellius. Josephus couples it with Bethel, and it is a coincidence that, where it occurs in 2 Chron 13:19, Bethel is named with it. The two places were probably not far apart. Mr. Robinson (i. p. 447) identifies it with *El-Tayibeh*, some eight miles north of Jerusalem. In the passage in the Chronicles referred to, the Kthib has Ephron עֶפְרַיִן, but the Qri Ephraim עֶפְרוֹן; perhaps a dual form like Mizraim, the Upper and Lower Egypt. It is mentioned also in the Talmud (Neubauer, p. 155). The Ephraim of St. John must not be confused with the wood of Ephraim of 2 Sam 18:6, or the Ephraim of 2 Sam 13:23, both of which are spelt with an Aleph like the patriarch Ephraim; or with the district called Apherema in 1 Macc. xi.34. Mr Robinson (l.c.) identifies it with Ophrah עָפְרָה of Benjamin (1 Sam 13:17; Josh 18:23). This may or may not be the case.[69] The Qri of 2 Chron. l.c. and the passage in Josephus are sufficient for my purpose. Whether the Qri be the right reading or not, it shows that such a place existed just in the region where, from St. John's account, we should expect it to be.

(2) *Bethany* (1:28). This is certainly the correct reading in this passage, and accordingly St. John has been charged[70] with gross ignorance as not being aware that Bethany was near Jerusalem. In the light of the accurate and

---

[69]It is noticeable that in the Codex Alexandrinus Ἐφραίμ is the LXX rendering of the other Ophrah the birth-place of Gideon, in Judges 8:27; 9:5. Eusebius, *Onom.* s.v. says 'now the village is called greater Ephraim'; cf. Jerome, *Opus* III. p. 203, who repeats the same statement. But if Mr Robinson's identification is correct, the Ephraim of St. John is the *Aphra* of Eusebius' *Onom.* s.v.
[70]By Paulus and Bolten; see Lücke, I, p. 394.

minute acquaintance with topography elsewhere displayed by the Apostle, such an accusation is hardly worth the trouble of refutation.

We may however briefly reply, first, that the writer carefully distinguished the two places, speaking of one as 'Bethany beyond Jordan' (1:28), of the other as 'Bethany the town of Mary and her sister Martha' (11:1); secondly, that he accurately described the Bethany of chapter 11 as 'nigh unto Jerusalem about fifteen furlongs off'; thirdly, that if we assume with most commentators the identification of Bethany beyond Jordan with 'the place where John was at first baptizing' (10:40), our Lord is represented at the time as out of Judaea (11:7, εἰς τὴν Ἰουδαίαν πάλιν), as journeying from the one Bethany to the other, a journey which occupies three days (11:39, τεταρταῖος γάρ ἐστιν), which takes Him into Judaea once more (11:7, Ἄγωμεν εἰς τὴν Ἰουδαίαν πάλιν), and into danger from a position of security (11:8). Personally I prefer to keep these scenes of St. John's baptism distinct, and to place the Bethany of chapter 1 somewhere in the Upper Jordan.[71] It was probably an obscure place. 'In any case,' as Mr. Sanday truly says (p. 45), 'the distinction between two places having the same name is a mark of local knowledge which is unlike fiction.'[72]

(3) *Aenon near to Salim* (3:23). Here again we are introduced by the Evangelist to fresh names. It is true that in Joshua 15:32 mention is made in the tribe of Judah of שִׁלְחִים וְעַיִן (Cod. A Σελεείμ, A.V. 'Shilhim and Ain'); but neither name corresponds exactly to the notice in St. John. Moreover the places mentioned in the Old Testament lie in the arid country south of Judaea (see Grove in Smith's *Dictionary of the Bible*, s.v. Salim). The most probable site of the Salim of the Fourth Gospel is that assigned to it by Eusebius and Jerome near the Jordan, eight Roman miles south of Scythopolis. In Jerome's time it was called Salimias. A Salim has been discovered by Van de Velde (*Memoir*, p. 345sq.) exactly in this position, six English miles south of Beisan (Bethshan), and two miles west of Jordan. The name Aenon fully bears out St. John's description of the place, 'there was much water (ὕδατα πολλά) there,' the plural noun indicating 'many fountains' or 'springs.' Evidently therefore Aenon was not situated on the Jordan itself.

---

[71]This is the view of Dr. Caspari, quoted by Sanday, p. 45.
[72]In Mark 8:22 there is a well-supported variant Βηθανιάν for Βηθσαϊδάν, which may contain some underlying foundation of fact pointing to a Bethany in the northeast of Galilee.

These last two notices are especially interesting as showing how carefully the successive stages of John the Baptist's preaching are brought out in the Fourth Gospel. We find him first at the lower fords of Jericho 'beyond Jordan,' ὅπου ἦν Ἰωάνης τὸ πρῶτον βαπτίζων (10:40; cf. Matt 3:1). We meet with him next at Bethany (1:28, A.V. 'Bethabara') 'beyond Jordan,' probably at the upper fords. Lastly, his headquarters are at Aenon, near Salim (3:23). Thus we seem able to trace his course northward, and the successive changes of scene bear out what we gather from the more general account with which St. Luke supplies us. Though John's native town is in the hill country of Judaea (Luke 1:39), yet he is apprehended and put to death by Herod, the tetrarch of Galilee (Luke 3:19, 20), and therefore must, before his arrest, have passed within Herod's jurisdiction. The minuteness of detail which in the Fourth Gospel characterizes the episodes in which John the Baptist takes part, becomes doubly significant when we consider the great probability that John the Apostle had been in his early days a disciple of the Baptist.

II. *The Writer was an Eye-witness of the Events Recorded.*

In a striking passage in one of his works Auguste Sabatier draws attention to two characteristics of this Gospel which run side by side—that though in its teaching it is the most dogmatic, yet at the same time in its narrative it is the most vivid of the Four Gospels.[73] We are apt to forget this latter point in the absorbing eagerness with which we fix our attention upon the sublimity of the doctrines inculcated. Yet this vividness of description is the best guarantee for the conclusion that the writer was not merely a Palestinian Jew, but an actual eye-witness of the events which he records. We shall be compelled to treat this part of our subject in a very cursory and incomplete manner.

(i) *The minuteness and exactness of detail which he exhibits.* Sometimes these minute notices stand more or less closely in connection with the progress of the story; sometimes they are detached personal reminiscences which apparently struck the writer at the time, and have dwelt in his memory since. Such a reminiscence, introduced apropos of nothing, is the incident recorded by St. Mark (14:51sq.) of the young man clad with the linen cloth, which has been generally interpreted as an allusion to the history of the

---

[73]A. Sabatier, *Essai sur les sources de la vie de Jesus* (1866), p. 34.

Evangelist himself. I shall divide what I have to say on this subject under the following heads: (1) Time, (2) Place, (3) Persons, (4) Incidents.

(1) *Time.* The chronology of our Lord's life can be gathered from St. John's Gospel alone. In the other Evangelists the incidents are often grouped together with little or no reference to their chronology. This is especially the case with St. Luke, who, having neither been present himself at the events, nor, like St. Mark, especially attached to one who was himself present, is of the four the farthest removed from the position of an eye-witness. The minute exactness of St. John's chronology shows itself most particularly in his record of the first (1:29, 35, 43; 2:1) and of the last week (12:1, 12 etc.) of the narrative, but it is present throughout (4:40, 43; 6:22; 7:14, 37; 10:22; 11:6, 17). It arises in great measure from the part which he himself has in the drama. It extends even to the hour of the day (1:39; 4:6, 52; 19:14), or, if not the hour, the time approximately (3:2; 6:16; 13:30; 18:28; 20:19; 21:3, 4).

(2) *Place.* We have had occasion already to allude to the increased definiteness to be observed in the Fourth Gospel in this respect. All the incidents are referred to their locality. Compare this feature with the other Gospels, e.g. St Luke's account of Martha and Mary, Luke 10:38, εἰς κώμην τινά, with John 11:1, ἀπὸ Βηθανίας, ἐκ τῆς κώμης Μαρίας καὶ Μάρθας τῆς ἀδελφῆς αὐτῆς. It runs through the whole narrative, e.g. 6:59, ἐν συναγωγῇ διδάσκων ἐν Καφαρναούμιν; 10:23 ἐν τῷ ἱερῷ ἐν τῇ στοᾷ τοῦ Σολομῶνος. Notice the precision with which on two occasions the distance of the boat from the shore is recorded, measured by the practised eye of the fisherman, 6:19, ὡς σταδίους εἴκοσι πέντε ἢ τριάκοντα θεωροῦσιν; 21:8, ὡς ἀπὸ πηχῶν διακοσίων, and for his greater chronological accuracy contrast the Fourth Evangelist with St. Luke in the scenes of St Peter's denial (18:15sq.), remembering that the narrator is 'the other disciple who was known unto the highpriest,' himself a spectator throughout the terrible tragedy.

In all these details we recognise the hand of the personal disciple, and it would be strange indeed if an author with such opportunities did not produce more exact and precise results than one who, like St. Luke, was the disciple of one who was not even himself a personal disciple.

(3) *Persons.* Sayings, instead of being left vaguely general, are attributed to the speakers by name, e.g. 1:41, 45, 46 (bis), 48, 49 of Andrew, Philip and Nathanael; 6:7, 8 Andrew and Philip; 6:68 Peter; 11:16 Thomas; 12:4 Judas

Iscariot; 12:21 Andrew and Philip again; 13:8, 9 Peter; 13:24, 25 Peter and
John; 13:36, 37 Peter again; 14:8 Philip; 14:22 Judas not Iscariot; 20:25sq.
Thomas; 21:3 Peter; 21:7 Peter and John; 21:15sq., 21:20sq. Peter. This exactness is more noticeable when we have an opportunity of comparing the
incidents with the Synoptic records, as in the miracle of the feeding of the
five thousand, where the objection on the part of the disciples is left general
(Mark 6:37, λέγουσι) instead of being placed in the mouth of Philip (John
6:7), or the feast at Bethany, where the loving ministrations of Mary (John
12:3) are vaguely assigned to 'a woman' (Matt 26:7; Mark 14:3, γυνή), and
where the expressed discontent of Judas (John 12:4) is robbed of half its
force by being generalized (Matt 26:8, οἱ μαθηταί; Mark 14:4, τινες). Or
again take the scene of the betrayal, where a flood of light is thrown upon
that part of the drama when we learn from St. John that it was St. Peter
(John 18:10) who with characteristic impulsiveness drew his sword in his
Master's defence.[74]

(4) *Incidents.* The Fourth Evangelist acquaints us with a number of details, which, though in some cases unimportant in themselves, add greatly
to the life-like character of his portraiture of events. The six waterpots of
water containing two or three firkins apiece (2:6), the thirty and eight years
during which the man lying at the pool of Bethesda had been afflicted (5:5),
the bag in which our Lord and His disciples kept their common fund (12:6),
the sop given to Judas (13:26), the three languages of the title on the cross
(19:20),[75] the four parts into which the tunic (τὸν χιτῶνα) and the cloak (τὰ
ἱμάτια) were divided (19:23), the water and the blood which issued from the
Savior's side (19:34), the weight of the myrrh and aloes used for the em-
balming (19:39), the orderly folding of the napkin which had been about
His head (20:7), and, in the last chapter, the side of the ship on which the
net was to be thrown (21:6) and the number of the fish which were drawn
up (21:11)—all these are instances of the miniature painting which is noticeable in this Gospel. What is the inference from all this? Minuteness is
not in itself an evidence of authenticity. But taken in conjunction with the

---

[74]The Synoptists are perhaps designedly vague (Matt 26:51, εἷς τῶν μετὰ Ἰησοῦ; Mark 14:47, τις
τῶν παρεστηκότων; Luke 22:50, εἷς τις ἐξ αὐτῶν). The name of the servant Malchus is also given
by St. John.
[75]The corresponding notice in St. Luke 23:38 is an interpolation.

other arguments which have been adduced, this fact is important, pointing as it does to an author who, as he wrote, had all the scenes clearly and vividly before his eyes.

(ii) *The naturalness of the record.* This is exhibited in two ways: (1) by the development of the characters depicted, and (2) by the progress of the incidents related.

(1) The characters. Some of these appear also in the Synoptic Gospels; others are new. Of the former class are Martha and Mary, Mary Magdalene, Peter, Judas, Pontius Pilate, Caiaphas; of the latter, Andrew, Philip, Thomas, Nathanael, the woman of Samaria, Nicodemus.[76] In the first group of instances we have an opportunity of testing the Fourth Gospel by other independent accounts. The Evangelist therefore must be found true to his fellow-Evangelists. In the second group we have no such external criterion to guide us; but the Evangelist must be found true to himself. We will select an example or two from each of the two classes.

(a) *St. Peter.* His character is sketched for us in clear outlines in the Synoptic narrative. We cannot fail to notice his eager, forward, impetuous nature. He is the self-constituted spokesman of the disciples. His eagerness to learn, his curiosity, his love of definiteness shows itself in the type of question which from time to time he puts before his Master. He will know the precise point at which forgiveness ceases to be a duty ('Lord, how oft shall my brother sin against me and I forgive him?' Matt 18:21); the exact reward which those who follow Jesus should obtain ('Behold, we have forsaken all, and followed thee; what shall we have therefore?' Matt 19:27). He will have one mysterious parable explained ('Declare unto us this parable.' Matt. 15:15), and he will know the exact range of the application of another ('Lord, speakest thou this parable unto us, or even to all?' Luke 12:41). Notice his eagerness to remark upon what is going on around him, whether it be the evidence of Christ's power ('Master, behold, the fig tree which thou cursedst is withered away.' Mark 11:21), or the current of popular opinion ('All men seek for thee.' Mark 1:37). His impetuosity leads him on two occasions to administer rebuke to the Lord Jesus Christ

---

[76]Hort adds the note: 'The characters of Martha and Mary are given in the first Essay (p. 37sq.); they are Mary and of Thomas are given above therefore omitted here.' They can be found in the preceding Appendix.

Himself, either alone ('Then Peter took Him, and began to rebuke Him, saying. Be it far from thee, Lord. This shall not be unto thee.' Matt 16:22), or with others ('Peter and they that were with Him said, "Master, the multitude throng thee and press thee, and sayest thou, Who touched me?"' Luke 8:45). His eagerness of faith and assurance is discernible throughout the whole course of the Gospel narrative. It prompts his confession at Caesarea Philippi ('Thou art the Christ, the Son of the living God.' Matt 16:16), his proposal on the Mount of Transfiguration ('Lord, it is good for us to be here. If thou wilt, let us make three tabernacles.' Matt 17:4), his confidence on the Sea of Galilee ('Lord, if it be thou, bid me come unto thee on the water.' Matt 14:28), his protestation on the night of the betrayal ('Though all men shall be offended because of thee, yet will I never be offended.' Matt 26:33). After the arrest, with a characteristic mixture of courage and of curiosity, he follows Jesus into the high priest's palace 'to see the end' (Matt 26:58). On the other side, we notice sudden revulsions of feeling, resulting, now in lack of faith ('Lord, save me.' Matt 14:30), now in lack of courage (the three denials, Matt. 26:69sq.), now again in unexpected self-abasement ('Depart from me, for I am a sinful man, O Lord.' Luke 5:8). Accordingly we find our Lord in the Garden rebuking Peter specially and by name (Matt 26:40; Mark 14:37), as though implying that his actions had in the most signal way belied his professions.

Such is St. Peter's character as delineated in the Synoptic Gospels. Before proceeding to test the record of the Fourth Gospel, we must turn aside to notice a charge brought against St. John by M. Renan (*Vie de Jesus*, p. xxviii. and p. 159) and reiterated by other critics (e.g. Lampe III p. 510). It is to the effect that St. John was jealous of St. Peter's reputation and endeavored to undermine it in his Gospel. The charge is false in every way. Compare St. John's account of the third denial (18:27) with that of St. Matthew (26:74) or of St. Mark (14:71), the one Synoptist writing for the Jewish Christians among whom St. Peter was especially honored, the other 'the interpreter' of St. Peter. Or again, remember that the rebuke 'Get thee behind me, Satan,' is confined to St. Matthew (16:23) and St. Mark (8:33), and is not recorded by St. John. These facts will show how gratuitous this offensive insinuation is. On the other hand, another antagonistic critic (Kostlin in *Theol. Jahrb. for 1850*, 2, p. 293) has supposed that the object of the twenty-first chapter is to glorify St. Peter and St. Peter's see. Thus one criticism serves to neutralise the others.[77]

We return to St Peter's character, as portrayed by St. John. It is in thorough accord with what we have already gathered from the other Evangelists. His curiosity comes out in the eager question with which he interrupts his Master's discourse in the upper room 'Lord, whither goest thou?' (13:36), in the expedient by which he endeavors to obtain through the medium of the beloved disciple the traitor's name (13:24sq.), in the anxiety which he shows to learn his brother apostle's destiny ('Lord, what shall this man do?' 21:21). He will not rest content with dark forebodings and mysterious intimations; he will know the facts, and know them definitely. Again, his ready profession of faith, which makes him now the mouthpiece of the apostolic band ('Lord, to whom shall we go? Thou hast the words of eternal life.' 6:68), now the revealer of his own deepest heart-utterances ('Lord, thou knowest all things; thou knowest that I love thee.' 21:17), is in perfect keeping with what the Synoptic narrative has led us to expect. His impetuosity shines out in every action which is recorded of him. In Gethsemane, without a thought for the consequences, he draws his sword and smites the high-priest's servant (18:10sq.); at the tomb, while the younger disciple stands awestruck and uncertain, he enters in without a moment's hesitation (20:6); at the sea of Galilee, he plunges into the lake (21:7), he drags the net to land (21:11). And the sudden revulsion of sentiment, of which such striking examples are recorded in the first three Gospels, has its complete parallel in an incident peculiar to the Fourth Evangelist—the washing of the disciples' feet ('Thou shalt never wash my feet.' 'Lord, not my feet only, but also my hands and my head.' 13:8, 9).

(6) *Pontius Pilate.* In the portraiture of the Roman procurator there is much in common between the Synoptists and St. John. Thus in all we see the abstract love of justice, inherent in a Roman magistrate, overborne by the desire of securing popularity, natural to a provincial governor. But his personal characteristics appear especially in the Fourth Gospel, and it is not

---

[77]M. Renan accepts the latter criticism, but supposes this last chapter to be a later addition by some other hand, in which amends are made to St. Peter. But the internal evidence of style proves chap. 21 (though probably a postscript) to have been written by the author of chaps. 1–20 (see the additional note at the end of this essay).

too much to say that we should not have apprehended his character as a whole without the light thrown upon it from this fresh source of evidence. Here at last we get to understand the man thoroughly in all the variety of his complex nature—his desire to purchase public favor at the expense of justice and yet his unwillingness to condemn Jesus, his cynical contempt of the subject-people, his sarcasm, his scepticism and yet his fear. It is only when, fresh from studying him in the Fourth Gospel, we turn once more to the pages of the Synoptists, that his scorn for the Jews as a nation is clearly discerned. However, when once we have found the clue, that scorn is evident enough. It appears in the form of his questions 'Art thou the King of the Jews?' (Matt 27:11); 'What will ye that I should do unto him whom ye call the King of the Jews?' (Mark 15:12); and especially in the title placed over the cross.[78] Apparently he could not lose the opportunity of insulting the Jewish rulers, whom he was obliged to gratify nevertheless. But when we read St. John's account, we see these lurid features of Pilate's character emphasized and lighted up under the glow which issues from the narrator's master-pen. With what persistency does Pilate evince his desire to shirk the responsibility of condemnation! 'Take ye him, and judge him according to your law' (18:31). Baffled here by the logic of facts, the inability of the Jews to condemn to death, he tries another loophole to escape from his dilemma. 'Ye have a custom, that I should release unto you one at the Passover; will ye therefore that I release unto you the King of the Jews?' (18:39). Foiled again by the malignant hostility of the crowd, he seeks to appeal to their pity by exhibiting his prisoner scourged and mocked. In vain. He is met by the cry, 'Crucify him.' Once more he would shift the responsibility on the shoulders of the chief-priests, 'Take ye him and crucify him, for I find no fault in him.' From the furious, raging mob he turns to meet the calm, impassive countenance of Jesus Christ. The sight only increases his perplexity. 'From henceforth Pilate sought to release him.' The struggle is ended by the twice-repeated name of Caesar (19:12), and the dread image thus called up before his mind of the suspicious, vindictive Emperor prevails at last over his sense of justice and of awe. He tries one last appeal, 'Behold, your King,' and then

---

[78]The scorn is lost in the form in which the question appears in St. Matthew (27:22). Though here again the climax of contempt is found in St. John's version, 'Jesus of Nazareth, the King of the Jews.' See above.

delivers Him unto them to be crucified. And if the wavering, vacillating temper of the governor is drawn in clearer outline by St. John than by the Synoptists, no less is his cynicism, his sarcasm and unbelief painted in deeper colors. 'Am I a Jew?' (The English fails to convey the withering scorn of the Greek original—Μήτι ἐγὼ Ἰουδαῖός εἰμι;), 'Art thou a King then?' (Οὐκοῦν βασιλεὺς εἶ σύ; We can imagine the intonation of the voice upon the final word σύ, as Pilate amuses himself with what he considered the fanaticism of his prisoner), 'What is truth?' And so the conversation ends, Pilate no doubt thinking that he had had the best of it, had secured the last word. Notice too how he repeats the expression 'the King of the Jews,' harping on the title which he knows to be offensive to his Jewish audience (18:39; 19:14, 15, 19, 22). And the Roman soldiers catch up the spirit of the Roman governor, who sets the fashion, and cry, 'Hail, King of the Jews' (19:3).

(c) *Philip.* Of the characters known only from St. John's Gospel the first in importance undoubtedly is Thomas; but there are others, which the Evangelist, with a few masterly touches, depicts for us, and which deserve more than a passing notice. There is in Philip a certain cautious, business-like way of looking at things which bespeaks much circumspectness of disposition. We remark this at once when we are introduced to him in the first chapter (1:43sq.). Unlike Andrew and the nameless disciple, he does not make the first advances himself; but he is found and summoned by the Savior. Yet when found, he accepts the call without hesitation, and finds a new adherent in his turn. But the mode in which he announces his discovery to Nathanael is characteristic. He keeps back the name as long as possible, and the place to the last word in the sentence, for Nazareth would prejudice any cause. When Nathanael demurs, he does not argue; he simply bids him try, 'Come and see.' Philip appears again upon the scene in the sixth chapter on the occasion of the feeding of the five thousand. Again it is Jesus who opens the conversation: 'Whence shall we buy bread, that these may eat?' (v. 5). The business question is put to the business man. It is answered in a business spirit. He makes the necessary calculation. 'Two hundred pennyworth of bread is not sufficient for them that every one of them may take a little.' But he does not reply to the question. It is left for Andrew to suggest a remedy. We meet with him a third time in the twelfth chapter, when certain Greeks come to him with the request, 'Sir, we would see Jesus.' Here again he does

not take the initiative. He will not act without consultation. 'Philip cometh
and telleth Andrew, and again Andrew and Philip tell Jesus' (John 12:20-22).
It has been suggested that Philip was the steward, the purveyor of the little
company, that he managed the commissariat; just as Judas was the treasurer,
the purser. Such a position at all events would suit his business-like character.
And it would account for strangers (12:21) applying to him first, as they may
have been brought in contact with him in this capacity.[79]

(d) *Andrew.* In two places Andrew is associated with Philip, and on both
occasions he appears not merely in contact with, but in contrast to, his
brother-Apostle. He is as eager and prompt as the other is slow and cautious.
While Philip is calculating the amount of bread required to feed the multitude, Andrew has hit upon an expedient (6:8, 9). While Philip cannot act
alone in bringing the Greek strangers to Christ, Andrew, as soon as he is
consulted, goes with him to tell Jesus. Thus he is quick alike to act and to
speak. It is this decision of character which made him the first to join the
Savior himself, and the first to bring another to the Savior (1:37, 40, 41). In
short, he has much of his brother Peter's eagerness, without that brother's
tendency to grievous falls. It is quite in accordance with this characteristic
that we read in the Muratorian Canon that Andrew was the Apostle to
whom it was revealed that John should write his Gospel, and that the revelation took place on the first night of the three days' fast.[80]

(iii) *The progress of events.* We cannot rise from the perusal of the characters as they appear in the Fourth Gospel without the assurance that we
have been introduced to real, living persons, described by someone who
knew them well. Individuality is seen to be stamped on every face. Exactly
in the same way, as we mark the progress of events gradually unfolded before
us in the narrative, our conviction becomes more and more settled that the
guide who conducts us has been an eye-witness of the incidents which he
records. In order to get the full effect of the extreme naturalness of the de-

---

[79] An early tradition identified him with the disciple who requested that he might first go and
bury his father (Clement Alex. *Strom.* iii. 4. 25, p. 522). This would be in keeping with Philip's
hesitating faith.

[80] 'Cohortantibus condiscipulis et episcopis suis dixit [Iohannes] Conieiunate mihi hodie triduum, et
quid cuique fuerit revelatum alterutrum nobis enarremus. Eadem nocte revelatum Andreae ex apos-
tolis ut recognescentibus cunctis Iohannes suo no- mine cuncta describeret.' Canon Murator. p. 33
(ed. Tregelles).

scription, we have only to read the historical portions successively, and to remark how vivid is the sequence of the narrative as it opens out from point to point. Or we may take a conversation like that held in the fourth chapter between our Lord and the woman of Samaria. We notice, first of all, the development of the conviction in the woman's mind. Starting with a contemptuous irony (v. 9), she passes by gradual stages into a growing respect mingled with curiosity (v. 11), then into wonder ripening into faith (v. 15). The conversation now takes another turn. There is a direct home-thrust at the vicious part of her character (v. 16). This she disingenuously parries. Convinced by this time of her questioner's spiritual insight, she attempts to divert into a general theological channel the conversation which was taking so inconvenient a turn (v. 19). Our Lord's answer contains a tacit reproach (v. 24), but she still shows her unwillingness to appropriate the lesson (v. 25), and quietly ignores all particular allusions (v. 25). Observe secondly, that the spiritual teaching of our Lord, which is so prominent throughout, arises naturally out of the external incidents. The presence of the woman with the pitcher at the well (v. 7) leads to the subject of the living water; the arrival of the disciples with provisions (vss. 8, 27, 31) to the reference to the spiritual food. In these two cases the point of connection is distinctly stated; in others it is mentally supplied by the recollection of the eye-witness. Thus the mountain of Gerizim towering above them, and the expanse of corn-fields stretched out at their feet, are each in turn taken advantage of as opportunities for inculcating spiritual truths. And the whole is woven together with a naturalness which defies all separation of its component parts; for the teaching and the incident are the woof and the web of the fabric. Thirdly, the amount of local and special knowledge contained in the incident is both considerable and varied. As we glance through the chapter, we notice that it demands a particular acquaintance with the well of Jacob (v. 5), the relations of Jews and Samaritans (v. 9), the depth of the well (v. 11), its history (v. 12), the mountain and the worship on its summit (v. 20), the social position of women (v. 27), the corn-fields and the harvest-time (v. 35). And all this intimacy with places and customs is not an excrescence merely, but an integral and essential part of the narrative. You cannot remove it without the whole structure falling to the ground.

Or take the scene enacted in the Judgment Hall (18:28–19:16). Observe at the outset the unartificial, the unsystematic, character of the narrative. The incidents are not grouped according to subject, but related in sequence as they actually occurred. Hence the history of St. Peter's denials is interrupted by other matters. The third denial interposes between the mention of the transfer from Annas to Caiaphas, and the transfer from Caiaphas to Pilate. On the other hand St. Luke (22:54-62) adds force to the episode by placing all three denials together. With St. John however dramatic propriety is sacrificed to chronological accuracy. Notice, in the second place, the gaps in the narrative. Jesus is first examined before Annas, then He is transferred to Caiaphas; but nothing is recorded of what happened at this second examination. We may perhaps infer from the silence of the Evangelist that he was not an eye-witness of this part of the scene.

Again, we cannot fail to be struck by the introduction of certain incidents which have no direct bearing on the history, but yet are not on this account excluded. A moment's consideration will explain their presence in the narrative. The fire of coals kindled in the hall (18:18), the goings in and goings out of Pilate (18:29, 33, 38; 19:4, 9, 13), notes of place and of time (18:28; 19:14)—such would be just the kind of circumstances which would impress themselves indelibly upon the memory of an eye-witness, and would inevitably rise up again before him as, years after, he recalled the memorable scene. Or consider the respective attitudes of the chief-priests and of the Roman governor. How natural the representation. On the one side, the Jews, with their fear of ceremonial pollution (18:28), their appeals to the law (18:30; 19:7), their inability to punish (18:31), their affected loyalty (19:12, 15). On the other, Pilate, that masterpiece of portrait-painting to which attention has been drawn already. Surely, whether we examine the details, or regard the picture as a whole, we are constrained to admit that all this is something more than *ben trovato*, nay, we may say with confidence *e vero*. And so we might pass in review other incidents; the calling of the disciples, the marriage at Cana, the man at the pool of Bethesda, the scene at Bethany and at the tomb of Lazarus, the washing of the disciples' feet, the declaration of the betrayal—all these bear stamped upon their face the impress of trustworthy and contemporaneous testimony. I will conclude this part of my argument by an appeal presented from a somewhat different quarter.

The writer of the Fourth Gospel often distinguishes the facts which he records from his commentary upon those facts, made when an interval of time had thrown fresh light upon their spiritual import. Is it Christ's prophetic language, 'Destroy this temple, and in three days I will raise it up'? We are told that 'when He was risen from the dead. His disciples remembered that He had said this unto them; and they believed the scripture, and the word which Jesus had said' (2:22). Is it the mysterious utterance, 'He that believeth on me, as the Scripture hath said, out of his belly shall flow rivers of living water'? The Evangelist's comment, made subsequent to the Pentecostal gift, explains it of 'the Spirit which they that believe on Him should receive; for the Holy Spirit was not yet given, because that Jesus was not yet glorified' (7:39). Is it Christ's announcement of results to issue from His coming exaltation, 'I, if I be lifted up, shall draw all men unto me'? It is explained as 'signifying what death He should die' (12:33). The prophecy of Caiaphas (11:51), the triumphal entry into Jerusalem (12:16), Christ's appeal on behalf of His disciples in the moment of the betrayal (18:9)—all form texts for the conveyance of spiritual truths viewed from the stand-point of the Evangelist's maturer experience. Some have maintained that the commentary is wrong. I do not assert this, nor do I allow it. But one thing at least is clear. If the fact or the saying had been invented for the sake of the comment, the fact or saying would in most instances have taken a different form and the correspondence would have been made more obvious. But the fact does not lead up to the comment, for the simple reason that the fact was already there, in absolute possession; and as, in the light of a fuller and clearer knowledge, the Evangelist draws out its hidden meaning, he will not venture to subserve the purpose of the application by diverging one hair's-breadth from the exact letter of the records.[81]

ADDITIONAL NOTES.

A. On the twenty-first Chapter. The Gospel was originally intended to end with the twentieth chapter. The conclusion of the narrative is significant, 'Blessed are they that have not seen, and yet have believed' (μακάριοι οἱ μὴ ἰδόντες καὶ πιστεύσαντες, 20:29), and the writer's own addition (vv. 30, 31) is evidently the original close to the whole.

---

[81]As Hort points out at this juncture, there was originally a third part to this essay, which is now found in the earlier discussion about John being the author of this Gospel. On the whole Hort leaves the essays as he found them.

The twenty-first chapter therefore is an after-thought. This distinction is no refinement of modern theorists; it is as old as the time of Tertullian.[82] But did it emanate from the same author or not? Clearly yes. The style is essentially Johannine. There is the same historic οὖν, so characteristic of St. John's narrative, and of his alone (vv. 5, 6, 7 (bis), 9, 11, 15, 21, 23); the same comparative absence in the narrative part of δέ (which is wrongly inserted by the scribes in v. 12); the same tendency to place the verb first (vv. 1, 2, 3, 4, 5, 7, 10, 11, 12, 13, 23, 25), especially with λέγει (v. 15sq.); the same abruptness of diction, the result of the avoidance of connecting particles (vv. 3, 12, 13, 16, 17). Again such sentences as Ὑπάγω ἁλιεύειν. λέγουσιν αὐτῷ Ἐρχόμεθα καὶ ἡμεῖς σὺν σοί. (v. 3); Δεῦτε ἀριστήσατε. οὐδεὶς ἐτόλμα τῶν μαθητῶν ἐξετάσαι αὐτόν Σὺ τίς εἶ; (v. 12); Ἀκολούθει (v. 19); Κύριε, οὗτος δὲ τί; (v. 21); σύ μοι ἀκολούθει (v. 22) etc. are features which are familiar to us from previous chapters, and should be compared with e.g. the narrative of 1:35sq. or 20:11sq. We find the same fondness for ἐκεῖνος (vv. 3, 7, 23), the same love of definiteness, e.g. τὰ δεξιὰ μέρη (v. 6); ἀπὸ πηχῶν διακοσίων (v. 8); ἑκατὸν πεντήκοντα τριῶν (v. 11); τοῦτο ἤδη τρίτον (v. 14), to which we have already drawn attention; the same vivid painting (e.g. vv. 7, 9 etc.) the same use of a parenthetic explanation (vv. 7, 8, with which compare 6:23). Favorite Johannine expressions are found, as the doubled ἀμὴν (v. 18), which is peculiar to this Gospel, τοῦτο δὲ εἶπεν σημαίνων ποίῳ θανάτῳ etc. (v. 19; cf. 12:33; 18:32), καὶ τὸ ὀψάριον ὁμοίως (v. 13; cf. 6:11 ὁμοίως καὶ ἐκ τῶν ὀψαρίων, which last is a word only used by the Fourth Evangelist). We notice the characteristic mode of designating places, τῆς θαλάσσης τῆς Τιβεριάδος (v. 1; cf. 6:1), and of describing disciples, 'Thomas called Didymus' (v. 2; cf. 11:16), 'Nathanael from Cana of Galilee' (ib., his abode specified as in the case of Philip 12:21), 'Simon, son of John' (v. 15 sq.; cf. 1:42), 'the disciple whom Jesus loved' (v. 7, 20; cf. 13:23; 19:26; 20:2).[83] Again there is the suppression of the author's own name, which would most certainly have been mentioned by a

---

[82]'Ipsa quoque clausula evangelii propter quid consignat haec scripta, nisi ut credatis, inquit, Iesum Christum filium Dei?' Tertullian, adv. Prax. 25. He refers however in three places to the twenty-first chapter (see Ronsch p. 290).

[83]The Evangelist is fond of marking his characters by some striking circumstance which serves as a label. Examples are the designation of Nicodemus (19:39; 7:50 from 3:2), and of Caiaphas (18:14 from 11:49). From a different spirit and with a different aim Carlyle exhibits the same tendency.

continuator of the narrative. Lastly, the delineation of the character of St. Peter, and of his relation to St. John, has all the refinement of our Evangelist. This is the case in the two scenes in which they appear in contact. The spiritual insight of St. John (v. 7) is matched by the impetuosity (vv. 3, 7, 11) and the curiosity (v. 21) of St. Peter.[84]

Thus, though an after-thought, this chapter was certainly written by the author of the Gospel. How soon after, it is impossible to say; but there is nothing in the style which requires us to postulate more than a few weeks or a few days. As all the manuscripts without exception contain the chapter, and there is no trace of its ever having been wanting from any copies, the probable conclusion is that it was added before the Gospel was actually published. After the Gospel was written and submitted to his friends, the Apostle may have heard that some misapprehension was abroad respecting himself, or that some disappointment had been expressed because no mention had been made of an incident which they had heard him relate, and which would naturally be interesting to his admirers. He may have then consented to add it as a postscript. Apart from the identity of style, it is hardly likely that the chapter was written after the Apostle's death, for in that case an event which threw so much light upon our Lord's mysterious utterance respecting the beloved disciple would scarcely have been passed over in silence. The question of the integrity of the last two verses of the chapter is an issue which has to be treated separately. The twenty-fourth verse is a confirmation or attestation of the truth of the narrative on the part of his friends and disciples, and it bears out the traditional account, given in the Muratorian Canon, of the origin of the Fourth Gospel. The last verse is evidently a *scholium*. Tischendorf declares that in the Sinaitic manuscript (‫א‬) it is written in a different hand from the rest of the Gospel, by the διοθωτης of the whole, and it is perhaps omitted in a valuable cursive (63).[85] However,

---

[84]Against such indications of identity of authorship, the objections commonly alleged (e.g. by Lücke) are powerless, e.g. the use of new expressions, as ἐφανέρωσεν δὲ οὕτως (v. 1), ἐξετάσαι (v. 12). Any writing or portion of a writing might be set aside on the same grounds. Thus, to take 20:30, μὲν οὖν is a *hapax legomena* in St. John, so is βιβλίον so is ἐνώπιον. Indeed the first and third phrases are rather characteristic of St. Luke; but the endeavor to press such arguments would justly be scouted as fatal to all fair criticism. The chronological difficulty of τοῦτο ἤδη τρίτον (v. 14) remains unaffected by the question of authorship.

[85]Dr. Gwynn kindly supplies (Oct. 4, 1892) the following information respecting this manuscript: 'I think there is no room for doubt that Cod. 63 has lost a leaf (or more) at the end, and that it

as it occurs in all the other copies, and these come from very various sources, we may safely infer that, if an addition, it was written by St. John himself, or by one of his immediate disciples.

B. *On the Conversational Character of the Gospel.*

The Fourth Gospel was addressed to an immediate circle of hearers. In this respect it differs from the other three, St. Luke's Gospel approaching most nearly to it in this respect. But Theophilus, if a real person, and not a *nom de guerre*, the type of a God-loving or God-beloved Christian, soon disappears out of sight. On the other hand, the Fourth Evangelist keeps his disciples before his mind. He has to correct misapprehensions, to answer questions, to guide and instruct a definite class of persons, and those persons his immediate circle of acquaintance. Hence he assumes a knowledge of himself in the case of those for whom he writes. He does not give his own name, because his hearers already know his personal history. For the most part however the reference to these disciples is indirect. They are before the Evangelist, but he does not address them in the second person. Instances of allusions to misapprehensions or to questionings rife in those about him are i. 41 'He was the first to find' etc., ii. 11 'This was the beginning of his miracles,' iii. 24 'John was not yet cast into prison,' iv. 54 'This again was the second miracle which Jesus did,' xviii. 13 'He (Annas) was father-in-law to Caiaphas,

---

when complete contained John xxi. 25. At first sight, one might be led to form an opposite opinion. For the last page of the ms., as it now is, is the last of a complete quaternion, and in it the text ends οἴδαμεν ὅτι ἀληθὴς ἐστίν ἡ μαρ/τυρία αὐτοῦ (the last ten letters being arranged in the middle of a new line). The final stop looks like a colon, but may be a period; and one might suppose that the scribe's reason for placing τυρία αὐτοῦ thus, was because his text was at an end. But on looking through the ms. one would find this supposition to be unfounded. It frequently happens that he ends a page with an incomplete line, longer or shorter, not ranging with the previous lines, either at its beginning or its end. Comparing the place with the ends of the three preceding Gospels, one finds a small bit of negative evidence. Each of them has, after its last word, the marks : These do not appear after τυρία αὐτοῦ. None of them has any subscription, or even Τέλος subjoined. So much for the text; but when we look at the surrounding scholia all doubt is removed. The ms. has in every page a body of continuous scholia, some half-dozen lines in the top margin, a pretty long column (in continuation) all down the outer margin, and six or eight more lines at the foot. As the scholia proceed, the scribe denotes change of subject commented on, by a numeral letter (sometimes), and always by beginning the new matter with a capital letter, in red. The last two lines of these are pure scholia and here you will observe: (1) that the scholium breaks off in the middle of a sentence, showing that there ought to be another leaf; (2) that this broken scholium referred to verse 25, as is proved by the word ὑπερβολικός and an equivalent phrase to the ἄλλα πολλά of St. John in 21:25. These facts seem to settle the question.' Compare Scrivener, *Collatio Cod. Sinait.* p. lix; C. E. Gregory's prolegomena to Tischendorf, N. T. (ed. 8), p. 479.

who was high-priest of that year,' xix. 34 sq. 'There came out water and blood.' Great stress is laid upon this last point, doubtless in allusion to some symbolism which is not explained, because they would understand it. So xxi. 14 'This was now the third time that Jesus manifested Himself,' xxi. 23 'The saying therefore went abroad among the brethren that that disciple should not die. Yet Jesus said not unto him. He shall not die' etc. Thus we find the Evangelist clearing up matters which the current tradition had left doubtful, or on which the popular mind wished to be further informed. Through the main part of the narrative we see these parenthetical additions, these conversational comments. At length (19:35; 20:31) there is a direct appeal to these disciples, for whom the whole has been written. 'He knoweth that he saith true, that ye might believe.' 'These things are written that ye might believe that Jesus is the Christ, the Son of God; and that believing ye might have life through His name.'

The Gospel however does not stand alone. Its connection with the First Epistle is both intimate and important. Its authenticity and genuineness are still further confirmed by this consideration, which brings out in clearer colors the circumstances under which the Gospel was written, and sets more vividly before us the relation of the Evangelist to his band of hearers. The Muratorian Canon points to this connection. The close association of the two Johannine writings warrants the inference that the author of the Canon treated the First Epistle as an epilogue to the Gospel. And this in fact is its true character. The Epistle was intended to be circulated with the Gospel. This accounts for its abrupt commencement, which is to be explained as a reference to the Gospel which in one sense preceded it. This accounts likewise for the allusion to the water and the blood (1 John 5:6sq.) as the witnesses to the reality of Christ's human nature, the counterpart of the statement in the Gospel narrative (19:35).

The evidential value of all this cannot be over-estimated. It presents us with a combination of circumstances which a forger would not have had the ingenuity to invent; nor, if he had invented it, would he have commanded all the circumstances necessary to carry out to a successful issue so stupendous an under-taking. [1867, 1868]

Appendix C

Lightfoot and German Scholarship on John's Gospel

Martin Hengel was in many ways the perfect person to discuss J. B. Lightfoot at length. On the one hand, like Lightfoot he was a historian, linguist and New Testament scholar, but his output was even more prodigious than Lightfoot's. On the other hand he was a professor at Tübingen, a far more conservative professor than his predecessors, including F. C. Baur and the school he spawned, whom Lightfoot was constantly debating with and challenging. Hengel, as you will see, was in some ways far more in sympathy with Lightfoot's reading of John than with his predecessors at Tübingen. We are pleased to present below Martin Hengel's fine essay, which is no longer in print. (BW3)

Bishop Lightfoot and the Tübingen School on the Gospel of John and the Second Century[1]
by Martin Hengel

1. The Tübingen Shock[2]

In Vladimir Soloviev's short story about the antichrist, at the beginning of

---

[1]This essay was first presented at Durham University in 1989 at the centenary celebration of Lightfoot's passing. It was then published in the *Durham University Journal* in a 1992 special edition. In addition to this article by Hengel, that volume included essays by C. K. Barrett and J. D. G. Dunn on Lightfoot as a New Testament scholar. Whereas the Hengel article appears here, the essays by Barrett and Dunn appear as appendices in volume three of this set. This reprinting is done with the kind permission of Durham University.
[2]I wish to thank John Bowden for the translation and Roland Dienes for typing the article into the computer and help in the redaction of the footnotes. In the second revision I was helped by Jorg Frey.

the great ecumenical council, which the antichrist calls in Jerusalem he is given an honorary doctorate from Tübingen University. The German translator, Ludolph Muller, rightly sees an allusion here to David Friedrich Strauss, and the Tübingen school founded by his teacher, Ferdinand Christian Baur, which lay the foundations for modern radical criticism of the New Testament.[3]

In the year 1835, David Friedrich Strauss, then twenty-seven years old and Repetent at the Tübingen Stift published his work *The Life of Jesus*, which contains a devastating critique of the historical value of the Gospels, and in particular of the Gospel of John. According to the verdict of his most recent biographer, it caused a devastating explosion 'like a fire-bomb thrown into the tinder-dry pietistic forest of Würrtemburg . . . *The Life of Jesus* ignited a conflagration which quickly spread throughout the whole of Germany.'[4]

However, this fire did not stop at the German frontier. Its sparks carried over to the whole educated world of Protestantism and European Enlightenment. In France, Ernest Renan could not have written his 1863 *Vie de Jesus* and the subsequent volumes of his history of early Christianity without the preliminary work of Strauss and the Tübingen scholars. Nor did the Anglo-Saxon world remain uninfluenced by it, though initially the influence was limited, and even now has been only partially investigated. Owen Chadwick comments, 'English deists seized upon Strauss, and used his name as a scourge.' The work, nearly 1500 pages long, was not read very much before the English translation, made by the young Marian Evans, who later became famous as George Eliot.[5]

According to an anecdote which came down to me from a reliable oral tradition, significant contemporaries already associated F. C. Baur, Strauss's teacher and the spiritual father of the Tübingen school, with the Antichrist. Shortly before his death in 1860, it is said: 'When the head of the Tübingen

---

[3]V. S. Soloviev, *Kurze Erzahlung vom Antichrist*, translated and explained by Ludolf Muller, Munich 1951, 56, 96f. n. 68.

[4]H. Harris, *David Friedrich Strauss and his Theology*, Cambridge, 1976, 66.

[5]O. Chadwick, *The Victorian Church*. Part 1: 1829–1859, London, 1971, rpr. 1987, 532; for the influence of German criticism on the Anglo-Saxon world, see op cit. Part 2: 1860–1901, London 1972 (rpr. 1987), pp. 68-70; 99-100; cf. further S. Neill, *The Interpretation of the New Testament 1861–1961*, London 1964, pp. 29-60; V. A. Dodd, 'Strauss' English Propagandists and the politics of Unitarianism, 1841-45,' *Church History*, 50 (1981), pp. 415-35.

school came in his lecture to the mysterious number of the Beast, 666, to
the exegesis of Revelation 13, he remarked to the student: "And as Hengstenberg (the spokesman of conservative Lutheranism) says in Berlin,
that's me.""[6]

However our theme for today is fortunately not the dispute over the
radical (or even anti-Christian) views of the Tübingen school of Baur, Strauss
and his other pupils, which lasted for a whole generation, but the question
whether and to what degree the work of Bishop Lightfoot, which is unique
in the nineteenth century, represents an answer to the aggressive theses of
the Tübingen scholars.[7] Here I am thinking particularly of his studies of
the Apostolic Fathers and the Fourth Gospel.

We have to presuppose that a scholar of Lightfoot's status, outstanding for
his tremendous capacity for work, and his stupendous range of reading,
knew the works of the Tübingen school, i.e. not only Baur and Strauss, but
above all Zeller, Schwegler, Hilgenfeld, Volkmar, and the young Ritschl, even
if he does not quote anywhere near as many modern authors as is the custom

---

[6]I received this anecdote from my teacher Otto Bauernfeind; he had received it from his teacher
E. von der Goltz, and von der Goltz had received it from his grandfather who had been a student
of Baur in Tübingen. Remarkably, not only Baur but Lightfoot was compared with the Antichrist.
See below.

[7]A very instructive recent contribution on Lightfoot is the essay of G. R. Treloar, 'J.B. Lightfoot
and St. Paul 1854–65: A Study of Intentions and Method,' in *Lucas; Review of the Evangelical History Association,* Sydney vol. 7 (December, 1989), pp. 5-34; On Bishop Lightfoot and the German
critics see also B. N. Kaye, 'Lightfoot and Baur on Early Christianity,' *Novum Testamentum* 26
(1984), pp. 193-224; C. K. Barrett, 'Quomodo Historia Conscribenda Sit,' *New Testament Studies*
28 (1982), pp. 303-320; R. Morgan, 'Non Angli sed Angeli: Some Anglican Reactions to German
Gospel Criticism,' in S. Sykes and D. Holmes (eds) *New Studies in Theology* I (London, 1980), pp.
1-30; idem, 'Historical Criticism and Christology: England and Germany,' *Studies in Theological
Diplomacy,* Frankfurt on Main, 1982 pp. 80-112; J. S. Andrews, 'German Influence on Religious
Life in the Victorian Era,' *English Quarterly,* 44 (1972), pp. 213-233; see further below on Lightfoot and his works. Cf. L. W. Bernard, 'Bishop Lightfoot and the Apostolic Fathers,' *Church
Quarterly Review,* 161 (1960), 423-35; C. K. Barrett, 'Joseph Barber Lightfoot,' *Durham University
Journal* 64/3 (1972), pp. 193-20; P. H. Richards, 'J. B. Lightfoot as a Biblical Interpreter,' *Interpre-
tation* 8 (1954), pp. 50-62; J. A. T. Robinson, 'Joseph Barber Lightfoot,' Durham Cathedral Lecture, 1981; H. E. Savage, 'Bishop Lightfoot's Influence: His Trust in Young Men,' *Durham University Journal* 77/1 (1984), pp. 1-6; Except for the 'sole very inadequate,' so the verdict J. A. T.
Robinson *The Priority of John* (London, 1985, p. xi n. 14) biographical collection edited by G. R.
Eden and F. C. Macdonald, *Lightfoot of Durham* (Cambridge, 1932), and an unpublished dissertation (D. J. Wilson, *The Life of J.B. Lightfoot, 1829[sic]–1889*) with special reference to the
training of the ministry, Ph.D. Edinburgh, 1956, there is no comprehensive biographical study
on Lightfoot. So the comprehensive study announced by G. R. Treloar in the article mentioned
above is deeply demanded. [Unfortunately, as valuable as Treloar's study on Lightfoot as a historian is, it is neither a comprehensive study nor a biography on Lightfoot. (BW3)]

today.[8] Nevertheless, he once gave a pupil the advice, 'If you write a book on a subject, you have to read everything which has been written about it.' Remarkable times, when this was still possible. Armitage Robinson who tells us this, also adds: 'His independence of predecessors was startling. . . . He refused to catalog the interpretations of previous writers, he will not even mention the names of other commentators, unless there is some special reason.'[9] In Lightfoot's case, we must always keep in view the tension between these two remarks.

All the other representatives of the Tübingen school were substantially older than Lightfoot: Baur 36 years older, Strauss, 20, Zeller 14, and even Ritschl, who later became the leader of liberal theology in Germany, 6 years older. When Lightfoot entered Trinity College, Cambridge in 1847, at the age of nineteen, the new radical criticism movement had reached its heights, and Miss Evans had just translated the Jesus book by the Schwabian 'arch-heretic' Strauss into English. That same year Baur's 'Critical Investigations into the Canonical Gospels' had appeared, in which he declared that none of the Gospels was Apostolic or written by the disciples of the Apostles, and moved their origins into the second century. Baur was most intensively concerned here with the Gospel of John; following his pupil E. Zeller, he put it around 170 A.D., i.e. shortly before Irenaeus' *Adversus haereses* (circa 190). 'In it New Testament theology reached its highest level and most complete form.'[10] According to Zeller and Baur, Valentinian Gnosticism, Montanism, and the Easter dispute did not presuppose the Fourth Gospel, but on the contrary were to be understood as its historical background. In John the contrast which according to Baur dominates earliest Christianity between particularistic Petrine Jewish Christianity and universalist Pauline Gentile Christianity, is transcended and superceded in the Hegelian sense. He looks

---

[8]It should be noted, that the very pages of this John volume prove that Lightfoot had read these scholars, with the possible exception of Volkmar, as they are all cited, or alluded to, in one place or another in Lightfoot's commentary on John. (BW3)

[9]J. A. Robinson, 'The Theological Influence of Bishop Lightfoot,' in *Lightfoot of Durham*, pp. 123-35. The quotations are on p. 135 and 124. [It can now be said that this is something of an exaggeration. He mentions plenty of commentators, including German ones (Meyer is one of his favorites), both in his articles being published here, and in the previously unpublished commentaries themselves. (BW3)].

[10]F. C. Baur, *Vorlesungen uber neutestamentliche Theologie*, ed. F. F. Baur, Leipzig, 1864, reprinted with an Introduction by W. G. Kummel, Darmstadt, 1973, p. 351.

down on Judaism and Paulinism as 'outdated standpoints' because 'in free ideality he stands above the oppositions and, adopting the standpoint of the absolute idea, sets himself above the elements of historical mediation.'[11] The sum of Johannine Christianity becomes identical with Baur's own theology, stamped by German idealism.[12] This is 'the elevation of the consciousness into the sphere of pure spirituality in which God is known as Spirit and all that is particular and limiting is taken up and transcended in the universality of the idea of God.' Here however 'the invisible being of God is opened up' by means of the Logos, 'and goes over into the human consciousness as its absolute content.'[13] In the Fourth Gospel, the apotheosis of man is completed in the form of the participation of the human consciousness in the absolute divine Spirit.

It is understandable that from this perspective, which almost makes the author of the Gospel a philosopher, and completely subordinates the contingent historical detail to the speculative philosophical overall view, the unknown author of the Fourth Gospel, for Baur a Gentile Christian from the second half of the century, comes very close to Gnostic speculation, and his picture of Christ (which is completely unhistorical), has to be interpreted in docetic terms. The young Baur had already acknowledged the pre-imminence of a philosophical perspective in historical research, and in his very first work he wrote the sentence which was to point the way forward for his whole life's work 'without philosophy, for me history remains eternally deaf and dumb.'[14] This priority of the absolute Spirit in Hegel's sense, coming to consciousness in history by means of dialectical movement, over contingent historical reality, then also led to his reconstruction of earliest Christianity, which overturned the whole traditional historical picture—though that did not mean that on each occasion he did not begin from specific observation on the text: for

---

[11]Ibid., p. 401.
[12]On F. C. Baur, cf. K. Scholder, *Theologische Realenzyclopadie* 5 (1980), pp. 352-359; F. W. Graf in H. Fries, G. Kretschmar eds. *Klassiker der Theologie* II München, 1983, pp. 89-110, 411-414 (bibliography); P. Hodgson, *The Formation of Historical Theology. A Study of Ferdinand Christian Baur*, N.Y. 1966; on the Tübingen School see H. Harris, *The Tübingen School*, (Oxford, 1975), U. Kopf, 'Theologische Wissenschaft und Frommigkeit im Konflikt: Ferdinand Christian Baur und seine Schuler,' *Berichte zur Wissenschaftsgeschichte* 11 (1988), pp. 169-77.
[13]See the previous note. Cf. the Introduction of Kümmel, p. xxv.
[14]See Gotthold, Muller, *Identitat und Immanenz, Zur Genese der Theologie von David Friedrich Strauss*, BSHST 10, Zürich 1968, p. 187 = F. C. Baur, 'Symbolik und Mythologie oder die Naturreligion des Alterthums,' I, Stuttgart, 1824, XI.

example, the tension between the two reports on the council of Jerusalem, Galatians 2 and Acts 15. However these only became fertile when he incorporated them into an overall view of earliest Christian history which was grounded in his philosophical pre-understanding.

According to him, and the pupils who stood closest to him, Zeller and Schwegler, only the four genuine letters of Paul came from the first century— Galatians, Romans, 1 and 2 Corinthians. So did the Judaizing Revelation of John, which he believed to have been written by the son of Zebedee. All the other New Testament writings are pseudepigrapha from the second century which convey the split between Paulinism and Judaism, or like the latest (the Pastoral Epistles and the Gospel of John), have already left it behind them. But Baur also declares the writings assigned traditionally to the end of the first or the beginning of the second century, the so-called Apostolic Fathers like 1 Clement, the letters of Ignatius and the letter of Polycarp, to be later forgeries.[15] The interest of Baur and his immediate pupils did not therefore lie in painstaking editing of texts, the thorough philological and theological exegesis of them, and a detailed investigation of their sources, but in the critical analysis of the particular 'tendency' of the texts, a presentation of their religious or philosophical doctrinal concepts ('Lehrbegriff'), and an overall reconstruction of the spiritual awareness bound up with them, along with its development. Baur was interested in understanding the whole history of the church and of dogma and their development down to the battles of the present. Grasping the sources and systematically steeping himself in this enormous amount of material was his strength, but his also too speculative fabrications, coupled with mistakes in detail, often made the whole enterprise questionable. Therefore, Hilgenfeld and Ritschl relatively quickly detached themselves from the school and went their own ways.

2. LIGHTFOOT AS HISTORIAN AND HIS WORK

Lightfoot notes this move very well in the second edition of Ritschl's *Die Entstehung der altkatholischen Kirche,*[16] which put Ritschl in more direct

---

[15]See e.g. J. B. Lightfoot, *The Apostolic Fathers,* I (London, 1890, rpr. Hildesheim and New York, 1973), p. 8: 'They (= Clement, Ignatius, Polycarp) are the proper link between the canonical Scriptures and the Church Fathers who succeeded them.' Cf. also pp. 55-55.353f.

[16]The subtitle was *Eine kirchen- and dogmengeschichliche Monographie,* Bonn, 1857, first edition 1850.

antagonism to the Tübingen school, and described the work as 'very able and suggestive.'[17] His own way of working and the goal that he strove for were, by contrast completely different; he was a highly gifted philologist and historian, always going by the text, by sources and facts, and antipathetic to any speculation. Before he made general statements, he examined any available detailed evidence with extreme care. Not only did he have a comprehensive knowledge of Graeco-Roman antiquity including archaeology and epigraphy, but he knew the Church Fathers and the languages of the Christian East: Syriac, Coptic, and Armenian. His argument, built up carefully, often took the form of scrupulously constructed lists of items of evidence; here—in complete contrast to his German conservative colleagues like Theodor Zahn—any hair-splitting logic and any forcing of proofs were alien to him.[18]

Shortly after Lightfoot's death, no less a figure than Adolph Harnack made a unique evaluation of Lightfoot's method and personality, though he had never met him personally. Let the greatest German theological scholar of that time speak for himself:

> Lightfoot was the most learned and worthy representative of the conservative critical school in England. In nineteenth century Germany we have no scholar in the conservative camp who could match him in the extent or accuracy of his knowledge. His editions and commentaries ... and his critical articles are of lasting worth, and even where one cannot agree with his conclusions, one can never pass over his arguments. His respect for his opponent, which marked him out—I cannot recall a single derogatory remark in any of Lightfoot's writing; the strongest form on which he commented on a quite untenable argument was to express amazement—brought him the utmost respect of all parties. Anyone who read him had to feel that here not only a scholar but a Christian was speaking, one for whom the supreme principle was ἀληθεύοντες δὲ ἐν ἀγάπῃ. There has never been an apologist who was

[17] J. B. Lightfoot, *St. Paul's Epistle to the Galatians*, London, 1890, rpr. 1902, p. 295 n. 2.
[18] But Lightfoot's method also had its limits, for his commentaries were primarily historical and philological. See the comment of Hort, 'in some ways the most acute thinker of the three' (C. K. Barrett, *Westcott as Commentator*. The Bishop Lightfoot Memorial Lecture, 1958, Cambridge 1959, p. 6), in letters to his friend John Ellerton. On the other hand see the positive remarks of Westcott concerning Lightfoot's Galatian Commentary in A. Westcott, *Life and Letters of Brooke Foss Westcott*, vol. 1, London 1903, p. 289 (see also p. 294 concerning *Philippians*, and p. 432 concerning *Colossians*).

less of an advocate than Lightfoot; therefore the German apologists were not to his taste. Moreover one would do him an injustice if one were to sum up his whole significance under the title *vindex traditionis*. He was an independent, free scholar not only by the standards of the official theology of the English church, but also in the absolute sense. He never defended a tradition for tradition's sake; but how often he rescued the tradition, which previously had not been defended adequately, and therefore risked losing its credibility! In this respect his great work on the Letters of Ignatius is above all to be singled out.[19]

Five years earlier, in a review in *The Expositor*,[20] Harnack had acknowledged, 'We may say, without exaggeration that this work is the most learned and careful Patristic monograph which has appeared in the nineteenth century.'

One special feature of Lightfoot's way of working was the way in which his academic work was based above all on the recovery of the text of early Christian writings, of which the significance and authenticity was disputed, and extensive commentary on them. From his time in Cambridge come the commentaries on Galatians (1865), Philippians (1868), 1 and 2 Clement (1869, with an appendix, 1877), Colossians and Philemon (1875). It was not until as Bishop of Durham that after thirty years' preliminary work he could finish his edition of the letters of Ignatius and the Letter of Polycarp as 'the core of the whole' (1885).[21] The five-volume complete edition of the Apostolic Fathers, which summed up the earlier editions of the text in an expanded form, had to appear posthumously, shortly after his death, in 1889.[22] Seriously ill, Lightfoot was working on the chapter on 'Peter in Rome' until three days before he died, and the manuscript broke off in mid-sentence. The extensive excurses, monographs in themselves, discussed not only all the questions of testimonia, textual tradition, and authenticity, which was so disputed, but also historical problems of the second and early third centuries up to Hippolytus of Rome. They also described the relationship between the church

---

[19]A. V. Harnack, *Theologische Litertuarzeitung*, 15 (1890), cols. 297-301; 207f. in a review of E. Hatch, *Essays in Biblical Greek*, Oxford 1889.

[20]Ed. by W. R. Nicholl, Third Series, Vol. II 1885, London 1885, pp. 401-414, 401 in the review of 'Bishop Lightfoot's "Ignatius and Polykarp"' (= *The Apostolic Fathers* II, 1-3, London 1885).

[21]Preface to the First Edition, *The Apostolic Fathers, II, 1* op. cit. (n. 10), IX.

[22]J. B. Lightfoot, *St. Clement of Rome* (= *The Apostolic Fathers* I, 1-2), London 1890. The second volume *Ignatius and Polycarp* (= *The Apostolic Fathers* II, 1-3), had been published in 1885 and came out in a second edition as soon as 1889.

and the Roman empire under the Antonines in connection with the relevant
texts. Apart from the outsider Hilgenfeld and the less convincing editions of
the Pseudo-Clementines and of Eusebius' ecclesiastical history by Schwegler,[23]
the Tübingen School had produced neither substantial editions of the text
nor comparable commentaries. In method and substance Lightfoot adopted
quite a different way, all his own. In my view, his work was more strictly
'historical-critical' in the real sense than the criticism of the Tubingen
scholars—which was to a large degree speculative. Within the framework of
the historical picture with which they had been provided by Baur, they offered a one-sided investigation of 'tendencies' which they claimed to dis-
cover in the early Christian writings.

3. LIGHTFOOT'S ARGUMENT AGAINST THE TÜBINGEN SCHOOL

But did Lightfoot allow himself to be influenced by the Tübingen scholars,
and was the perspective of his research defined by their radical critical results? In the not particularly frequent cases in which people have thought
back to this greater scholar who died a hundred years ago, this has often
been asserted quite emphatically,[24] but most recently the view has been put
in question almost as decisively.

A first reason given is that the works of the Tübingen school found relatively little visible recognition in the sphere of official theology in England
between 1850 and 1870, and only among some free-thinkers like Marian
Evans alias George Eliot or twenty-seven years later, the author of *Supernatural Religion* which was published anonymously.[25] However the surprising success of this attack on the New Testament, the ammunition which
came not least from Tübingen, shows that the time for such attacks was now

[23]A. Schwegler, (ed.) *Clementi Romani quae feruntur homiliae* . . . Stuttgart, 1847; idem (ed.);
Eusebii Pamphili Historiae Ecclesiasticae Libri X, Tubingen 1852, Cf. for the later edition the
negative verdict on Schwegler's text critical work by Eduard Schwartz (GCS, *Eusebius Werke* II/3
Leipzig 1909, XLVf.). On Schwegler cf. the biographical sketch by E. Akerknecht, 'Albert Schwegler, Historiker und Philosoph,' in *Schwabische Lebensbilder* IV, Stuttgart 1948, pp. 312-40 (lit).
[24]Cf. J. A. Robinson, op. cit.; A. C. Headlam, 'Bishop Lightfoot's Place as a Historian,' in *Lightfoot
of Durham*, op. cit., pp. 136-45. S. Neill op. cit. p. 55 writes on Zahn and Lightfoot: 'They had
identified the precise point at which the Tübingen theories were most open to attack; if the attack
were successful here, the champions of the Tübingen theories would have no power to defend
themselves elsewhere. The theories had been killed stone-dead.' The point to which Neill refers
is the dating of the writings of Clement and Ignatius.
[25]Volume 1 and 2 1874, Volume 3 1874, see Owen Chadwick, op. cit. Part 2, p. 7of.

ripe, even on this side of the channel, at a point in time when Tübingen's radicalism had lost the battle in Germany. When Lightfoot began to write against *Supernatural Religion* in 1874–75, he probably did so not only out of personal concern, because in connection with it close friends were under suspicion and under attack, but also because of the danger arising out of the historically untenable criticism which the work contained. He had seen it coming, and he had incomparable resources for countering it.

The other object[ion][26] to excessive stress on the Tübingen School lay 'in the . . . surprising paucity of Lightfoot's references to Baur, which are far less common than the popular picture of Lightfoot would require.'[27] But when we reflect that (although he had read everything on the question) Lightfoot goes completely by the sources, quotes other authors relatively seldom and, as Harnack already observed, writes polemic about them even more rarely, it is striking how often and sometimes how sharply on occasion he attacked Baur or the Tübingen School, or, as he could also say, the 'Tübingen fallacy,'[28] or 'a modern school of critics'[29] and their 'historical speculations.'[30] Of all

---

[26]Hengel's translator seems to have erred here. He surely means objection not object. (BW3)

[27]C. K. Barrett op. cit. p. 309. The argument is repeated by B. N. Kaye, op. cit., p. 198. But I am convinced that Lightfoot and his friends saw the importance of Baur's work right from the beginning. For instance, in the first volume of the *Journal for Classical and Sacred Philology*, which appeared in four volumes during 1854–59 (rpr. Amsterdam, 1970) founded and edited by Lightfoot among others, appeared a review of Baur's 'Das Christenthum und die christliche Kirche der drei ersten Jahrhunderte,' by Westcott. He speaks about Baur's book as an 'authoritative statement of the critical school of which he is the founder and ablest representative' (p. 281). Also noteworthy is the fact that the *Theologische Jahrbucher* which were edited by Baur and Zeller, had always been registered under the title *Baur's Theologische Jahrbucher*, which since the journals were listed in alphabetical order, were the first in this list of journals.

[28]*Essays on the Work entitled Supernatural Religion*, reprinted from the *Contemporary Review* (London, 1891 2nd ed.) 1889 (1st ed.), p. 12. The first part appeared in December 1874 and the last in May 1877. Though from the beginning intended for publishing in a permanent form, the author hadn't enough time for it until 1889, cf. H. W. Watkins, *The Quarterly Review* (no. 351) vol. 176, 1893, p. 86f. The intended completion with notes was never realized. This drawback had been attacked by John Owen in his review in the *Academy* (No. 913 from 2nd November 1889, pp. 280-82). About the original articles he comments: Lightfoot 'succeeded in pointing out various shortcomings, both in textual scholarship and of critical inference, which certainly implied both inadequate equipment and an *animus* wholly irreconcilable with impartial and trustworthy investigation.' But questionable for him was the unchanged reprint because 'the author of *Supernatural Religion* had in subsequent editions of his book modified so largely many of the passages inculpated in the bishop's essays that their criticism was already out of date. Dr. Lightfoot seems herein to have forgotten the first canon of controversial writing, which requires that the controverted matter to be taken from the very latest form' (p. 281).

[29]Ibid. (Essays), p. 251, cf. 101.

[30]*Galatians*, op. cit. p. 295, n.1.

the contemporary authors Baur and the Tübingen scholars e.g. Volkmar, Schwegler, and Hilgenfeld (whose growing distance from his old friends he noted with pleasure) are those whom Lightfoot quotes by far the most often in his works on early Christianity. And when he quotes them, he mostly contradicts them.

So when in the few obituaries on Lightfoot, pupils and friends referred to this point, which in my view was decisive for his life's work, they were probably reflecting more than a popular picture.

Armitage Robinson, a personal pupil of Lightfoot's from his group of the Auckland Brotherhood, describes the effect of the *Apostolic Fathers* with a quotation from Lightfoot himself: 'He had knocked . . . "the last nail in the coffin of the Tubingen theory."'[31] In the memorial address given on the fiftieth anniversary of Lightfoot's death, Bishop Eden in retrospect struck up an almost hymnic tone. The battle of the trio Lightfoot, Westcott, and Hort 'seemed to us humbler students to be a battle of the giants for the citadel of Faith.'[32]

But we do best to let Lightfoot himself speak. In the Preface to his *Letters of Ignatius*, published in 1885, he ends it by pointing out that friends had criticized him 'for allowing myself to be diverted from more congenial task of commenting on St. Paul's Epistles; but the importance of the position seemed to me to justify the expenditure of much time and labor, in 'repairing a breach' not indeed in the 'House of the Lord' itself, but in the immediately outlying building.'[33] By directing the force of his concentrated historical argumentation against some, as he pointedly says, 'academic terrorism' (a harsh word, but what scholar has not come across this phenomenon?) working with 'moral intimidation'[34] he raises at the same time

---

[31]Op. cit. p. 133, cf. 128.
[32]G. R. Eden, 'A Sermon preached before the University of Cambridge,' (24, November, 1929), *Lightfoot of Durham*, op. cit, p. 154. On B. F. Westcott, cf. A. Westcott, op. cit., C. K. Barrett op. cit. H. Chadwick, *The Vindication of Christianity in Westcott's Thought*, Cambridge, 1961. O. Chadwick, *Westcott and the University*, Cambridge, 1963. D. L. Edwards, 'Lightfoot and Westcott,' in *Leaders of the Church of England 1828-1944*, London 1971, pp. 207-222 and comprehensively F. Olofsson *Christus Redemptor et Consummator. A Study of in the Theology of B. F. Westcott*, Uppsala, 1979. On Hort cf. A. C. Hort, ed. *The Life and Letters of F. J. A. Hort*, 2 vols. London, 1896. Th. B. Strong, 'Dr. Hort's Life and Works,' *Journal of Theological Studies* 1 (1900), pp. 270-386. E. G. Rupp, *Hort and the Cambridge Tradition*, Cambridge, 1970; M. E. Glasswell, in *Theologische Realenzyclopaedie* 15, pp. 584-86, and comprehensively the recent monograph of G. A. Patrick, *F. J. A. Hort, Eminent Victorian*, Sheffield, 1988.
[33]*Apostolic Fathers II/1* op. cit, p. xv.
[34]He writes, 'If the ecclesiastical terrorism of past ages has lost its power, we shall in the interests

the question: on which side is freedom from the pressure of a tendency greater? He replies: 'To the disciples of Baur, the rejection of the Ignatian Epistles is an absolutely necessity of their theological position. The ground would otherwise be withdrawn from under them, and their historical reconstruction of early Christian history would fall in ruins on their head.'[35] By contrast, for the other conservative side, the question of their authenticity was of secondary significance. For them the whole canonical witness of the New Testament had not lost its value. Here it becomes clear that Lightfoot's thirty-year occupation with Ignatius and the other Apostolic Fathers was motivated not least by the aim of rejecting the destructive theories of the Tübingen scholars on the origin of the writings of the New Testament.

In the *Quarterly Review* of January 1893 an anonymous writer (he was in fact H. W. Watkins) published the most extensive assessment of the great scholar after his death.[36] Watkins already points to the connection between the editing of the letters of Ignatius and the Tübingen school. By contrast, in his short article in the *Dictionary of National Biography*, Hort, Lightfoot's close friend and ally, saw the excurses on James and 'St. Paul and the Three' in the *Commentary on Galatians* as the 'most important contribution to the Tübingen controversy.' But his further comment that Lightfoot's conclusions were 'not a refutation of conclusions of the Tübingen scholars' but 'a rival interpretation and a rival picture' is his own interpretation—from a later time, and more critical.[37] That Lightfoot himself understood his interpretation rather as a refutation is evident from his remark in the preface to the Galatians commentary: 'If the primitive Gospel was, as some [compare the Pauline τίνες, Martin Hengel] have represented it, merely one of many phases of Judaism, if those cherished beliefs . . . were afterthoughts, progressive accretions, having no foundation in the Person and Teaching of Christ, then indeed St. Paul's preaching was vain, and our faith is vain also. I feel very confident that the historical views of the Tübingen school are too

---

of truth, be justly jealous of allowing an academic terrorism to usurp its place.' Ibid., p. xi.

[35] Ibid., XI/XII. Cf. also the similar verdict in his *Essays on the Work entitled Supernatural Religion*, op. cit, p. 64.

[36] H. W. Watkins, op. cit., pp. 73-105; pp. 84f.

[37] F. J. A. Hort art. 'Lightfoot, Joseph Barber,' in *Dictionary of National Biography* ed. by S. Lee vol. xxxiiii (London, 1893), pp. 232-40; here p. 238.

extravagant to obtain any wide or lasting hold over the minds of men.'[38] This prophecy was not fulfilled in that way. The criticism of the Tübingen scholars also had lasting effects behind which we can not go back.

Be that as it may, Lightfoot the exegete wanted to make his contribution to the refutation to the deadly danger presented by the Tübingen scholars, and this contribution was greater than any other in the English-speaking world. The critical references to the Tübingen school and its representatives, in the first place Baur, but also Schwegler, Volkmar, Hitzig, and in the second place Hilgenfeld and Ritschl, permeate his whole work from his first commentaries to the posthumous collection of articles. Despite his restraint, all in all Lightfoot quotes them well over a hundred times; in other words he argued against their theories all through his life. It was not only the results which, in his view, threatened the very foundations of the Christian faith, but the speculatively destruction and constructive methods which keep irritating this exceptional and reticent scholar, and indeed embittered him.[39]

Otherwise, it is hard to explain a remark towards the end of his detailed account of the dispute over the authenticity of the Epistles of Ignatius in his *Essays against Supernatural Religion:* 'But even if we set Polycarp aside (as evidence for their authenticity, M. H.) it would hardly be rash to say that the external evidence for at least two-thirds of the remains of classical antiquity was inferior' (to the evidence for the letters of Ignatius—M. H.).[40] Lightfoot said that as a classical philologist of high standing, who on this point was probably superior to most of his theological contemporaries. He continues: 'We Christians are constantly told that we must expect to have our records tested by the same standards by which are applied to other writings. This is exactly what we desire and what we do not get. It is easy to imagine what would ensue if the critical principles of the Tübingen school and their admirers were let loose on the classical literature of Greece and Rome.' In other words he censures the presumptuous criticism of his opponents as being basically unacademic and unprofessional.

An illustration of how the anger of despair over absurd assertions of his

---

[38]Op. cit. Preface to the First Edition 1865, XI cf. p. 295 n.1.

[39]Having done my own research on this topic I can agree with my friend Prof. Bammel who wrote me in a letter on the 31st of July, 1989: 'Baur is das Lebensproblem für L[ightfoot] gewesen (wie Schweitzer für Dodd).' Generally, I feel confirmed by the study of G. R. Treloar op. cit.

[40]*Essays on the Work entitled Supernatural Religion*, op. cit. p. 82. The article was first published in 1875 under the title 'The Ignatian Epistles.'

opponents could suddenly overcome this scholar notable for his tranquility and self control, when he was discussing just a small point: 1 Clement played only a secondary role in the historical construction of the Tübingen school—in contrast to the letters of Ignatius and the traditions about Polycarp. However, it had to be unauthentic and late so that the Gospels and almost all the other writings of the New Testament could be put back into the second century. Baur was only peripherally occupied with the letter. He was more interested in the person of Clement as allegedly a pupil of Paul or Peter and as the legendary pseudepigraphical author of the Pseudo-Clementines, which he over-estimated to a ridiculous degree and dated much too early. In his view Paul's letter to the Philippians, which was a forgery, mentions this Clement at 4:3 and identifies him anachronistically with Titus Flavius Clemens, nephew of the Emperor, who was executed by Domitian for Christian leanings.[41] The letters and the Pseudo-Clementines were then attributed to this legendary Clement, supposedly related to the Emperor. In this way 1 Clement appeared in Rome in the first half of the second century as a mediator between Jewish and Gentile Christianity. In two articles Volkmar (following the Heidelberg Old Testament scholar Hitzig who was a supporter of Baur) had claimed that the letter was written at the earliest in the time of Hadrian (117–138), as the book of Judith is mentioned in 1 Clement 55 and reflects in allegorical form Trajan's unsuccessful expedition to the east (114–117) and the reign of terror in Judaea in 116–117 under his general Lucius Quietus, whom Hadrian had executed when he seized power.[42] 1 Clement must therefore have been written some time later. Baur

---

[41]F. C. Baur, *Paulus der Apostel Jesu Christi, Sein Leben und Wirken, seine Briefe und seine Lehre. Eine Beitrag zu einer kritschen Geschichte des Urchristentums*, Stuttgart, 1845, pp. 471ff. cf. J. B. Lightfoot, *St. Paul's Epistle to the Philippians*, London and Cambridge, 1868, p. 168; *Apostolic Fathers*, I.

[42]G. Volkmar, 'Ueber Clemens von Rom an die nachste Folgezeit, mit besonderer Beziehung auf den Philipper- und Barnabas Brief, so wie auf das buch Judith,' *Theologischer Jahrbuch* 15, (1856), pp. 287-369; 'Ueber Euodia, Euodius, und Anaclet,' *Theologischer Jahrbuch* 16 (1857), pp. 147-51. Lightfoot referred to this in *Apostolic Fathers*, I,I op. cit. p. 346; cf. also F. C. Baur, *Lehrbuch der christlichen Dogmengeschichte*, Leipzig, 1867 (rpr. Darmstadt, 1974), p. 82; *Vorlesungen*, op. cit. p. 41ff.; *Das Christenthum und die christliche Kirche der drei ersten Jahrhunderte*, Tübingen, 1860 (rpr. with an introduction by U. Wickert, Stuttgart-Bad Canstatt 1966 as Vol. 3 of F.C. Baur, *Ausgewalte Wirke in Einzelausgaben* ed. by K. Scholder, p. 134 n. 2 reference to Volkmar). A. Schwegler, *Das nachapostelische Zeitalter in seiner Hauptmomentum seiner Entewicklung II*, Tübingen, 1846 (rpr. Graz, 1977), pp. 125-33. In his view the name of Clement is a mere cipher ('Tendenzbegriff') 'Er bezeichnet immer und ueberall *die Tendenz der Vermittlung*

took up this conjecture of his pupil's without delay and resorted to it often. Lightfoot spent two and half pages reporting Volkmar's peculiar theory in detail—he wanted to demonstrate its absurdity for all to see. Then he breaks off: 'I shall not attempt to dissect this theory in detail for it would be mere waste of time to do so. Those who wish to see it torn into shreds have only to consult the criticisms of Hilgenfeld and of Lipsius'—i.e. Volkmar's German critics. Nevertheless, additional arguments follow for more than another page, showing his knowledge of rabbinic literature.[43]

Lightfoot ends with a methodological consideration of true and false criticism, which leads into a tempermental attack not on Volkmar but on Baur, the head of the school. 'Ingenuity often wears the mask of criticism, but is not infrequently the caricature of criticism. Ingenuity is not necessarily divination; it is not wholesome self-restraint, is not the sober weighing of probabilities, is not the careful consideration of evidence. Criticism is all of these, which are wanting to its spurious counterfeit.'[44] True historical criticism has nothing to do with the critic's fantasy. So much for Volkmar. But then Lightfoot turns to the chief culprit, who credulously took over the absurd hypotheses of his pupil and from whom this fantastic method of fabrication emanated. First of all he cites the 'apostate' Hilgenfeld ('I have always been amazed that Volkmar's theory found favor with Baur'). Then comes the verdict: 'No man has shown himself more ready to adopt the wildest speculations, if they fell in with his own preconceived theories, than Baur, especially in his later days—speculations which in not a few cases have been falsified by direct evidence since discovered. Nothing has exercised a more baneful influence on criticism in the country of critics than the fascination of his name. While he has struck out some lines which have stimulated thought, and thus have not been unfruitful in valuable results' (Lightfoot's sense of justice does not let him pass over these valuable promptings, even in his devastating criticism) 'the glamor of his genius has on the whole exercised a fatal effect on the progress of a sober and discriminating study of the early records of Christianity.'[45]

zwischen Judenchristen und Heidenchristen zum Behufe der Verwirklichung einer katholischen Kirche' (p. 130).
[43]*Apostolic Fathers I, I op cit.*, p. 356f.
[44]Ibid., p. 357.
[45]Ibid., p. 357f. '(Volkmari) sententiam . . . Baurio placuisse semper admiratus sum.'

This completely unexpected and at the same time fundamental attack on Baur in a 'dissertation' on 1 Clement while recognizing the stimulus which emerged from his genius, shows how baneful Lightfoot thought the influence of the Tübingen church historians to be. Baur was too ready to neglect the detail of what the text said or to do violence to it (in order to bend it in his direction) in favor of his wider-ranging historical constructions.

Lightfoot's criticism was supported by a series of sometimes sensational discoveries of patristic texts extending over the whole of the second half of the nineteenth century (see his 'direct evidence since discovered'). Above all, step by step these showed that it was impossible to put the Fourth Gospel as late as 170. The discoveries included books IV-X of Hippolytus's *Refutatio omnium haersium*, discovered in 1842 and first published in 1851 as the work of Origen.[46] This showed that the Gospel of John had already been used by Basilides or his pupils and other early Gnostics. There was also in 1846 the Armenian translation of Ephraem's commentary on the Diatesseron, from which it became clear that John formed the framework of this earliest Gospel harmony,[47] the complete text of the Pseudo-Clementine Homilies,[48] the previously unknown conclusion of which contained a clear quotation from John 9:3,[49] or the Syriac translation of the seven authentic letters of Ignatius. The list could be continued further.[50]

4. ANALOGIES AND DIFFERENCES

The attempt I shall now venture to make, to arrive at a just definition of the relationship between Baur and Lightfoot, comes up against a number of difficulties, because of the nature of the subject-matter.

---

[46]Cf. M. Markovich, ed. 'Hippolytus, Refutatio omnium haeresium,' *PTS* 25, Berlin (1986), pp. 5f.

[47]See now L. Leloir, 'Ephrem de Nisibi Commentaire de l'Evangile, concordant ou Diastesseron,' *Sources chretienne* 121, Paris 1966, pp. 25ff., cf. also pp. 22f.

[48]Ed. by A. R. M. Dressel, *Clementis Romani quae feruntur Homiliae viginti nunc primum integrae, Textum ad Codicem Ottobonianum constituit*, Göttingen 1853, rpr. in Migne, PG. 2, Paris 1866, cols. 19-468.

[49]Hom XIX 22, 6 cites John 9.2f. (B. Rehm ed.) *Die Pseudoklementinen I, Homilien: GCS* 42, Berlin 1953, p. 265. Cf. also Hom XI 26.3 Quotation of John 3:5 (ibid., p. 167). Without convincing arguments, G. Volkmar contested always that the above mentioned passages were quotations from the Gospel of John, see his 'Ein neue endecktes Zeugniss fur das Johannes-Evangelium,' *Thelogische Jahrbucher* 13, 1854, pp. 446-62.

[50]On the Gospel of John in the 2nd century see now M. Hengel, *The Johannine Question*, London and Philadelphia 1989, pp. 1-23.

1. Despite some analogies, a real comparison is hardly possible, since the analogies are more external and eventually bring out the difference more strongly:[51] *firstly*, the interest in historical truth—yet attempts to approximate to it in very different ways; *secondly*, stupendous diligence and comprehensive philological and theological education—but which for the most part lead to such very different results; and *thirdly*, the link with the church—but which for the Tübingen professor became increasingly weak and for Lightfoot became increasingly dominant. He devoted a large part of his time to his church duties, first of all as a Canon of St. Paul's in London and then above all as bishop in one of the most important dioceses of England, and in so doing also sacrificed his academic plans. Both the commentary series on the letters of Paul and the *Apostolic Fathers* remain incomplete; a planned history of the fourth century was never written; the edition of the Pseudo-Clementine Recognitions went through several hands and did not appear until seventy-six years later.[52]

Because of the widespread repudiation of him which increased the more time went on, Baur removed himself increasingly from church duties and also gave up his office as Frühprediger at the Stiftskirche of Tübingen, whereas the Professor in Cambridge and Canon of St. Paul's, where he was also advisor of the Queen, and even more the Bishop of Durham, who was regarded as one of the best preachers of his time, took these duties increasingly seriously. Even today his sermons are worth reading. Finally, moreover, Baur lived eight years longer than Lightfoot, who had worn himself out prematurely in his twofold profession as bishop and scholar, and the Tübingen scholar could therefore look back on a much more extensive and complete work.

2. Lightfoot faced not just a single adversary but a whole group which emerged with a relatively well-defined programme, 'a modern school of critics.'[53] Baur appeared to him only as 'its most determined and ablest

---

[51]See B. N. Kaye, op. cit.

[52]B. Rehm/F. Pascke eds. *Die Pseudoklementinen II, Rekognitionen in Rufins Ubersetzung,* GCS 51 Berlin 1965, IX ff. In his preface the editor describes the way the Lightfoot manuscript, which eventually formed one of the sources of the GCS edition, passed through several hands.

[53]*Essays on the Work entitled Supernatural Religion* op. cit., p. 251, originally 'Churches of Gaul,' August 1876. Cf. also above.

antagonist.'[54] Lightfoot can therefore—in fact certainly quite wrongly—describe Hilgenfeld 'as the successor of Baur, and the present representative of the Tübingen School (though it has no longer its head-quarters at Tübingen),'[55] who nevertheless had generously to bring back the dating of the Gospel of John from A.D. 170 to 150. Sometimes he also simply speaks of 'German criticism,' which in addition to the closer and more distant pupils of Baur also included Credner, de Wette, Lipsius, Harnack, etc. So he contradicted Matthew Arnold, who criticized an all too eccentric British author (Samuel Davidson), by pointing out: 'an extravagance of this sort could never have come from Germany where there is a great force of critical opinion controlling a learned man's vagaries and keeping him straight,'[56] since Lightfoot had had quite different experiences: 'I confess that my experiences of the critical literature of Germany have not been so fortunate. It would be difficult, I think, to find among English scholars any parallel to the mass of absurdities which several intelligent and very learned German critics have conspired to heap upon two simple names in the Philippian Epistle, Euodia and Syntyche.'[57] First of all he mentioned Baur, who puts the letter near to the Gnostic systems of the second century because of the hymn in 2.6-11[58] and attaches most importance of all to the mythical person of Clement in 4:3,[59] in whom the Pauline and Petrine churches are combined. Schwegler then made the two ladies allegorical representatives of these two parties and Volkmar and Hilgenfeld had spun out this fable even further. So when the author of *Supernatural Religion* appeals to such authorities, 'I have my own opinion of the weight which such names should carry with them.'[60] On Hitzig, the Old Testament scholar in Heidelberg, he goes on to observe: 'The learning of this curious pamphlet keeps pace with its absurdity. If the reader is disposed to think that this writer must be laughing in his sleeve at the

---

[54]J. B. Lightfoot, *Biblical Essays* (London, 1901 2nd ed.), p. 10. In the article entitled 'Internal Evidence for the Authenticity and Genuineness of St. John's Gospel,' originally published in *The Expositor*, 1890.

[55]Ibid.

[56]M. Arnold, *Essays in Criticism*, London and Cambridge, 1865, p. 57 quoted by Lightfoot in his *Essays on the Work entitled Supernatural Religion*, op. cit, p. 24.

[57]Ibid.

[58]F. C. Baur, *Paulus*, op. cit., p. 458ff.

[59]Ibid., p. 470.

[60]Lightfoot, *Essays on the Work entitled Supernatural Religion*, op. cit., p. 24f.

methods of *the modern school to which he belongs* (my italics) he is checked by the obviously serious tone of the whole discussion. Indeed it is altogether in keeping with Hitzig's critical discoveries elsewhere.'[61] There were limits and when these were exceeded, Lightfoot could react with bitter irony.

3. It is remarkable that, as far as I can see, David Friedrich Strauss, who was the first to draw all eyes to Tübingen as a result of his *Life of Jesus*, and whose influence in the world of culture far surpassed that of his teacher Baur, is never mentioned in Lightfoot's published works, not even in his argument with *Supernatural Religion*, where one would inevitably have expected a reference. This looks more like a deliberate *damnatio memoriae*.[62] As a student, Lightfoot must have read the *Life of Jesus* closely. His friend Hort mentions it in 1851, when he was twenty-two, in a letter to the Religious Socialist, Charles Kingsley. First of all he mentions Strauss in the same breath as the philosophers Emerson and Francis Newman, saying that he is afraid that 'our orthodox Epicurism' could develop in this direction. However the 'cold laborical criticism' of Strauss's book does not seem to him to be the greatest danger. Unbelief in England must not take on any German form; it does not grow so much through theology as through a failure to take note of 'questions concerning social relations.'[63] Here Lightfoot may perhaps have adopted a rather more critical attitude than his contemporary and friend.

Two years later, at twenty-five, shortly after his nomination to be a Fellow of Trinity College, Cambridge, Lightfoot won the Norrisian prize with an essay of sixty handwritten pages. This essay has only recently been rediscovered and published. In it he presents a perspicuous rejection of Strauss' thesis that the Gospels, and thus earliest Christianity, do not basically go back to the historically unique activity of Jesus i.e. to God's revelation, but are the fruit of the contemporary world of Jewish culture. Here already we

---

[61] Ibid., p. 25 n.1.

[62] The careful reader of these three volumes will see that this statement is no longer quite true. Strauss does come up for mention in this now published material. Largely, however, it is true. Lightfoot knew Strauss's work, but practiced benign neglect when it came to mentioning it. Perhaps a distinction should be made between what he allowed to be published in his lifetime and what he said in lectures at Cambridge, which is the source of the bulk of this freshly unveiled Lightfoot material in these three volumes. (BW3)

[63] A. F. Hort, op. cit. I, p. 187: 'Lightfoot continued: ". . . above all, that which daily more strongly appears to me to lie at the root of all social problems, the relation of the sexes, will be the *prominent* subjects of unbelief."'

see the mastery of the historian. Neither the incarnation nor atonement by the cross of Jesus—the basic themes of the Fourth Gospel, which Strauss considered to be mythical through and through—can be derived from the Judaism of Palestine and the Diaspora. Christian faith rests on a personal revelation of God in Jesus of Nazareth and cannot be reconciled with an immanent systematic development of the history of mankind. In a last paragraph he argues with Baur's thesis that the first apostles' faith was a crude Jewish Christianity under the influence of Ebionitism, and that this shaped the course of church history.[64] Here we already see the basic lines of his later work on the Apostolic Fathers. 'We have seen how a consciousness of the weakness of their position has induced our adversaries to seek a connecting link between Judaism and Christianity; the same desire too has led to their denial of the authenticity of the Apostolic writings. Some period must elapse, they argue before the full development of the system, but nowhere is this exhibited more perfectly than in some of the St. Paul's Epistles and St. John's Gospel—they cannot therefore have been productions of the first century.' Thus the argument of his opponents. Over against this he sets out the argument, the detailed implementation of which became his life's work: 'We have remarked how the remains of the earliest Fathers, the contemporaries of the Apostles, support the existence of teaching either oral or in writing, such as is exhibited by these controverted books; we may also advert to the incongruities, which are presented by the theory of our adversaries, considered independently.'[65]

4. A real comparison between Baur and Lightfoot is most possible where both begin with the authenticity of a text, i.e. in the case of the four letters of Paul which Baur considers to be authentic. Professor Barrett's comparison

---

[64]It is far from clear that the essay Hengel is referring to here is in fact the one he wrote for the Norrisian prize. See appendix C: "Lessons of History from the Cradle of Christianity" in volume 3 of this series. (BW3)

[65]J. B. Lightfoot, 'On Strauss and Christian Origins: An Unpublished Manuscript,' ed. and Introduced by B. N. Kaye, *The Durham University Journal*, 79, 1987, pp. 165-200, here p. 200. In their introduction the editors state: 'The reply to Strauss was the first sign of an active interest in the Apostolic Fathers, the outcome of which thirty years later was again partly intended as a control on the effects of speculative critical theories on the New Testament writings, especially the Gospels. . . . The main issue, and the method for dealing with it, has been discerned at the outset, and was developed with much greater learning and conviction over the next thirty-five years. To the recognized influence of Baur and the Tübingen School, on the direction and character of Lightfoot's scholarship must now be added that of D. F. Strauss.'

of the two scholars' exegesis of Gal. 2 and Acts 15 shows that there is no
absolute opposition here.[66] For despite Lightfoot's tendency to harmonize
the various reports, he does not simply deny some tensions between the
earliest Apostles and Paul, and Baur does not consider Acts to be completely
unhistorical, despite its tendency towards mediation and its late origin.
However, beyond the 'Pauline island' the opposition becomes unbridgeable.
Therefore, Lightfoot could not but see an essential part of his scholarly work
as consisting not least in the refutation of the Tübingen speculations that the
writings of the New Testament originated late, in the second century, especially as here a pantheistic understanding of God, wholly shaped by the
dominant philosophy of the time, was associated with historical hypotheses
which seemed to be too often fantastic and destructive.

5. THE RELEVANCE OF THE APOSTOLIC FATHERS FOR LIGHTFOOT

Towards the end of the 1850s the trio Lightfoot, Westcott, and Hort discussed
the editing of a series of commentaries. Lightfoot himself wanted to concentrate on the letters of Paul and therefore yielded to Westcott the Fourth
Gospel which he loved so much, whereas Hort, after overcoming certain
hesitations arising out of his more marked critical tendencies, was to take
over the Synoptic Gospels and Acts.[67]

---

[66]See the essay by Barrett in the appendices of vol. 3 in the Lightfoot Legacy.

[67]Originally they all wanted to participate in the Bible Commentary projected by William Smith. In
this former plan Lightfoot had to comment on Acts, Westcott on Daniel and most of the Apocrypha and Hort on the Gospels, Wisdom, and Ecclesiasticus. As in 1859 the Smith Commentary had
not really gotten off the ground (and was finally abandoned in 1863), the publisher A. MacMillan
initiated this commentary only on the New Testament. See Barrett's article in volume 3 of Lightfoot
Legacy and the correspondence between the three friends. A. F. Hort, op. cit., I, p. 396, 417-24; A.
Westcott, op. cit., I, pp. 204-08. Concerning the internal problems mentioned above cf. especially
the letter, which Hort wrote to Lightfoot on 1st May 1860: 'If your idea is to have an uniform
commentary, which shall demonstrate that the final results of accurate and honest criticism do not
disturb 'orthodox' assumptions, you are quite right not to admit a coadjustor who cannot feel
certain of having equally good luck. . . . At the same time, as far as I can see at present, I should
shrink from transferring myself to other books of the New Testament in your scheme on the
ground that you could not trust me with the Gospels . . . and I could not work freely at any book
of the New Testament if I were under obligations to produce results of a predetermined color.' And
a little later in the same letter 'If you make a decided conviction of the absolute infallibility of the
New Testament practically a *sine qua non* for co-operation, I fear I could not join you, even if you
were willing to forget your fears about the origins of the Gospels' (I, pp. 418-20). Here the limitations of Lightfoot were obvious (see below). But that he entrusted Hort with the Synoptics and
Acts in spite of his doubts, may demonstrate that his attitude was not that kind of narrowness, that
was widespread in the Anglican orthodoxy of his day. He 'did not censure' see below.

Basically, here in a decision of which he himself was perhaps not aware, Lightfoot took on those texts in which he could most successfully develop his philological and historical genius specifically over against the Tübingen faction. In the case of the Gospel of John, as with the Synoptics, his historical scope would have been considerably limited by his reluctance to engage in any substantial 'negative' criticism in the sphere of the New Testament canon, but in the case of the Epistle to the Galatians, written by the historical Paul, which was decisive for Baur's assumptions, he could counter, based on the biblical text, the exaggerated Tübingen theses that the earliest Apostles were Judaistic and legalistic and advance a convincing argument for the authenticity of Philippians, Colossians, and Philemon, which even the supporters of moderate criticism like Hilgenfeld, Ritschl, and Davidson in Britain had to acknowledge. It was almost a sixth sense which, as far as his main academic work was concerned, took him out of the sphere of the New Testament canon which fundamentally constricted him, and led him to the Apostolic Fathers. When he said that his edition of the letters of Ignatius was the most important motive of this new task and 'the core of the whole' (see above), he was indeed conscious that by the apparent detour he could most surely ward off attacks on the canonical apostolic testimony of the church.

Here, by way of Clement, Ignatius and Polycarp, the post-apostolic writers of the early 2nd century, he could bring relief, above all to the Gospels which were so much under attack and in particular to the Fourth Gospel, which was most severely threatened. There existed a longer recension of twelve letters of Ignatius and a middle recension of seven; in addition there was a short Syriac version published by Cureton in 1845/49 of only three letters.[68] Since the Reformation the authenticity of the letters had often been disputed by Reformed authors, because of their stress on the monarchial episcopate, but defended by Catholics and Anglicans; later the arguments for the authenticity of the middle recension became increasingly strong, but in the decade after their discovery especially the three Syriac Letters propagated by Bunsen were regarded as original. Lightfoot was also initially inclined to follow this hypothesis of the three letters whereas Baur argued against Bunsen that all the letters were forged.[69] By contrast, in 1873

---

[68] Cf. J. B. Lightfoot, *Apostolic Fathers* II, 1, p. 657.

[69] F. C. Baur, *Die Ignatianischen Briefe und ihr neueste Kritiker. Eine Streitschrift gegen Herrn Bunsen,*

Zahn had defended the authenticity of the middle recension with its seven letters. Zahn's position was finally corrected and endorsed by Lightfoot and put in a comprehensive and convincing historical context: he dates the martyrdom of Ignatius 'within a few years of A.D. 110, before or after.' As Ignatius presupposes a written Gospel, and cites the Gospel of Matthew and also is familiar with the spiritual world of the Johannine Corpus, indeed probably also knew the Gospel,[70] we are given a *terminus ad quem* for these writings which matches Irenaeus's information that the evangelist John of Ephesus and the Lord's disciple lived until the time of Trajan (A.D. 98–117).[71] The figure of Polycarp is of no little significance for this Johannine tradition, as Irenaeus refers to him as the bishop of Smyrna, who died as a martyr at an advanced age, as well as being a pupil of John and the apostles, and reports that he himself had heard him in his youth. The Tübingen scholars and German critics generally had to condemn the letter of Polycarp and the letter of the community of Smyrna with its report of the martyrdom of their bishop along with the letters of Ignatius: 'It has been reserved for the feverish and restless criticism of our day to impugn its genuiness.'[72]

As the letter of Polycarp to an abundant degree draws on the letters of Paul, but also very clearly at one point on 1 John and other Johannine traditions,[73] for Lightfoot this is a clear indication that there can be no question of a 'personal antagonism between St. Paul and St. John and an irreconcilable feud between their respective schools,' as the Tübingen scholars claim.[74] Here too, as with the letters of Ignatius: 'If therefore the Epistle be accepted as genuine, the position of the Tübingen school must be abandoned.'[75] In his edition, the gifted historian now succeeds in bringing the disputed texts into the context of the history of the Roman province of Asia, pagan politics towards the Christians and the development of the

---

(Tübingen, 1848). Lightfoot refers to this dispute in his *Apostolic Fathers*, II, 1, p. 283. The attacked book of Chr. J. Bunsen was *Die drei achten und die vier unachten Briefe des Ignatius von Antiochen.* Hamburg, 1847.

[70]See Hengel, op. cit. pp. 14f. Cf. also 'The Titles of the Gospels and the Gospel of Mark,' in my *Studies in the Gospel of Mark*, (London, 1985), pp. 71, 167 n.45.

[71]Cf. M. Hengel, op. cit., pp. 80f; 133.

[72]Lightfoot, *Apostolic Fathers*, op. cit., II, 1, pp. 604.

[73]Cf. M. Hengel, op. cit., p. 15f; 153f. ns. 93-95.

[74]*Essays on the Work entitled Supernatural Religion*, op. cit., p. 95, originally 'Polycarp of Smyrna,' May 1875.

[75]Ibid., p. 96.

church in the second century. At the same time he shows that he is a perceptive textual critic and exegete, an expert in Roman history down to the last detail and a master in the description of material, presenting all the essential texts in the original. Thus the five volumes of the *Apostolic Fathers* became a treasure chamber, the riches of which are inexhaustible even for today's reader. In his refutation of *Supernatural Religion* he made good use of this work to combat attacks on the Gospels by demonstrating that in the second century the Gospels are far more widely and better attested than his opponents would concede. That was true not least of the Fourth Gospel also, and as scholarship has advanced it has completely confirmed this picture sketched out by Lightfoot. New texts which Lightfoot could not yet know, like the Gospel of Peter, the Egerton papyrus, Melito's Homily on the Pascha, Ephraem's Commentary on the Diatesseron (which has now been discovered in the original Syriac), the Syriac Odes of Solomon, the Epistula Apostolorum, a number of texts from Nag Hammadi and finally three further papyri of John from the second century, attest the age and the significance of the Fourth Gospel in this early period.[76]

Balance was thus restored to the chronology of early Christian writings, and Harnack's great history of early Christian literature down to Eusebius, which appeared between 1893 and 1904, i.e. a few years after Lightfoot's premature death, often agreed with Lightfoot in decisive points of chronology. However, we have to add that this *agreement was mainly over the extracanonical literature of the second century.*

6. LIGHTFOOT'S LIMITATIONS AND MERITS AND THE BREAKTHROUGH OF HISTORICAL CRITICISM IN ENGLAND

Here we come up against a limitation of the great scholar, which could not yet be overcome at that time either in New Testament scholarship in England or with leading conservatives in Germany like Theodor Zahn. This was a conception of the inviolability and authenticity of the canonical scriptures which still did not understand the widespread phenomenon of pseudepigraphy and because of too narrow an understanding of inspiration at this point applied modern moral criteria to the ancient writings. The canonical

---

[76]The relevant material is collected in the first chapter of my *The Johannine Question,* op. cit.

scriptures of the New Testament had to come from authors associated with them. It will be remembered that around the middle of the last century, when Lightfoot, Westcott, and Hort began their academic work, the possibility of biblical and theological criticism in Great Britain was still very much more limited than in Lutheran Germany. Just a few examples shall illustrate this: In 1836 the appointment of R. D. Hampden, a friend of Matthew Arnold, as professor in Oxford caused great rumor, because he was suspected of being 'heretical' and therefore 'unfit to instruct the youth of Oxford.' Eleven years later Prof. Hampden became the Bishop of Hereford and a fierce discussion about his orthodoxy broke out anew.[77] A few years later, in 1853, Frederick Denison Maurice lost his chair at King's College, London, because he ventured to doubt the eternity of the punishments in hell.[78] At the same time the Bishop of Natal designate, Colenso, was reprimanded because he had agreed with Maurice and in 1863 he was subsequently deposed as bishop in South Africa because he had doubted some of the numerical information in the Pentateuch.[79] Against this background we have to call Lightfoot and his friends, with their constant application of the philological-historical method, moderate liberals. Westcott doubted whether he could allow himself to be ordained priest because of the Arnold/Hampden affair, and Hort, an admirer of Maurice, was also deeply disturbed.[80] In 1856 the Old Testament scholar Samuel Davidson had to give up his post at the Congregationalist Lancaster College because he doubted the Mosaic authorship of the Pentateuch.[81] But in the long run, pressure for more freedom

---

[77]Cf. Owen Chadwick, op. cit. pp. 112-121 and pp. 237-49. The quotation is from p. 115.

[78]Ibid., pp. 545-49.

[79]Ibid., p.550f.

[80]Cf. the letter of Westcott from December 1847, where he wrote about Hampden (A. Westcott op. cit., I 94f.): 'I thought myself that he was greviously in error, but yesterday I read over the selections from his writings which his adversaries made, and in them I found systematically expressed the very strains of thought which I have been endeavoring to trace out for the last two or three years. If he be condemned, what will become of me? I believe he holds the truth; if he be condemned, I cannot see how I shall ever enter the Church.' And then turning on to the older friend of Hampden, Matthew Arnold, he remarks: 'If he were a heretic, I should be satisfied to be one too.' Concerning Maurice, held in high esteem by Hort, cf. his letter to Westcott from 29th June 1852, where he defends Maurice against his friend: 'that I regard him as a man to be valued and loved, far more than admired and glorified.' A. F. Hort, op. cit. I p. 223. Concerning Colenso his opinion is quite different cf. Ibid., p. 473.

[81]Cf. O. Chadwick op. cit. I, 407. On Davidson, see S. Davidson, *Autobiography* (ed. A. J. Davidson), London 1899, and shortly R. Bayne, 'Davidson, Samuel (1806-1899)' in the *Dictionary of National Biography*, Supplement vol. II, ed. S. Lee, London, 1901, pp. 115f.

to deal with the biblical texts without the fear of church repression could not be resisted. The dispute over *Essays and Reviews*, which appeared in February 1860,[82] with the arguments of various respected authors for a more flexible understanding of the doctrine of inspiration and a stronger historical perspective, once again aroused a storm of indignation. Hort was more inclined to see its positive side while Westcott wanted to attack it;[83] Lightfoot wisely held back. He felt that his task lay not so much in excited discussion of general dogmatic problems, like the particularly controversial question of verbal inspiration, as in peaceful historical and philological argumentation. Lightfoot's own philological work was largely fitting in line with the concept uttered by the Oxford philologist and commentator on St. Paul, B. Jowett: to 'read the Bible like any other literature'—as to the 'externals of interpretation.'[84] By resorting to this in principle he was implicitly

---

[82]*Essays and Reviews*, ed. by H. B. Wilson, London 1860. For the debate on *Essays and Reviews* cf. O. Chadwick op. cit. II, 75ff. The contributors were H. B. Wilson himself, R. Williams, B. Powell, M. Pattison, C. W. Goodwin, F. Temple, and B. Jowett.

[83]Cf. A. Westcott, op. cit., I, pp. 212-16. His son wrote the activities of his father in this affair: 'He was most anxious that Lightfoot and Hort should join with him in preparing a reply to the controverted volume. For his own part, he felt this to be so important that he would gladly lay aside all other work that he might be free to point out some *via media*' (p. 212). In a letter from 25th February 1861 Westcott confessed: 'It would be impossible to find opinions more opposed to my own than those of the Essayists, and for this very reason, I am most anxious to see the error calmly and clearly pointed out, and not merely shrieked at. As far as I have seen, those who have written against the Essayists have been profoundly ignorant of the elements of the difficulties out of which the Essays have sprung' (p. 215). Cf. also A. F. Hort op. cit., I, pp. 436-45. Hort saw their own position between the Essayists and the 'mere orthodox assertion' (p. 436f.). He drafted a 'Declaration' in which he wanted to protest against 'the violent and indiscriminate agitation' directed against *Essays and Reviews*. He saw that 'suppression of free criticism must ultimately be injurious to the cause of truth and religion' (p. 439). Hort based his engagement in this controversy because in his eyes the Essayists 'represent the cause of freedom of thought and criticism' (p. 440). The planned mediating volume should be edited under the title 'Revelation and History.' In a letter Hort described the whole planned arrangement: 'Lightfoot takes "the preparation for the Gospel," i.e. the stages of Jewish history, the work of the different nations of antiquity, and the special calling of Israel. Westcott takes "the witness of God in His Son," in short, the Incarnation as an historical revelation of God, especially with reference to miracles. I am to take the development of doctrine out of revelation, including the progress within the NT and going on to the epochs of Church History since the close of the Canon, especially since the growth of a Scripture and of its use' (p. 442). Unfortunately, Lightfoot retired from the plan, so that his article about the 'praeparatio evangelica' never came into being.

[84]B. Jowett, 'On the Interpretation of Scripture,' in *Essays and Reviews*, 337f., 377f. Cf. G. R. Treloar, op. cit., p. 13f. On Jowett cf. J. Barr, 'Jowett and the Reading of the Bible Like any other Book,' *Horizons in Biblical Theology*, 4-5 (1982/83), pp. 1-44. On Jowett as philologist see H. Lloyd-Jones, *Blood for the Ghosts. Classical Influences in the Nineteenth and Twentieth Centuries*, London, 1982, pp. 16-19. Lightfoot had critically reviewed Jowett's Commentary on St. Paul in his *Journal of Classical and Sacred Philology*.

avoiding the historical narrowness of an extremely doctrinal orthodoxy and resisting a conception of inspiration which was all too rigid.[85] At the same time he saw very clearly that the progress of New Testament scholarship could not be held back by eternal church measurements; all that counted in this spiritual battle were the arguments arising from the texts themselves, which philologians and historians could see. According to an unpublished lecture manuscript Lightfoot taught students at Cambridge not to fear the application of philological and historical methods to Biblical texts: 'The timidity which shrinks from the application of modern science or criticism to the interpretation of Holy Scripture, evinces a very unworthy view of its character. If the Scriptures are indeed true, they must be in accordance with every principle of whatever kind. It is against the wrong application of such principles, and against the presumption which pushes them too far, that we must protest. It is not much knowledge, but little knowledge that is the dangerous thing here as elsewhere. From the full light of science in criticism we have nothing to fear: the glimmering light—which rather deserves the name of darkness visible—hides and distorts the truth.'[86]

So it is no wonder that Lightfoot's relatively free application of philological and historical methods provoked furious attacks by the exponents of the literalist approach to the Bible. The *Churchman* considered his Commentary on Galatians as 'a very painful instance of the boldness of unbelief in the present day' and associated Lightfoot with Thomas Paine, Voltaire and Richard Carlile,[87] and a certain E. B. Elliott, a distinguished Evangelical who was mostly interested in Biblical Prophecy, boldly interpreted the 'Man of Sin' in Second Thessalonians in the light of contemporary history. So not only Baur, but also Lightfoot was compared with the Antichrist.[88]

---

[85]'Lightfoot was among the few who did not censure, and to that extent identified himself with the liberals' (G. R. Treloar, op. cit.). On Lightfoot's position towards the doctrine of inspiration, cf. Ibid., pp. 9-11: 'Lightfoot defined inspiration as "a moral and spiritual power" which "does not transmute its agents but molds them."' (p. 9, citing Lightfoot's *Biblical Essays*, p. 226).

[86]Lecture Manuscript on Acts I–VIII, cited by G. R. Treloar, op. cit., p. 11. Compare the description of the manuscript Ibid., p. 25, n. 25. And see below.

[87]*The Churchman* (7 September 1865), pp. 1070-71, cited by G. R. Treloar, op. cit., p. 21.

[88]For the attack against Lightfoot, E. B. Elliott, 'Prophetic Articles in Smith's Bible Dictionary,' *The Christian Observer*, March 1846, pp. 214-18, in reference to J. B. Lightfoot, 'Thessalonians, Second Epistle to the,' in William Smith, *Dictionary of the Bible*, Vol. III, 1863, pp. 1482-84; Cf. G. R. Treloar, op. cit. p. 21. Edward Bishop Elliott (1793–1875), was the Evangelical vicar of St. Mark's Church, Brighton, he wrote a commentary on the Apocalypse, and he expected the Mil-

The outcome of the controversies was finally to prove him right; in 1863 there appeared the first monograph by R. W. Mackay, *The Tübingen School and its Antecedents*, with the sub-title 'A Review of the History and Present Condition of Modern Theology,' which combined a sharp attack on the conservatism that prevailed in the Church of England and English theology with the demand 'that the Tübingen School . . . , as representing the progressive spirit of true Protestantism and of sound learning, must be the basis of all future research in relation to the New Testament.'[89] In 1867 there followed a critical investigation of the Fourth Gospel and the Johannine corpus by John James Tayler which took its bearings completely from the modernistic Tübingen scholars,[90] and then in 1874 came the anonymous and polemical *Supernatural Religion* which I have already mentioned several times.[91] This caused Lightfoot to take up his pen to refute with historical critical arguments in the best sense this violent treatment of historical reality by an anonymous author who constantly appealed to the Tübingen scholars and other German writers. The breakthrough of historical criticism could no longer be stopped, or, as Robert Morgan has recently put it: 'In the 1870s the iron curtain began to be lifted.'[92]

With the support of a Theological Translation Fund fostered by liberal theologians, critical theological literature began to be translated into English and published. Among the first titles, Baur's book on Paul appeared between 1873 and 1875, and in 1875 his *Church History of the First Three Centuries*. In 1882 Davidson, now an old man, produced the second edition of his *Introduction to the Study of the New Testament* in two volumes totaling around 1100 pages of text. 'In his earlier treatment of the material (1848/49) the author still defended the authenticity of all the New Testament writings, including II Peter.'[93] Meanwhile he had changed his views radically. Like

lenium at the end of the nineteenth century. Cf. *Dictionary of National Biography* XVII (ed. L. Steven), London 1889, p. 268, and E. R. Sandeen, *The Roots of Fundamentalism, British and American Millenarianism, 1800–1930* (Grand Rapids: Michigan, 1978), pp. 82ff.
[89]R. W. Mackay, *The Tübingen School and its Antecedents,* Covent Garden and Edinburgh, 1863 pp. X-XL.
[90]J. J. Tayler, *An Attempt to Ascertain the Character of the Fourth Gospel; especially in its Relationship to the Three First,* London and Edinburgh, 1867.
[91]The author was W. R. Cassels, cf. O. Chadwick, op. cit., II, p. 2of. with n. 1.
[92]R. Morgan, *Historical Criticism and Christology,* p. 86.
[93]O. Pfleiderer, *Die Entwicklung des protestantischen Theologie seit Kant und in Grossbritannien seit 1825,* Freiburg i. Br. 1891, p. 483.

Supernatural Religion, he worked through the whole of German critical literature and largely followed the moderate criticism of Hilgenfeld. His wholly positive picture of the Tübingen school is significant: 'Though this School as represented by Baur and Schwegler has carried its speculations too far, the important advance it has made in the criticism of the New Testament cannot be reversed. Modified it may be: but its mark upon early Christian literature is deep and permanent. In correcting its excesses moderation must be carefully preserved, for examples of backwardism are usually weak. A few faults of the 'Tendenz-Kritik' leave its basis secure.' *Supernatural Religion*, also receives high praise: 'The learned work furnishes efficient aid to rational inquiry, and deserves to be studied by all lovers of free investigation. The assaults which were made upon minor details leave its main position unharmed.'[94] The reference here was of course above all to Lightfoot's attacks in *The Contemporary Review*.[95] Lightfoot himself is mentioned only six times in the voluminous work; Westcott, who had written his very successful *Introduction to the Study of the Gospels* in 1851, is mentioned incidentally only once, and Hort not at all. In his refutation of *Supernatural Religion* Lightfoot mentions Davidson not even once, instead he is referring directly to the Tübingen critics.[96] That despite—indeed perhaps because of—his dependence on German criticism Davidson did not defend his critical stand-point any more convincingly than the Tübingen scholars earlier is evident from his remarks on the attestation and dating of the Fourth Gospel. He follows the approach of Hilgenfeld, for whom he has particular respect, and puts it around 150.[97] The letters of Ignatius are not treated any more graciously: 'But the so-called Ignatius is not an apostolic father, and the productions bearing his name were not prior to the middle of the second

---

[94]Samuel Davidson, *An Introduction to the Study of the New Testament*, I, London, 2nd ed. 1882, pp. V-VI in the Preface to the second edition.

[95]Ibid., p. V. Davidson wrote about a reactionary spirit towards the Tübingen school.

[96]Of course Lightfoot knew Davidson's *Introduction to the Study of the New Testament* (in its first edition of 1848/49) very well. He cited it with critical comment in his essay on 'The Mission of Titus to the Corinthians,' published in 1855 = *Biblical Essays*, op. cit., pp. 271-84, see p. 275 n.1.

[97]S. Davidson, op. cit. II, p. 390, 417. He refers to Hilgenfeld as an 'indefatigable scholar' (vol. I, V), but he did not appreciate Davidson to the same degree. I came to see this during my year's study at the Wissenschaftskolleg in Berlin, where I borrowed Davidson's NT-Introduction from the library of the Kirchliche Hochschule in Berlin. The copy I used was given and personally dedicated by the author to Hilgenfeld, who obviously never had used the book; the pages were not yet cut open.

century.[98] Although Davidson's work, in contrast to *Supernatural Religion*, could not have any great influence, since it was a technical theological textbook, it is important for progress of theological criticism, which after the 1860s was unstoppable in England also. Here reference was still made to the radical results of the Tübingen school whereas in Germany a moderate criticism had long since been established. The importance of Samuel Davidson for the development of critical New Testament scholarship in England is also unknown in Germany.[99]

7. Lightfoot and the Fourth Gospel

In conclusion, one has to say that the continuation of historical research into early Christianity in the last century has proved both the Tübingen School and Lightfoot *both* right *and* wrong. The picture of the church and its literature in the second century still largely corresponds with the outline which the Bishop of Durham drew for us. Moreover we must grant that he, and Irenaeus with him, are right in thinking that the Johannine corpus presumably came into being between the latter part of Domitian's reign and the early period of the reign of Trajan. However, the question of authorship, which is still disputed hotly (or denied in resignation) is quite another matter. Nowadays only a minority still regards the apostle John, son of Zebedee, as the author and faces the difficult time of reconciling the strangely unreal statements of the Johannine Christ with the Synoptic logia tradition. The only possible expedient here is to assume that the disciple exercised the same creative freedom that Plato exercised in his later days towards his teacher Socrates. The Paraclete gives the disciples the freedom to project the exalted Christ in union with the Father on to the earthly Jesus.[100] This approach was not yet open to Lightfoot, even if sometimes he wants to distin-

---

[98]Ibid., II, p. 328.

[99]W. G. Kummel, in his comprehensive history of research, (*Das Neue Testament Geschichte der Erforschung seiner Problem,* 1970 2nd ed.; English translation, *The New Testament. The History of the Investigation of its Problems,* London, 1973), does not mention Davidson with a work. Besides Lightfoot, Westcott, and Hort he refers only to two other British scholars of the 19th century: Hatch who died the same year as Lightfoot (1835–89), and Streeter (1874–1937). Even such great scholars as Swete (1835–1917), Burkitt (1864–1935), Conybeare and Sanday (1843–1920) remain unmentioned. It seems as if British New Testament scholarship up to World War I was a *terra incognita* in Germany.

[100]Cf. Hengel, op. cit., p. 104f; 130f.

guish between historical event and evangelist's comment.[101] His unshakeable conviction that this most divine book was indeed the work of "the disciple whom Jesus loved" guaranteed him access to the *ipsissima vox Christi*, Jesus' own testimony about his unity with the Father, his Incarnation, and his atoning death on the cross. Or, as Robert Morgan puts it in connection with Lightfoot's interpretation of John: 'If Jesus really *was* the incarnate Son of God, then it was natural to expect that honest historical research (as opposed to a tendentious rationalism which excluded the miraculous as an *a priori*) would reveal this.'[102]

However, it is necessary to add here that in the first half of the nineteenth century in Germany too, the leading liberal theologians, above all Schleiermacher, argued for the originality of the Fourth Gospel. Schleiermacher's lecture on the *Life of Jesus*, completely orientated on the Gospel of John, appeared posthumously in 1864, thirty-two years after they were given and were subjected to devastating criticism by Strauss. But in contrast to Schleiermacher, who as Albert Schweitzer put it, sought 'not the Jesus of history, . . . but the Jesus Christ of his *Glaubenslehre* (translated into English as *The Christian Faith*),'[103] wisely and with restraint Lightfoot did not write any *Life of Jesus* or even give lectures on it in the light of what was historically possible. His argument for 'the internal and external Evidence for the

---

[101]*Biblical Essays*, op. cit., pp. 190ff. The article is printed from lecture notes with the same title as the article cited above 'Internal Evidence for the Authenticity and Genuineness of St. John's Gospel.'

[102]Robert Morgan, *Historical Criticism and Christology*, p. 87. A good deal of Lightfoot's pupils kept his conservative views on the authenticity and authorship of the Fourth Gospel; so the Archdeacon of Durham H. W. Watkins in his study *Modern Criticism Considered in Relation to the Fourth Gospel*, London and New York, 1890; J. Armitage Robinson, who republished his book on *The Historical Character of St. John's Gospel*, London and New York, 1908, in 1929, where he reproduced (pp. 7-11) a Cambridge lecture of 1901 from 'The Study of the Gospels,' London 1902, pp. 126ff. with the comment: 'After the interval of twenty seven years, I have no desire to speak otherwise today.' Similar views were still held by A. C. Headlam, *The Fourth Gospel as History*, Oxford and New York, 1948.

[103]F. D. E. Schleiermacher, *Das Leben Jesu*, Vorlesungen an der Universitat zu Berlin, im Jahr, 1832. Aus Schleiermacher's handschriftlicher Nachlasse und Nachschriften seiner zuhorer herausgegeben von K.A. Rutenik = F. Schleiermacher, *Samtliche Werke*, 1 Abth. 6 Bd. Berlin, 1864. Strauss had already become acquainted with the Schleiermacher lecture through a student's lecture notes during his Berlin visit in 1831/32. The verdict of A. Schweitzer is to be found in *Von Reimarus zu Wrede, Eine Geschichte der Lens-Jesu-Forschung*, (Tubingen, 1906), p. 61; the second edition came out in 1913 under the new title: *Geschichte der Lebens-Jesu-Forschung*, also Tubingen (since that time many reprints). English Edition—*The Quest for the Historical Jesus*.

Authenticity and Genuineness of St. John's Gospel'[104] posthumously put together from notes is most times convincing in connection with the external attestation to the Gospel in the second century, and the same is true with internal evidence, in so far as it demonstrates that in contrast to prevailing German criticism the author came from Palestine. The linguistic investigations of Schlatter, the parallels of Billerbeck and Odeberg, archaeological results and the discovery of texts—to mention just Qumran here— have endorsed this impression. But here too Lightfoot clearly saw the limitations of an historical argument.

If we are more restrained at this point than Lightfoot in our judgments on access to the historical Jesus and see the discourses of the Johannine Christ primarily as the development of the evangelist's theory and not, say, the very words of Jesus, this is because of the further development of the historical method and theological reflection. The truth of Christ as the Λόγος θεοῦ revealed to us cannot be bound up with the human work of historical proof.

In a study published immediately after his death in *The Expositor* (February-March 1890), which goes back to lectures given in 1871, but which was prepared by Lightfoot for publication in 1889, the year in which he died, the great scholar stresses that he understood his argument for the originality and authenticity of the Fourth Gospel as *secular* historical work: 'I have treated this as a purely critical question, carefully eschewing any appeal to Christian instincts. As a critical question I wish to take a verdict upon it. But as I could not have you think that I am blind to the theological issues . . . connected with it, I will close with this brief confession of faith.' And then follow those much-quoted words:

> 'I believe from my heart that the truth which this Gospel more especially enshrines—the truth that Jesus Christ is the very Word Incarnate—the manifestation of the Father to mankind is the one lesson which . . . will do more than all our feeble efforts . . . , the one study which can fitly prepare us for a joyful immortality hereafter.'[105]

---

[104]Lightfoot, *Biblical Essays*, op. cit. 'External Evidence for the Authenticity and Genuineness of St. John's Gospel,' pp. 123-93; Additional Notes pp. 194-98. [See the introduction and the first appendix to this volume. (BW3)]

[105]Ibid., p. 43 in the reprint of the article from *The Expositor*, quoted in n. 50. Cf. *Lightfoot of Durham*, op. cit., p. 185; J. A. T. Robinson, *Joseph Barber Lightfoot*, op. cit., p. 19.

Here a clear distinction is made between the faith which is the basis of true life and salvation and 'all our feeble efforts'—and who labored harder for historical truth than Lightfoot did? Over his plain bed in Auckland Castle hung a simple engraving by Durer with the inscription 'Es ist vollbracht—it is finished.' Bishop Moule, who tells us this, remarks: 'To my dear Tutor, deep within the heart of his most noble life, the Incarnate Christ of Atonement and Resurrection was all in all—salvation, desire, motive, life, way, and end.'[106]

Rightly understood, on this basis Joseph Barber Lightfoot, historian and theologian, Christian and bishop, can still become our tutor today.

---

[106]In *Lightfoot of Durham*, op. cit., p. 15.

Author Index

Adler, 170
Aelian, 13, 97, 172
Aeschylus, 14, 198
Akerknecht, Erwin, 334
Alford, Henry, 17, 90, 106-7, 112, 118, 124, 128, 130-32, 138, 147, 151-52, 164, 171, 176-77, 184, 190, 196-97, 202
Ambrose, 14, 170, 172-73, 235
Andreas of Caesarea, 264
Andrews, J. S., 328
Apollinaris, Claudius, 215, 228, 232, 237
Apollonius, 209
Aristobulus, 84
Aristophanes, 14, 146
Aristotle, 14, 271
Arnold, Bill, 30
Arnold, Matthew, 343
Assemani, J. S., 263, 279
Auger, 148
Augustine, 14, 146, 170, 172, 180, 190, 262, 283
Barclay, J. M. G., 24
Barr, J., 351
Barrett, Charles K., 21-22, 24, 28-30, 33-34, 326, 328, 332, 335-36, 346
Barton, Stephen, 24
Basil, 14, 90
Basilides, 46
Bauckham, Richard, 42
Baur, F. C., 36-38, 43, 48, 63, 75, 208, 326-27, 329-30, 331, 335, 339, 342-47, 354
Bayne, R., 350
Beeler, 201
Beer, Bernhard, 181
Beker, M., 118
Bekker, Immanuel, 142, 153
Bengel, Johannes, 17, 191
Bernard, L. W., 328
Bleek, Friedrich, 207, 276
Boeckh, Philipp August, 17, 280
Bretschneider, Karl Gottlieb, 17, 125, 208
Bright, William, 264
Brown, 104
Browne, Harold, 285

Bunsen, C. J., 17, 244, 247, 258, 263, 348
Buttmann, Alexander, 17, 125, 136
Buxtorf, Johannes, 132-33, 144, 163, 183, 199, 278, 299, 302
Caius, 210
Cassels, W. R., 353
Cave, William, 17, 107
Cerinthus, 45
Chadwick, Owen, 327, 334, 336, 350, 353
Chrysostom, 90, 165, 168, 283
Cicero, 291
Clement of Alexandria, 14, 73, 84, 89, 95, 112, 197, 209-11, 233, 240-43, 255-58, 260, 283, 318
Clinton, Henry Fynes, 17, 211, 215, 228
Cotcher, 109
Cotelier, Jean-Baptiste, 17, 246
Cranfield, C. E. B., 24, 30
Credner, Carl August, 18, 343
Cureton, William, 18, 227, 279
Cyprian, 14, 89, 235
Cyril of Alexandria, 168, 283
Dachs, S., 163
Davidson, Samuel, 354-55
Delitzsch, Franz, 126, 135-36, 144
Demosthenes, 14, 46, 122
Dionysius Areopagiticus, 14, 223
Dodd, C. H., 35
Dodd, V. A., 327
Dodwell, Henry, 244
Dressel, Albert R. M., 45, 260, 341
Dunn, James D. G., 21-22, 24, 34-35, 326
Eden, George R., 7, 26, 328, 336
Edwards, D. L., 336
Elliott, Edward B., 352
Epictetus, 142, 165
Epiphanius, 14, 44, 91, 107, 179, 184, 211, 213, 231, 237, 251, 255, 257, 262-64, 285, 304
Etheridge, J. W., 84, 212

Euripides, 15, 95
Eusebius of Caesarea, 14, 84, 89-90, 103, 111, 122, 135, 143-44, 168-69, 202, 207, 209-12, 218-22, 228-30, 234-35, 237, 242-43, 248, 251, 255, 262-64, 279, 286, 302-3, 308
Ewald, W. H. A., 18, 84, 91, 102-3, 138, 163, 167, 169, 179, 223, 184-85, 277, 280, 284, 290, 304
Fabricius, Johann Albert, 15, 264
Falina, 181
Franckel, 162, 292
Fries, H., 330
Garenkis, 135
Gesenius, W., 18, 274, 276-77
Gfrorer, August F., 287-88, 290
Glasswell, M. E., 336
Godet, Frédéric, 157, 161
Goodwin, C. W., 351
Gotthold, Muller, 330
Graf, F. W., 330
Gregory of Nyssa, 15, 90
Greisbach, Johannes J., 305
Grimm, Wilibald, 271
Groddeke, 163, 299
Grotius, H., 275
Gruter, 118
Gundert, E., 198
Harmer, J. R., 26, 31
Harnack, Adolf von, 7, 332-33
Harris, H., 327, 330
Headlam, Arthur C., 25, 334, 356
Heliodorus, 15, 118
Hengel, Martin, 22, 326, 337, 341, 348, 355
Heracleon, 103, 257
Herzel, 109
Herzog, 114, 290
Hilgenfeld, A., 48, 179, 208, 224, 257, 340, 343, 354
Hippolytus, 15, 46, 89, 179, 190, 193, 249, 252-57, 259, 263-64, 283, 341
Hodgson, P., 330

Scripture Index

The Lightfoot Legacy Set

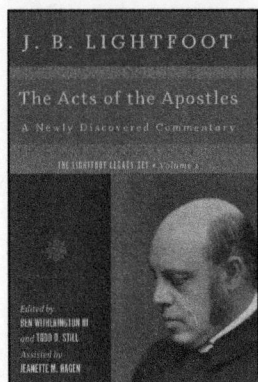

The Acts of the Apostles:
A Newly Discovered Commentary
978-0-8308-2944-6

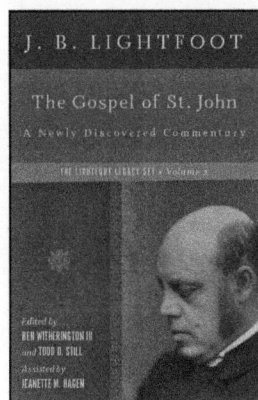

The Gospel of St. John:
A Newly Discovered Commentary
978-0-8308-2945-3

Forthcoming:

The Epistles of 2 Corinthians and 1 Peter

Finding the Textbook You Need

The IVP Academic Textbook Selector
is an online tool for instantly finding the IVP books
suitable for over 250 courses across 24 disciplines.

ivpacademic.com

www.ingramcontent.com/pod-product-compliance
Lightning Source LLC
Chambersburg PA
CBHW030806100426
42814CB00015B/397/J